REMAKING OUR SCHOOLS

For the Twenty-First Century

A Blueprint for

Change/Improvement

in our Educational Systems

Robert L. Arnold
Professor of Education, Emeritus

Ithaca Press
3 Kimberly Drive, Suite B
Dryden, New York 13053 USA
www.IthacaPress.com
Copyright © 2013 Robert Arnold
Remaking our Schools for the 21st Century
A Blueprint for Change/Improvement in our Educational Systems
All rights reserved under International and
Pan American Copyright Law, including the
right of reproduction in whole or in part,
without the written permission of the publisher.
Requests for such permission should be addressed to
Ithaca Press, 408 East Marshall Street, Ithaca
New York 14850
Cover Design Gary Hoffman
Book Design Gary Hoffman
Manufactured in the United States of America
9 8 7 6 5 4 3 2 1
Library of Congress Cataloging-in-Data Available
First Edition
Printed in the United States of America
ISBN: 978-0-9839121-7-0
www.RobertLArnold.com

Table of Contents

Dedication..................................v

Foreword..................................vii

Preface The role of theories in the change processes of our public educational systems....................ix

Introduction The Difficulties of Communication in the Systemic Change Process...................1

Chapter 1 Remaking Our Schools for the Twenty-First Century – What it will take to fix it?..............17

Chapter 2 The Constructive Assessment, Recordkeeping and Evaluation System (CARES)......................89

Chapter 3 Individual Development and Behavior – A Knowledge Base for Change.....................131

Chapter 4 Group Processes and the Public Schools.......209

Chapter 5 The Structure of Education From a Systems Point of View...................................261

Chapter 6 Teacher Education for the Twenty-First Century 291

Chapter 7 How Can Change Be Accomplished...........331

Chapter 8 A Solutions Generator......................387

Bibliography............................397

Appendix A What Professional Educators Know and Are Able to Do.................................401

Appendix B Sample Workshop Process-Recordings for Goals 2000 Project..............................421

Appendix C Rituals of Intimidation by Rory O'Day (With permission from Sage Publications)..............461

About The Author..........................473

Dedication

There are so many people who have contributed to the development of the ideas in this book; inevitably there will be some who will be left out of this dedication. Everyone with whom I have worked, students, faculty, community persons, children, and family members have my sincere thanks.

I'm especially mindful of the contribution of Dr. Charles Lahey who introduced me to the proposition that young learners would enjoy and profit from engagement with the tools and orientations of historical research, viewing history as a way of creating meaning rather than simply a body of knowledge to be consumed.

The work of Dr. Philip Phenix, of Teachers College Columbia University expanded the insights developed with Lahey to include all ways of knowing as creative disciplines. This lent credibility to my own experience with Geography that stemmed from growing up on a nearly self-sufficient farm, living in the out-of-doors, and encountering the physical world of which I had little or no recognition of its potential for learning in the academic world at the time.

Many conversations with one of my best friends and most respected colleagues, Tom McGrath, led to many refinements in my work and most importantly, lent invaluable support for the importance of these efforts.

Likewise, Drs. Arthur Newgarden, David Elliott, Paul Bardis, Kathryn Smith, Marie McGrath, Ralph Gabrielli, Manny Bernstein and Barry James all have provided me with expanded insights and motivation to pursue what is often viewed by others as unrealistic, abstract, and perhaps revolutionary ideas.

Sid Couchey, a cartoonist/visual poet, contributed immeasurability with his insight, his sense of humor and steadfast integrity.

Clarke Mitchell, whose creative inspiration has been most appreciated in helping to translate the mundane into new and fresh ideas.

Joanna and Ro Piekarski deserve a very special recognition. Throughout the many years of our association, they have demonstrated an undaunted commitment to changes in education that can lead to a more productive life for all citizens. Their support of my work has been demonstrated many times over, through their active participation in the promotion and dissemination of fundamental principles of learning and development.

The undergraduate and graduate students with whom I have shared my ideas and heard theirs have contributed immeasurably to my growth and development. It is gratifying to learn of their appreciation for the experiences we shared.

Lastly, my family, and especially my wife, Mary Sue, who have put up with my indignation and frustration over the shortsightedness of educators and politicians, I owe a gratitude that cannot be adequately expressed in words.

Foreword

This book is a rare opportunity for the world to take a look into the mind of an amazing American educator. Professor Arnold was a major part of a university's teaching staff that helped prepare teachers for their careers.

Bob Arnold taught students the way he fiercely believes they must be groomed: the teacher needs to inspire rather than require: to work as a partner with each student in order to discover that student's strengths and to cultivate their interests, rather than drilling a prescribed, narrow curriculum.

It reads much like the journal of a courageous master educator—-his successes and failures.

To change the conventional one-size-fits-all educational system has always been one of the most difficult habits to change, historically. The vested interests are huge, from the top down, including test companies and highly paid administrators.

This is a book about a lifetime of promoting education instead of schooling.

Professor Arnold shares with us his successes and failures, all of which can give us insights about some things we can do and other things we better not, if we are going to change and improve the system.

Patching the system has never worked. It must be totally changed to that teachers and students can be trusted, for one thing. For another, we must stop seeing schools as machinery to control others, or a race of some kind. Instead, we need to see it as a cooperative adventure that helps encourage each student to prepare for the pursuit of his or her interests and find the best of him or herself.

Robert L. Arnold

Bob recently told me that one of the main things that inspired him to write this book was a moment of time I shared with him: after years of being a psychotherapist, I suddenly realized my clients were just as often damaged by conventional schooling as they were by other factors, such as poor parenting. So when I was asked to heal a child in school, I learned to look hard at the school he or she attended. Often the conventional schooling system or a terrorist teacher was a major dynamic in damaging the child.

I believe a journey through this manuscript can be considered a journal of the thought, actions, hopes, and dreams of Bob Arnold, Professor of Education, Emeritus.

This is a book that is useful to any student of schooling or education where the scholar is interested in finding pearls of wisdom. Reading it is a little like being in conversation with Bob, a bit like an interview, a lot like the life history of one man's heroic actions to change the insanity of conventional schooling, which is based on the blueprints of the Prussian army, into an enriching experience that educates its students into being successful lifelong learners.

The current authoritarian practices that sometimes have worked in prisons and in the military are destroying the very qualities in students that this country desperately needs and wants.

We have been mesmerized to believe that we are successful because of that old time teaching. But if most of us thing about it, those who are successful have gotten over it. It is time for us to replace the stale, outdated conventional system that restricts the student and the teacher, and crushes creativity. Yet the conventional belief of good scores on tests as the measure of educational progress is so ingrained in our society, and so damaging to students, that we must unite and rebel and demand the kind of individualized education that Professor Arnold recommends.

—*Emmanuel (Manny) Bernstein, PhD.*

Preface

The role of theories in the change processes of our public educational systems

A theory is a statement of our individual beliefs and assumptions. Our theories define our interpretation of the meanings we place on our experience. Theory defines the facts as we perceive them, including those that pertain to education. We act on our theories whether or not they can be supported by evidence.

Theories can be based on reputable research and study, they can be based on little or no evidence, and they can ignore previously verified research and insight. A theory that is verified in our personal experiences and found consistent with the experiences of others who have studied the matter in depth is considered appropriate. Appropriate theories are also strengthened when supported by other theories of similar stature.

An inappropriate theory is one that does not reflect adequately a verifiable view of reality. These theories yield inappropriate, distorted or limited facts that often challenge the value of appropriate theory. For instance, everyone has a theory of the uniqueness of every individual. This theory is verified in our personal experiences and in the experiences of many scholars who have studied these matters in depth. Yet, a theory of learning and intellectual growth adopted by today's decision makers defines changes and growth in individuals as simply statistical improvement in the scores recorded on a one-size-fits-all standardized test. This position is the result of flawed, limited or inappropriate theory about learning and change. In today's educational arena, inappropriate theory is being used extensively by those in authority to support their biased version of facts.

Much of the resistance to change in our public educational systems and the lackluster record of failed schools stems from an extreme conventional wisdom (accepted by many members of the lay public and regrettably by many if not most of our educators) which assumes that theories are just untested ideas and have little value in the examination of the processes and problems of schooling. Taking another extreme position, persons in authority currently claim to be operating on legitimate theories even when they are shown to be contrary to established facts.

Conventional wisdom and a distorted reality has allowed, if not caused, educators, laymen and decision makers to routinely dismiss the insights of numerous authorities who have studied and written extensively about individuals, their growth and development, both alone and in groups. When asked, many will steadfastly claim that theory is useless in solving the problems of education and others will claim inappropriate theories are indeed valid. Unless the lay public knows the difference between appropriate and inappropriate theories, and understands appropriate theories that provide a comprehensive view of the school, they will likely go along with the positions of authorities. Acceptance of conventional wisdom and inappropriate theory has led schools to conduct instruction in a manner that ignores the verified findings of experts in the fields of communication, human development, individual behavior, group processes, learning and epistemology.

Recognizing the shortcomings and problems in our public educational systems is seriously hampered by a lack of sound/appropriate underlying theory that can identify reliable 'facts." Unfortunately, confounding any efforts to correct this situation is the public's conventional wisdom that is a by-product of the very school system we are trying to understand. Unlocking its hardened categories and eliminating its rigid adherence to conventions is a formidable task.

If this were not difficult enough to correct, add the existence of a strong and relentless pursuit of profits envisioned by corporate entities for business in the vast educational market. Corporate interests have been successful to date in spreading their version of facts since the public knows and accepts so few appropriate theories applicable in the educational enterprise that corporate-sponsored marketing strategies have easily prevailed.

Remaking Our Schools for the Twenty-First Century © 2013 by Robert L. Arnold attempts to explain appropriate theories for public use in improving the public schools. It is a book to be studied, contemplated and most importantly internalized, making possible significant progress in designing sustained improvements in the conduct of education in this country.

There are at least **six clusters of interrelated theories** explained and utilized in this book, applied to an in-depth study of what is happening in education today, and importantly, what could be happening if only there was widespread understanding of and commitment to verifiable assumptions and beliefs. These six clusters of theories define the facts about schooling far differently than those of the decision making authorities.

In the first cluster are the interrelated theories of human behavior, human growth and development, including learning. These theories were developed by scholars from different parts of the world and at different points in time. Their messages are un-mistakably consistent about biologically-based and experientially-influenced developmental realities. The absolute uniqueness of each individual has centrality in these many "appropriate" theories authored by such scholars as: Jean Piaget, Viktor Lowenfeld, Lawrence Kohlberg, John Dewey, Benjamin Bloom, Eric Erikson, Abraham Maslow, Lawrence Kubie, Howard Gardner, William Glasser, Lev Vygotsky, Albert Bandura, Jerome Bruner, Robert Gagné, and many others.

The second cluster contains theories of communication between and within humans, and communication within groups of individuals, especially those groups engaged in team development within compatible organizational structures. Many of these theories evolved from the efforts of those who participated in the National Training Laboratories that originated in Bethel, Maine in the late nineteen forties, under the direction of Kurt Lewin and Leland Bradford. Other familiar names associated with these efforts are: Goodwin Watson, Carl Rogers, Warren Bennis, Kenneth Benne, Ronald Lippitt, Chris Argyris and many others. Sound, appropriate theory in the field of group dynamics, especially group/team development, holds a key to the transformation/change and improvement in our formal educational institutions that now harbor extreme competitiveness and social disorder. This system must be changed into one that promotes cooperation and individual productiveness, consistent with the group development theories.

The third cluster features a central theory developed by Philip Phenix in the nineteen sixties and reinforced by a plethora of supporting positions that deal with the origins and nature of knowledge and knowing from an articulated epistemology. The subject matter theories developed by the Federal commissions of the nineteen sixties, particularly in the areas of mathematics education and biological sciences, along with the enlightened discovery/inquiry approach in the disciplines of history and geography created by this author and Charles Lahey, have extended the credibility of Phenix's theory of six realms of meaning. Each realm is found to contain creative/constructive methodologies and structures that encompass all academic disciplines.

The work of Phenix is broadened with the contribution of Jean Piaget whose theory of knowledge and knowing is epigenetic – it covers the nature of knowledge and knowing from early childhood to all later stages of development. This cluster of theories addresses the need for re-defining subjects of the school from isolated bits of information to be consumed by individual students within arbitrarily organized groups, to an experience-based organization that utilizes the creative construction and communication of meanings using the legitimate processes of organized yet creative ways of knowing and communicating.

The fourth cluster deals with systems and systems theory applied comprehensively to the nature, organization, rationale, and function of the existing school system and that of an effective school system and school curriculum. Bela Banathy, Charles Reigeluth and Jeannette Olson deserve much attention as modern conveyors of systems design "A New Educational Technology." These authors owe much to the work of such persons post World War II as: Ludwig von Bertalanffy, Anatol Rapport, Kenneth Boulding, William Ross Ashby, Margaret Mead and others. Systems theory and systems design provide a systemic and reputable substitute for the current "school system" as an organization for raising up our generations of youth to become mature adults. We have learned to live with an antiquated and ineffective system based on invalid assumptions and beliefs about individual development and behavior, including learning. Systems theory is the hope of the future in education to replace our antiquated and ineffective delivery systems.

The fifth cluster includes a new theory of assessment, recordkeeping, evaluation, and reporting designed to modify and eventually supplant the need for standardization and standardized testing. Central to this cluster is the Constructive Assessment, Recordkeeping and Evaluation System (CARES) developed and field tested by this author. This theory places each unique individual learner in control of his or her record of growth and development that will serve personal needs in ways beneficial to all learners, his or her employers, researchers, parents and many others. This system utilizes modern communications technology in ways that enhance learning and preserves a record of accomplishment that will follow each learner.

The sixth cluster deals with teacher education. It has long since transcended discussion that teachers play a key role in the learning of our youth and our adults. A theory of the effective teaching/learning transactions owes much of its clarification to Leland Bradford within the larger systemic model for modern, twenty-first century schools. Prior and subsequent theories can be integrated into this comprehensive model. A new in-depth approach to teacher education will evolve from the applications of these appropriate and essential theories.

Remaking Our Schools is the product of sixty years of experience by this author within our systems of education beginning at home, continuing in the elementary and secondary school, into teacher education, graduate school and culminating in numerous reform efforts across this land. Each time a resistance to change and suggested improvements were encountered, a search into the origins of that resistance was sought and a conceivable change-strategy was formulated. "Remaking Our Schools" is the product of those efforts.

The Introduction to *Remaking Our Schools for the Twenty-First Century* summarizes an essential theory of communication that identifies the difficulties of gaining acceptance of proposals that deviate from the status quo and provides direction for overcoming obstacles to learning and change.

Chapter one places our change processes in an historical context. The philosophical rifts between a child-centered and subject-centered school experiences have prevented most credible change from being sustained; pendulum swings have existed between these incompatible positions reflected in the rhetoric of change, if not in the actual attempts at change, observable throughout the last century and the beginning of this twenty-first century.

When and if learners utilize the processes of coming to know that are found in the academic disciplines, this can bridge the gap between the subject-centered concerns for conveying to students a fixed amount of pre-defined subject matter and the child development concerns for honoring individual perception and creativity. This child development view of individuality is incompatible with a fixed, imposed common core content-orientation.

Engaging learners at their level of development in legitimate disciplinary processes as practiced by specialists in all fields of inquiry and communication can become an essential ingredient in sustained processes of change. This proposition is supported in this chapter by a brief glimpse into the personal experiences of this author that shaped the philosophy and theory of change expressed in this treatise.

No proposal for change and improvement in the way we educate our youth will be sustained without addressing the need to assess and evaluate outcomes achieved by individual learners. Here, "The Constructive Assessment, Recordkeeping and Evaluation System" (CARES) is presented as a workable, field-tested alternative to the present systems of assessment and evaluation used in our schools and advocated by most decision-makers.

The current approaches through standardization of learning activities, coupled with the use of standardized tests of outcomes reduces acceptable levels of learning to the recall of isolated bits of pre-defined content; it simply ignores the realities of individual development and behavior and has the potential for destroying the creative and critical thinking capabilities of all but a few learners. Chapter two addresses the dimensions of a new and comprehensive assessment and evaluation system that utilizes modern electronic technologies in support of individual and collective learning opportunities for all levels of learning.

Since the existing assessment and evaluation paradigms are so entrenched in the psyches of decision-makers and the lay public, it will take a powerful argument to displace that orientation. Utilization of systems theory, which has a profound legitimacy in the scientific and engineering world of today, has a real potential for displacing the standardization orientation that is being promoted by those in charge.

Chapter three contains a summary of numerous developmental and learning theories that can be validated in our personal experiences and in the extensive experiences of authors including Jean Piaget, Viktor Lowenfeld, Lev Vygotsky, Lawrence Kohlberg, Robert Gagné, and many others. Without internalization of these theories, the educational community and the lay public will not fully understand what is happening or not happening in our schools. Nor will they appreciate the extent to which ignoring these propositions has led to and will continue to lead to the creation of educational practices that severely limit the possibilities for healthy individual and collective development in our society.

Since learning can best be facilitated with consensus building therapeutic communication, it is imperative that an understanding of group dynamics, especially group development is understood and practiced. There is rich literature on this topic that expresses theories revealing the major problems in the way our schools are currently organized and conducted. For example, schools are organized around groups that are no more than collections of individuals where individuality is compromised. Reliable theories of group dynamics discussed in Chapter four provide a far different set of facts about how instruction should be conducted in our schools.

Chapter five describes what a system of education might look like if the principles of learning and development, group processes and compatible organizational structures, along with a re-orientation in our ways of constructing knowledge are honored, for individuals alone and in groups. This chapter addresses the need to revise the way the school system is organized and run and a constitutionally-based democratic structure and process for governance is featured to replace the authoritarian structures that govern most of our public schools today.

Without a revised teacher education component in the proposed systemic model, very little will likely be changed in the system or sustained beyond short excursions into new and isolated territory. Current teacher education programs are utterly absurd when considering the need for developing expertise in the theory and practice of sound principles of individual development and learning, group dynamics and a re-defined theory of knowledge and knowing.

Chapter six outlines a skeleton plan for teacher education that is designed to establish a genuine teaching profession. This chapter features a masterful article written in the late 1950's by Leland Bradford that identifies many of the dimensions of making a professional educator. It provides a profound example of what it takes to be a truly facilitative professional. Implementation of this model is only likely to happen when the total system is re-constructed or re-designed from the bottom up as outlined in the chapters of this treatise.

Chapter seven contains an explanation of three manageable components of the change process considered essential in achieving lasting and legitimate change in our educational programs. Leadership in the change process must pay particular attention to these three components of change.

Chapter eight suggests a procedure ("A Solutions Generator") to aid the readers in examining the internal workings of their local school districts, revealing the systemic inconsistencies that likely exist. This will stimulate a beginning dialogue for bringing about change and improvement at the local level.

There are three Appendices referred to in the text. One outlines what a professional educator needs to know and be able to do, the second contains an example of workshop activity for bringing about change, and the third is a published article that describes in detail the existence of significant forces that often prevent change from occurring.

Introduction

The Difficulties of Communication in the Systemic Change Process

If you are expecting a quick fix for the ills of education, you won't find it here. "Real," sustainable change will take at least a full generation of students with their teacher/facilitators to take control of learning.

This change process must start early and continue throughout the childhood days and beyond. It must be constructed upon a sound philosophical and theoretical base that can be verified in our experiences and in the experiences of others, especially in the experiences of those who have studied these matters in depth. Systemic change is needed that will require the concentrated efforts and support of concerned citizens throughout this country and countries throughout the world. Anything less is just tinkering with an antiquated system.

In September of 1989, Robert Muller, former Assistant Secretary-General of the United Nations, defined the objectives for a "World Core Curriculum," most relevant today given the current obsession in this country with mandating a common core curriculum that proposes to be evaluated with a one-size-fits-all standardized test. According to Muller, objectives for a real common core curriculum are "…to give children **(to provide learners with the opportunity to meaningfully construct**) (emphasis added) (1) a good picture of the home into which they are born–from the infinitely large realm of the universe and our planetary home down to the atom and the infinitely small, (2) a correct picture of the family into which they are born–namely, the human family with its great variety of natural and cultural common features and infinite diversity, (3) an accurate picture of the time flow into which they are born–from paleontology, archaeology, and history to the future, and (4) a sense of their important, personal, miraculous lives in this wondrous creation, with the physical, mental, sentimental, and spiritual qualities, and the role they can play to further humanity's progress during their life on earth."

How these objectives and more can be achieved is the subject of this book.

The purpose of this treatise is to connect with all concerned citizens interested in real change and improvement in education within the USA and elsewhere. *Remaking Our Schools* can and must become our national and international priority.

The audience for this treatise begins with the lay public. Without stirring an interest among members of the public, the entrenched ideas often shared with the educational establishment will be perpetuated. Our educational system will continue to be considered a "sacred cow," untouchable and institutionalized, regardless of the evidence of its possible negative impact on individuals and society.

Needed is a thorough analysis of the systemic elements that support the qualities for success, complete with a sound rationale for their justification. With this analysis we will recognize that failure in the general education programs of our schools is in large measure responsible for negative attitudes and aggressive actions we are experiencing in this modern world. Individuals cannot spend their growing years immersed in nearly meaningless activities for the satisfaction of those in authority without many developing deep resentment and frustration. These frustrations become embedded in their being and for too many that frustration is eventually taken out on fellow human beings. We have developed a population that is far more interested in aggressive sport, exploitation, and warfare, than learning to understand our world and the human beings within it. This, I believe, is attributable to experiences or lack of experiences offered to students in their general education programs in our conventional public schools.

That is not to say that our schools have had little value. They have served as a resource for a limited number of learners; those with motivation to find meaning in their lives or find the information necessary to achieve a diploma or a license to practice in their chosen field. However, the vast majority of our students do not have the necessary motivation or vision to pursue a long range plan for a better life. Most are bogged down with ineffective strategies for learning such as memorization of pre-defined information that the schools are noted for.

The plan for change proposed here calls for a major overhaul of our conventional schools. This plan is not a "fixer-upper," it is a re-design from the bottom up. It offers an alternative that is dynamic and systemically sound. It features innovations that can replace the existing schools with institutions that will produce individuals in our global society who are far more competent, compassionate, and healthy.

The field-tested components of this plan are explained in this treatise. They are based on the personal experiences of this author over seven decades, spanning the full spectrum of teaching and learning from early childhood, to graduate and post graduate education and supported by many whose published works are detailed in this text.

There are five main innovations in the proposed design that address needed and essential changes.

The first and most fundamental innovation addresses the need to establish a validated and widely shared knowledge base that will guide decision-making in our schools. That knowledge base must be comprehensive and instructive about what is known and can be verified regarding human growth and development, including learning, for individuals within groups and institutions.

The second addresses the need to establish an individualized, computer-based assessment, record-keeping, evaluation, and reporting system that is consistent with and complementary to what we know and can verify about human growth and development.

The third addresses the need to install a legitimate and constructive set of strategies for learning using the methods and materials of a full range of ways of knowing and communicating the academic disciplines within six "realms of meaning."

The fourth addresses the need to organize information/data necessary for the pursuit of personal meanings and personal competency. Information must support the conduct of individual and collective investigations, interpretations, and communications using electronic storage, accessing, and communication technologies.

The fifth addresses the need to replace the existing authoritarian structures and decision-making procedures with a democratically-based organization. While the school has a business component it is not a business, it is a social institution that must employ strategies that recognize the full range of individual needs and aspirations. Democratic participation will foster the use of strategies that will cost less money by encouraging far wider participation and responsibility for establishing and maintaining a viable, effective, and dynamic school system at all levels of education.

Remaking Our Schools for the Twenty-First Century is not a slogan; *it's a **Blueprint for Real Change in Our Educational Systems***.

1. *What is different about this effort?* **This is grassroots, low budget, no glitz view of the processes and products of education from a systems point of view—a comprehensive rather than a piecemeal attempt to bring about a better school.** It proposes to recognize and capitalize upon the potential for learning during every hour of the day, three hundred sixty-five days of the year, throughout each person's unique lifetime. Learning is not to be reserved for the time between nine and three; it knows no summer vacation. Personal experiences that lead to learning are found

throughout life as it occurs in all its manifestations, day after day, night after night.

2. *How much of one's personal experience is utilized and valued in our current educational systems?* Not much, if any.

3. *Why is this so?* Schools are primarily dispensers of pre-defined information, much of it trivial and reflective of the biases of its organizers, packaged for consumption by students with a promise that someday the information will become relevant. The students are taught, that is informed, about many things, but what is actually learned is infinitesimal. Scores on a test provide little evidence of what has actually been learned.

4. *What are the reasons for this?* Our conventional schools are not organized for effective learning. Learning results from an internally stimulated, individualized, creative process, beginning with simple responses to stimuli/experience in the real world and gradually building to a level of competent problem solving; learning is much more than an externally imposed requirement to be reflected in test scores. Evidence shows that the nature of learning and human development is not adequately understood in our schools, the nature of group processes and communication are not being implemented, the arrangement of subjects to be consumed defies logic, and the way we humans come to know is essentially ignored. In the plan described here these needs are addressed.

5. *What are the results of shortcomings among educators and the lay public?* The natural curiosity of young learners is frequently and severely diminished before the age of ten. Resigned boredom (or not so resigned) for many grows with every day thereafter; the great escape is eagerly sought—graduation and making money—or dropping out of school to find something better. If something better is not found, frustration is understandably taken out on the human and material surroundings. The alternative is to stay in school and fill in the blanks for homework, subordinate personal ideas to the pronouncements of so-called experts; dutifully, or not so dutifully, conform to the demands of the system, attend classes, do

homework, commit to memory what is hoped will be on the test, pass the test and move on to the next class, or, flunk the test and drop out of this perceived prison-like environment in exchange for more grief.

6. *What must we do to change this situation?* Everyone has a set of beliefs and assumptions that we hold about life, including what we understand about education that guides much of our behavior. We must change those beliefs and assumptions that are wrought out of ignorance about the fundamental foundations required for an effective education. What we know and can be verified in our own experiences and in the experiences of others about the nature of human development and behavior, including learning, must be understood and acted upon. What we know and can be verified about the nature of communication and group processes, especially group (team) development, must be acted upon. The subjects to be investigated must be organized to reflect the creative processes required of learning, including an integration of all ways of knowing in all realms of meaning. The school as a social system, not a profit-making business, must be studied to reveal its inconsistencies with what we know about individuals, groups, and ways of knowing, and make the needed changes. The role of facilitators of learning needs to be oriented toward guidance of each individual's unique search for meaning, the results of that learning to be shared with others who are engaged in that search as well. These are the components of a foundation for education at all levels from pre-school to post graduate school and beyond that must replace the current shifting rhetoric and the piecemeal approach to educational practice and change. These components form the basis for a written constitution and by-laws that will guide decision-making toward an effective school system.

7. *What else needs to change?* The assessment, recordkeeping, and evaluation systems in our schools must be replaced with a system that recognizes the wide world of personal learning opportunities for each unique individual, utilizing the

electronic input, storage, manipulation, and communication capabilities of modern technologies. Focused on the mastery of personally constructed systems, this will free each learner to capitalize upon the many opportunities and experiences that occur in everyday life. A complete record of learning generated by each individual will provide the evidences required for determining success or failure of learners and the system within which they are working.

8. *What would be the result of these changes?* Students who learn how to learn will become lifelong learners, pursuing personally meaningful searches for making sense out of their lives and the vast universe. From an orientation with systems concepts, learners will be constantly looking to develop what A.N. Whitehead, a noted philosopher/mathematician, called "an eye for the whole chessboard, for the bearing of one set of ideas on another." This orientation aids the complex processes of problem solving and recall. It fosters a real sense of humility as one discovers a place among the many dimensions of this universe and beyond. It will develop sincere compassion for the needs and aspirations of all peoples, regardless of age, race, ethnicity, or economic standing. It will fulfill the promise of humankind to be human. Democratic processes will become more than a slogan to be pronounced but will become procedures to be engaged.

9. *How soon can a change be made?* "Change is a process, not an event." (Hord et.al., 1987)

Change must begin at the earliest levels of education and gradually spread to all other levels including higher education and on the job.

If teachers are better prepared they will be able to help bring about changes in how schools conduct their business. However, I spent fifty years in teacher education working tirelessly to change the primary orientation of schools as dispensers of information to one of engaging students in *real learning* that has lasting personal meaning for each student. The lessons from this experience show how difficult it is to bring about these needed changes.

I worked in laboratory schools and conducted courses in foundations of education and teaching social studies using a discovery approach. I supervised student teachers and observed teachers at work in many different settings. I set in motion a number of experimental programs that were designed to help point the way to a better system of education. I served as a consultant to many school districts and funded projects throughout New England, the Carolinas, Ohio, and elsewhere. I submitted two elaborate charter school proposals only to receive a hostile attack for even suggesting that things could be different.

I have spent a long career attempting to convey the messages of change to numerous groups throughout society, including the educational community and the lay public. These efforts, while assisting many in realizing the possibilities for change, far too many have not heard the message. This has led me to examine the realities of communication.

Just when I thought my messages had been heard by another I got additional feedback and realized I have not communicated as effectively as I originally thought. Frustrated with this realization, each time I found difficulties in communicating, I have attempted once more to clarify my message. Every teacher has faced this reality after the results of their lessons are evaluated. What they thought they taught is seldom what was fully internalized or learned. Frustration with this event has led to instruction and assessment/evaluation that has been reduced in education to the recall of simple concepts and isolated terminology.

In a face to face encounter, we have the advantage of gestures and expressions with direct feedback that adds meaning and context to our messages. We feel satisfied when the feedback received seems to validate our assumption that our message is clear and it has been received as we intended it.

When we try to convey our messages in writing, we then

have to substitute our varied skills of verbal communication for skills in composing messages with printed words, carefully strung together in such a way as to make our meaning clear. This requires a skill not everyone has mastered. Depending upon the complexity of the message, it may require extraordinary skills and extensive elaboration to convey our meanings, especially since the receiving person is not there to provide immediate feedback. Besides the written word, workshops are useful, as are audio-visual presentations and social networking.

The message about the need for systemic change and what it involves, supported by its rationale and underlying theory is the thesis of this book. Understanding the intricacies of communication is essential to aid the reader in building a foundation for understanding its content.

The first crucial element in any communication is the fact that input stimuli, messages from others, no matter from where or how they originate, is assimilated or received into pre-existing patterns of thought and insight. This means each individual has already established a personal orientation that filters whatever is contained in the communication. Many, for instance, have already established their orientations to the nature and processes of education, based upon distilled and often vague memories of school experiences. This influences and often controls the interpretations of whatever messages of systemic change are presented.

These pre-existing structures reflect the residue of past experiences that reside essentially at an unconscious level. These pre-existing structures filter the communication and change or distort it to conform to its pre-defined orientations, no matter how hard we try to convey exact meaning in our messages. This is an important reason for the difficulties of convincing educators and the public that our schools need changing, now.

The messages received can be recognized and assimilated thus reinforcing pre-existing structures, or, they are not recognized and they create dissonance. Some messages are perceived to require immediate responses since they are automatically related to past experiences, while others are variously massaged with meta-cognition (inner speech) within the internal processes of mentation. Messages that are massaged, that is, organized, incubated, and stored, are eventually encoded in language forms for expression to others. Encoded language can take three forms as Bruner explained, namely, enactive, which includes outward, observable behavior, iconic which is the language of imagery, and symbolic, the language that represents our thoughts in various symbolic codes (Bruner, Jerome, 1968).

New structures can lead to new representations in the form of enactive, iconic or symbolic language. Enactive language is non-verbal, iconic language is pictorial/graphic, and symbolic language is composed of symbols that are in the form of words, gestures or mathematical/logical constructs.

The receiver of an encoded message must assimilate and decode the message in a way similar to how the sender processed the message at the start of the sequence, if the meanings conveyed are to be similar to those received. The internalized, encoded messages either reinforce pre-existing structures or they challenge them. When challenged, the message can be ignored or it can lead to ideation, incubation, or storage. Challenged messages can potentially lead to the adaptation of prior-held beliefs and assumptions, provided there is a willingness to entertain possibilities.

When two or more persons are involved in a communication transaction, the encoded output from one person is the input for the other. Input is assimilated into that person's pre-existing structures as it is decoded. Those structures can determine what is to be accepted or modified to conform to that person's personal orientation. When the challenge is accepted, it can lead to ideation, incubation, or storage. If rejected, the message becomes distorted and even discarded. When pre-existing structures are adapted as a result of the challenge, change has occurred and these adapted structures are transformed and represented in enactive, iconic or symbolic language—changes in behavior.

The continued exchange of one person's encoded output to the other's input leads to a process of validation of the intended meanings in the communication. Validation is sought through back and forth exchanges that may require several or more opportunities to determine the shared meanings. Satisfaction is reached when the encoded message has been similarly decoded and both parties to the transaction feel good about the communication. This is referred to in group process literature as "consensual validation."

It is important to note, even with a high degree of satisfaction, the messages are only similar, not identical, due to the vast differences in personal backgrounds of the individuals involved. The message intended is never exactly the message that is received. Acknowledging this fact is the first step in the realization that improvements in communication are incremental, requiring time, active engagement and a supportive environment in which to approach satisfaction in achieving a consensus.

There are at least six factors that act as intermediary influences between two or more persons in a communication transaction. The first is the quality of the social context, whether supportive or threatening; this will either enhance or diminish the satisfaction of meanings intended and received. A threatening environment potentially shuts down the stage of ideation and incubation, since a direct and immediate response is often required.

The second influence is equilibration, a term borrowed from Jean Piaget. It refers to the energy level, need, and motivation for engaging the conversation. Obviously, if there is a lack of energy, need, and motivation present in the communication, it will not be actively engaged.

The third influence is the level of maturation or stage of development. A communication framed in adult's symbolic language will not compute as intended with a youngster at the pre-operational or pre-logical level. Language at that level is limited to signs that denote meaning, void of more sophisticated subtleties. Enactive and creative iconic language-forms are most appropriate as a medium for communication at this pre-operational/pre-logical level. Symbolic language used by adults is gibberish to the pre-operational, pre-logical youngster, but the accompanying non-verbal language is more readily processed.

Individuals at the concrete operational level, the level when logical capacities emerge, can assimilate limited symbolic meanings if they are attached to concrete and direct experiences. Most symbolic language is out of reach for individuals at this concrete level of maturation since it is not directly attached to concrete examples.

Individuals at the formal operational level, the level that abstract reasoning, hypothetical deduction and higher thought processes emerge, meanings offered in symbolic language forms can and will be assimilated.

The fourth influence has to do with the level, type, quality, and quantity of experience encountered by each participant in the communication transaction. For example, a person listening to a lecture in biology, or any discipline where technical terms are used that have symbolic meanings to the lecturer, comes across to the listener as gibberish or as different information than that intended by the lecturer, if the listener does not have the experiential background to sufficiently decode the intended meanings.

The importance of this reality cannot be overstated. Much of the instruction in our schools involves messages with more or less symbolic meanings, served to students as passive receivers with limited background for assimilating those messages. It matters little whether the messages are relayed through electronic media or by *Sesame Street* type presentations. Related personal and concrete experience is required to develop a readiness for assimilating and internalizing more fully the intended message. Otherwise, the message remains superficial.

What is often determined to be failure on the part of the student in getting the message is likely to be failure on the part of the teacher in not providing the pre-requisite experience that would prepare the student to assimilate the intended messages. This experience must best be concrete and direct. Only after much deliberation does symbolic language get attached to the meanings derived from concrete experience. This is as true for college students and other adults as it is for concrete operational and formal operational children. The main difference is in the time that it takes to generate the level of symbolic meaning and the complexity of the message that can be entertained.

The failure to communicate effectively in an instructional setting generates the justification for remedial treatments. Remediation most often involves more repetitions, which eventually can bring about approvable outward expressions that resemble Pavlov's dogs reacting by salivating. These procedures result from a violation of basic principles that underlie the nature of effective communication and add additional costs for education. Most importantly, they create severe social deprivations for learners who are designated as failures.

The fifth intermediary influence is self-awareness, the recognition of inner cues and clues. Self-awareness is developed over time through introspection, validated or challenged with the assistance of others who provide perceptual feedback.

The sixth intermediary influence that exists with all parties to communication transactions is the physical/biological potentialities of each individual. Each person has a unique hereditary/genetic/developmental background, personal health status, and state of wellness. These states of being may maximize the potential for hearing and reacting to communications or they may minimize that potential.

The basic elements of communication are illustrated in the following chart.

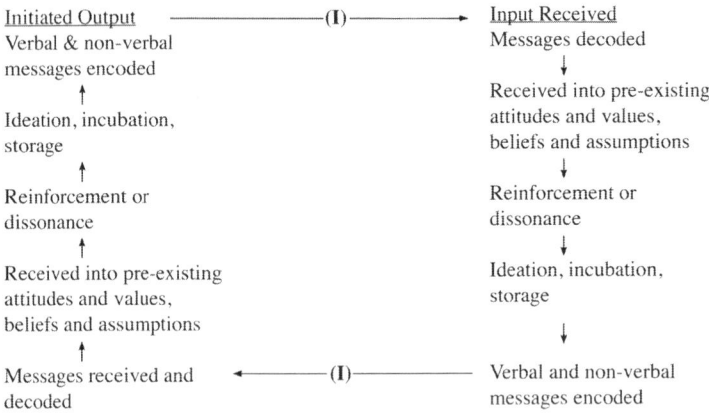

Communication Cycle

Initiated Output — (I) → Input Received

(Intermediary Variables diagram)

(I)
Intermediary Variables

Quality of the social context

Energy level, need and motivation

Level of intellectual development

Level, type, quality and quantity of experience

Self awareness

Physical/biological potentialities

As I attempt to convey the message of systemic change, I am faced with the realities of the effects these intermediary influences have over my communication. Even though I believe the shortcomings of the existing school system are threatening our democratic way of life, there seems to be reluctance in many to entertain that possibility. A positive message is more readily received than a negative one. This reality may account for avoidance of a penetrating examination of the problems in our schools.

In this era of visual communications through electronic messaging, there seems to exist a disturbing level of impatience with detailed printed words as a means of conveying meaning, especially if it involves careful study and prolonged thought-processing. Assimilating complex messages requires a dedicated commitment that is difficult to fit in with the busy lives of most Americans who consider "Tweets" to be sufficient communication. They got that way by being bombarded with disconnected sound bites in school that are reinforced through the media.

The audiences for the messages about systemic change in our public schools are young and older adults who theoretically are capable of "higher thought processes." They may, and often do choose to dismiss important issues without taking the time for full examination. This places a heavy burden on the power of the stand-alone written word without the benefit of further elaboration to gain appreciation of the full meanings attempted to be conveyed.

Perhaps the most challenging aspect for conveyance of these messages of change is the fact that substantial amounts of background information are missing, which is needed for establishing a full appreciation for the propositions about to be presented in this treatise. This information, as much as possible, will be summarized from original works that are represented in a library of sources, too extensive to be fully included here. The reader is asked to engage the materials with patience and perseverance.

Widespread and sustainable changes in education in the U.S. can only be achieved when the American public, including educators, determine which educational processes and structures will result in the development of compassionate and competent citizens. *Remaking Our Schools* is an attempt to help with this determination.

The work of Lawrence Kubie, MD, a psychiatrist whose impeccable credentials and a mile-long resume of critiques of the processes of education is featured extensively throughout this treatise. His basic premise and mine is that "...we do not need to be taught to think: indeed that is something that cannot be taught. Thinking processes actually are automatic, swift, and spontaneous when allowed to proceed undisturbed by other influences. Therefore, what we need is to be educated in how not to interfere with the inherent capacity of the human mind to think." (This does not mean to imply a laizze faire attitude but rather an active supportive transactional relationship.) "We need also to be helped to acquire the tools of communication…" (*Kubie*, Lawrence S. 1961)

Although much of Kubie's writing occurred in the 1950s and 60s, his framework for understanding the human mind has not been altered, simply elaborated and refined. It is profoundly relevant in today's understanding of the educational processes. Take, for example, this Kubie statement: "My point is that education will continue to perpetuate a fraud on culture until it accepts the full implications of the fact that the free creative velocity of our thinking apparatus is continually being braked and driven off course by the play of unconscious forces. Educational procedures that fail to recognize this end up by increasing the interference from latent and unrecognized neurotic (rigid-emphasis added) forces." This reality is pervasive in today's educational arena and is being compounded by the efforts of those more interested in profitmaking than turning the public into thinking, mature individuals.

How many decision makers in today's educational reform movements even begin to understand the pervasive meaning of these important words? The answer is not encouraging. Their immaturity is witnessed everywhere. Unfortunately, as Kubie states: "We cannot be wise yet remain immature. Maturity requires the capacity to change, to become different, to react in varied and unanticipated ways. All of these words describe different facets of this same human need: and none of it is attainable as long as the human spirit remains imprisoned in its masked neuroses. That is the ultimate challenge to the value of any educational process in any culture." That is the challenge this book is designed to address.

Chapter 1

Remaking Our Schools for the Twenty-First Century – What will it take to fix it?

The attitudes and values, beliefs and assumptions that direct behavior, including how we view education, are developed gradually over time from past experiences, many of those experiences have occurred in our elementary, middle and secondary schools. Some of these assumptions and beliefs are valid and some are invalid. Determining the validity of our assumptions and beliefs about education should become a never-ending process of examination and re-examination based on our personal experiences and those of others. That is an essential process of change and growth, pivotal in the efforts to change/improve our schools.

As Hord, et al. made clear in their writing, *Taking Charge of Change*, (1987) published by the Association for Supervision and Curriculum Development (ASCD) "Change is a process, not an event...change is primarily about individuals and their beliefs and actions, rather than merely about programs, materials, technology or equipment (although all of these elements are important)."

Individuals have led movements, each focused on the improvement of education, each based on a particular set of assumptions and beliefs. Assumptions and beliefs professed in one movement are often in conflict with those of another movement. An historical perspective can help establish the facts regarding the results of the evolution of change and reform that has taken place over the last century in our conventional public schools.

Historical Relevance

How much progress have we been able to achieve with the current emphasis on high stakes testing and drill/regurgitate methodology? In 1993, Bela Banathy, a leading advocate of systemic change in educational institutions had this to say in the first chapter of a book that sounded the alarm about the need for systemic reforms. "The ship of education is sailing on troubled waters. One national report after another highlights the current 'crisis' of a 'nation at risk,' pointing out dangerous currents and menacing shoals. There is an ever increasing realization that unless we change the course, the ship will sink. But people are still trying to 'rearrange the chairs' on the deck of a sinking ship" (Reigeluth, C.M., Banathy, B.H., & Olson, J.R. 1993).

In 2012, the rearrangement of the chairs is still going on.

What have been the changes before and after these pronouncements?

There has been a long standing and continuing rift between the advocates of child development and those of a subject matter orientation that plagues the possibilities for any meaningful change in education. Unless we find a solution that bridges this philosophical conflict it can be expected that any changes will be short lived. Creating such a bridge is a major thrust of this book.

The child development advocates have maintained the ideal that each child is unique and must be recognized as having a creative capability for interacting with and uniquely making sense out of life in all its manifestations. This ideal is often expressed in less than precise terminology as part of the personal orientations of teachers who work with learners every day of their professional lives, who recognize the uniqueness of each individual.

The subject matter advocates have maintained the point of view that since there is a vast library of information, assembled over time, there is far too much to be processed by individuals who attend school. Therefore, a pre-selected portion of that library (a common core curriculum) is identified by so-called experts, reflecting their particular biases, packaged for instruction. The learner is supposed to consume the pre-selected information and show some evidence of recall and conformity with the offerings of its programmed conclusions. This is believed to adequately prepare students for any eventuality the future may bring. This subject matter orientation places the learner in a consumptive mode, interfering with and often denying the creative potential for constructing personal meanings from the experiences of individual human beings.

The rift between these subject matter concerns and those of the child development advocates can be better understood when reviewing national trends in educational change, at least the change reflected within the rhetoric, over the last one hundred years or more. It demonstrates where we have been, where we are now and what the future may hold.

There have been pendulum swings between the advocates of these opposing views beginning with the early years of the twentieth century. Subject matter concerns were dominant in those years. Later in the 20s and 30s those ideas were challenged by the progressive movement led by John Dewey. While the results of progressive schools were inspirational in suggesting a dramatic change in the way schools conducted their learning activities, the subject matter advocates eventually won out and the pendulum swung back toward the subject matter side.

A few remnants of the progressive movement remained in the Project Method of William Heard Kilpatrick (1918) where units of work became the predominate elementary classroom activity. This was a plan that placed emphasis on the acquisition of subject matter and the skills necessary to read and write, while allowing the learners an opportunity to participate in classroom decision-making.

This effort still remains essential in the lesson plans of many elementary teachers, even today, though the lessons are often designed and packaged for consumption apart from the learners who are supposed to buy into the plans and master their pre-defined contents.

To assist in understanding and evaluating how successful this approach to education has been, a brief review of another event of the early 1950s is useful as background information. Prior to the Russian *Sputnik*, committees of educators met to review the test questions that teachers used in their teacher-made and standardized tests in an effort to improve instruction. Thousands of questions were examined and placed in categories. Three handbooks emerged from this effort. One has been commonly referred to as Bloom's Taxonomy of Educational Objectives–Cognitive Domain. Actually, this taxonomy was the result of the work of an educator led committee, chaired by Ben Bloom of the University of Chicago.

Two other handbooks were published, one dealt with the Affective Domain and the other with the Psycho/Motor Domain. Neither of these two handbooks received the recognition they deserved, presumably because they didn't deal with the subject matter concerns of the school and due to the nature of the dimensions of life they dealt with, the handbooks appeared less precise and were often viewed erroneously as less scholarly.

Since these handbooks represented a separation of the cognitive from the affective and the psycho/motor dimensions of human behavior, it contributed to the lack of understanding of the interconnections between these three dimensions important in understanding human activities.

In Bloom's Taxonomy of educational objectives, cognition is arranged from simple to complex. The first level is simple recall of information—knowledge of facts, events, theories etc. The next higher level of cognition is called comprehension. This involves translation, interpretation and extrapolation referred to in common language as simple understanding. The next level is called application. This refers to the individual's ability to link with what has been understood about personal experience, but on a fairly limited basis. Following application is analysis. This involves the taking apart of what was understood at the application level and applying it to understanding more of the details involved in any subject. Once the subject matter is taken apart, it is re-constructed and elaborated at the synthesis level, as a creative proposition, unique to each individual. Synthesized cognition leads to critical (and creative) evaluation, the most complex and mature level of cognition.

It was around the time of this publication that Professor Lahey and I, while employed at SUNY Potsdam, were developing a *Discovery Approach to the Teaching of Social Studies*, featuring the methods and materials of historians and geographers in a setting that encouraged inquiry. We used Bloom's terminology to frame our arguments about the importance of our approach to teaching and learning, focusing on the achievement of synthesis and critical/creative evaluation. Our plan demonstrated a counter proposal to the unit approach in classroom instruction that typically deals with isolated bits of information primarily at the knowledge level.

The unit plan was severely challenged when the Russian *Sputnik* flew into space in 1957 ahead of the U.S.A. A near panic erupted that recognized the inadequacies of our math and science programs. The mainstays of the subject matter orientation, college professors, were called in to solve the problem. Mathematicians and scientists headed up massive federally funded projects to study the nature of their disciplines and prepare classroom methods and materials designed to more effectively teach their subjects to unsuspecting elementary and secondary level students.

In spite of limited effectiveness, as witnessed by the inadequacies of math and science outcomes measured today by standardized tests, this was a very fruitful period that resulted in an intellectual examination of education generating many calls for reform. The "New Math" and improvements in the biological sciences grew out of this effort with an emphasis on discovery.

This effort coincided with the Vietnam War protests and a growing dissatisfaction with the way our country conducted its business and the perceived lack of opportunity for finding personal meaning in life's experiences. Today, a cursory view of progress reveals the reality that not much improvement has resulted from this effort.

At this time, based on a successful experiment that featured one teacher/group leader with the responsibility for "teaching" all the subjects of the freshman curriculum with a group of elementary education majors enrolled in a New Jersey State College, there was an attempt by this author to bridge the gap between these competing philosophies.

This led to the design of a comprehensive teacher education program called the "Open Curriculum." This program was begun at a New York State college and it lasted two years before the forces of convention did it in (Arnold, R. 1967).

The efforts at reform, which included school design as open architecture and open education, were quickly replaced in the Reagan era with what was labeled a "back-to-the-basics" subject matter orientation. With regard to concerns about the quality of our conventional education, Reagan commissioned a study group to investigate. Their report emphasized what was perceived as a nation at risk since the quality of education in this country was thought to be nearing a crisis. Ronald Reagan's National Commission on Excellence in Education submitted a report called *A Nation at Risk: The Imperative For Educational Reform* (1983). This report stimulated widespread concern about what to do about our failing schools. The report opened the flood gates for a plethora of proposals for change. (A recent report in 2012 involving Condoleezza Rice, a former Secretary of State, under the second Bush administration, indicates approval of the common core curriculum and the use of standardized tests as the solution to all the ills of education, another example of rearranging the chairs on a sinking ship.)

An outgrowth of dissatisfaction emerged among educators that led to a push back on the back-to-the-basics effort that was called the constructivist movement. This was stimulated by a re-discovery and re-emphasis on the work of Piaget and other child development advocates who had been around for many years. This served at the time as a rationale for the child advocate positions and the pendulum swung temporarily toward the child development side. The concept of systemic change emerged from these proposals.

In 1993, a book was published that presented "the results of a NATO Advanced Research Workshop on educational systems design as a new educational technology. The objective of the workshop was to advance our knowledge about the comprehensive systems design approach for improving educational systems" (Reigeluth, C.M., Banathy, B.H., & Olson, 1993). The fact that this report resulted from a NATO organized effort indicates a perception that problems in education were not confined to the boundaries of the USA.

There were twenty eight separate contributors to this report and all of them accepted the notion that systemic change in our schools was needed and they each contributed to this effort by exploring the dimensions of system's theory, its processes and change strategies.

When the first Bush administration took office following the Reagan era, the President declared himself to be the "education president." The New American Schools Development Corporation was formed to take on the task of reforming our schools. It was proposed that this corporation would raise private capital to fund thirty proposals to address a redesign of American education. It hired the Rand Corporation to write the RFP (request for proposals) which featured forward looking concepts of what might be accomplished. It was so convincing that this author organized a team to help design a comprehensive response to the Rand produced guidelines. Our proposal received a ranking of seventeenth among over six hundred proposals submitted for the redesign of American education.

Shortly after hearing encouraging news about our ranking that supposedly gave us eligibility to receive funding under this program we received word that sufficient private investment could not be secured and only a handful of proposals instead of thirty were selected for implementation. When the announcement of these proposals was finally delivered by the commissioner of professional football, nearly all the participants originally involved had vanished. The funded proposals offered gimmicks for presenting subject matter to passive learners, reflecting traditions that were in place when the *Nation at Risk* report was published. So much for the education president.

Prior to the *Sputnik* event, there was a growing movement in education to focus only on observable behavior when defining or evaluating the progress of educational instruction and learning. There was little room it was thought for a "fuzzy-minded" concern for unobservable behavior like higher thought processes. A book on how to write "behavioral objectives" became the talk of the profession. This represented the behaviorist orientation of Skinner and others (Mager, R. 1962).

The behaviorist orientation was picked up in the late 1980s and early 90s by the educational research establishment in its efforts to legitimize the teaching "profession" that was under siege from the criticism of the Reagan report. It was thought that legitimacy could be obtained if change became research-based. Educational research was/is based on studying mostly isolated variables that did not and cannot possibly account for the complex social events of education. Yet, there was/is blind acceptance of this notion.

It was thought that since higher thought processes are generally unobservable, focusing on the outward, observable behavior of the learners was the best first step in the way to improve the quality of education. This legitimized the testing movement and its narrow definition of learning and led to the emergence of learner evaluations based on a concept of "central tendencies"; that established the rationale for grade level placements and hierarchal categories of excellence.

After the first Bush administration had failed to capitalize on the movement to reform our schools, President Clinton's administration initiated what was called "Goals 2000." This was a forward looking proposal that encouraged cooperative decision making at the local levels of education in hopes that increased participation would bring about significant changes. This represented a pendulum swing back toward the child development side of the conflict.

Again, this author organized a team of educators to pursue a comprehensive redesign particularly focused on the formation of a rural school consortium in upstate New York. This project was initially funded on a five year plan that would attempt to bring a systems approach to the planning and implementation of educational reforms. The initial stages of this project were focused on the development of a validated knowledge base that included what we know and can verify about learning and development, individually and in groups and institutions.

After two and one half years of funding, the project was canceled ostensibly as a result of complaints about changes that were occurring from members of administration and school board members conveyed to the State Education Department. The project was cancelled without any consideration of the progress that had been made, no interviews were conducted with the principals of the project, nor the faculty members who had made real progress having developed a sincere belief that something positive was happening. Once again they became disillusioned with the arbitrary decision making processes they had so often endured in the past. A sample of the process recordings developed from workshops conducted in the *Goals 2000 Project* that faculty members had experienced can be found in Appendix B.

During the second Bush administration, two important

initiatives emerged—the charter school movement and the "No Child Left Behind" legislation.

The Charter School legislation emphasized systemic change, at least on paper. It allowed almost anyone to propose changes under rules established for judging success. This movement allowed profit-making enterprises to enter the lucrative public school business. In the early years of the movement, even foreign corporations established charter schools that were funded by our taxpayer money, extracted from the public school budgets. This tendency for private capital to promote these efforts that allow profits to be made is widespread today and growing rapidly.

Since the guidelines for charter schools seemed inclusive and open-ended, this author organized a team of educators to submit a charter school design that was built on a legitimate systemic change model. In New York State, charter schools can be approved through two state agencies, the State University of New York and the New York State Education Department. Our first submission was entered through the SUNY agency since many of the principals in our project were employees of the State University at Plattsburgh, NY. (It is important to note that the administration of SUNY Plattsburgh decided not to support any charter school proposals, especially ours, without any discussion with its principals who were long time faculty members of the education and liberal arts departments of the college.)

Earlier, the Educational Research and Demonstration Center on the Plattsburgh Campus had been closed and its resources and faculty, over twenty positions, were transferred to the formation of a business school. This meant that the laboratory school for pre-service elementary and secondary school teachers no longer existed in spite of the fact that a relatively new building had been erected with extensive facilities for educational research and demonstration including one-way vision observation windows, closed circuit television etc. at a cost of millions of dollars. Legislation to prevent this move was approved overwhelmingly by the state legislature, but it was vetoed by the governor, claiming that it would usurp the authority of college presidents. It's important to take note of the fact that teacher education is still the largest major on that campus, even without a campus laboratory school.

Our proposed charter school was designed to help fill the void left by the closing of the laboratory school. We proposed a regional school as a center of inquiry into teaching and learning that would involve all the area schools in this rural region, including the colleges that were contributing to the preparation of teachers. We intended to house our school in a building which was originally part of the Plattsburgh SAC base that had been recently closed. Our proposal was a comprehensive redesign that required extensive documentation and background information. The proposal was literally four inches thick, with many appendices that displayed the work of this author, supported by the literature of systemic change. It was proposed that a sound knowledge base, a set of valid beliefs and assumptions, would be required as a foundation for sustainable and effective changes in education.

This proposal met with a hostile attack by the reviewers of the project and the sponsoring agency. The treatment of this effort prompted an investigation by a *New York Times* writer, but nothing substantial ever resulted from our response. The proposal also met with local resistance especially from private parochial interests within the area.

Determined to push forward in spite of our disappointment with the SUNY agency, we decided to submit our proposal through the New York State Education Department. The same proposal was submitted under a new title that included the governor's name, having written to him for permission. Since we included a letter to the governor that stated if we did not hear from him to the contrary, we would proceed to use his name in the title. He never responded to the request, so we proceeded on the basis of our request.

Like the SUNY response, we received a hostile attack for

suggesting our version of the charter school requirements. As the team leader for the project, this author attended the meeting when the NYS Board of Regents voted to officially reject the proposal. It was obvious that these individuals did not agree with the contents of the project, or possibly did not know what the project was about, since they one by one voiced their disapproval with mostly a no-comment negative vote. The chair of the Regents had only to say, "I wonder if the Governor knows his name is used in the title of this project." One of the Regents was a member of the same faculty as the authors of this project, and he took this opportunity especially to voice his disapproval. This was clearly a decision from a subject matter determination that disregarded the requirements for process that is represented by the child development orientations.

The charter school movement has gained considerable momentum in recent times with federal support in an effort to stimulate change in the way public schools are conducted. While it can be said that this movement adopted a systemic change model, its implementation of systems theory is far from what was identified by Bela Banathy and his colleagues during the NATO workshop mentioned at the beginning of this writing. Like other efforts at what was referred to as systemic change it has become nothing more than what Banathy saw as rearranging the chairs on the deck of a sinking ship.

The bipartisan legislation of the second Bush administration was granted the slogan, "No Child Left Behind" as recognition of the need to improve the education of all students. This effort featured a widespread testing program using a rationale based on the need to know what is happening in the schools of this country. Its "need to know" necessitated the use of standardized testing. The subject matter advocates, once again won out, accepting a blind assumption that the standardized test was an adequate measure of learning.

Numerous articles have been published challenging this assumption. One article is of particular interest, written by

Marion Brady, a frequent contributor to the *Washington Post*. Titled "Unanswered Questions About Standardized Tests" in the April 27, 2011 edition of the *Washington Post*. He stated:

"Standardized tests are enhancing and destroying reputations, opening and closing doors of opportunity, raising and lowering property values, starting and ending professional careers, determining the life chances of the young, and shaping the intellectual resources upon which America's future largely hinges.... You might think that with so much riding on the tests, every civic-minded person in the country would be demanding transparency, proof of validity, assurance that every item on every test had been examined from every possible perspective. If you think that you are wrong.... This vast experiment with kids' minds and America's future was put in place without broad national debate, without in-depth research, without trial pilot programs, and without answering posed questions again and again by those who know something about teaching – know about it because, unlike those making policy, they've actually taught."

It was during this time, in the second Bush administration, that an RFP (request for proposal) was distributed dealing with "Teaching American History."

Quotes from the reviewers of a grant proposal ("America's Past, Through the Eyes of Local History") that this author developed for a local school system illustrates a major detriment to making significant changes in education. As a frequent grant writer, I have witnessed, first hand, the lack of background and common sense among reviewers (selected in the name of democracy).

There is a troubling willingness to discount any ideas that depart from the predefined parameters of the grant requirements. This stifles any significant innovations. It is reasonable to assume that this pattern will not be altered in the present efforts at reform.

The positive statements by reviewers of our grant proposal (America's Past Through the Eyes of Local History) submitted to the United States Department of Education under a 2003 program entitled "Teaching American History," could lead one to conclude that it was truly worthy of serious consideration. For example, reports from reviewers indicated: "The project has a focus on technology in classrooms...; the report is very clear, thoughtful, and interesting... The application presents a strong case for using local history to stimulate student interest in larger national issues in American history... The responsibilities of the management and staff positions are well defined."

Wouldn't you agree that recognition of these strengths could be encouraging news? Wrong!

Other reviewers pointed to perceived weaknesses that outweighed the strengths.

In illustration it was concluded that: "The project does not specifically describe *a plan for teaching **traditional** American history*. The grant does not describe how the project will *improve teacher knowledge* of American history. The project is local based and useful for local history making it *likely to exclude topics found in a **more traditional** American history class*." (Emphases added)

What they apparently meant by "traditional" American history is the presentation of pre-ordained conclusions (the facts) offered in various texts for consumption by the students, typical of what goes on in classrooms across this country. Traditional American history precludes individual interpretations, thus it precludes intelligent decision making. When the individual learner is treated as a consumer of the "wisdom" of others, some of which is biased and suspect, this we believed encourages disengagement and boredom.

These reviewers most likely had no frame of reference they could draw upon about what the processes proposed would be like. This is first of all a study of the local community using the methods and materials of relevant disciplines. It is not the study of history as a subject in the curriculum. Motivation to pursue an in-depth study of the local community has intrinsic value since it involves each learner's personal life in the present and its origins from the past. The materials and methodologies of history, geography and anthropology are employed to aid each learner in addressing constructive learning objectives that result in the intrinsic rewards of accomplishment. Furthermore, since the object is to develop/construct a model of the local environmental relationships, over time, where one starts in this investigation will invariably end up with consideration of all the other related variables within the system or model.

These reviewers were acting in concert with the mandated subject matter orientation of the U.S. Office of Education. Today, the mandate is to raise test scores presumably to improve educational outcomes.

What follows are excerpts from the text of our rejected grant proposal that addresses all of the concerns of the reviewers, had they been able to visualize the processes. The value of the local study has traditionally been discounted and this would be changed when it is recognized that the local community is part of the larger community with obvious ties to the national and international scene. A local study has the distinct advantage of concrete experiences that produce conclusions that are easily verified through direct experience. Not only does the study of the local community link directly with the national and international scene, its study would significantly aid the development of insightful uses of the local resources for the enhancement of its citizenry.

> Introduction: This project is offered as a prototype plan for teaching American History through in-depth study of local communities in the rural Adirondack Mountain Region in Upstate New York and adjacent communities of the Champlain Valley. Crown Point Central School is the LEA for this project positioned in the richly-historical Lake Champlain Valley along the eastern edge of the Adirondack Mountains.
>
> The Champlain Valley has been the site of the French and Indian Wars, major battles of the Revolution and the War

of 1812, and continues to be a major connector between New York City and Montreal, Canada.

Crown Point has a typical small rural central school with 356 students, 42 instructional staff and a total of 79 employees.

There are five essential interdependent elements in this plan aimed at significantly improving the short-term performance outcomes in American History instruction at the 4th, 5th, 7th, 8th and 11th grades and the long-term recall of important events and personalities of our Country's past. Each of the elements listed below are addressed in the narrative in the order in which they appear.

A. Teaching strategies that engage students in methods and materials as historians and geographers, viewing American History through in-depth study of the learner's local region.

B. Sourcing of primary data required for local historical study through involvement of selected community repositories–regional museums, libraries, restorations etc.

C. Individualized assessment, evaluation, record keeping and reporting strategies that are compatible with historical and geographical study.

D. In-service and pre-service programming designed to engage teachers and teacher candidates in methods of historical and geographical study adapted to the various grade levels of students.

E. Project normative and summative evaluation strategies that ensure program integrity and accurate reporting of findings.

This project plan is based on the following assumptions:

History as a discipline is different from history as a school subject. The discipline of history features a process for constructing and internalizing an understanding of past events and personalities through the collection and authentication of pertinent raw data and the reporting of findings in a synoptic narrative form.

Competent historians maintain high standards through the application of the rules of scholarship for their discipline. Criteria used to judge the value of an historical account, among others, are as follows: (1) Is the narrative clear and organized for readability? (2) Is the information about past events comprehensive and has the information (data) been authenticated? (3) Is the narrative account internally consistent? (4) Is the account supported in the works of others? (4) Or, does the account state a unique interpretation based on the study of particular, authenticated facts?

Similarly, geographers have a set of criteria that gauge their standards of excellence.

In this project, the outcomes of students' historical study will be judged on a basis similar to those employed by the history professionals.

Alternatively, history as a school subject is a collection of selected conclusions about historical events organized randomly for consumption by students in the instructional setting.

Selected topics of typical American history instruction are taught to students at several levels of their school experience–in New York State it is included in the 4th, 5th, 7th, 8th and 11th grade curriculum. What has been learned is evaluated essentially through both teacher-made and State tests that measure the short-term retention of the conclusions of others and limited demonstration of skills in interpreting documents. In New York State, performance outcomes are assessed by State Tests at multiple grade levels.

Noteworthy is the fact that American History topics are repeated many times over, based on the recognition over time that one attempt at instruction would not likely result in retention of these "important" facts, so they are repeated and repeated, again and again.

There doesn't seem to be a recognition that students of the elementary grades, in particular, present developmental capabilities that can significantly affect performance on standardized tests and these differences are not accounted for in the typical evaluation process.

In the plan here it is proposed that the methods of history and geography as disciplines can and should be employed by learners in the instructional setting recognizing developmentally appropriate experiences, with expected outcomes that will far exceed those resulting from the repetitive teaching of history as a school subject. Learning how to learn can result in preparation for a lifelong, sustainable commitment to seeking valid interpretations of past and current events and to the principles articulated in our "founding documents."

Learning that is committed to long-term memory, continuously expanded, valued and utilized in life's on-going transactions has been organized by the learner into recurring patterns or principles. These patterns in American history are developed over time through meaningful study of the events and persons who have shaped and continue to shape "America's struggles and achievements" beginning with the study of the local setting.

Acquiring the patterns of relationships among the variables that relate to historical events gives the possessor lasting intellectual power and increased effectiveness required for thoughtful and active citizenship in a democratic society. The study of local history develops these patterns that can be personally verified. This study establishes a frame of reference for learning and for recognizing patterns in events that are remote to the learner in time and location.

One need only watch the facial expressions of students when the family name of one's ancestors appears on the map of an 1868 Historical Atlas of the home community to realize the positive connections that a local study can make with the past.

To identify with historical events remote in time and place, students need to develop and validate a conceptual frame of reference based on in-depth studies of the history and geography of their local region. The local region is a microcosm of American History that connects to the events of our country and the rest of the world.

Each local community has social/cultural characteristics that link with the greater state and national fabric. Each community exhibits economic and political events that cannot be separated from the state and national scene.

While the particular elements found in each geographical setting may vary, the categories among environmental variables that form a pattern of relationships remains constant.

The study of the local community links the patterns of history and geography to the personal lives of students in the present, and since the local community is a part of the larger national and international community, the local study provides learners with powerful motivation for continuing to investigate and internalize the interconnected lessons of history in the larger context. Availability of primary source documents beyond the local setting, will need to be provided learners—the raw data for reconstruction of the history of these other regions—for learners who reside in California, the Champlain Valley and elsewhere.

An example of data about the past for the Township of Crown Point drawn from Gordon's Gazetteer of 1836, will illustrate some of what can be found that interrelates and serves as the basis for seeking connections with the larger American experience. Comparable data needs to be made available for the present, also.

"Crown Point, organized 7th March, 1790; N. from Albany 100 miles; along the lake the surface for the breadth of four miles is level, and the soil, principally clay loam; high mountains pervade the west; drained centrally and eastwardly, by Putnam's creek. Crown Point, whence the name of the town and the ancient Fort, is situated at the N.E. extremity, and is formed by an extensive deep bay on the W, skirted by a steep mountain, and on the N. and E. by the body of the lake.

The fort, St Frederick, was built here by the French, in 1731, on the bank of the lake, but was subsequently blown up; and its site is now marked by a heap of stones. After capture of this post, in 1756, Fort Crown Point was erected about 47 feet above the level of the lake, Lat. N. 44o 3' long. W.73o29' from London. May 14th, 1775, it fell into the hands of the Americans, but was evacuated in 1776, and re-occupied by the British..."

"The Township of Crown Point is reported to have 2189 inhabitants, of which there were 477 voters. The town contains 27129 acres, and 12313 were improved. There were 15 school districts. The assessed value of real estate was 81155. Crown Point had 2537 cattle, 671 horses, 9217 sheep, 1160 swine, 4 grist mills, 14 sawmills, 3 fulling mills, 4 carding machines, 1 trip hammer, 2 asheries and 2 tanneries. Crown Point village has a post office, a Presbyterian church, a tavern, store, several saw mills, a blast furnace, and clothing works. Much lumber business is done here."

An in-depth analysis of these data reveals an obvious connection between Crown Point, as with all other communities, and the larger American experience. Tracing the evolution of Crown Point from its beginnings (socially, economically, politically and geographically) to the present, linked to each significant event of the American experience and compared with neighboring communities establishes a lasting frame of reference.

Personalized, and integrated connections, together, of an authenticated image of "life in all its manifestations" is what historical study entails

Raw, primary-source data for the study of local history and geography has been essentially unavailable for classroom use due primarily to its limited market value. There is therefore a vital need to provide this information, packaged specifically for use in the classrooms of our rural communities, required by learners to develop their conceptual frames of reference in history and geography.

The conduct of instruction in the disciplines of history and geography is dependent upon the availability of materials relevant to the location, events, and timeframe being studied. In a plan such as this (that involves the use of local artifacts, documents and other primary source information) without such materials readily available in the classroom, the teacher is forced to rely on prepared texts, workbooks, ditto sheets, CD's and other pre-digested information organized for instruction. This material is generally focused on isolated topics taught randomly and often superficially within the typical curriculum. Most students exposed to this type of presentation of history will find it nearly impossible to sustain an interest or develop a lasting and verifiable knowledge of American history.

Distribution of primary source materials of a local area, especially one that has a limited number of potential buyers, there is therefore limited commercial value. Repositories house what materials are available and students are encouraged to visit from the local schools. These occasional visits, while important, do not become a regular resource for learning. Hence, these collections, only tapped sporadically, have limited impact on learning in the school. This must be changed.

Teachers bring knowledge of subject matter, and much more, to the teaching/learning situation. Ongoing professional development must attend to all dimensions of behavior that affect the teacher's capabilities for bringing about student learning. The teacher's knowledge of subject matter, being one of those dimensions, must be continuously expanded, reaching higher levels of sophistication. **To accomplish this, teachers must engage in continuous historical study the same as their student learners. The same holds true regarding all other disciplines within six "realms of meaning."**

A detailed record of this learning process is necessary for helping the learners shape conclusions regarding their study and serves as a reminder of the facts included as the learning sequence continues. Being able to access this personal record of developmental experiences gives the learner intellectual power and increased motivation to learn.

Needless to say, this project was rejected for funding since it took a comprehensive view of systemic change as it applied to the learner oriented study of history and geography. Since it included a strong emphasis on the learning process, it was possibly viewed by the subject matter advocates as less that rigorous.

Since the "No Child Left Behind" legislation was in place when the Obama administration came aboard, its basic testing objectives were not only upheld but were increased under an extended plan called "A Race to the Top." Billions of taxpayer dollars were appropriated along with contributions from various philanthropic sources to support the proposed raising of standards and standardizing the curriculum and testing programs across this country. The U.S. Office of Education concocted a plan to coerce states to comply by offering large sums of money, if they agreed to establish a common core curriculum and uphold the objectives of a "Race to the Top."

It can be said that this effort supports a systemic change strategy, and the recent experiences with corporate-designed tests administered to determine progress made in achieving learning objectives lends testimony to the systemic results of this effort. Those results have indeed changed the system, but the changes represent collateral damage, not yet fully recognized, even by the parents and their teachers who have endured the results of implementation of this "race to the top."

It is not surprising that corporate interests have seized upon the opportunity to transform the public school into a profit-making enterprise since the charter school movement has laid the groundwork for such involvement. It is understood that the market for educational products is huge and will grow exponentially if corporations are allowed to take control of education. And since the market for production and distribution of saleable products requires consistency across national boundaries, and the larger population, standardization is a necessary ingredient in this effort. The common core curriculum and further standardization is inevitable, at the expense of individual learners who are all unique, including their DNA, their experiences and what they have done and will do with their experiences.

This treatise, *Remaking our Schools,* is yet another attempt to gain support for a systemic change model, but this is one that truly considers a comprehensive view of systems designed for maximizing learning and human maturity. It emphasizes a plan to bridge the gap between the subject matter concerns and the child development advocates. This is proposed to be accomplished through re-defining the content of the curriculum in terms of an implementation of academic disciplines as creative processes for learning and communicating.

Personal background

Following is a brief glimpse into some of the processes of change and validation experienced by this author over many years that helped build the foundation for the beliefs and assumptions about education expressed herein. It illustrates much of what was found in education that needed changing and what could be changed when we know how.

I'm the youngest of a family of twelve children, six boys and six girls. We grew up on a farm with few amenities, but rich experience. We didn't have electricity, we read by kerosene lamps. We had some running water when a windmill pumped to a reservoir on the hill above the house from the brook that ran through the farm. The water flowed by gravity to the house. When the wind didn't blow, or the pump was broken, we would hitch up a horse on a wagon or sleigh and transport some water from the brook in wooden barrels. Pails of water were brought into the house as needed.

We raised most of what we ate along with what we bagged through hunting and fishing. My mother and older sisters made most of our clothes, darned our socks and cooked our meals on the kitchen wood stove. That stove heated the water for the family needs. Our baths occurred in a metal tub about three feet in diameter and a foot or so deep, with handles. This tub was transported to wherever the bath was to happen. About three inches of water was about all I wanted to transport upstairs to my bedroom.

The farm was located in the beauty of the Adirondack Mountains where the winters are very cold and the summers, very short. We could hear the corn growing in late August. It seemed to be hurrying to get the most out of the short time between spring and fall. I was assigned the "old long-horned cow" to milk when I was seven or eight. From then on I was gradually immersed in the daily chores of a farmer trying to scratch a living off the glacier-riddled, rock-covered land.

During the Second World War, as a teenager, I was practically running the farm since my older siblings were either in the armed services or working in a defense factory and had moved away. My father was in his sixties so he delegated to me many of the responsibilities that accompany caring for a herd of cattle to milk, caring for the sheep and the hens, and feeding the hogs and the horses. I would arise at my father's call at five o'clock or earlier, go to the barn and milk the cows by hand, bring the milk to the kitchen and begin cranking the cream separator. Cream gave us cash from a distant creamery.

Raw milk was part of our diet as was the butter we churned from the cream we saved for that purpose. Much of the skimmed milk was used to nourish the calves and when mixed with grain it was fed to the young hogs to fatten them for servings of tasty pork at our kitchen table. We raised the food for the animals on the farm, corn and hay for the cattle, oats and hay for the horses, and potatoes that were boiled in a potash kettle for the hogs. Potatoes were another source of cash, along with trees for pulp wood sold to a paper mill, and logs sold to the local saw mill. We tapped the maple trees for syrup, sugar on snow and maple candy. We raised buckwheat that was ground into flour for our pancakes.

During the winter and spring months, I would find time

in a busy schedule to establish a trap line for foxes, beaver, and mink. This provided me with some spending money.

Any machinery we used during the Second World War had to be kept operating by sheer creativity. I was the designated mechanic since I loved to tinker with machinery. Tires were not available, so ours were patched and worn. Gasoline was rationed, so the old Chevy didn't go far on the allotted gallon or two of gas. The fenders were held together with hay wire.

We managed to purchase a new Farmall tractor built in 1942; it served us well, much better than the team of horses that I disliked, or the old "Fordson" tractor with its temperamental magneto.

These are only a sample of the experiences that were part of a routine of planting and harvesting, hunting and fishing for food and recreation, and caring for the animals seven days of the week.

I didn't know my grandparents on either side of the family. My grandfather on my father's side died at age 92, in the spring of 1932, six months after I was born. I used to tell my students that my grandfather fought in the Civil War. "Sure" they said, "Tell us another story." Actually grandfather was wounded in the Battle of Drury's Bluff, and had a plate in his scull to prove it. He later became a scout for the Union Army with special orders from President Lincoln to collect "intelligence" from Southerners. A myth passed down through the family was that Grandpa died picking stone out in the field at the farm, placing them neatly on the many stone walls that bordered our fields. Actually he died at his oldest son's home in a nearby village.

His eldest son, Eli, seemed ancient to me when I was a teenager. He was about the same age as I am today. He loved to fish in his declining years and often he would get me in trouble. He would quietly dig some worms and seek me out to whisper in my ear, "Let's go fishing." This was all I needed to be convinced to sneak off with him when I was supposed to be splitting wood or cultivating the corn.

When I was about to enter my educational career at the age of five, they closed the one room schoolhouse that still stands vacant about a mile and a half down the road from our farm. This marked the beginning of consolidation/centralization of school districts in our area, resulting in a move to build elaborate edifices now referred to as "campuses."

My father was the trustee of rural District #10. He must have been sold a "bill of goods" that my educational opportunities would be better served in a union school ten miles up the road in the opposite direction. He couldn't have thought expenses would be reduced when a school taught by one teacher was exchanged for a school where eight teachers were needed to teach the same curriculum. In retrospect, they may have closed the one room school when they heard I was coming.

I'm told by my five brothers and six sisters who attended the one room school, it wasn't just one teacher, there were a whole group of older students, parents, and the teacher helping to instruct the students in reading, writing, and arithmetic. They all pitched in bringing in the wood to keep the fire going. They had concern for the health and welfare of their fellow/neighborhood students.

Nevertheless, I crawled up the stairs into the bus at 7:15 a.m. and rode the bumpy roads for an hour or so, while it picked up students from neighboring districts along the way that had also joined the move to a bigger school.

When I was about to graduate from the eighth grade and enter the union high school, that high school was closed and the ninth graders were sent six miles further up the road to a central school—adding another half hour to the trip. The sales pitch was the same, it will cost less to educate if everyone is herded into a central location where their lives can be more completely controlled. Here there were umpteen teachers all teaching their specialty and I was supposed to be grateful for all the attention I was getting.

Incidentally, when I started school, the school buses were owned, maintained, and operated by individuals (under scrutiny of state inspectors) who contracted with school districts to transport their students. My brother, who lived at the outskirts of the most distant district from the union school, owned and operated his bus. He contracted with several districts along the route. When centralization occurred in our area, there were four such entrepreneurs. They similarly lived at the outskirts of their district and would travel to the central school and wait until school was dismissed to make the return trip.

As soon as the central school got organized, it took over the bus runs, purchased buses, set up a garage, hired mechanics, hired bus drivers at minimum wages, etc. etc. In the morning, the buses that were housed near the central school would travel to the outskirts of the expanded district and return to the school with the students. The buses would collect the students at the end of the school day and travel to the outskirts and then return to the bus garage. This meant the buses traveled twice the distances the private owners would have traveled. Surely the decisions that led to centralized bussing would not have given much consideration to the exorbitant expense, but likely had to do with the need to maintain control.

After graduating from high school, I enrolled in a nearby liberal arts college in hopes of becoming a lawyer. Several weeks went by before reality set in and I realized that I couldn't afford to pay for the tuition and travel to and from classes. I left that college and enrolled late in Potsdam State Teachers College where tuition was minimal and they offered me employment to pay for room and board. My father was not in favor of my going away to college since he needed help on the farm. But, I couldn't wait to escape the tediousness that I associated with farm work.

My educational experience in elementary school and high school was less than rewarding. I can recall only one teacher who ever visited my home. He taught high school chemistry and physics and he liked to fish trout. The trout stream that ran through the farm attracted his visitation.

No one else seemed to care what my life was like. The

only link between the school and my life came when I was attending a social studies class in high school taught by a very strict, stern lady who was feared by everyone. During the war, butter was scarce so I would slip a pound of it to this teacher now and then, and as a result I was treated more appreciatively than my colleagues.

I didn't have time on the farm to study or read books (especially by kerosene lamp) so I used the long bus ride as time to finish my homework. This often meant copying another's homework or memorizing the history regent's review book in anticipation of a test that was administered every day at the beginning of each class. It was at that school that I received a 76 on my report card for physical education.

I started teaching for pay as a junior high school social studies and English teacher in a centralized school district in 1952. This junior high was departmentalized as was the high school.

Teachers were supposedly assigned to their post according to their expertise in their subject. That apparently didn't apply to me. I was doing my "student teaching" at the time and the regular teacher became ill so the district administration decided that it would be cheaper to pay me a nominal fee rather than hire a substitute, so I was hired, even though I was not qualified for the job. I spent much of my class time disciplining the class.

The students rotated from class to class trying to absorb what so-called "specialists" were passing out in their lectures, classroom activities, and homework. Each week the students were tested for what they retained from the week's classes. The test results were recorded as an average grade to be reported on the quarterly report card so parents could interact with the "learners" about the grades they received and what they were presumed to have learned. If the average resulted in less than a seventy-five (or sixty-five on State tests) the student failed, even if the grade average was only one point too low. Many of us have experienced this procedure and have felt the anxious moments before and after report cards were sent home.

Using test scores to determine how much was "learned" was then as now viewed as essential to "objective" assessment. However, I remember getting that seventy-six in physical education. For the life of me I do not know what I did wrong, except I do remember being "whistled" for double-dribbling, though I didn't know what that was. Back on the farm where I grew up we didn't pay much attention to double dribbling. Nevertheless, I often wondered how a 76 was arrived at without the "objective tests." It remains a mystery.

As a teacher, I learned early-on that being "objective" meant keeping an accurate score of the grades obtained by each student on tests, combined with an attendance record. There was always a section of the report card for recording a more subjective judgment about the personal conduct of each student by checking off important things like whispering too much, or not living up to his or her potential, or failure to complete homework, or just being un-cooperative.

My previous experience in the college's laboratory school allowed me an opportunity to do creative things like planning and executing the development of a tree plantation for a local landowner. Everyone in my class was involved in that experience and a grade expressed as a percentage seemed to be impossible. Instead of using a percentage point grading procedure, I was encouraged to arrive at a grade of A, B, C, D or F. Of course in my group no one got a failing grade if they actively participated in the project. And even in cases of absence, we were able to arrive at some solution such as substituting other activities in which the student could succeed.

Contrasting my junior high public school teaching experience with the laboratory school experience, it seemed obvious that alternatives to the way teachers could assess and grade their students was possible. But still, a judgment had to be made based on some arbitrary criteria that sorted students into those who were successful at various levels of pre-defined "excellence" and those who didn't live up to the arbitrary standard.

These two experiences in 1951 and 1952 left me feeling ambivalent about how to handle the assessment and evaluation of students and even whether or not a teaching career would meet my personal needs.

After graduating with a license to teach kindergarten through the ninth grade, I was encouraged by a college administrator to go to graduate school to study school administration. I knew about as much about that as I did about teaching, which in retrospect was precious little. Nevertheless, I trudged off to graduate school in NYC, married, and deferred from the draft during the Korean conflict. My wife began her shortened teaching career at this time and ended it when she became pregnant with our first son.

They didn't allow pregnant teachers to remain in the classroom when they began showing signs of their condition. She was not too happy with her teaching job anyway since her administrator taught next door and frequently monitored her every move.

In the early fall while my wife was teaching, I tried to work part time cleaning hen houses to help make ends meet while attending graduate school at night and on Saturday. This didn't work out well so an opportunity to teach occurred when a friend took a leave from her third grade class and left her position open. I got her job.

That class was an experimental group that was demonstrating a "reading" system designed and promoted by a rich lady who was on a mission to straighten out education. She had texts written for use in the elementary grades whereby students were immersed in phonics to learn to read and spell. Her texts included social studies and science, at least as she understood them. The directions to the teacher included what questions to ask of the students, what the answers were supposed to be and what was supposed to be done to get the right answers, including how to reprimand the failing students.

She came to my class to demonstrate to other teachers how her spelling instruction was to be handled without memorization. She listed on the board ten words in order and spent several minutes on each word to ensure understanding about its spelling. When finished, she asked the students to describe what had happened. Little Teddy in the back row said proudly: "We memorized ten words."

Her reaction was so intense that she sat down heavily and the chair legs broke off and there she sat on the floor with her wide brim hat cocked sideways on her head. This marked the end of an interesting day with this "innovative" reading program. Incidentally, Teddy missed by one point the cut off score on the achievement test that was used to determine promotion to the fourth grade, and after a serious negotiation by me, Teddy passed.

I tried to make my program more relevant to my students. I organized them in smaller groups so they could talk to one another. This prompted the principal to inform me that the janitors would not sweep the floors and I was to put the desks back in rows, the way I found them. I simply said, give us a broom and we will sweep the floors. This didn't sit well with this administrator.

On another occasion, this principal, returning from his three martini lunch, came to my room and began reading the riot act to me in front of my class because my window shades were not adjusted "properly." I physically removed this school official from my room.

A third incident that I recall involved a visitation from the principal during a creative writing and storytelling experience. Of course, this activity was not allowed in the rigid schedule and rules mandated by the district for their "innovative" program in reading. One youngster was relating a dream he had experienced the night before. The details of that dream were very bizarre that involved his mother; and it struck this youngster as very funny. The subject matter was viewed by the principal as a serious moral problem that needed to be corrected immediately. After all, we couldn't condone humor when it relates to such a serious subject without an immediate reprimand.

There was no interest in finding out more about the meaning the student attached to the incident, those ideas and feelings just didn't matter. I couldn't wait to be let out of that prison even to go into the Army.

Of all the classes I attended during my master's program in elementary administration, only one seemed really interesting to me. This was a course in Human Administration. School finance was at the bottom of my list. I was happy to volunteer for the draft during that experience, thinking that I would get the uneasy burden of facing going to war, off my back.

Since I was suspected to have a potentially serious arthritic condition that plagued my everyday activity and I wasn't much interested in the class work of the master's program or my teaching experience, I thought I would be rejected as unfit for military duty and could get on with my life. However, I was sent to Fort Dix for infantry training. While there, I was offered an opportunity to become a CIA agent or go to officer's training school; all I had to do was enlist for many more years of service beyond the two years I was supposed to serve as a draftee. Needless to say, I turned down the offers.

There was one aspect of my farm experience that came in handy since I could drive a truck. I was asked to take a test to drive army vehicles including jeeps and "duce-and-a-halfs." As a driver I often chauffeured my first sergeant on his routine visits to the troops in the field. I was often challenged by the "regulars," as a lowly PFC draftee, perhaps because I had a master's degree and a high score on the army's aptitude test.

Not long after being assigned to "Dog Battery" I was transferred to headquarters and became troop information and education NCO. This job involved signing out a jeep and traveling to other batteries that surrounded Pittsburgh. I kept bulletin boards updated in the "day rooms" with the latest newspaper clippings and occasionally would hold classes to help the recruits understand what was going on in the world.

The education level of most of these GI's, who were mostly Afro-Americans from the South, was below the sixth grade. Many could not read since they quit school to help support their families. I tried to address this problem by starting educational sessions designed to help these soldiers obtain an eighth grade certificate and occasionally a high school GED.

Although I felt great when I finished basic training, I began to feel increased pain from my arthritic condition due in part to the more sedentary life of serving in a *Triple A Battalion* with a low level of physical activity. I visited "sick call" but was often told that I just wanted to get out of duty.

Finally, I was referred to Carlyle Barracks for an evaluation. The doctor in charge explained that there was nothing physically wrong with me. He concluded that I was an educated type who had learned to find ways of avoiding duty. After a heated discussion, I convinced this doctor that I would gladly trade with him anytime if he would like to take my pain and discomfort. As a result of this altercation, he called in a civilian specialist who took one look at my x-rays and stated: "This soldier has a special form of arthritis called ankylosing spondalitus." As a result of this diagnosis, I was transferred to the Valley Forge Army Hospital where I spent my remaining days in the U.S. Army.

While at Valley Forge, I received every known treatment for my condition including liberal ingestion of cortisone, ACTH, and gold salts along with physical therapy and radiation treatments to the spine. I would sit for hours in the hospital hallways agonizing over the thought of curtailment of physical involvement and substitution of mind-based activity. Even though I had a master's degree at the time, I didn't feel confident that I could survive simply relying on my intellect since my experience with education had taught me to mistrust my own abilities. I had always relied on physical capabilities to make a living. Now I was faced with giving up what I had great confidence in and substituting another activity about which I was unsure.

After ten months in the hospital, I was discharged with a rating of one hundred percent disability. I arrived home and spent several months in a veteran's hospital where I met my life saver. He was an Austrian-born physician who specialized in rheumatology. After a long interview where I told him of my many attempts to cure my pain, including acupuncture, he looked me straight in the eye and said: "You are a fool if you think there is a cure for this condition. What you must do is learn to accept that fact and take measures to maintain a more-healthy life style." He said he would keep me in the hospital until he taught me how to minimize the pain and control the condition.

He said it involves three aspects that I must religiously obey. One is a healthy diet, including eating a good breakfast, two is a routine of exercise, and three is adequate rest. It took me about three years to fully accept his treatment schedule, but when I did the episodes of increased inflammation subsided. I began to listen to myself and recognize indicators that would portend an extended bout with increased discomfort if I didn't make some preventative adjustments.

A position opened at the Campus Laboratory School where half of my student teaching experience occurred and I was accepted as a sixth grade teacher. This Campus Laboratory School was the only community public elementary school in Potsdam, employing both college and public school personnel, working side by side. I taught a typical class of students with various levels of development as I had been accustomed to seeing others teach; assigning chapters in the text and giving tests.

I did try to squeeze in some projects that interested both me and my students. One project involved building a model house to scale. The parents of one student were building a new home so the incentive was there to try our project. We visited the construction site and talked with carpenters, electricians, and plumbers about their work and especially about how the house was being built. We went back to our classroom and assembled our materials –wood, piping, glass, light fixtures etc. We designed a plan for our house and followed construction procedures as we had seen them at the building site.

We cut out floor joists that were equivalent to two by sixes and studs that were equivalent to two by fours. We laid out the boards on our plans and proceeded to construct the house; first the floors, then partitions, and finally the roof. Our innovation included (in 1956) roof-mounted solar heating panels and baseboard heating units in every room. We decorated and furnished every room in the house.

When finished we entered the house in a science fair. It was stolen. The students were heartbroken so we decided to rebuild the house. This time we knew exactly what was needed so we set up a mass production line and assembled the house in a matter of hours; the original house took months to build. We took photos of every phase of the project and constructed a photo essay complete with descriptive narrative.

Plainly, this project embraced many subjects and mastery was evident throughout the class. Nevertheless there was always the presence of criticism that "real" subjects were not being given the importance they deserved. This fact was made perfectly clear at parent conference time.

One of my students was the daughter of a former history professor who taught American History from a documents point of view. I had taken that course and others from that professor. He came to the conference with "blood in his eye." The essence of his complaint was that I was a terrible history teacher. To that I agreed. However, I reminded him that I had taken courses from him and if I was so terrible it wasn't all my fault. As a result of this conference, I made a major change in the way I taught social studies/history and geography.

This professor was completing his doctoral dissertation wherein he had traced the events of the early 1800s based on the papers of an entrepreneur who opened the territory of

St. Lawrence County in Upstate New York. These papers contained diaries, contracts, letters, testimonials, and lots of data. He had constructed an image of what life was like during those years, using the papers and related histories as the sources for reaching his conclusions. He had written the narrative—the history of this period—based on the original documents.

He made me a proposition that he would furnish our class (moving to the seventh grade) with the same documents he had used, for them to construct their own histories about the development of their neighborhoods. He agreed to help by showing how to use the methodologies of historians without giving the students any answers.

Students recognized many of the names mentioned in the documents; they had seen many of the places involved in the development of the county. I knew they would be motivated to dig deeper into understanding how their own community and other adjacent communities developed.

Since I didn't have a better plan we agreed to work together with these seventh graders to present history as a discipline with rules for the conduct of inquiry. This was in direct contrast with history as I had treated it as a collection of facts to be memorized and passed back on a test for which students would receive a grade. Since the official seventh grade curriculum was New York State History, we didn't have to petition for permission to engage in our project.

Our class began our inquiry by first discussing the overall goal we wanted to achieve which was to create a complete and accurate image of the evolution of the communities within the county and the state. This image had to be based on verifiable facts drawn from authentic documents, supported by direct observation and the interpretations of experts in these matters.

We found terms from records that were unfamiliar as well as those we understood. One unfamiliar term, ashery, that appeared often in records of the early eighteen hundreds led to an extensive search for a picture or diagram of an ashery, or perhaps a description by one who was familiar with the term. After much effort, we found a sketch of an actual ashery that once existed in St. Lawrence County. We needed that visual experience to adequately conceptualize the realities that surrounded the appearance of asheries—what an ashery looked like, what the process entailed, how many people were needed to run the operation, etc.

We learned that asheries played an important role in the early development of a temperate wilderness region. We found that asheries produced a cash crop for those who were clearing the land of its trees before roads were built. Ashes could be shipped over rough terrain in barrels after the wood from the forests was burned to an ash.

Ashe (potash) was needed by the textile industry as a bleaching agent used to prepare fabric for dying. The textile industry was willing to pay for potash from St. Lawrence County even though their mills were located many, many miles away, in the textile mills of New England Ashes were also needed to produce soap for local consumption.

Whenever we saw asheries listed among the facts, we knew that the area was being cleared for farming, predating the development of improved roads that allowed logs to be hauled to a saw mill that was built by a waterfall. This mill and others would use the water power to turn a water wheel that powered the saw that produced lumber for building houses and barns. This was the level of technology available at that time, before the advent of the steam engine that could be located almost anywhere. The mills became the focal point for a village complete with homes, stores, and professional services. We developed and verified our concepts of the facts we needed to put together a complete image of life in the early 1800s in St Lawrence County.

To keep our facts organized, we decided to construct a model of our county within our classroom. This model was three-dimensional, made out of a wood frame and paper mache and measured to scale; it took up much of the classroom space.

At the bottom of this model we showed a cross section of the bedrock and any existing mineral deposits we found to be located there. This information came from published maps and narratives mostly from government agencies. The bedrock of St. Lawrence County featured three distinct types, sedimentary sandstone and limestone, and granite-associated igneous rocks. Each of these rock types were located and accurately placed on the model that resembled a block of earth cut out and displayed as it would look from the top and sides.

When we finished painting the rocks and minerals, as they would appear on the sides of our model we then laid relief features on the surface. This information came from U.S. Geological Survey maps, aerial photos, and firsthand observation. The land over the granitic type rocks featured the mountainous terrain of the Adirondacks. Iron ore was found in this area. The sandstone area supported a plateau at a lower elevation north of the granites. This plateau bordered the limestone area, which featured a nearly level plain. The overall regions of terrain sloped from the south to the north and bordered on the St. Lawrence River. The river and stream systems all flowed north from the mountains to the plain and emptied into the St. Lawrence River. There were numerous waterfalls associated with the breaks between these three types of bedrock; these were the sites for mills that were the heart of emerging village life.

We gathered information about plant types and animals found in each region and placed this information on the model. We investigated the literature on the flora and fauna and spent considerable time out in the field observing these plants and animals in their habitat. We conducted soil tests throughout the regions. Using soil maps developed by State and Federal Agencies, we correlated our findings with those official publications. We then located on the model the different soil types imposed over the terrain and river valleys. Weather and climatic information was then determined for each region and this information was also included on our physical model.

As each layer of information was developed and placed

on the model, obvious relationships began to emerge for each student. The terrain influenced the water drainage patterns waterfalls were related to the bedrock, the soils related to the terrain, rocks, and weather, different types of vegetation related to the drainage patterns, animal habitats related to their needs for survival, etc. The landscape showed the potential for human endeavors such as farming, manufacturing, mining etc.

These relationships were the direct result of placing accurate, personally-verified information on a physical model that was tested for accuracy and clarity. The students discovered these relationships with little intervention from their teacher. They summarized their findings in a narrative with illustrations to communicate what they each understood. They developed the basis for retention and transfer of this information important to understanding other regions with similar and different objects, processes, and relationships.

This exercise in model construction resulted from a need to accurately conceptualize the variables found in the physical and social/cultural environment. This model was built to help visualize what existed and exists in the student's local surroundings. Since it was all about the local regions, the information was easily verified through firsthand observations and personalized conversations.

Once a completed set of relationships was recognized there emerged a sense of structure, an organization that formed a foundation for not only extracting maximum meaning about the familiar, but also for transferring that structure to the understanding of areas remote in time and place.

This part of the exercise was what physical geographers do for a living. They assemble verifiable data drawn from a multitude of disciplines including, geology, mineralogy, hydrology, topography, pedology, botany, biology, chemistry, physics, meteorology, climatologic, cartography and astronomy. Based on these data, the geographer organizes, describes and communicates assumptions about what exists or has existed and distributed in areas throughout our local areas and the universe. Like the exercise my students and I experienced, they employ model construction and a regional organization complete with a written narrative with maps and diagrams etc. to communicate their findings.

For the first time in my teaching career, I drew upon the variety of experiences I encountered growing up on the farm. I tilled the soil and worked around rocks left by the glacier. I knew trees by name since I spent many days and months cutting and transporting logs to market, tapping maples for sap to be made into syrup and peeling balsam and spruce trees in the springtime for transport to a pulp mill to be made into paper. I recognized types of animals including fish, birds, deer, bear, and coy dogs. I knew where berries flourished, I ate the seeds from the beech tree, I trapped beaver and foxes to earn money for myself, I lived in the out of doors experiencing all types of weather, I saw the full moon, trampled through the snow in the dead of winter and dug potatoes and carrots in the fall. There were very few aspects of the environment that I hadn't either experienced directly, or picked up in conversations with those who had experienced those things.

When these rich experiences were taking place, however, I paid little attention to their importance and since teachers didn't seem to care about what I experienced or what I knew (they were glued to the texts and tests) the values I had gained were downgraded. In fact, I grew to be ashamed of my existence and thought many times that there must be something better to look forward to. Neither my teachers nor I knew the profound importance of mastering the local setting as a preparation for mastering those settings remote in time and place.

The seventh graders and I knew how important these personal experiences could be when given a chance to prove ourselves.

We had succeeded in achieving a high level of mastery in a subject matter that had many ramifications. We had prepared ourselves to understand the social, economic, and political realities that took place over time in our region.

We began our historical journey together, all of us having a limited level of real understanding of history. The main advantage I had over the students was age and experience. We acquired the documents and data that had been assembled by our college historian, and we began our effort to piece together an image of what life was like in the early eighteen hundreds in St. Lawrence County, in upstate New York State.

The documents we received included letters and diaries of important people who lived in the county during its early stages of development. Most of the documents related to the work of a land development entrepreneur who had connections with European banking interests. Using his wealth, he helped fund the French Revolution and in this country, the War of 1812. Many of those documents contained descriptions of people and places familiar to us who were living in the area. Family names sparked a motivating force that sent students to local archives to trace their family tree. Census data, gazetteers, written histories, regional artifacts, and historical restorations became the sources of raw data that we analyzed, reconstructed, conceptualized and made sense out of in our efforts to describe the nature and evolution of the social, economic and political events and processes that occurred over time in our county, community by community.

We found several sources of data particularly useful. Gordon's *Gazetteer of New York State*, published in 1836, contained tables of facts summarized from census data. It listed the dimensions of the county in square miles; that which was improved (cleared of forest) and that which was unimproved. It listed how many asheries were operating in each township throughout all the counties of New York State. It reported the number of cattle, hogs, sheep, and horses counted by the census takers. It listed the value of real estate, the number of schools and scholars and how much the schools cost to run.

The narrative illustrated, in detail, the values and attitudes of people who lived there during those times. For instance, groups of people were classified in the records as idiots, lunatics, and Indians; in that order.

This document located and enumerated the number of saw mills, the grist mills, trip hammers, woolen mills, and the breweries.

Along with Gordon's book, we researched other histories that contained important facts and interpretations that we could use in our investigations. We got a copy of the census of 1845, from the State Archives. We read historical novels. Every known resource that our history consultant directed us to, served to be tremendously valuable to us as fledgling historians.

As we continued to piece together a picture of activities and events we summarized our findings and placed the information on the model we had constructed to show the natural and physical geography of the region. There was a growing awareness of the interrelatedness of the natural physical setting, and the social, economic, and political activities. By tracing these activities over several decades, we discovered patterns of changes that occurred and events that remained constant.

Church affiliation and attendance in schools was found in each era. There were numerous school districts throughout the county linked to the distance that could be walked by students to get to school. Potash was gradually being replaced by increased lumber production when the roads were improved to allow their transport.

We found an evolution that was matched to one that appeared in a short history of another New York State region written by James Frost. His treatise was called *Life on the Upper Susquehanna*. This evolution was shown to begin with a frontier economy where the land was being cleared and where subsistence living was predominate.

When farmers produced a surplus, people began to trade their surplus products for things they needed or wanted. This marked the beginning of a capitalistic economy supplanting the self-sufficiency and bargaining of prior times.

As transportation improved with the building of improved roads, canals and railroads, some goods could be produced elsewhere more cheaply even though they were grown some distance away. The availability of cheaper goods meant that local products could not compete in the marketplace, so adjustments had to be made. This initiated an era of adjustment to a regional or national economy. Experimentations with different crops and other products resulted, some were sustained, and some did not survive. It was easy to extrapolate to the adjustments to a world economy that exists today.

We found how governments at the local, county, state, and federal levels interacted with the events of people on the farms and in the villages. A good example of local governments serving the people occurred when roads were being built. The township boards passed laws requiring stumps to be cut at a certain height to allow wagons to pass over them. When the stumps were too high, the wagons would get hung up and spill their loads. When townships would pass laws that were different from their neighboring townships, such as allowing stumps to be left at a higher level, the standard wagon could not pass through. The county would then step in and pass a law requiring all towns to cut their stumps in the roads to a standard height. Then wagon manufacturers in the villages could build their products to be used throughout the counties.

The same held true for roads across all the counties. The state would then require all counties to conform to a standard stump height. Likewise the federal government would require states to conform to the rules for road construction so that interstate travel could be maintained. It was obvious in these examples that a role for government was to regulate for the common good to better serve the people.

An interesting finding that linked directly with events that were happening in current times had to do with the building of the St. Lawrence Seaway. In early days of the 1800s, grain shipments from the mid-west came by way of the Great Lakes to Ogdensburgh, New York and Prescott, Ontario. Here the grain was off-loaded from lake vessels and stored in grain elevators on both sides of the St. Lawrence River. The grain was then transferred to smaller boats that could shoot the rapids on their way to Montreal where shipment to foreign countries originated.

The Seaway dams and locks made it possible for ocean going vessels to pass over the rapids and continue out to sea. Town and village officials along the river judged that increased shipping would inevitably occur so they proceeded to build elaborate docking facilities. Much to their disappointment, the ocean going vessels passed right on by their new port and went out to sea. These communities had apparently misjudged the lessons of history that are repeated over and over again concerning the effects of improved transportation routes linking large metropolitan centers that bypass many small communities along the way, leaving them to decline or find other sources of survival.

When we finished our version of the history and geography of St. Lawrence County for a period of forty years, beginning in 1800, we reported our findings in a narrative. There were sections that described what we had found about the physical setting. There were sections that discussed our findings about the social, economic, and political realities. Our conclusions in the final section illustrated the relationships we discovered between all the other sections.

Writing the narrative provided sufficient motivation for honing our skills of writing, so attainment of these skills became an important byproduct. Because we had discovered the value of clearly communicating what we were experiencing, the opportunities for improving our language skills were frequent and relevant as were refinements in our mathematical skills.

We arranged a meeting with our history consultant to discuss our findings and make comparisons between ours and his conclusions. We discovered the areas where there was agreement, and areas where our interpretations and conclusions differed from his.

There was a lively discussion between these seventh grade students and the college level historian that showed the real nature of history being that which is constructed by humans who view facts from their perspective, sometimes differing significantly from those of others.

The myth that history is absolute as written in the texts was replaced with the realization that history is the product of humans who make decisions that must be continuously authenticated. When those conclusions do not stand the test for accuracy, verifiability, and clarity, they must be treated not as absolute certainty but rather as a product of the search for meaning that is always subject to review.

The students and I then applied our skills and expertise to the study beyond our county during the times before 1800 and after 1845. We now knew what we must do to produce history that could be verified including what data was required, what we needed to do to conceptualize those data; and what was involved in piecing together an interconnected narrative and image of what life was like at a particular place and time. We applied our skills across the state, first contrasting what we knew about St. Lawrence County with adjacent counties and then more distant counties, eventually covering the entire state. As each region was addressed we became more efficient and critical. We developed a high degree of self-confidence that was based on personally verified skills and insights. We knew that these skills could be transferred to the study of any area throughout our country and the world.

I continued with this class into the eighth grade where the social studies curriculum was American History. Having previously recognized regions that had distinguishable characteristics gave us a direction for approaching the study of American History. We could approach our study as regions based on geographic characteristics, or based on cultural commonalities, or economic potential or political boundaries etc. The choice was ours. We used written documents, federal census, and many government publications that were similar to documents found about our region.

When westward expansion continued in our country, we found variations that were particularly interesting. In our county trees were abundant, so wood was used as lumber for buildings and a source of heat from wood burning stoves. But, on the plains of the mid-west there often were few trees for lumber to make houses. There was an abundance of sod from the grassland terrain, and these sods were used to build a shelter from the elements. These sod houses were supplanted by wood framed houses only when transportation allowed lumber to be offered for sale at a reasonable price in these areas. These eighth graders referred extensively to a book written by Billington called *Westward Expansion*, a book normally used in college classrooms (Billington, Ray Allen and Ridge, Martin, 1949).

Grasslands were correlated with climatic data, particularly rainfall that was much different from our local weather and climate. As was plainly evident to us, the foundation we had developed from studying our local region in depth, gave us the opportunity to create a more complete image of life in a more distant and different setting.

Without that locally verified study we would not have been able to develop and connect with rich concepts of more distant places and times.

We traced events that were of national significance, including conflict resolution (wars) and expanded governmental regulation and support. We learned of the structure of governments, local, state, and national. We visited the state government in action, met the governor, talked with legislators, and attended a session of the state's highest court. We studied the constitutions of the state and our nation, and saw firsthand the three branches of government in action. Our image of the entire United States was filled with details that were linked to our understanding of St. Lawrence County and New York State.

While still in the eighth grade, we tested our insights and skills by taking the New York State Social Studies Survey Exam.

This test was usually administered at the end of the ninth grade after students had taken world economic geography. Since we had not taken a formal course in world geography, we were not expected to do well on this exam.

However, we aced the exam. How is that possible? We had developed insights and skills that would transfer easily to areas throughout the world. We knew how to approach this subject, and what factors were needed to fully understand the subject matter. When these test scores were shared with local school superintendents, they concluded that we must have cheated.

As a byproduct of this experience, I later developed an assessment technique that required model construction—iconic models that look like the object they represent. Since mastery of natural/physical phenomena, social, economic and political realities requires the development of a structure of the interrelatedness of data from each of these categories, in the nineteen seventies I set about designing a way of finding out what people know about these matters. I had made a listing of major elements found in each sub-category under each of the four major headings, natural physical, social, economic, and political.

The directions for the test ask the test-taker to draw a three dimensional model that represents the essence of what they understand about selections made from each of twelve environmental categories. They are asked to start with the bedrock category and select one or more rock types, draw them on the three-dimensional model as they would appear in real life, then select items from the minerals category that would be found correlated with the bedrock. This information is to be added to the model. Then appropriate elements from the relief category, such as hills and valleys, are correlated with the existence of certain bedrock and mineral deposits.

This procedure is continued until selected items from every category are included on the model, illustrating an interrelatedness of all the items. The title of the test was/is "The Environmental Relationships Test."

This *Environmental Relationship Test* has been administered to hundreds of students and adults, including specialists in areas that relate to each category of factors found in the environment. It was once listed by "Educational Testing Service" among other possible ways of assessing competency. I received one inquiry about this test and that came from India.

While administering this test to college science department specialists, the dean of science tried to cheat by sneaking a peek at his neighbors drawing. I found one professor in a group of twelve who could actually construct a verifiable model of an environment. To test to see if this professor simply memorized the exercise from some previous experience, I asked him to change the amount of rainfall and reconstruct the model based on this change. Of course, he was able to do this since he had developed a real sense of the patterns, structures, and organization of elements within the environment. He had developed this expertise as a field biologist with ample concrete exposure to the many variables and patterns of relationships found in different settings. Like this expert, our class of junior high school students developed a similar grasp of the elements and relationships that exist in our environment.

The results of administering this test revealed nearly a total lack of awareness of the interrelatedness of all the factors in a given area, whether one's home town that is experienced daily or other areas of the country or the world. It also revealed a predominate lack of skill in illustrating three-dimensionality. Most of the test-takers showed skills that ordinarily appear with 7 to 10 year olds. It seems that our educational system has allowed its charges to remain arrested in their growth that first appeared at these early age levels.

The consequences of such a lack of awareness of the interrelatedness of specific factors of the environment, for given times and places, are very troubling. How can decision makers act intelligently when they do not have a conceptual framework that includes all the elements of the setting in which they live and the interdependence of one element with another?

Judgments made in this intellectual vacuum have led us to make decisions about important matters that have caused destruction of our environment and the lives of human beings. It is the direct result of educational processes that emphasize memory of the conclusions of those who do not generally have an orientation to interdependency and in many cases have reached erroneous conclusions that remain untested and lead to potential disaster.

The Environmental Relationships Test

In this test, the learner is presented with common terminology that is recognizable by everyone who speaks English and has attended our public schools. This terminology relates to each part of the environment and the learner is asked to construct a personal view of the perceived/conceived relationships between each part and to express the results in a three dimensional representation—an iconic model. Considering what architects and engineers do when studying and designing a plan for a city block or a home development project, model building is central to this activity. They deal with systems of communication, transportation, aesthetic design, plumbing, heating, structural integrity, etc. as parts to be integrated into the whole and this test looks at the general abilities of learners to do the same.

A three-dimensional, cross-section of a segment of the earth's environment, often used by geographers and geologists to communicate their ideas, is an example of an iconic model at the synthesis level of cognition which the examinee is asked to construct. The following illustration shows such a model with enhanced labels and an expanded diagram for additional emphasis:

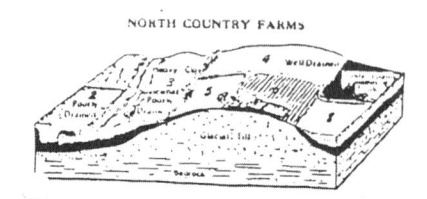

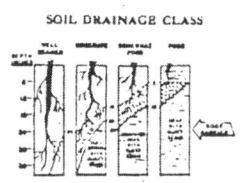

The amount of detail contained in the model is governed by the intended message and capabilities of its author, based on what is known. The richness and accuracy of the concepts illustrated in the model are variable factors in the communication, circumscribed by one's level of developmental maturation. For those who have reached the levels of concrete or formal operations, (the more mature developmental capabilities) who cannot represent accurate concepts within an iconic model, may not have adequate skills for drawing, or incomplete or unavailable concepts or both. A person at the pre-operational or motor sensory levels (the less mature levels) would not be expected to deal logically with the construction of the model.

There are twelve categories that list the common terminology which should trigger a concept of the parts. These parts are ultimately included in the construction of the model, illustrating the relationships the test taker perceives/conceives.

In the bedrock category is listed sandstone, limestone, shale, gneiss, granite and slate with a suggestion that other elements can be added if they fit the category. This feature applies to all the categories listed below.

In the minerals category is listed iron, oil, coal, talc, cooper etc.

The relief category contains mountains, hills, undulating terrain, valleys, plains, and plateaus.

The soils category contains a listing that includes, sand, gravel, loam, clay, sandy loam etc.

The vegetation category includes deciduous trees such as maple, beech and poplar, evergreens such as pine, balsam, spruce, cedar, broadleaf evergreens and grasses.

The animal category includes deer, bear, antelope, tigers, alligators, insects, birds of all kinds etc.

Weather/climate category contains high pressure, low pressure, wind, tornado, hurricane, rainfall, snowfall, growing season, temperate, torrid, arctic etc.

The location category lists latitude and longitude along with directions east/ west/ north/ south.

The manmade objects and alterations category includes buildings, machines, landscape alterations etc.

The social category lists customs, manners, religions, arts, education, recreation, etc.

The economic category lists businesses, banks and finance, trade, capital, investment, profit and loss, etc.

The political category lists courts (local, state, and national), boundaries, political organizations, state and federal constitutions, democracy and voting, etc.

What follows are typical responses from hundreds of college students, majors in teacher education, tested in the mid-seventies, including those who had taken environmental science, all of whom had passed the NYS Regents exam in Earth Science.

Test results for these students were rated with Bloom's Taxonomy of Educational Objectives from simple to complex cognition, namely knowledge or awareness of, limited comprehension, application, analysis, synthesis and critical evaluation.

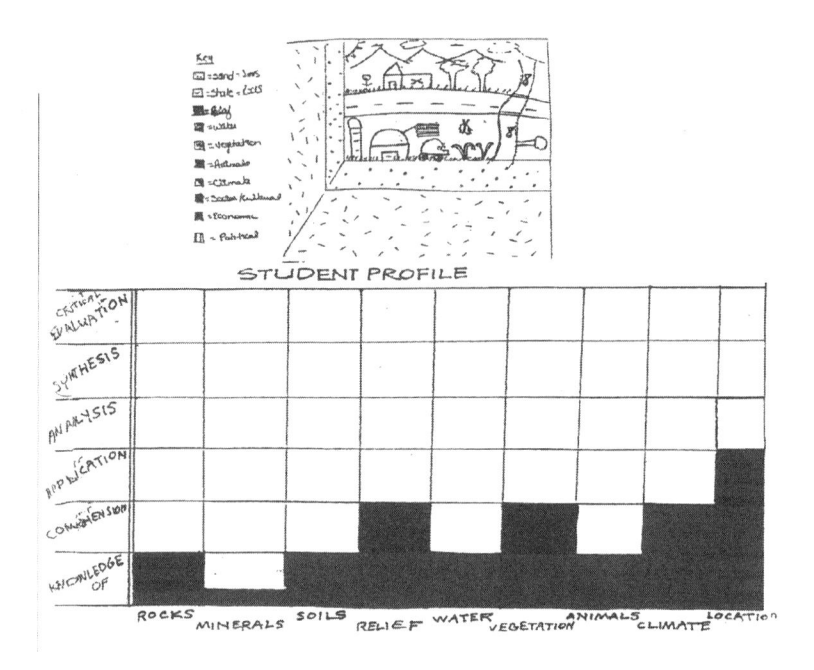

Students with this profile obviously do not perform much above the level of recalled knowledge. While completing the test, students with these deficiencies observably exhibit a sinking realization of their ignorance about matters once covered in their texts, but long since forgotten and impossible to retrieve.

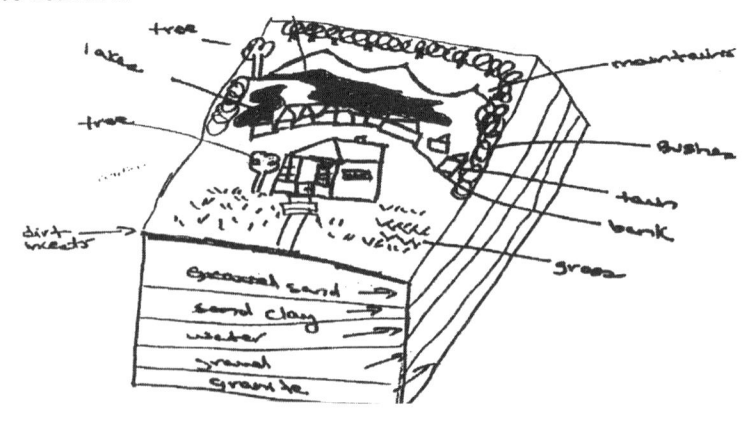

Take particular note of the house depicted in this model.

The front of the house shows beginning three dimensionality, while the rear of the house is two dimensional. The ability to represent the third dimension usually emerges between the ages of seven to ten years of age. This twenty-one year old not only cannot draw three dimensionally, but has regressed from using capabilities she or he developed by ten years of age.

Results from administering this test to all ages revealed nearly a total lack of conceptualization of the parts and the interrelatedness of all the variables of a familiar area, one's home town, or areas of the country or the world. It also revealed a predominate lack of skill in illustrating three-dimensionality.

For the individual to conceptualize the results of experiences indicated in each of the listed categories, those experiences should have been direct and purposeful or at least direct experiences that were carefully contrived to aid in gaining important exposure to the variables of any region and their integration or synthesis within a model. These requirements have obviously not been met.

Why is this so important? This involves just the world in which we live. It is the world from which we get our food, breathe our air, obtain our resources, and manufacture our goods. Ignorance about this world allows us to ignore global warming, pollute the environment, profit from its destruction, and view human societies through stereotypical lenses.

A working model of the interrelatedness of the variables of our world that is essential to recognizing and judging the validity of actions taken by humans is missing. It should be obvious to everyone that general education in our conventional schools has failed to produce this intellectual orientation and there seems to be a reluctance to admit to this reality.

We are left with an educational enterprise that has allowed somewhat effective, but isolated specializations to develop for a few that reflects high levels of individual motivation to achieve, (mainly to make money) without the awareness of or concern for the relationships of one set of ideas on another or one set of actions on another.

Taking a cue from this evidence, we must re-organize our schools to develop the basic general education that is mandated if we are to resolve our national and global problems before it is too late, if it is not already so.

The Discovery/Inquiry Approach To The Teaching Of Social Studies

The outgrowth of the work begun with the partnership of a classroom teacher and a college history professor went beyond the development of "The Environmental Relationships Test." We developed what we called "The Discovery Approach to the Teaching of Social Studies." Based on the obvious success of these teaching-learning experiences, we set about trying to convince teachers and schools to adopt our approach to change.

We held workshops across the state and in varying parts of the country. I did a demonstration for several hundred teachers at an annual meeting of the National Council for the Social Studies. A group of students were found from the St. Louis area and brought to the auditorium on a Sunday morning for the purpose of demonstrating the "Discovery Approach." I had assembled materials from local sources that these students could relate to and we pieced together an image of life that occurred in their home town area at an early period in their history.

The demonstration was well received, but nothing developed from that experience. I wrote a chapter for a publication of the National Council for the Social Studies discussing the essence of the Discovery Approach. (Powell, Thomas F., 1969)

One person from a Liberal Arts College in New England wrote a letter of appreciation and encouragement, but this was the only response.

My colleague and I also assembled and published *Inquiry, A Source Book for the Discovery Approach to Social Studies*. (Arnold, Robert and Lahey, Charles, 1965) We found that documents needed to conduct this approach required prior assembling. These included those documents for the local, state, and the nation.

Teachers could not be expected to search out and duplicate these necessary materials. So we selected some of the more generative documents of our local area and the state that would point the way for other collections to be made through local historians. Our sourcebook was published, but only a hand full of schools ever bought the book.

Most educators probably did not understand the importance of this learning process nor did they know where the documents would be found. Such a problem could not be solved without a serious effort and much work, far too much to expect educators to find the time and energy to do the job. Nevertheless, I kept trying to find ways of making the teaching materials available to teachers for a price they could afford and provide training that would help them find their way to a more profitable study of history and geography.

Professor Lahey noted in his book commissioned by the State University at Potsdam as part of a celebration of its history, that he and I received praise for the *Discovery Approach* from Laura Shufelt, curriculum bureau, New York State Education Department. She said in response to an observation of Arnold's classroom in the Congdon Campus School, "We have long given lip service to the aim of teaching pupils to think. It seems as though Dr. Lahey and Mr. Arnold are endeavoring to put this aim into practice." She continued to note that she "…was impressed with the wealth and variety of materials that had been accumulated and the aids and devices that had been created in classroom use. However, she understood and acknowledged as we did about "…the effort required both in finding and making those materials and in inspiring pupils to find and make them." One of the major obstacles to the use of similar procedures is the heavy burden of work on the teacher and the real challenge to his inventiveness and ingenuity…" Of course, she did not attempt to follow through with recommendations for government funding to make these materials available for classroom use (Lahey, W. Charles, 1966).

Our experimentation occurred in 1957 through 1960. We included in our book sections that discussed such concepts as the importance of discovering (constructing) an organization, a pattern, a structure among many isolated facts.

Subsequent to publishing our *Discovery Approach to the Teaching of Social Studies*, a very popular book appeared entitled *The Process of Education* (Bruner, Jerome. 1960) that reported the results of a Woods Hole conference on science and mathematics. Remember that in 1957, Sputnik roared into space ahead of us causing an outcry about the deficiencies of our science and mathematics programs in our schools. Subject matter commissions were established to restructure these subjects. The Woods Hole conference furthered the dialogue in this endeavor. This new publication appeared in 1960. Educators went wild over this book. More copies were sold that year than the Bible.

The author/editor of the book was a noted Harvard psychologist who reported about the need to teach *the* structure of these disciplines as opposed to teaching isolated facts. He maintained that structures could be identified and taught to students in an intellectually legitimate/honest way at any age.

He cited at the time a relatively unknown psychologist/biologist, Jean Piaget, as support for his contention. Educators saw this treatise as a bridging of the gap between the subject matter specialists and the child-centered teacher/educators. Educators were feeling left out of the dialogue about math and science since there was a conclusion that the way teachers taught math and science had failed, there was a need to turn to the "experts" in subject matter for more effective direction.

One simple word "the" that was attached to the word "structure" was a warning sign to me. The Woods Hole report indicated that "the" structure of a discipline could be taught effectively to almost anyone. This may seem trivial, but it has profound implications.

In our treatise on structure, based on several years of experimentation, we argued that a sense of structure is developed through the practice of the methodologies of the disciplines, and that a sense of structure comes about through unique and individualized findings. In our opinion, structures that evolve through individualized efforts are by definition opposed to the idea of "the" structure. We found that individual structures when evolved using methodologies of each discipline, such as geography and history, when shared, were similar but not identical to others that resulted from the same participation.

It is important to understand that an "objective" testing mentality requires a clear definition of what is to be "learned" so that a test can be constructed to measure the extent to which an individual can recall that which is mandated to be learned. The proposition that "the" structure of a discipline can be identified fits a testing orientation; structures are viewed as inclusive of interrelated facts rather than just isolated facts.

Designing tests to measure the mastery of a concept that is arbitrarily established for all to grasp, simply ignores the existence of individual perceptions that are often more insightful than that established by the experts. An attempt to find a way to recognize individual perceptions applying an open-ended set of criteria for determining what has actually been learned is found in other chapters.

Discussions with the author of the Woods Hole report over these differences resulted in a confrontational response that led nowhere. It became obvious that my standing as a skeptic could not compete with the Harvard-backed assertions, no matter how limited they turned out to be. The subject matter specialists, the representatives of their disciplines, went about their work and published such noted programs as "the new math." Go to any school today and see what happened to those efforts, since our math and science programs are still regarded deficient.

We frequently hear these days that our schools are failing. One suggested solution says we need to increase teacher's salaries and recruit an army of new, brighter teachers. Another solution is to offer parental choice, assuming that when given the opportunity, parents will seek out the best schools for their children, as if parents, the products of our schools, know what constitutes effective education. A third solution is to fund charter schools, assuming they would create positive changes in how our schools function.

Changing Assumptions And Beliefs

In all cases the proposed solutions are simply naive. We can pour in tons of money and offer many choices, but if the fundamental premises, the assumptions and beliefs, upon which schools are based, are not altered, the result will be more of the same. Only a few incremental changes in test scores will likely occur. These changes will be far from what is needed to make our schools more competitive and our citizens better educated.

Changing assumptions and beliefs is prerequisite to improving and sustaining sound educational practices, and the process requires time and a personal, emotional commitment. A new set of beliefs that stems from a shared and validated knowledge base presumably can, over time, establish a new educational institution more responsive to the needs of people in this twenty-first century.

A shared knowledge base for professional educators, parents and the lay public must contain constructs (theories) that can be relied upon for their validity. These constructs need to be continuously tested against our individual experiences and validated in the experiences of others.

A validated knowledge base contains at least the following five categories: (1) What is known and can be verified about how individuals learn and develop, (2) How communication occurs and how groups and institutions develop maturity, (3) How what we know is constructed and communicated, and how the disciplines within all "realms of meaning" contribute to this effort, (4) What is known about the organization and evolution of the existing school as a social system, and (5) What each professional educator knows and can verify about his or her personal characteristics that impact the job of helping others learn and develop, alone and in groups.

A validated knowledge base, that contains foundational assumptions and beliefs identified within the categories above, will define and shape the curricular experiences required of professional educators. That in turn will define and shape what is offered for learners in the school of the twenty-first century.

The educator, as a person and a professional, plays a pivotal role in determining the effectiveness of the school system in achieving its mission of producing intelligent decision makers and compassionate human beings. Importantly, the organization and evolution of the school system as we know it today needs to be understood so that informed change in that system can take place that encourages competency among its teachers.

Since instruction occurs in group settings, and institutions are composed of groups, professional educators must draw from the basic literature of communication and group processes, and in particular, group/team development. This aspect of the knowledge base must include assumptions about how groups function at varying levels of development and what interventions can support positive growth toward maturity.

There are multidimensional elements in human development and behavior that influence the processes of learning both in positive and negative directions. These elements include physical/social/emotional factors, intellectual levels of maturation, and moral and aesthetic orientations. The professional educator must have a clear grasp of what constitutes individual development and how behavior changes as the individual progresses from one level of capability to the next.

What learning is and how it takes place must shape and guide the actions of professional educators.

Understanding the nature of knowledge and knowing requires a re-evaluation of what it means to know and how the disciplines (within all realms of meaning) can serve as effective strategies for learning. This will define the content and processes of the curriculum that reflects a recognized theory of knowledge, an epistemology.

The basic personality of the professional educator is central to the facilitative roles required of a helping professional. The professional educator must continuously engage in self-evaluation with a goal to achieve consistent levels of "self-actualization." Self-actualization is defined as a state of being whereby the individual is utilizing his or her maximized potential.

The elements of the knowledge base must feature an interdependence of its parts. Inconsistencies among the parts must be reconciled through personal investigations and validation by others, especially by those who have delved deeply into the subject matter. A validated knowledge base (an assumptive underpinning) is always subject to review and modification when new and more insightful formulations are discovered. When these changes are internalized, personal behavior will change.

A validated assumptive/knowledge base provides guidance for decision making by the professional educator; it serves as a perceptual filter, an evaluative framework for making judgments about individuals, groups, institutions, and the content and processes that form the substance of curriculum. A validated knowledge base will ensure the development of constructive learning environments for every learner, regardless of age, race, or social standing. The nature of the curriculum and instructional strategies, combined with assessment, evaluation, record keeping and reporting procedures are shaped by the assumptions contained in the knowledge base.

Inquiry into the substance of this knowledge base and

its implications for curriculum and teaching must become a continuing professional activity for both the pre and in-service teachers.

Competent professionals must be granted the freedom to decide the appropriateness of any activities that are engaged by their students. Lessons produced apart from the group of learners, and taught by a teacher, whether prepared by outside "experts" or by the teacher, will significantly diminish the processes required for learning. Implementations require constant decision making in instructional settings with learners engaged in planning and executing their educational programs in partnership with their teacher/facilitators.

I worked for fifty years with pre-service and in-service teachers, supervising student teachers, watching closely how the schools are run, observing the roles and responsibilities of personnel, studying the ways the curriculum is structured and delivered, and most importantly, observing how all of this was effecting each student. I envisioned ways to improve the school with a view to bringing all the variables into alignment in an effective system. The variables discussed in this treatise are based on direct observations that have been woven into a design to bring about needed changes in our schools in this twenty-first century.

Throughout my professional experience, I have learned that education does not have a shared set of beliefs/assumptions about how individuals learn and develop, alone and in groups. As a result, schools are conducted essentially at the whims of officials and practitioners who (perhaps unknowingly) do harm to their students.

I observed significant differences in teachers' personal orientations that shape the programs they implemented in several thousand classrooms I visited throughout my career. I found consistently about 90% of the observable personal orientations among teachers and administrators appeared to be based on closed, highly categorized and rigidly maintained points of view. Routines considered safe and repetitive dominated the classrooms where the characteristics of those who were within the 90% group were found. The other ten percent had more open-ended orientations where creative exploration was pursued and maintained, where ambiguity was expected and plans to pursue meaningful activity were made cooperatively.

I found ways to bring about more open-ended orientations with most of the 90% group with whom I worked, by engaging them in a penetrating self-examination that led to their reconstructing personal orientations that were getting in the way of productive and constructive life-experiences. Once these individuals constructed a set of assumptions and beliefs that were authentically supported by their personal experience and those of others, especially having support from those who were considered scholars in such matters, they gradually changed not only their teaching/learning styles but their entire lives to accept a more productive, open-ended, less stressful and more satisfying orientation.

I observed that in spite of courses offered in the academic programs of teacher education, a predominate position taken among educators was based on generalities about human development and behavior, much of which was passed down from past generations of educators and seldom examined for validity. Those with more rigid orientations were most often guilty of this position.

I concluded that much of what these teachers and administrators had been introduced to in their course work at college was not learned, that is, not internalized as beliefs and assumptions that would guide their behavior as educators. In response to this reality, I set about to arrange hands-on activities that revealed to them characteristics of individual development and behavior that could be validated in their own experiences, gradually peeling-away the response patterns that were stereotypical and out of sync with reality. Once the old generalities were replaced by personally developed insight, connections were made between these insights and classroom activities. Changes then began to emerge.

All levels of education are organized around various sized groups of students. In most classrooms what was happening was functionality at the lowest level of group process, the level of dependency. I found that the maintenance of dependency required disciplinary tactics aimed to control each individual within the group. These tactics were time consuming and unproductive. The more rigid educators believed that turning over decision making to students, however limited, was considered a lack of leadership and a breakdown in a necessary order of the school.

I found through my study of group dynamics that achievement of the level of consensual validation requires passing through the difficult stage of independence, characterized by assertion of individual points of view. Since these points of view are often conflictive, it is necessary that teachers/group leaders have the skills to manage this difficult stage of development, which teachers don't appear to have. What was observed in the conduct of small groups indicated an unawareness and a reluctance to acknowledge that highly productive and individually satisfying groups exhibit what is called, consensual validation in its communication patterns, a goal worthy of attainment. (Bennis, Warren, et al. 1969). This level of functioning provides the necessary support for the pursuit of individual interests and an acceptance of the need to engage the priorities of others including those advocated by institutional authorities.

Knowing little about the developmental sequence of groups, most of those with the more rigid orientations condemned openness as inappropriate and potentially destructive. What seemed not to be understood is the fact that assertions of independence represent a necessary stage in the sequence that begins with dependency, moves to assertions of individuality, and develops into interdependency and consensual validation, the most mature level of group functioning.

The fact that most groups at all levels of education are operating at the level of dependency, unable to grow to a more mature state, there is a stagnation found in the classrooms that contributes immeasurably to the lack of individual productivity and the acceptance and practice of frequent anti-social behavior.

I found the reliance on textbooks or textbook substitutes was dominating the classrooms conducted by the more rigid educators. Those who did not have much confidence in self-insight were found to be prevalent among the teachers and students in rigid classrooms. In this group the role for teachers defined them as the conveyors of isolated bits of information and students as consumers of that information. This orientation to teaching and so called learning is at the heart of many of the problems relating to a lack of achievement among many students at all levels of instruction.

When viewing what the sequence in development of learning is that culminates in problem solving abilities, I found that sustained learning is far more than the recall of information, which is measured by many tests in utilization today. Learning is a cumulative process of creatively transforming personal experiences into patterns of meaning, leading to problem solving abilities.

I began my teaching career offering the content of each subject of the curriculum as I understood it in the same style I had observed in others; the teacher was the conveyor of information, supported by textbooks and instructional media, conducted in groups where students were dependent on the teacher and where the student was supposed to dutifully assimilate isolated bits of information or suffer the consequences. This was happening in nearly all classrooms I visited, even those conducted by educators with more flexible, open-ended personal orientations. Members of this group were often reluctantly enduring this procedure in order to keep their jobs.

By sheer luck, outside of preparation courses for teachers, I was introduced to the disciplines of history and geography as ways of creating knowledge. I discovered when using these creative processes with my teacher education students and younger students it produced insights that I had never witnessed before, far superior to anything that I had experienced as a student or as a teacher. This initiated an intense inquiry into the nature of all the disciplines as they were organized by Phenix, (Phenix, Philip, 1964). His schematic features six realms of meaning, what were formerly randomly organized subjects to be consumed by the students. This organization features interdependent, creative processes for engagement of reality that produces the skills and insights necessary for continued lifelong learning and effective communication.

I witnessed the nature and uses of assessment and evaluation procedures in every school I visited. These assessment devices, especially standardized tests, were instrumental in shaping the classroom procedures and the content conveyed to the students. Few other forces in the conventional school have such an influence in directing the nature and outcomes of the school experience.

Standardized tests were designed not to aid students in determining their problems in learning, but rather to segregate students into categories based on the test scores and the schools on the basis of comparative success. The misuse of these tests had extensive negative consequences. Although individual achievement in developing the skills and insights necessary to live effectively and participate intelligently in a democratic society are legitimate goals, the achievement of those goals has been seriously hindered by the widespread uses of standardized tests that lump the test takers together as if they are all the same.

I have dedicated a large portion of my investigations to the development of a system of education with a focus on developing a more effective and developmentally/experientially compatible approach to the assessment and evaluation of learning outcomes. Initiated with younger learners and pre-service teacher education students, the Constructive, Assessment, Recordkeeping and Evaluation System (CARES) was developed. It has been field-tested in college classrooms and adopted for use in elementary and secondary classrooms. The products of learning, documented through the use of this system, have been nothing less than extraordinary.

Although much information is introduced within the classrooms of our schools, very little is actually learned. The evidences produced by surveys of adults have found an appalling lack of retention of what was undoubtedly taught at perhaps several points along the sequence of grade levels.

This lack of recall is largely attributable to the perceived need to efficiently cover large amounts of subject matter thought to be important in the lives of every student. Lacking records of experiences that would reveal what was actually accomplished with those experiences throughout the years, the conventional schools have become dispensers of information with very limited internalization by the students. Over time, personally developed records can be constructed and re-constructed by each learner that could result in the development of emerging patterns that greatly enhance the ability to reconstruct one's memories or after images of personal experience.

Personal diaries for some have always served well the ability to recall significant events, but in a limited format. The CARES model expands the individually developed common diary to include a detailed record of personally important information that can be accessed and reconstructed with the click of a mouse when the need arrives. Computer technologies give the storage and accessing of personal learning records an accepted advantage over anything used in the past to record the progress of learners. As experience tells us, grades in the registrar's office tell little of the nature of learning or the actual degrees and dimensions of success.

Records kept with the application of the CARES model (discussed in detail elsewhere) are evaluated and reported using stringent criteria selected from the field of systems analysis.

The advances in communication technologies have been

exponential. Yet, the uses of this technology have been limited mostly to searches by dependent learners for the generalities of so called experts, or the exchanges of trivia among the broader populations. The potential for this technology has stirred a revolutionary movement in other parts of the world where populations have faced exploitive treatments by despotic leaders. Unfortunately, educators apparently do not feel a similar need to eliminate the long term, life-altering practices of authoritarian leadership in our schools and among our high level decision makers. Frustrated by these communication inventions, educators are seemingly unable to create a system that will more fully harness their vast potentialities for enhancing learning and the development of competence.

Devices are available to almost every student in our society that can capture images of everything encountered in the search for personal meaning; recording those meanings in a complete record can be maintained, massaged periodically, and shared by others. What a shame if this potential is viewed to interfere with the conduct of instruction.

Probably the most controversial suggestion from my experience that I make about systemic changes needed in education, would be a change in the administrative organization. Our society has increasingly become dependent upon the decisions of persons granted authority by our legal and political systems. So much so that it is felt that without a "strong" leader we cannot maintain an orderly society.

Facing this same problem in 1776, our forefathers set out to declare independence and argued out a design for decision making that involves three departments of governance, the judicial, the legislative and the administrative/executive branches. These departments/branches were expected to function with a balance of power under the direction of a written constitution and bill of rights.

This organization was designed to function even in the face of conflicting points of view, requiring of course an educated public and an educated leadership. (Given the conduct of our current governing officials one cannot help but wonder what kind of education these people received.)

Given the habit of living in an overly dependent society, and a serious problem with lack of competency among a large portion of our citizenry, a grave danger exists from within our democratic organization that is now seemingly an unrecognized reality.

Recognizing that schools are organized and function primarily under an authoritarian structure with hierarchical decision making, I set out to define an alternative that is compatible with the other propositions in education I had refined over the years. Since our nation's form of governance has served us well for the past many years, I designed a written constitution and bylaws that can be installed in our schools featuring an instructional branch, an administrative branch, and a quality assurance branch.

This constitutionally-based organization is supported by a statement of beliefs and assumptions about human learning and development and institutional organizations that enhance the growth of maturity, validated in our experiences and supported by scholars who have studied these matters indepth. This system would modify, if not eliminate, the makeshift, piecemeal attempts to reform and improve education in this country.

Without this change, we are left with having to live with the various styles of authoritarian leadership that may be entirely despotic or at best benevolent. We will continue to endure the tactics of leaders who claim to be consultative. These leaders are also authoritarian, but give the impression of democratic processes until those processes do not conform to his or her positions (Likert, R. 1967).

In a truly democratically run school, the levels of participation by all stakeholders would necessarily be increased and the processes of intelligent decision making enhanced when all participants are familiar with and committed to the underlying assumptions and beliefs that maintain stability in a democratically-run system.

No individual teacher or administrator can effectively manage the complex dimensions of becoming educated in this or any other day and age. As others have said, "It takes a whole community to raise a child." There are human and material resources within every community that must become integrated into the planning and functioning of an effective system for educating all our citizens. A community center that engages all members of the community and draws in resources from other communities will profit from the varying points of view and the sharing of proven skills and procedures. Unlike the conventional school, a community center that engages special skills, both professional and self-developed, for responding to the needs of all learners, will inspire and promote the development of the unique capabilities of everyone involved.

I spent over fifty years in teacher education as a professional educator. Little did I realize at the time of my attendance in a teacher education program as an undergraduate, just how inadequate this was in preparing me for the complexities of teaching. I struggled to maintain throughout my formal education a commitment to learning as I had lived it from the days I spent working on our family's nearly self-sufficient farm. In contrast, I witnessed fellow students cramming for tests, memorizing nearly useless generalizations and moving from class to class almost never referring to the bearing of one set of ideas on another. My experience in self-reliance and integrated life experience did not serve me well in classes where an overly dependent relationship with teachers and reliance on a prepared subject matter was expected.

I set about designing a teacher education program that incorporated all the findings I have mentioned above and more. This model for teacher education has relevance at all levels of instruction since the principles of development and learning know no artificial boundaries designated separately for children, young adults, and adults. The model takes into account the deficiencies that manifest themselves in the capabilities of today's young people. It recognizes the need to establish a foundational knowledge base that cannot just be covered in the curriculum but must be mastered in the processes of becoming a competent teacher and citizen. This knowledge lays the groundwork for sustained and consistent implementations, once these persons are working with learners in the transactional processes of helping them come to know and appreciate the wonders of this universe. Teaching that is defined as sharing, rather than telling or lecturing, will go a long way toward improving the quality of education for every individual.

Teacher education that emphasizes logical and powerful arguments for changes that are based on the scholarly literature today receives mixed responses from participants, dependent upon how they are introduced to this material. For those who are taught (the conventional way) to accept the arguments and find ways to implement them in their teaching activity find it difficult to translate systems theory into practice. This explains what has happened in most teacher education programs today.

Those who are immersed in direct teaching and learning experiences will find motivation to examine the theories when they explain what is happening and what could be happening. With sustained investigations that validate the language and concepts of these theories they are internalized and they translate into practice.

Teachers, who cannot cite these powerful arguments by drawing support from the literature, do not create the impression they belong to a respected profession. Absent this capability, they will be more easily manipulated to perform in ways that are totally inconsistent with what they may assume and believe intuitively. A prime example is the currently mandated approach to assessment that treats all learners of the same age as being the same. No teacher assumes learners are all alike, yet most teachers today go-along with the trend to do so. They conform to the demands of the system fearing that confrontation would lead to their dismissal or being subjected to various tactics of intimidation. (See Appendix C for elaboration.)

Chapter 2

An Overview of the Constructive Assessment, Recordkeeping, and Evaluation System (CARES)

Perhaps Bud Blake did not realize the full significance of his cartoon that follows. This profound statement sums-up what is mostly unexamined about instruction in our schools. "Does he know any other tricks? Sure! We taught him all of 'em! ... But this is the only one he learned."

Tiger — **Bud Blake**

TIGER © KING FEATURES SYNDICATE

Teaching and learning, as we have come to know them, are distinctly different things. In today's conventional schools we teach, that is, we cover the text and test for simple recall. We refer to the incremental changes in test scores as learning. Since the amount retained and available for use is infinitesimal, as compared to the amount of information that has been "taught," to refer to this as significant learning reveals a major problem.

What is Learning?

Learning for Stripe (the dog) is not presumed to include

higher thought processes; it simply refers to being able to repeat a task that was drilled into him until he was able to automatically reproduce the trick at a later time. This is stimulus-response learning at its best.

Robert Gagné's model of learning combines behaviorist's viewpoints of stimulus-response learning with those of the cognitive and developmental theories. His work explained what learning is, so that we can understand what happens with Stripe revealing the parallels that happen with our students in the typical classrooms of our schools.

Educators were undoubtedly "taught" about Gagné's theory, but did they learn it? Judging from observable behavior, they did not. Robert Gagné's eclectic insights have seldom been acted upon or even retained by teachers, educators, parents or the lay public. Current test makers do not appear to have a clue about this theory, or perhaps they know it but it doesn't fit with their objectives to commercialize the schooling processes.

All learning begins with experience, called a stimulus, which yields an initial automatic response unless there is some anatomical restriction that prevents a response. This condition is presumed to be the same or similar for Stripe as it is for human learners. If specific stimuli are repeated enough times, simple associations are developed.

In Stripe's case, his master probably offered rewards with goodies that dogs like to eat and provided positive, encouraging statements and stroking that communicated approval. The responses that gain approval act as a reward that encourages a continuation of those responses.

Teachers, typically give rewards for behavior judged to be approvable and punishments for unacceptable responses. The withdrawal of rewards, such as denying recess, is well known by all of us. An "A" brings great satisfaction since parents, teachers, and our society grant approval, even when the "A" only represents what Stripe demonstrated in Blake's cartoon.

That is, the ability to perform a trick automatically after sufficient reinforcement and repetition has been employed.

The next higher level, learning of associations, is assumed to be similar for the human learner as for Stripe.

Associations are responded to first by physical actions, and later by verbal. A physical response by Stripe is easy to recognize, as for example, salivating, according to Pavlov, and might even be followed by a bark that might signal a reaction to the reward.

A physical response followed by a verbal one is likewise easy to recognize in a human learner. For humans, recognizable language patterns and utterances of words emerges at this developmental level. This marks the likely near-terminal learning-outcome for Stripe, but only the beginning for the human learner.

The next level of learning for the human learner is multiple-discrimination. At this level the simple physical and verbal associations become the building blocks for deliberate internal intellectual manipulation and decision-making (cognition) that Stripe is assumed to be incapable of accomplishing. Language that represents the objects and actions in the immediate world begins to emerge at this level for human learners.

Multiple-discrimination involves looking at one's experiences from various vantage points, leading to groupings based on discovered commonalities—the classification of objects and events in differing ways, using different criteria. These may be differences in color, texture, or social dimensions etc.

These discriminations are the forerunners of concepts or mental images, which are the definitions or points of view held by the learner that can be manipulated and retained for later use. Recognizable language that represents the thoughts and actions of the individual emerges at this level.

This level was described by Jean Piaget as "concrete operations" in *The Growth of Logical Thinking from Childhood to Adolescence* (Piaget, Jean and Inhelder, B., 1958).

Importantly, concrete, direct experience is necessary to

fully develop this concrete operational level of learning that gradually evolves into higher level intellectual capabilities.

Concepts of objects and events are personal points of view that may or may not be validated or based on verifiable evidence. These points of view are elaborated over time with continued exposure with the subject matter encompassed in the concepts. Eventually, recognizable regularities or simple rules begin to emerge. These rules are substituted for multiple concepts and used to interpret life's experiences in a more sophisticated manner than was possible at the prior level.

These rules, developed internally, emerge into principles that are verified as representative of a more reliable and integrative insight than the prior simple rules. These principles guide intelligent intellectual behavior and influence physical behavior when consistently acted upon.

Principles develop into laws that apply to the interpretations of a wider variety of phenomena; laws are even more inclusive and generative than rules and principles. Personally constructed laws provide the learner with intellectual power that motivates and stimulates investigation and verification of conclusions, one's own and those of others. Validated laws provide the necessary ingredients for problem solving, the pinnacle of the learning hierarchy.

Adult learners who have reached the biologically-based developmental level of "formal operations" described by Piaget (a level of capability that is characterized by the ability to think abstractly and deal with hypothetical deduction) can progress from the level of stimulus-response through the entire ladder of learning in a shortened timeframe, as compared to younger learners, provided the prerequisite concrete experiences have been engaged. The younger learners, with developing intellectual capabilities, are restricted in their learning by less mature developmental capabilities, regardless of their experiences.

Assessment and evaluation procedures that reflect a limited definition of learning, that matches Stripe's capabilities, dictate the nature of our schools and their classroom procedures and instructional materials.

If we want to change/improve education, a fundamental requirement is to change the assessment and evaluation system, where current practices are primarily focused on the lower levels of learning (typical of Stripe) with only token concern for higher thought processes.

To meet the need for assessment and evaluation procedures that are individualized, yet standardized, the "Constructive Assessment, Record Keeping and Evaluation System" (CARES) was created and field tested over the last thirty years by this author. This approach grew out of what is generally known as systems design.

The CARES Model is a computer-based system for gathering and storing experiential data; storing these data in an organized record of personal experiences, allowing the manipulation of stored data through the construction of models/systems, obtaining validation of the models through sharing and comparing output by developing a narrative or other forms of expression and finally, identification of new areas of investigation.

A basic premise of the CARES model builds upon what Alfred North Whitehead (a noted philosopher/mathematician) stated in his book *Aims of Education and Other Essays,* published in the early twentieth century. Whitehead stated that what students need is "An eye for the whole chessboard, for the bearing of one set of ideas on another." The whole chessboard is viewed here as involving systems, wherein the parts are perceived and conceived to be interrelated and a change in any one part brings about a new pattern of relationships.

How does the CARES Model Work?

It is one thing to criticize the use of standardized tests that are designed to measure evidences of learning, but it is another to present a viable alternative that has the potential to eradicate the ills of the current standardized movement.

"The Constructive Assessment, Recordkeeping and Evaluation System" (CARES) is just such an alternative. Its acceptance by educators, parents, and the-public-at-large, hinges on an understanding of how the system works and how it addresses the needs of the twenty-first century student. Here is an attempt to describe this system, hopefully in terms understandable by everyone who has attended a conventional school.

Educational assessments are made of specific subject matter. In the case of current assessments using standardized tests, the questions are supposed to sample the content that each student has presumably been exposed to through instruction in various classes. These common-core subjects are labeled, mathematics, English/language arts, history, science etc.

The topics taught in these classes are selected by so-called authorities, like the writers of textbooks or members of the state or federal curriculum committees. Teachers are expected to arrange these materials for instruction, always mindful of the need for students to pass the standardized achievement tests that are supposed to certify what has been learned. With the current widespread use of standardized tests, corporations commissioned to design those tests have acquired significant influence over if not control over what topics are included in instruction.

Each area of content covered in classes contains mainly generalizations and conclusions reached by others, presented to students for consumption through the aid of prepared lesson plans, audio/visual media, teacher lectures, or demonstrations, supported by textbooks and workbooks and worksheets.

Much of the "study" of the content is relegated to homework that often amounts to filling in the blanks on pre-designed worksheets. This is generally an exercise in matching-up whatever is in the text or presented by the teacher with each question on the worksheet. For many students this is a relatively meaningless exercise, but it assists short term memory sufficient to enable passing a standardized or teacher made test. Databases of the internet are mainly searched to expand or validate what was or is being taught in the classroom and reinforced by homework.

This type of instructional program is organized into compartmentalized units that are offered in departments, each area of the curriculum treated as a separate and isolated experience.

This type of program is subject-centered. Teachers are the conveyors of the content prescribed for each subject; with the help of instructional materials and equipment that includes the computer, all assisted by a "teacher's guide" which often includes the answers to questions posed in the body of the texts—thus creating nearly "teacher-proof" instructional materials and procedures used in today's classrooms.

Students are the consumers of the information conveyed by the teacher and the texts. *Learning is defined as "remembering" a specified amount of the content covered in the pre-defined curriculum.*

Everyone knows from experience, nearly all the material covered in this type of instructional program is forgotten, seldom to be resurrected again, once the tests have been passed. Even more troubling, the possible relationships between subjects are not understood and the isolated information is not only forgotten, it becomes useless information that stifles creativity and operational intelligence.

How does the CARES model differ from the current use of standardized tests in a subject matter oriented curriculum? As with the conventional curriculum and instruction, the CARES assessment and evaluation model is also inextricably linked to the content of the curricular program. But this is where the similarities end.

The CARES model starts, not with subjects (the canned conclusions about the past and present) but with the universe, the real world, itself, as viewed from four interconnected sub-parts of a vast system. These interconnected sub-parts are (1) the natural physical features, (2) the social/cultural activities, (3) the economic activities, and (4) the political activities of human beings, the inhabitants of our natural/physical universe.

Investigations into the nature, function, and interconnectedness of the sub-parts of the system we call our universe, today and in the past, is the focus of the general education curriculum. These investigations are learner centered, not teacher centered.

An attitude of science is central to this program. It is basically a process of gaining a point of view based on investigation, observation and experimentation. Science is considered to be a frame of mind that every learner must adopt to gain profit from exposure to the many variables contained in this universe. Curiosity is at the heart of this scientific orientation.

Here is an example of a comprehensive system to be approached in early childhood and eventually mastered as a result of reality-based experiences, facilitated with the contents stored in computerized folders containing many files. This system is best initiated with a focus on the local environment, which includes the natural physical characteristics, and the social, economic, and political activities. The focus is on "Life in all its manifestations" (Whitehead).

Mastery of a system requires an individual's extensive knowledge/awareness of each part, and through experience and reflection, that knowledge is raised to the level of "an eye for the whole chessboard" with insight into the bearing of one set of ideas on another—an integration that represents a level of principles and laws. Today's computer-based technologies can aid this process.

Mastery occurs when the learner has developed levels of higher intellectual capabilities indicated by the formation of concepts, rules, principles, laws, and finally creative problem solving abilities. Stripe is presumed to be incapable of functioning at these levels.

One of the many criticisms of today's "high stakes testing" is that teachers teach to the test. Not only are the tests selectively narrow in scope, they force the teachers to spend much of their time in and out of the classroom nervously preparing for their students to answer the secretly-selected questions of the test-makers. Job insecurity and prolonged anxiety are the direct results of such a process. Teachers are compelled to teach to the test regardless of their insights into the fallacies and shortcomings of this process. This inflicts severe psychological stress that diminishes the very capabilities of teachers so needed in creating effective educational experiences.

Emphasis on tests has always been a reality in our schools, only now the intensity has vastly increased due to anxieties over a need to raise "standards" and make our students more competitive in a global society.

Standards are primarily described as the ability to perform the prescribed "tricks" that have been taught, resulting in the development of intellectual capabilities rarely above the level of multiple discriminations with little or no insight into what constitutes personally validated concepts, principles and laws.

Fortunately, some students, on their own, act on their experiences independently and progress to significantly higher rungs on the learning ladder. However, these occasions are all too infrequent; most of the school population never experiences these higher levels of performance, at least in relation to their school experiences.

Although the test-makers have recently improved their tests by asking more performance-based questions than prior tests that were predominately in a multiple choice or forced choice format, the correct answers are still prescribed and failure to answer correctly is reflected in the final score. The correctness of specific answers on the test is often unknown to the students or to their teachers.

The tests are not diagnostic; they are designed to provide data for evaluating the performance of the school and now for evaluating the performance of the teacher on very narrowly-defined criteria. The statistical scores are reported in minute increments (ex. one tenth of one percent) as if complex human behavior can be reduced to a single statistical number. School authorities, politicians and the lay publics are tethered to the concept that each increase in small increments in the general population of students shows significant "progress" in "learning." This conclusion results from a widespread confusion and ignorance about what learning is and how it comes about.

Learning is an internal process of elaboration as can be seen in Gagné's work, from simple responses to specific and varied experience, associations developed from repeated exposure leading to concept formation and development of patterns that eventually result in problem solving abilities. Simple regurgitation of facts and generalizations or drilling the definitions of sophisticated theories is at the lowest levels of the learning process, and as we all know well, these "facts" are easily and willingly forgotten.

In response to the limitations of the "one size fits all" type of assessment, teachers tried what became known as "portfolio" assessment. Attempting to provide more credible evidence of what individual students actually experienced and perhaps learned. The "portfolio" was a collection of documents (papers) and recordings that represented the work of each individual student.

The results were often bulky collections of examples of student work that were supposed to be evaluated so as to produce a grade for the report card. This task demonstrated many difficulties in evaluating each portfolio. The subjective nature of evaluation attacked a long-standing belief in pre-ordained "objective standards." This led to resistance to the idea of a creative portfolio and re-assertion of the "validity" of the one-size-fits-all "objective" test.

Trying to counter the criticism of subjectivity, groups of teachers, together, would attempt to reach a reasonable agreement as to the value of each portfolio. Clearly, this approach could not be sustained, partly because it was unwieldy, but mostly because it challenged the established "objective" testing mentality.

A necessary requirement for an effective system of assessment and evaluation is consistency with the developmental characteristics of each student, which the portfolio assessment tried to accommodate. In the "one-size-fits-all" approach, developmental differences in students are virtually ignored. Students, and ultimately their teachers, are penalized for failure to produce the correct answers on tests, even if that failure is due to the lack of the developmental maturity needed to make informed choices.

In the portfolio approach, individual differences were subjectively muddled in an attempt to objectify the often random, but authentic collections of materials displayed in the record.

In this era of digital storage and retrieval, an effective system of assessment and evaluation can and must employ the latest technology. Today, nearly all students have access to computer-based communication instruments, the cell phone, the computer and the internet. Each day there are advances in the use of this technology in everyday life. But many schools view aspects of this technology as unwanted competition in the "teach to the test" procedures. Frequently cell phones are banned from the school and often the internet is used only to bolster the pre-selected information important in the school's standardized curriculum. Students are accustomed to using these devices as entertainment or to exchange trivia.

The CARES model incorporates technology in every aspect of learning, and in the assessment and evaluation process. The cell phone and portable computers with their various capabilities frees students to interact with every aspect of everyday life wherever it occurs, and to convey their reactions and ideas to others, including the school, if only it would recognize that potential.

How many of us agonize over the loss of memory about what were once significant events in our lives. What a waste of valuable information. Using the latest technology, the CARES model relies upon the collection and electronic storage of the record of experiences, as they have occurred throughout one's life, those that happen by circumstance as well as those directed by individual curiosity and those encouraged by the formal educational establishment.

Imagine what would happen if each of us could retrieve with the click of a mouse pertinent information from the many experiences we have encountered beginning with early childhood, and have available our personal record so that we can revisit and study/reconstruct what we have made of our past experiences.

Records must reflect the developmental differences of individuals, so due to relative immaturity in young children the record originates with the aid of adults and the responsibility for record keeping is gradually transferred to individuals as their capabilities mature.

The record is maintained as a documented listing of experiences and illustrations of what has become of those experiences as they are reflected upon. In this way, the responsibility for learning and record-keeping is gradually shifted to each individual, with assistance from the teacher/facilitator and other adults, including parents.

The CARES model has a built-in procedure for evaluating the products stored systematically in the record. The record is organized around systems concepts, drawing once again upon the wisdom of Whitehead when he noted that "the only legitimate curriculum for the school is life in all its manifestations." This translates to mean the focus of schooling must be on the examination and construction of meaning in our lives, its objects, and events, and the activities of other human beings wherever and whenever they exist or have existed.

Of course, there are skills required to shape the analysis of one's own and other's experiences such as mathematics, dealing with quantity and spatial relationships, and other languages, including the language of computers, the arts and scientific formulations.

Mastery requires an ability to construct systems and subsystems from life's experiences; this is the overarching goal.

Mastery of language skills will best occur in the context of learning that develops a need to organize and communicate one's personal discoveries.

Any part of a system must be related to all the other parts that make up the whole. As Whitehead maintained, the "inert" ideas that are simply taken into the mind and never put into fresh combinations are not only useless, they are harmful. Think about this. How much of our education involves simply taking into our minds isolated, inert ideas that are never placed into fresh combinations. If Whitehead was right, and I believe he was, instruction that is full of useless information is harmful to the general population of students.

The development of language for communicating with ourselves and others must follow a continuing natural recognition of whole words and phrases that represent the real meanings as seen through the eyes and heard through the ears of each individual. This must replace the near mindless exercise of drilling young, intellectually immature students in repetitions of isolated letters and sounds.

Analysis of the nature of language parts becomes meaningful when it coincides with the appropriate developmental level that develops later in the emerging intellect of each learner. To introduce exercises in the parsing of language at the level of pre-operations (pre-logical) is a waste of valuable time at its best and harmful to the developing intellect at its worst.

Subjects taught in our schools are an accumulated set of conclusions formatted mainly in textbooks and other canned storage vehicles, conveyed to students through various forms of media and demonstrations by the teacher. The student is generally a passive receiver of this information.

Students' interpretations are often disallowed as they are

forced to commit to memory those conclusions that are presented in the prescribed curriculum. This process is reinforced through the use of "high stakes" testing wherein the students are required to match their answers to those of the test makers, which were presumably derived from the conclusions of "experts" accepted on faith for their authenticity and validity.

The CARES model seeks an alteration from typical subjects to "realms of meaning" and provides a new direction for aiding learners in becoming competent in their own lives, but also more competent in assessing the value of the conclusions and representations of others, even those found currently within outrageous media advertising. The CARES model includes a reorganization of the way we view the common core school subjects.

Each discipline can be viewed as a sub-system, as part of larger systems. A discipline is a process of creating meanings using tools and constructions that follow a set of rules and assumptions derived from the efforts of those who have focused and are focusing upon creating meaning in their worlds. Disciplines are process oriented, compatible with the CARES model, and compatible with child/human development and behavior.

In place of subjects, the CARES model recognizes the need to focus on meaning in the context of real life situations. Instead of the typical listing of subjects of the school curriculum, here the curricular content is framed as the living universe, investigated using a concept of academic disciplines within six "realms of meaning." Philip Phenix, an educational philosopher who studied the various ways human beings create meaning, published this schema in a book in 1964 entitled, *Realms of Meaning: A Philosophy of Curriculum for General Education.*

Phenix categorized these realms of meaning as (1) *empirics*, embracing all sciences including social science; (2) *synoptics* which includes history, geography and cultural anthropology; (3) *esthetics* which includes the arts and architecture, (4) *symbolics* which includes all forms of language and mathematics [updated to include the languages of technology systems-engineering, electronics and computers], (5) *synnoetics* which is self-knowledge and (6) *ethics,* which includes morality.

All disciplines in each of six "realms of meaning" have established methodologies and organizing principles for creating products in their particular domain. These methodologies are constantly changing/improving as new experiences occur that challenge or extend the existing formulations. Those who participate in the construction of meaning using these modes of inquiry and expression readily recognize the need for change in response to new discoveries. The following illustration of Phenix's concepts serves as a summary of his model:

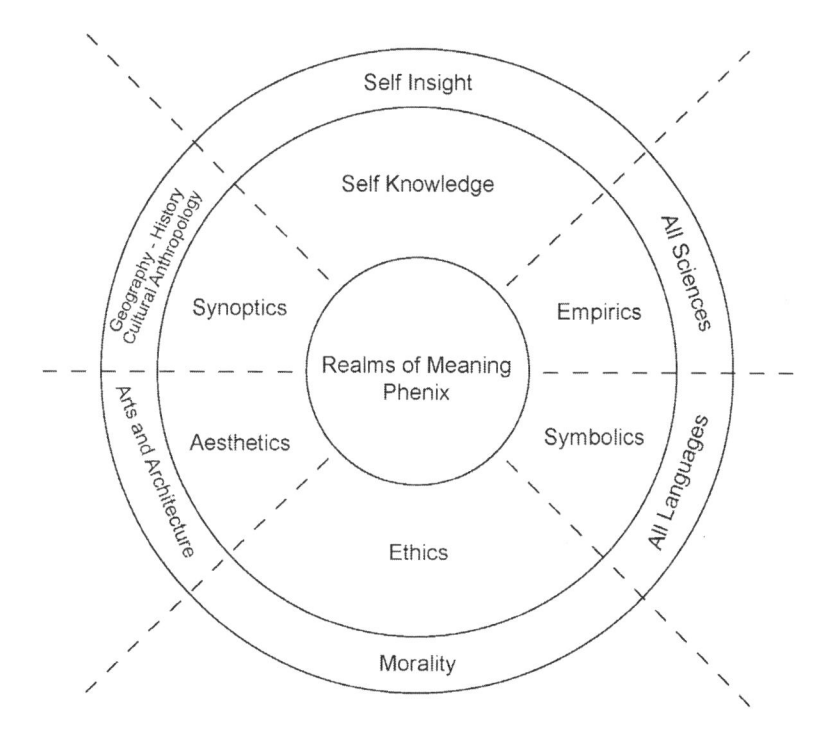

Each of these categories contains disciplines that are grouped according to specific domains held in common from the standpoint of their processes and organizational structures. When viewed from a process point of departure, the disciplines are compatible with the construction of meanings, essential in organized educational experiences. This constructive/creative orientation contrasts dramatically with the conventional view of subject matter as essentially pre-defined conclusions of the so-called experts, offered to be consumed by students.

When students in our schools and colleges utilize the methodologies of the disciplines, exciting things will routinely happen as was demonstrated in the work cited earlier with junior high school students in geography and history. Students will learn how to learn, utilizing and identifying with the very best approaches to creating and communicating meaning about life in all its manifestations. They will develop the need and the skill for communicating effectively about validated and important personal discoveries and create relationships/integrations among the various ways of knowing.

History, Geography, and Cultural Anthropology, as disciplines dealing with the present and the past, are considered synoptic, and seek within a narrative, to integrate findings from each of the sub-categories listed below. This synoptic orientation must play a major role in the processes of integration and the reality of interrelatedness among all the variables in life's manifestations.

Art serves as the expression of personal meanings in unique and creative forms. It has a significant role in communication and in defining the essence of reality for individuals and societies.

The following file names provide the broad framework of sub-categories to be investigated, first in the local surroundings and later in other areas throughout the world. Any media and experimentation that reveals graphically the nature of objects, processes, and events of every region under study will be essential.

The subjects covered in these categories represent topics that are encountered over a period of years. For simplicity sake, they are divided like this, but in the actual application, the boundaries between each discipline and its contents are blurred because children will learn through discovering patterns instead of learning specific narrow conclusions with no context.

The first sub-category described here relates to those experiences with the natural/physical characteristics of any region of the universe, including manmade alterations. Keep in mind, these sub-categories are parts of a whole that are to be investigated using established, construction methodology drawn from the disciplines, and the results recorded when the parts of the system are being experienced. Parts of the first sub-category are listed in common language in the nine categories shown below. As each part is encountered in experience, learners turn to the materials and methods of relevant disciplines for guidance in their inquiry. The results of these investigations are utilized in the construction of models of the whole system, one part at a time. This organization is repeated for all sub-categories that follow.

1. Rocks and minerals: This is the domain of Geology and Mineralogy among others.

2. Soils: This is the domain of Pedology/Agronomy

3. Relief features: This is the domain of Cartography

4. Vegetation: This is the domain of Botany

5. Animal life: This is the domain of Zoology/Biology

6. Water and drainage patterns: This is the domain of Hydrology

7. Weather and climate: This is the domain of Meteorology and Climatology

8. Location and evolution: This is the domain of Astronomy and Cosmology

9. Manmade objects including buildings, machines, landscape alterations etc.

This is the domain of architecture/engineering, and systems design

10. Other

The second sub-category identifies experiences that reveal

the social/cultural characteristics. These are the domains of Sociology, Education, Psychology, Anthropology and others:

1. Customs and manners
2. Religion
3. Recreation
4. Heritage and ancestry
5. Social and service organizations
6. Education
7. Community art and architecture
8. Communications methodology
9. Any other social/cultural factors

The third sub-category contains experiences with economic activities and institutions.

These are within the domain of Economics:

1. Trade and commerce
2. Banking, stocks and money
3. Agriculture
4. Industry
5. Transportation
6. Employment opportunities and requirements
7. Profit and loss
8. Purchasing/shopping
9. Retail and wholesale
10. Any other economic factors

The fourth category relates to experiences with political activities and realities. These are within the domain of political science:

1. Boundaries–Village, City, Town, County, State, Nation, Other Nations
2. Laws and courts–local, state, federal, international
3. Constitutional guidelines
4. Governmental structures and procedures
5. Political organizations
6. Voting and democratic processes
7. Agencies of government

Underlying all of the above topics are ways of learning

and communicating that include such disciplines as chemistry, physics, and mathematics.

Each of the above categories suggests activities to be offered to learners. As they experience these topics, using developmentally appropriate methodologies of the disciplines, their experiences are recorded in a personal record. Over time, an extensive record will provide opportunities to remember and revisit past events and to re-structure the earlier responses to reflect up-to-date interpretations. Completed files will interrelate as more and more experiences are recorded and connections between contents previously stored in the files are discovered.

The ultimate model to be constructed for any region, for any point in time, includes topics from all the above files. This provides a structure for more fully understanding the systemic parts and their relationships to the whole. Acquiring this sense of structure will help enormously in recall of information and in bringing to bear important conclusions with a direct impact on the tasks of current problem-solving. The construction of these relationships and their implications will become the hallmark of competence.

Four folders, one for each category— natural/physical features, social, economic and political activities—are maintained in the computer, each containing files that relate to the sub-parts and the experiences with these sub-parts encountered in the real world. The number of computer files maintained in the CARES model reflects the variables identified within an environmental system. The initial number of parts suggested here is thirty, as listed later in this chapter. These may change as investigations proceed and new classifications are developed.

Even experiences and reactions to those experiences at the earlier stages of development necessarily would be entered into the learner's record with the assistance of adults. The number of parts encountered in these early years would be limited; however, those that are experienced will be recorded. Later investigations will fill in the gaps.

Pertinent confidential data is inserted for the files including name, date of birth, local address, and identifying passwords.

When the learner is mature enough to remember past events, the record that contains enough descriptive information and conclusions will trigger the memories of learners at a later time and reveal to the learner events that happened before the ability to reconstruct events emerges.

Investigation begins by identifying the historical/geographic region under study. Entries into the record are dated for future reference. Since individual learners experienced the events, they will be able to recall/reconstruct relevant details. This recording is assisted by adults until learners eventually develop the full capabilities for logical analysis and record management, when they can deal with more elaborate, abstract and hypothetical propositions.

An in-depth study of the local environment leads to the transfer of important organizational principles that are adaptable to environments wherever and whenever they exist or existed. The local setting provides many opportunities for concrete, direct, and purposeful experiences with each and every variable that exists in a manageable, accessible area or region.

Heretofore, a local study was thought to be unimportant as contrasted with the major events of the world, and relevant materials were seldom made available due to a lack of sales and profit-ability with limited locally-related markets. Here a local study is considered essential to the development of insights that will transfer to more remote events and locations.

Starting from the earth's sub-structure and moving upward to the outer-reaches of space, the variables are identified and computer files/folders are arranged to provide storage of a record of those direct experiences with each variable and the reactions to those experiences.

Files within the natural physical features folder:
1. Rocks and minerals
2. Relief features
3. Soils
4. Drainage patterns
5. Vegetation
6. Animals/biological creatures
7. Weather
8. Climate
9. Location and manmade objects and alterations

Files within the social/cultural folder:
10. Social networks/communications methodology
11. Customs and manners
12. Arts/architecture and education
13. Recreation
14. Religion
15. Family structures/heritage

Files within the economic folder:
16. Money/checking/credit cards
17. Banks, banking and accounting
18. Employment/management/employees, Unions
19. Agriculture and industry
20. Business/corporations /Insurance
21. Profit/loss
22. Investment/dividends
23. Savings/interest
24. Federal Reserve/currency
25. Credit/mortgages/contracts

Files within the political folder:
26. Boundaries/local/state/national
27. Laws, courts/local/state/national
28. Constitution/state/federal
29. Government/local/state/national
30. Political parties/voting

Faced with the extensive listing of the thirty parts to be engaged, entered into the record and transformed into personal meanings, one might ask, "Isn't this process too complicated and time consuming?" A fair question, but there are some pertinent considerations when implemented that make the process not only manageable, but exciting.

The linear listing above of thirty topics reflects an organization of subject matter familiar in the conventional school. Viewed in this manner, it encourages an instructional procedure one topic at a time, leaving the integration of topics to chance. The probabilities of an integration occurring is very low. Without this integration of ideas, which the human mind is fully capable of accomplishing, isolating the information deprives the individual of the powers of creativity. As long as the topics remain isolated and disconnected, the achievement of mastery is nearly impossible.

The first task is making this listing more manageable and more reflective of higher thinking processes. The same listing (slightly modified) is arranged in a different format. The circular format reminds us that all the topics are potentially interrelated and a search for this interrelationship is the central theme that organizes the curricular experiences. The illustration below shows that interrelated model.

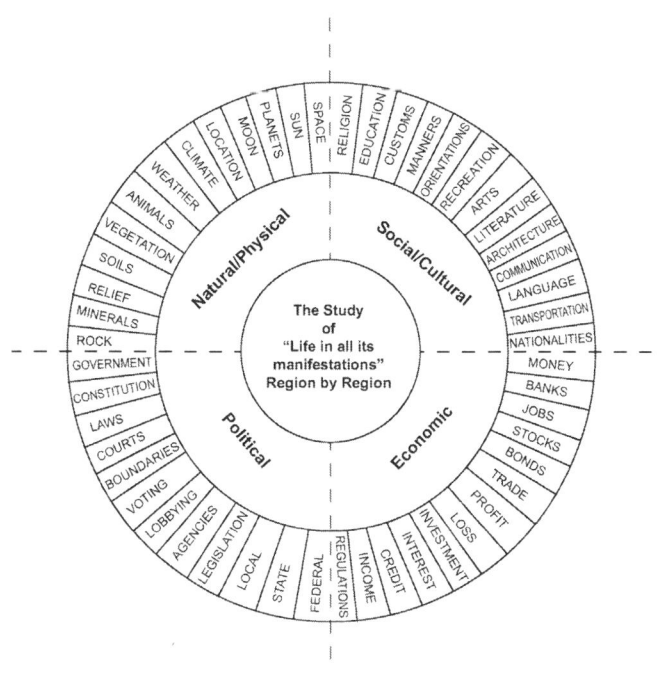

In the normal course of events, both within the school program and outside, learners explore, question, and reach conclusions about what they experience. Inevitably, experiences leave an impression that is based on the evidence of what was observed/experienced, conditioned by the impressions of others. Photographs may have been taken, ideas may have been generated, and the experience is remembered for whatever it meant at the time it occurred. If this information is not summarized and kept in a record it invariably will lose significant details over time and perhaps the whole memory of the incident will be lost. This is a significant loss of valuable information that ultimately can be related to other information and generalized in one's statement of personal assumptions and beliefs with far wider applicability.

It matters little which variables in the system are approached or in what order. The interests of each learner can be honored since the end product is the construction of models that contain all the variables of the system; the point of departure will ultimately be linked to all the other variables. Think of this as a puzzle with a thousand pieces. You start by getting an overview of the image you are trying to create and you then begin piecing together the border and interlocking parts. Gradually all the pieces are placed in a relationship and the image becomes clear. Individuals select the pieces that most interest them and the process ends up with a completion of the task.

While this analogy helps in understanding the process, in actuality the process is more complex than simply putting together a puzzle. Each person will perceive and conceive the parts of the system somewhat differently and will construct a unique final picture. This is what's called synthesis" in Bloom's Taxonomy. Cognitive synthesis is unique to each individual and this presents a unique problem in achieving an accurate evaluation of the individual products of inquiry. The CARES model is designed to address this problem.

There are six steps in this learning process:

Step 1: Identifying the components of a system to be mastered. This process is ongoing. There is defining and redefining as the individual proceeds with learning.

Step 2: Translating/conceptualizing the components of a system and inserting evidences into the record. Conceptualizing the content of each component will require accumulation of experiences and a translation of those experiences into personalized language forms.

Step 3: Model building that will aid the process of organizing and reorganizing the findings. The models can be in the form of iconic, symbolic or analogies that can be either iconic or symbolic.

Step 4: The learner formulates in various language forms the levels of mastery achieved to date. Synthesis and critical/creative evaluation occurs, facilitated by the models noted in the previous step.

Step 5: Verification of the validity and usefulness of the newly constructed system is aided by comparing and contrasting with other's formulations, especially those formulations generated by experts in that field.

Step 6: During the process of verification, each learner will isolate the hypotheses untested and the questions unanswered. This will invite continuation of inquiry at an even higher intellectual level.

In an effort to satisfy the need for stringent evaluative criteria that can be applied to all learners, yet individualized for each learner, the following criteria are used in the CARES model.

Evaluation criteria applied to student-generated constructions (systemic records)

(1) Clarity and organization. A record that is disorganized lends very little to one's insights. *It is here that grammar and spelling are continuously dealt with **in context**.*

(2) The information entered into the record should be an accurate reflection of the learner's viewpoint.

(3) The files in the record must be comprehensive. Gaps in the record are identifiable and these gaps indicate the experiences that must be afforded the learner. The teacher must provide this experience or point the learner in the direction of acquiring it.

(4) The record must clearly connect with the personal experiences of the learner and when appropriate, the experiences of others, especially those drawn from the accounts of experts in a particular topic, etc.

(5) Each of the major categories must reflect internal consistency. This means the learner must examine the entries for instances of internal contradictions that they are aware of. They may deliberately choose to either alter them or simply know that they exist and for the time being leave them as they are and later re-visit them.

(6) The materials in the record should help the learner identify questions that are unanswered and hypotheses that are untested. With this there is an open invitation to pursue

further those areas that have not been touched by current processes.

Each individual will differ from peers in terms of the time it takes to master the system, the degree of complexity in the constructions, the number of uses that can be described for the system, and the nature and consequences of change that can be anticipated

It is important to note that the first encounter with any of the variables (parts of the environmental system) will be understood as gross impressions; details will be missing. With each additional visitation/encounter, more details are observed and recorded. This reality suggests that learners need to revisit their experiences several or more times to be able to tease out a more fully-developed conceptualization of what exists to be understood.

It is possible to revisit experiences with each variable in our worlds several times during the course of the years of elementary education and these re-visitations are greatly enhanced if a record of past experiences has been maintained. Extended visitations will lead to the development of patterns that greatly reduces the complexities of the world and immeasurably improves recall of specific facts.

The active pursuit of meaning on the part of each learner is the orientation of this program and the assessment, record-keeping, evaluation and reporting procedures are designed to support this orientation. The teacher's role is that of facilitator of a transactional process of selecting, seeking, defining, examining, organizing, storing, and communicating meanings constructed by individual learners, including the teacher in partnership with the learners.

A systems orientation encourages learners to creatively construct their own models of their interpretations of objects, events, and processes, the gathered information/experiences found throughout the universe. Taking account of the many variables found in this booming buzzing universe is made meaningful and manageable by using the CARES model. The CARES model is systems oriented.

Starting in the local environment and expanding into other environments/regions throughout the world (and beyond), each learner investigates first hand and through the vast library of computer-connected data sources, the parts of systems, records experiences and interpretations in computer/storage programs, and constructs integrations among what most often remains isolated, disconnected information in the conventional system of education.

Since the universe is a vast network of sub-systems that make up the whole, it is necessary that the whole universe be organized into identifiable categories each learner will engage. To help keep track of the findings each learner has constructed/discovered there is a need to maintain a complete record of the accumulated experiences encountered with each variable, one part at a time. Each encounter is recorded with the personal interpretations, validated with support from others (especially those who have studied these matters in depth) and personally organized through an integration into models refined with the assistance of adults who have pursued similar investigations and expressions of meaning in their lives.

Having a complete record containing the summaries of past experiences available with the click of a mouse enables each learner the opportunity to revisit those experiences, reconstruct their meanings, and re-integrate the updated versions in the construction of ever-evolving systems. This element of recordkeeping prevents the loss of important information that is easily forgotten without a record. Valuable information is most often lost in the processes of the conventional schooling where records consist primarily of letter or numerical grades, not very useful for either the learner or any other interested party.

A listing of similar files/folders can pertain to other locations and time periods. Files can also be identified for any sub-systems such as the human body, the field of mathematics, other courses of study, and all other systems.

When the Constructive Assessment, Recordkeeping, and Evaluation System is employed from the earliest possible times in the lives of children, continuing at least throughout formal education, and for adults attempting to create more productive lives, the following characteristics and outcomes of learning will occur:

This system will utilize the unique, cumulative learning opportunities of every individual, inside and outside of school.

(2) Continuity in learning will occur; one episode building upon another.

(3) A systems orientation will reduce complexities to manageable elements, enabling individuals to make sense out of and more control over a booming, buzzing world and universe.

(4) Integration and construction of meaningful relationships between sets of ideas and subject matter will be constructed.

(5) Personally developed and validated frameworks for understanding elements of the universe in which we live will be the result.

(6) A continuous search for meaning in life's experiences will personalize any formal schooling experiences.

(7) The process of gaining self-direction and personal-competency, with open-sharing of ideas and validation through comparisons with the lives of others, will lead to far more productive citizens, more productive human communication and yes indeed, more sensible and productive governing processes.

To get started recording experiences that can lead to the construction of a workable model, any form of electronic storage is formatted to receive the recordings as they occur with the natural/physical, social/cultural, political and economic parts of the world. Each region under study will require separate storage formatted in a similar manner to provide easy access to the full record.

The process starts by transferring data from one's memory, from notes and from the computer, digital camera and the cell phone to the appropriate category and sub-category.

Data are accumulated over time and periodically entries are reviewed and restated as integrations of discrete information.

Once this integration happens, original data can be moved to a permanent file in another storage folder, catalogued for future retrieval and use. In this way the current record reflects just the most up-to-date constructions the learner has defined. The permanent file will serve to document the process of experiential re-constructions that resulted in each learner's current conclusions.

Access to a collection of experiential records will enable the learner to constantly consider re-construction and elaboration of personal conclusions. This record will be supplemented by the writings of others in both fiction and non-fiction. The completed record will be summarized for efficiency in communicating with employers, teachers, parents, and researchers.

The current summaries will have a rich and extensive data base that will be used to support the conclusions as they are challenged through self-reflection and through the shared ideas and opinions of others.

If the task of engaging students in learning seems overwhelming, remember that insights into complex systems emerge over time as each individual is encouraged to experience life in all its manifestations, one experience after another, and communicate those experiences in a variety of forms. If sufficient time is allowed for every individual to achieve mastery, the whole educational experience will produce lasting and significant results.

Experience happens from infancy to graduate and post-graduate levels, it continues throughout one's lifetime. When the record of experiences is maintained by organizing the responses to those experiences so that they can be retrieved and elaborated throughout time, it will maximize the learning processes and alter behavioral outcomes.

When individual learners achieve higher levels of integration and elaboration of their experiences, they vastly improve their capabilities for recall and for solving complex problems with an element of humility. The cumulative record of the learner's information-processing, relating each of the parts of systems, is maintained to aid conceptualization of each part and integration of the parts into a dynamic relationship that represents mastery.

A system is defined as any perceived whole composed of functionally related parts. Any set of interrelated parts can be viewed from a systems point of view, thus the parts are identifiable, and interrelationships among the parts can be uniquely constructed by each learner. The record contains a table of contents, continuously updated, that identifies the parts of each system to be mastered.

Each category (a file in the CARES model) that appears in the table of contents contains recordings of experiences, and learner transformations of those experiences. The transformations appear in four forms: (1) enactive behavior, recorded as video, (2) iconic models that resemble the objects and events that are communicated visually and in common language, (3) symbolic models that utilize all formalized language forms including mathematics and technical symbol systems, and (4) analogical models that utilize both iconic and symbolic forms that are indirectly stated as analogies.

Models are simply representations of some subject of inquiry—an object, event, system or process. Learner-generated models serve four functions—an organizing function, a heuristic orientation to the pursuit of meaning, prediction and measuring. Iconic models look like the subjects they represent, symbolic models are mathematical/logical language constructions, and analogical models represent, with familiar models, unobservable objects, events, systems or processes.

The process of relating the achievements within each file to all the other files is begun when each file in the record is periodically reworked and restated at a more integrated/sophisticated and detailed level. The object is to develop a synthesis within and between files and restate that synthesis for use in understanding and communicating with the efforts of others engaged in their processes of learning.

Some of the materials that are used in reaching a higher level of insight can then be purged from the current record and stored in a research file for future use. These files would contain information that identifies the topic and date of the inquiry and the original descriptive information about the experiences that was used in arriving at conclusions that remain in the current files.

To make this process concrete, let's assume that the system to be mastered focuses upon the local community—your town, county, village or city, etc. Inquiry into the local setting must precede that of more distant settings both in time and space so that direct, firsthand experience can be facilitated and personal conclusions directly verified. What is learned at this level forms the foundational patterns for insight about other settings wherever and whenever they occur. A recognition that insights into the elements of the local setting are missing in today's instruction contains the origins of problem-solving abilities among our populace.

The parts of this system are (1) the natural/physical features such as the rocks, minerals, soils, relief, water and drainage patterns, vegetation, animal life, weather, climate and location, along with manmade products and alterations. (2) The human patterns of events contain social/cultural factors including customs/manners, education, communications, religions, and recreation; political factors including boundaries, laws, constitutional matters, courts, elections, government organization, and economic activities which include jobs, banking, trade, indebtedness, profit, loss, sales and marketing.

Each of the items mentioned are the titles of files that

will contain accounts of direct experiences in the community that fall within each title. For example, a trip to a local rock formation will be recorded in the record in visual and narrative form, reflecting what the learner saw and understood that had meaning for him or her. The attendance at the local Town Board meeting likewise is recorded and placed in its appropriate category. Trips to museums and historical landmarks are recorded. Each experience with the parts of this system is recorded and accumulated over time.

As more experiences are recorded, it will become necessary to organize those findings and conclusions to help clarify them for future use. Eventually the interrelationships between the categories are constructed and the results are recorded as integrations. The findings in each file are restated as a pattern of relationships or a system. Recognizing the interdependence of each of the separate categories is a discovery of immense importance.

With today's educational emphasis on specializations, the recognition of the interdependence of systemic parts is often lost. This allows individuals to make decisions based on limited awareness of the consequences of their actions which are often destructive and dangerous in today's complex world.

An example of this lack of systemic awareness is seen in the current world financial crisis. Frequently, we hear that no one knew this problem was coming. How could they if only a few parts of the system are understood? A system is like a house of cards where the cards are integrally related. When a card falls, the others are affected. Constructing interrelationships is fully within our grasp if we have an educational orientation toward the construction of systems of meaning.

In step one, the teacher and the learner(s) cooperatively develop the listing of parts that will ultimately make up the system to be constructed and validated by each learner. The listing of parts (the record's table of contents—each part represents a file for the record) becomes the statement of goals taking into account what is required by the curriculum of the school, what is presently known about the subject drawn from within the group and from others. The listing is subject to change as inquiry proceeds. New parts may be added or some listed initially may be removed as more insight is developed.

Agreed-upon listings of parts are translated into learning objectives that provide structure for building toward mastery that is continuously tracked in the record.

In step two, the performance objectives include experiencing, then translating those experiences into personal language forms, followed by interpreting and personally connecting the new experiences with related ones from the past, analyzing the experiences and finally inserting all of the results into the record under each appropriate file. This process is continued for each file of the system being constructed.

It is of utmost importance to have access to a rich bank of information from all types of media. The more direct or life-like the experiences, the richer the concepts will become. Richer concepts will lead to greater possibilities for making connections that build toward the construction of meaningful systems.

It is the teacher's responsibility to provide information-rich experiences for each of the parts in the table of contents. It is the learner's responsibility to translate those experiences into personalized language forms and insert the results into the record. The uses of modern communication technologies will aid this process immeasurably.

In step three, the records of experiences contained in each file will accumulate extensively over time. When evidences are sufficient, integration or synthesis will occur within each file. These integrations will then be represented by models that summarize the meanings derived by the learner. The models should include both iconic and symbolic representations to ensure that the uses of words are supported with a conceptual underpinning. When models are constructed that represent the syntheses of ideas, the accumulated evidences that were used to construct the model can then be removed from the file and placed in a permanent file and catalogued for future reference.

In step four, as models are constructed within files, logical connections develop between concepts in multiple files that result in even higher levels of integration or interfile connections. It should be noted that a learner who hasn't reached a level of logical capabilities, will represent appropriately ideas in illogical or partially logical ways, no less important than more sophisticated logic and hypothetical deduction.

Many students reach capabilities of consistent logical analyses first as concretely logical and later at a level of more abstract symbolism. Piaget's formulation describing a pre-operational intellect, concrete operations, and formal operations offers useful guidelines for determining expectations for each learner. These are explained in detail in later chapters.

Higher level interpretations result in more elaborate models that show the relationships of discrete experiences in a completed synthesis—the development of a meaningful system. A synthesis gives rise to critical evaluation and creative manipulation that takes the form of a formulation used to communicate the results of one's inquiry to others. This communication can take many forms including written narrative, demonstration, artistic representation, or performance.

In step five, one's system is constructed and communicated to group members, facilitating a process of comparing and contrasting individual constructions. This input from others serves to validate the content of the record and challenges the author to support and perhaps change the contents to reflect new information. In this way, the record provides the evidences that support the learner's constructions of meaning, thus it facilitates retention, examination, and validation of the evidences.

Since the learner has constructed the record from personal experiences, the defense of that record is not difficult. Since the record provides a snapshot of current understandings, it can easily be modified and updated as new evidences present themselves. Once constructed, the structures of meaning are in place that will not be lost and new information is thereafter assimilated into those structures.

For example, a learner who has constructed a comprehensive and validated model of all the dimensions of the local setting, currently and in its past, will make meaningful connections with people and places remote in time and place.

The Constructive Assessment, Record Keeping, and Evaluation System (CARES) presents a new vision and value specification for the kinds of learning outcomes we want our students to achieve. It has been classroom-tested in a variety of subject areas and institutional settings ranging from childhood to middle school, high school, junior and senior colleges.

Its implementation requires:

(1) A staff development program to establish the practical and theoretical dimensions of the strategy,

(2) A demonstration within a manageable instructional unit, followed by gradual expansion into other units, one geographic area at a time. With the aid of guidelines already available, each teacher can begin immediately to install the system within any subject area and shift the major responsibility for record keeping from the teacher to the learner. The guidelines ensure the orderly shift from existing procedures to the new CARES model.

(3) This model does not preclude the use of conventional tests but their frequency and importance would be greatly reduced and they would need to become more diagnostic of student needs. Installation of this system will require active support from the various levels of administration and will require intensive educational efforts involving the parents and lay public.

The Constructive Assessment, Record Keeping and Evaluation System (CARES) is a computer-based strategy designed for use in any curricular area or sub-division where mastery is the desired goal. Mastery is defined as the ability to discriminate, synthesize and evaluate the functioning parts of any system defined for study, and to represent in various language forms, the origins and products of that construction.

The CARES model facilitates individual achievement of mastery by generating organized, accumulated evidences of experiences and learner-developed competencies; a record useful to the learner, employers, school officials, parents and researchers. Its focus is on learner-constructed systems of meaning that begin with identification of the individual components of the system to be mastered; continues with accumulation of records of learner experiences and concepts that pertain to each component of the system; is followed by transformation of the records into models, and the eventual development of a synthesis among all of the parts.

Records of each component of an identified system are maintained in computer files for each topic, reflecting the achievement levels of cognition as outlined in the *Taxonomy of Educational Objectives: Cognitive Domain* (Bloom et al., 1956) Each file contains personal notes and drawings that describe discrete experiences as they happen, and the learner's translations, interpretations, extrapolations, applications, analysis, synthesis and critical evaluation of those experiences. Such a system would transform our outdated and outmoded general education that is failing our students and our society.

This personal record is like a greatly expanded diary, scrapbook, or autobiography. With today's capabilities for electronic storage and retrieval, a complete record of experiences for every individual is possible. Instead of brief entries made at the end of each day, this record will contain pictures of significant events, personal surroundings, and individualized engagements that take place throughout one's lifetime—beginning with pictures and recordings of the events of infancy, noting the date the events took place, physical changes such as rolling over in the crib, beginning to creep and walk, the utterances of language from mimicking to recognizable words and phrases etc. Imagine what a powerful tool this record will become for each individual to gain in personal insight and appreciation of others.

Gradually the topics of the record will reflect focused investigations into the broader aspects of the local community and eventually those of other more remote places and times. The full implications of such a record can only be imagined. Personalized educational experience that develops extra-ordinary competencies will become commonplace.

In summary:

Constructive Assessment, Recordkeeping and Evaluation System (CARES)

A completed record contains computer files representing each variable/parts of any system to be mastered. "Mastery is defined as the ability to differentiate/conceptualize the parts of a system, create an integration or synthesis of the parts, illustrate the synthesis by constructing models—iconic, symbolic or analogic—anticipate the consequences of change within the newly constructed system, freely compare and contrast the system with formulations created by others, modify and utilize the system to interpret and solve problems."

In general, there are six steps in the process of constructing a validated system. (1) Defining/re-defining a listing of parts of the system to be mastered. (2) Accumulating experiences and translating/conceptualizing the parts and inserting experiential evidence into a computerized record. (3) Model building by organizing and re-organizing the findings stored in the record. (4) Synthesis and critical/creative evaluation formulated into communications of the levels of achieved mastery. (5) Verification through comparing and contrasting one's findings with others. (6) Identification of a new system that grows out of the prior constructions.

The following criteria apply to the emerging, individualized records of learners with developmental capabilities at or above concrete/logical operations. (Piaget)

1. *Clarity and Organization*: The record and all of its subparts must be logically arranged with a brief explanation for the basis of the particular organization, with definitions for each file or classification written with correct spelling, grammar, sentence structure etc. All written statements and visual representations (example – charts, graphs, models, etc.) must be error-free with regard to formal language usage – spelling, grammar, sentence structure, etc.

2. *Accuracy or Plausibility*: Explanations, whether they come from the learner or from authors on the internet, from books, etc. must be verified as accurate, or at the very least, plausible as determined through logical analysis.

3. *Comprehensiveness*: Inclusion of materials must be representative of the total possible items that fall within the scope of the file.

4. *Support from Personal Experience*: All explanations and statements of beliefs must be supported as much as possible by and/or derived from personal experience. *Support from Others' Experiences*: Support for personal beliefs wherever possible must be supported by others, especially those of experts drawn from literature.

5. *Intra-File Consistency*: Each file must contain ideas, propositions, etc. that are found to be internally consistent (non-contradictory). Any possible inconsistencies must be identified.

Inter-File Consistency: Materials contained in each file should not be conflicting with the contents of other files without identifying these possible conflicts that inhibit integration.

6. *Generativity*: Hypotheses untested, ideas in process, and creative solutions must be identified.

7. Other to be specified

Evaluation, applying these criteria, encourages unique constructions by each individual.

Here is an example of a comprehensive system to be approached in early childhood and eventually mastered as a result of cumulated experience with the contents of each file. This system focuses on the local environment which includes the natural physical characteristics, and the current social, economic and political activities. The focus is on "Life in all its manifestations" (Whitehead). An in-depth study of the local environment leads to the transfer of important organizational principles that are adaptable to environments wherever and whenever they exist(ed).

The number of files reflects the number of variables identified within this environmental system. The initial number and the contents may change as investigations proceed and new classifications are developed. The above criteria are only used to the extent that they are applicable with learners of the earlier stage of development – pre-operations. The range of experiences and reactions to those experiences at the earlier stage necessarily would be entered into the learner's record with the assistance of adults. As this record is kept, learners will eventually develop the capabilities for logical analysis and record management when they can deal with more elaborate, abstract and hypothetical propositions.

Starting from the earth's sub-structure and moving upward to the outer- reaches of space, the variables are identified and files are arranged to provide storage of a record of the direct experiences with each variable and the reactions to those experiences.

File 1. Rocks and minerals
   2. Relief features
   3. Soils
   4. Drainage patterns
   5. Vegetation
   6. Animals/biological creatures
   7. Weather
   8. Climate
   9. Location and manmade objects and alterations
   10. Social networks/communications methodology

11. Customs and manners
12. Arts/architecture
13. Recreation
14. Religion
15. Family structures/heritage
16. Money/checking/credit cards
17. Banks, banking and accounting
18. Employment/management/employees/unions
19. Agriculture and industry
20. Business/corporations /Insurance
21. Profit/loss
22. Investment/dividends
23. Savings/interest
24. Federal Reserve/currency
25. Credit/mortgages/contracts
26. Boundaries/local/state/national
27. Laws, courts/local/state/national
28. Constitution/state/federal
29. Government/local/state/national
30. Political parties/voting

A listing of similar files can pertain to other locations and time periods. Similarly organized files can be identified for each of the sub-systems of the human body, the field of mathematics, courses of study, and all other systems.

When the "Constructive Assessment, Recordkeeping and Evaluation System" is employed from the earliest possible times in the lives of children, continued at least throughout their formal education, and for adults attempting to create productive lives, the following characteristics and outcomes of learning will occur:

(1) This system will utilize the unique, cumulative learning opportunities of every individual, inside and outside of school.

(2) Continuity in learning will occur; one episode building upon another.

(3) A system's orientation will reduce complexities to

manageable elements, enabling individuals to make sense out of and control over a booming, buzzing world.

(4) Integration and construction of meaningful relationships between sets of ideas and subject matter will be constructed.

(5) Personally developed and validated frameworks for understanding elements of the universe in which we live will be the result.

(6) A continuous search for meaning in life's experiences will personalize any formal schooling experiences.

(7) The process of gaining self-direction and personal-competency, with open sharing of ideas and validation through comparisons with the lives of others, will lead to far more productive citizens, more productive human communication and yes indeed, more sensible and productive governing processes.

Chapter 3

Individual Development and Behavior

This chapter is admittedly long. It features the work of numerous authorities on the subject of individual development and behavior, summarized from volumes of published works. Had these developmental theories, models or constructs been featured in separate chapters, an important message would have been diminished if not lost. The core message regarding the interrelatedness of these many dimensions of individual human development would not have received its proper due.

Numerous authors have tried to clarify the elements of personality that are required of persons entering into an effective helping relationship with learners. It has long since transcended debate that what the teacher brings to the teaching-learning transactions, in addition to a knowledge of subject matter (no matter how expansive or limited) makes a great difference in the quality of the experience and learning engaged by students. The teacher who encourages self-actualization in students most often exhibits a high degree of self-actualization as well.

What follows is an excerpt from a profile of dimensions of personal orientation, based on Maslow's theory of self-actualization and adapted by Everett Shostrom in the construction of the Personal Orientation Inventory. This illustrates some of the positive dimensions of personality that are required for effective facilitation of learning in others, applicable to all learners as well. When these self-actualizing characteristics are present in the teacher's behavior, there is an increased likelihood that a healthy and supportive relationship with students will be developed.

When the opposite personal characteristics are present, for example, time incompetence, outer-directedness, rigidity in the application of values, etc. there is a strong likelihood that the relationships established will be less than desirable for encouraging learning. Positive characteristics must be considered essential when certifying teachers for the most important job of our time and must become essential objectives for the education of our youth:

1. Time competence – lives predominately in the present rather than predominately in the past or in the imagined future.

2. Inner directedness – independent, self-supportive rather than outer-directed and overly-dependent on others.

3. Flexible in the application of values rather than rigidity in the application of values.

4. Sensitivity to own needs and feelings rather than insensitivity that often leads to self-denial.

5. Freedom to express feelings behaviorally rather than fearful of expressing real feelings.

6. High degree of self-worth rather than low self-worth.

7. Acceptance of self in spite of weaknesses rather than self-rejection or self-doubt.

8. Vision for human kind as essentially good as opposed to seeing human kind as essentially evil.

9. Vision of opposites of life as meaningfully related as opposed to seeing   opposites of life as antagonistic.

10. Acceptance of feelings of anger or aggression rather than denial of feelings of   anger or aggression.

11. Capability for exhibiting warm interpersonal relationships as opposed to distancing oneself with difficulty expressing warm interpersonal relationships.

12. Acceptance of values of self-actualizing people with tolerance for ambiguity as opposed to rejecting the values expressed in each of the dimensions above.

Self-actualization is not readily achieved unless the prerequisite needs are essentially met. These needs begin with food and shelter, safety, love and belonging, and self-esteem. When these needs have been met, the individual is better prepared to utilize his or her full potential. When self-actualization is a dominate characteristic in the behavior of both teachers and students, the need to know and understand, and appreciation for the beauty and subtleties of the universe are greatly increased.

The work of teachers requires the full utilization of human potential, with heightened sensitivity to oneself and to the lives of those with whom they work. It requires a high degree of insight into the nature of human nature and how it can be effectively nurtured into a lifelong commitment to learning and change. Teachers must become careful observers of student behavior.

Teacher education programs must screen for desirable and undesirable personality characteristics exhibited by those who choose to become teachers and other education professionals. Clearly, there are characteristics if left unchanged that should preclude individuals from licensure in this helping profession.

Self-actualization can be achieved at any level of maturation, although it is somewhat different at each stage of development. A self-actualized person at the pre-operational level (absent logical capabilities) exhibits many creative and interesting expressions of meaning that result from experiences. These expressions and perceptions are pre-logical; therefore, they do not require empirically supportive, reality-based evidence or justification. The need to know and to understand is not limited by a reality test, but rather is wide-ranging and spontaneously creative. Fulfilling this need for creative, imaginative responses to life's experiences is an example of self-actualization for a youngster at this stage of development.

When concrete operational capabilities emerge, the individual can apply logical constructions to direct and purposeful experience. When these constructions lead to personally important discoveries, the motivation to know and understand increases, as does the level of appreciation for the value of knowing.

Once an individual reaches the most mature developmental level of formal operations, infinite possibilities can be entertained and modes of expression become paramount.

Appreciation for the beauty of knowledge and knowing increases with each act that leads to achievement of insight and sensitivity.

Erik Erikson constructed a view of the processes and products of experiences that result in the formation of personality characteristics (Erikson, Erik H., 1993). Erikson's model illustrates both the negative and positive dimensions of psycho-social development across the full spectrum of life. When more negative experience dominates one's life, unconscious response patterns will be developed that reflect more intellectually restrictive characteristics. For instance, a lack of trust in early childhood often results in a diminished feeling of autonomy, which can lead to a reluctance to take initiative or to achieve industriousness, and that can result in a confused sense of identity.

There are eight levels illustrated in Erikson's model which he viewed as an epigenetic chart. The chart features on the one side a cumulative listing of the following hierarchically arranged positive items: (1) trust, (2) autonomy, (3) initiative, (4) industry, (5) identity, (6) intimacy, (7) generativity, and (8) ego-integrity. On the opposite side is a listing that states the opposing negative features of the first list beginning with (1) mistrust, (2) self-doubt, (3) guilt, (4) inferiority, (5) role confusion, (6) isolation, (7) stagnation, and (8) despair.

All psychological realities emerge in a social context. Psycho-social experiences are seldom, if ever, all positive or all negative; they are somewhat in between. Negative experiences that are not resolved or re-constructed will likely result in negative response patterns and more restrictive behavior in everyday life.

A more healthy psycho-social development begins with the establishment of trust—trust in other human beings and in the conditions of the environment. A trusting psycho-social relationship is one that protects one from harm, yet it allows for the expression of autonomy, a positive factor, while a lack of trust results in mistrust, the beginning of restrictive response patterns.

The experiencing of autonomy leads to initiative that builds a broader repertoire of experiences to act upon and file for future reference. Unable to take initiative, out of fear or a lack of self-confidence, deprives the individual of valuable data for future development and learning. Having a broad spectrum of successful initiatives to draw upon, those individuals are in a position to self-select areas of interest that are perceived to warrant their concentrated attention or sustained industriousness in one's chosen field of expertise.

With limited initiative and restrictive orientations that prevent or limit the engagement of new experiences, the individual is deprived of possible opportunities for growth, and behaviorally exhibits insecurities that disrupt and narrow his or her perceptual field.

When one has an extended, in-depth experience with any subject, object, or event, the self-discovery of potential aptitudes and interests is a likely by-product. This discovery contributes to a sense of identity as a unique person.

One, whose experiences lack depth and analysis, is likely to have a weak sense of identity and is more easily influenced by perceived external social concerns than by any internal sense of direction or rationale. Role confusion is the result of not having a rich understanding of who one is or what one is capable of doing.

A clearer sense of who one is, as a unique person, allows one to relate more easily, empathically, intimately with others, giving other persons the space to be themselves. Support from others and social acceptance of one's self leads to more generative, self-actualizing experiences in life.

More generative experiences throughout the most productive years of life lead to a sense of accomplishment, and satisfaction with those accomplishments that result in a personal reconciliation with death.

Since professional educators are in charge of social settings that either contribute to or detract from full development of potential in individual human beings, understanding the possible consequences of interventions they might use with groups is mandatory. Interventions that result in a lack of trust and its evolving restrictions must be eliminated.

Lawrence Kubie, MD, a psychiatrist wrote extensively about the shortcomings of our educational systems. In his book, published in the early 1960's entitled, *Neurotic Distortions of the Creative Process*, he presents a model for understanding aspects of mentation that appears to be seldom understood by educators, and for that matter, by most of the lay population. Understanding the mind and the processes of mentation reveals an essential element in what is required of the professional educator, essential to any possibility for improving education.

The current preoccupation with the workings of the brain, its anatomy, and physiology is important, but it does not adequately reflect the full spectrum of its product, the creative mind. Recent research with the use of MRI scans focused on brain sectors that relate to certain thoughts may at some time locate the brain response patterns that govern mental processes. In the meantime, it is sufficient to assume their existence based on extensive clinical experience and study.

Kubie's model relates to adult mental processes, reflecting full capabilities for symbolic representation, logical memory, meta-cognition and deliberate action. Individuals at less mature levels have more limited sensory apparatus, limited experience from which patterns of response are learned and limited language to express the results of their experiences.

Pre-logical and early concretely logical capacities limit the mental processing of hypothetical propositions. Negative experiences engaged at these less mature levels cannot be as easily rationalized or sorted out as they can with more developed language, logic, and self understanding. Once this adult model of mental processes is understood, the limitations that relate to earlier levels of maturity can be more easily seen and understood.

There are three aspects of adult mental activities identified by Kubie and supported in the literature on concepts of mind and in clinical experience in dealing with distortions that become troublesome to the individual. These three interrelated dimensions are the unconscious, the pre-conscious and the conscious mind.

The pre-conscious, according to Kubie, is the central processing unit of the mind, using computer terminology. All experience is initially and automatically processed at this level. The pre-conscious has capabilities for creativity that are almost never fully experienced by individuals, and seldom if ever recognized by the school.

The pre-conscious is postulated by Kubie as the mental processor with extraordinary capabilities. It can receive input from multiple senses, simultaneously. It is inclusive of information. It can process information/data at lightning speeds and produce creative output that results from an automatic process of combining and re-combining the individual elements of one's experience. This processor is capable of phenomenal creative capacities when allowed to flourish.

What we experience in dreams is presumed to offer a glimpse into the nature of the pre-conscious processor in action. Dreams produce elaborate combinations of experience in symbolic form. These experiences are articulated during the dream in a split second. When this dream occurs in the process of awakening, it is understood, consciously.

The pre-conscious processor has capabilities to creatively integrate bits of experience, provided it is not interfered with by previously developed unconscious response patterns that severely limit or distort the input and shuts or slows down the processor.

Since we are never free of unconscious patterns of response acquired from past experience, the pre-conscious mind is never fully free to function at its peak of capabilities. It is always influenced by the residue of past experiences, both positive and negative—the attitudes, values, stereotypes, and personal orientations learned from the past. Fears that lead one to avoid experience, joys that lead one to seek more, are prevalent all the time. Those fears and joys are what is left of past experiences, the details of which have been easily and usually forgotten.

The unconscious response patterns (like the computer's operating programs) are characteristics reflected in our personalities that can either impede one's productive experience or enhance that experience. Experiences engaged at all levels of maturity have both positive and negative results.

When positive, the individual exhibits more personally generative response patterns, that is, response patterns that enhance the creative processing of day-to-day experiences at a pre-conscious level. When negative, the individual likely will exhibit restrictive response patterns that slow, distort, and occasionally shut down the pre-conscious creative processing of experience. Kubie described this as neurotic (or rigid) distortions of the creative process.

These restrictive patterns interfere with the full utilization of innately creative potentialities that every human being possesses. Children at a pre-logical level are naturally free to express their reactions to experience with relatively little interference, except by adults who attempt to extinguish their behavior or try to "teach" what would be obvious to older youngsters who have reached a more mature level. Unlike younger learners, adults with a full range of mental apparatus can confront the results of negative experience and modify somewhat their unconscious response patterns, if they choose to.

However, before the individual is mature enough to be

able to rationalize and reconcile or reason about the impact of negative experiences, basic values and beliefs are formed that often continue to reside at the unconscious level where they restrictively influence current behavior. Because they are part of an unconscious pattern they are difficult to reconstruct and change. Due to this situation, patterns of behavior continue to be predictable elements of one's personality, and are often viewed as being more or less permanently in place by the age of five or six. If this were true, however, therapy would have no effect in altering personality defects; clinical experience suggests otherwise.

Modifying the patterns once they are in place is not easy; an active role is required on the part of each individual in confronting and changing the pattern and its resultant behavior. This process sometimes requires therapeutic interventions that are designed to help reveal the origins and consequences of the patterns that prevent or limit one from becoming a more fully functioning person. One such intervention is hypnosis which limits conscious awareness and taps more directly into the freer pre-conscious stream, thus revealing presumably a more reliable estimate of what is happening at the unconscious level.

Over a fifty year span while working with pre-service teachers, I used a classic film entitled *Unconscious Motivation* to introduce the importance and functionality of the unconscious. This film was developed at Indiana University many years ago. The film was carefully choreographed to provide a reasonably concrete example of what the nature and influence of the unconscious mind is that the viewer would easily relate to, short of engaging in psycho-analysis. The subjects in the film were two young volunteer college students, a male and a female, and an interviewer whose only presence was his voice.

The film begins as the students are being hypnotized, and while in a pre-conscious state, were told a story about an event that happened during their childhood that would manifest itself in their adult lives. Since this story was relayed to the two subjects as events that happened in their lives, they were able to internalize the story as if it actually happened to them, presumably because they were freer to assimilate the message than they would otherwise have been during a fully conscious state of being.

The story told to the subjects was roughly the following: You were walking in the park and you came upon a small purse containing some coins that belonged to a friend. Instead of returning the purse to your friend you went to the store and bought some gum. You took the gum home and hid it. Your mother found the gum and asked you where it came from. You lied to your mother.

You were so worried that you had stolen money from your friend and lied to your mother about it. Your feelings of guilt about your actions will stay with you as an adult. The subjects then dreamed about the events and were subsequently returned to a state of full consciousness.

The interviewer asked the subjects how they felt and they first answered typically that they felt fine. Upon further inquiry they both admitted that they felt at "loose ends," that something didn't feel right. The dream lasted only seconds, but the subjects felt that it lasted a half hour. The male particularly, exhibited obvious distress; he was biting his nails and rubbing his hands. The female didn't seem to indicate the same level of distress, although she did indicate that she didn't feel right.

The interviewer then proceeded to help them reveal to themselves and to each other the basis for their anxiety. Word association and Rorschach tests were used to provide information that would help them re-construct what had happened that was related to their feelings.

Since the subjects had been told the same story, they were in a position to compare each other's perceptions and validate each other's conclusions. Of course, the interviewer knew the story they had been told, so his questioning was pre-determined. Unlike the same situation in real life, the interviewer would not have prior knowledge of the events and therefore would have a much more difficult time getting to the bottom of a problem that only the subject could know and probably would be reluctant to disclose this easily.

When the full story was reconstructed, the subjects expressed great relief. The male seemed to feel that the story had been something that actually happened to him, while the female felt the story had been told to her. In either case, they both had felt the effects as they were manifested in nervous responses and feelings of uneasiness. However, for the male the episode seemed more real and therefore more stressful than that experienced by the female. The differences in reaction raises the possibility that the male at that time was more open to experience and the female more guarded in her experience.

While my re-enactment of the message does not do complete justice to the real impact of this film, it is clear, I believe, that it illustrates that one can better understand the relationship of the unconscious in shaping current behavior by considering its message. In the absence of intensive psycho-analysis, one would have difficulty appreciating the role of unconscious motivation. This film is as close to the actual experience as can be staged that I have seen during my many years as a teacher of teachers.

During a forty year span of my work with pre-service teachers, other than me, no one on the faculty ever viewed this film. The records of the film library validated this assertion. This is a possible indication of the relative lack of interest in the subject of the unconscious other than a fleeting reference to the subject. This college, it must be noted, offers two psychology majors.

All types of sensory input, according to Kubie, derive from personal experience, whether enteroceptive, as from within the body's interior, proprioceptive, as from deeper layers of skin, muscles, tendons, or joints, or exteroceptive, as from distant receptors such as through the eyes and ears. Experience can be direct and purposeful, or it can be simulations of life, or it can be encountered as verbal language, either as signs or symbols. In any event, experience, to be most meaningful, must connect with prior experience that either integrates into previously developed structures or challenges those structures that can lead to change.

Sensory input is creatively processed at lightning speeds at a pre-conscious level, with more or less openness and spontaneity. The manner and extent of processing at the pre-conscious level is governed by the previously learned and/or biologically-programmed unconscious response patterns that contain uniquely organized long-term memory (ROHM), however available or unavailable that may be. The unconscious response patterns govern the perceptual filters that allow only certain information to be processed and that information which is processed, to be interpreted and massaged in an individual's biased way at the conscious level.

The pre-conscious processor, in conjunction with conscious verbal and non-verbal capacities, organizes communications utilizing short term memory (RAM) along with current sensory input and available long term memory (ROHM)—a process referred to as cognition and meta-cognition.

The conscious aspect of mentation occurs when we logically organize our recognized thoughts and ideas (concepts) and attach or encode our language forms that communicate the meanings to others and to oneself. Conscious manipulation of the products of the pre-conscious results in an integrated response to that which is generated at the pre-conscious level, conditioned by the response patterns that resulted from past experience.

I have come to realize that many specialists in the area of inquiry and practice in psychology and psychiatry have developed a mystique about what they know and do, and they have convinced most of the lay public and educators that much of this aspect of life is off limits. The common message has been that "messing" with the mind is a potentially dangerous enterprise and should only be handled by trained professionals. Ironically, teachers are "messing" with the minds of their students all the time; unfortunately, they do this by avoiding those deeper dimensions of one's inner workings and instead, focus selectively on what is presumed to be conscious activity. Superficially, I might add.

Kubie's message added a significant dimension to the development of a comprehensive proposal for change in education that I have been on a mission to accomplish. For me it identified what teachers and other educators needed to know about the mind when "messing" around in this "forbidden" field.

Kubie illustrated in his model what he viewed in the 1960's as the relationships of the three dimensions of mind—the conscious, pre-conscious and the unconscious. His model presented the three dimensions each positioned generally within one third of the area of a rectangle. The middle third or center of the rectangle depicted a predominance of pre-conscious activity. The unconscious dimension was extended from its assigned area of dominance on one side of the rectangle, shown under the pre-conscious dimension. The conscious area of the triangle was positioned in the remaining third portion, indicating a clear relationship between the unconscious and the conscious. Taken together the three dimensions were shown to be inter-connected, operating interactively.

Neurotic Distortion of the Creative Process

Conscious	Pre-conscious	Unconscious
CS dominance	PC dominance	USC dominance

Conscious Yearnings Needs Urges More Deeper Automatic   Symptomatic
purposes wishes   auto personal patterns   compulsions
                              impulses trends drives

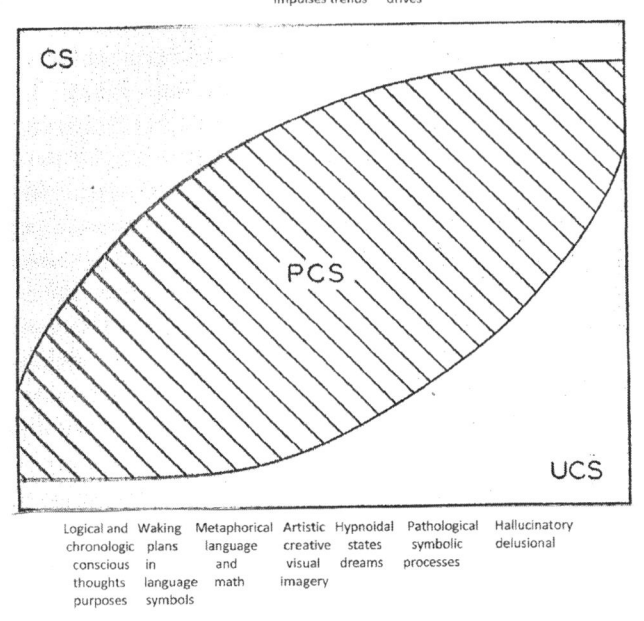

Logical and Waking   Metaphorical Artistic Hypnoidal Pathological Hallucinatory
chronologic plans   language   creative states   symbolic   delusional
conscious   in   and   visual   dreams   processes
thoughts   language math   imagery
purposes   symbols

"The figure above represents hypothetical relationships somewhat crudely but attempts to indicate something of their complexities. The shapes of the curves, their points of origin and insertion, the areas they subtend are all hypothetical. Even the implied assumption that their interrelationships can be expressed in quantitative terms is only a working hypothesis. Therefore the diagram is not to be taken literally. It is designed rather to illustrate complex interrelationships as they may be assumed to occur in nature (i.e. human nature), in which the concurrent action of preconscious processes frees our psychic apparatus, and more specifically our symbolic processes, from rigid anchorage. At the conscious end of the diagram, this anchorage is to fixed and literal relationships to external realities. At the unconscious end of the diagram, there is if anything an even more rigid anchorage to unreality, because the unconscious symbolic relationships which dominate at this end of the spectrum are unmodifiable by experience as long as they remain unconscious. The flexible and creative contribution made to our psychic processes by the concurrent play of unconscious process is illustrated in the middle band."

Over many years of study and thought about this model and how more recent information could be combined with it, the construction of a new model became necessary. This new model emerged from discussions with both graduate and undergraduate teacher education majors over many years and the model is still a work in progress since new scientific developments occur frequently. What follows is a description of a process that was developed with pre-service teachers, frequently used to stimulate thoughts and applications about heretofore ignored or superficially dealt with topics presented mainly in psychology classes.

Since computer terminology has become more commonplace in recent times, most people have heard terms like the central processing unit (the CPU), random access memory (RAM) and Read Only Memory (ROHM). They know about bits and mega-bytes, computer speeds, and computer programs. These concepts can be easily related to dimensions of mind, making a connection with familiar terms applied to more abstract and unseen phenomena.

This discussion begins with a circle with broken lines, located in the center of the illustration. The circle circumscribes the interrelated internal dimensions and the broken lines indicate that the system is not closed but is interacting dynamically with the other parts. This initial circle is labeled the central processing unit, the CPU, otherwise known as the pre-conscious processor.

The beginning illustration is shown below.

The conscious dimension of mind interconnects with the pre-conscious processor. Conscious awareness emerging from the pre-conscious is organized with pre-logical and logical capabilities and translated into language forms used for meta-cognition (inner language) and for communicating thoughts and concepts with others. These languages both verbal and non-verbal can include mathematics, native and foreign languages and computer languages.

Consciousness is a characteristic of cognition. Cognition starts with simple awareness derived from the pre-conscious, it then expands with experience to form associations, verbal and motor chains, multiple discriminations, concept formation, rules and laws and finally problem solving abilities with creative and critical evaluation skills (Robert Gagné). The interface between dimensions of consciousness and pre-conscious processes is illustrated below:

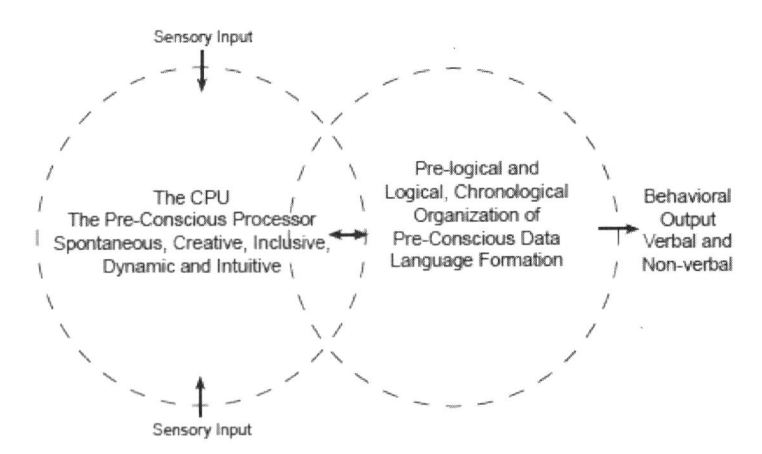

It is important to note that the CPU also receives input from the conscious patterns and particulars of our thoughts and actions as well as from other sensory mechanisms such as sight, sound, taste, touch, and smell; some add extra-sensory data as well. Conscious manipulation of data through language and organization, such as classifying, generalizing, and systemic modeling, occurs essentially during our waking hours and often "tweaked" during pre-conscious activity. Conscious output is manifested in both our verbal and non-verbal language and in other dimensions of our behavior. The pre-conscious manipulation of experiential data occurs during our sleep or during episodes of daydreaming, and in addition, during simultaneous and continuous experience leading to interactions between the conscious and pre-conscious dimensions of mind during our waking hours.

Cognitive processes are more limited in their scope and slower than pre-conscious processing. Cognition is more directed and less spontaneous; it is focused and variously organized. Cognitive capabilities, to be maximized, require active engagement with the constant output from the pre-conscious, during both waking hours and during sleep.

Organizing at the cognitive level can be enhanced through the employment of a full range of disciplines or organized ways of knowing and communicating. These disciplines are grouped within six realms of meaning, empirical, synoptic, esthetic, ethics, symbolic and synnoetics or self-knowledge (Phenix, Philip 1964).

Those who have employed these disciplines have produced a vast library of insights available to learners who are naturally in search of expanded meaning.

Conscious, cognitive processes employ random processing of current memories as well as long term memories that are stored from past experiences. Remote, long term memories are difficult to access due in part to their existence in the unconscious. In addition, long term recall suffers from significant memory losses. To enhance the accessing of long term memory the use of systematic recordkeeping is required. Such a system exists in The Constructive Assessment, Recordkeeping and Evaluation System (CARES).

The pre-conscious is never completely free to function fully. It is always influenced by the unconscious residue of past experiences that can slow down and even stop the processes altogether.

The role of the unconscious is pervasive and influences the functioning of the other two dimensions of mind. In the unconscious resides the residue of past experiences, what has been learned, valued, and believed including attitudes and orientations with life, mostly void of the details that once produced these products. The unconscious houses stereotypes and prejudices. It can also house an open orientation to accept new and different views of life's experiences. It can be rigid or flexible in its response patterns.

The unconscious is much less dynamic than the potentially creative pre-conscious. The unconscious dimensions reflect each of our personalities. Its orientations tend to be repetitive until they are changed by actions inner-directed by the individual. Because these orientations, for better or worse, reside in the unconscious, they are difficult to access and often require therapeutic interventions or shared disclosure to bring about a change.

All input from the outside world or from internal processes are conditioned by the pre-defined orientations or patterns of response that reside in the unconscious. The unconscious acts as a filter for that input. It shapes the pre-conscious processes. Response patterns residing in the unconscious reflect both positive and negative orientations that are selectively projected onto each and all experiences as they are happening. This distorts or modifies the processing to conform to the orientation of the imposed unconscious response patterns.

A negative response pattern will likely distort the perceptions of an object, event, or process to conform to the pre-defined negative orientations. A more positive response pattern derived from more positive experiences will modify the view of experiences as more open-ended opportunities for learning that will create greater acceptance of the ambiguities of life.

A more complete model is illustrated below. Keep in mind its components may be altered as new information is gleaned from research on the brain and other neurological realities.

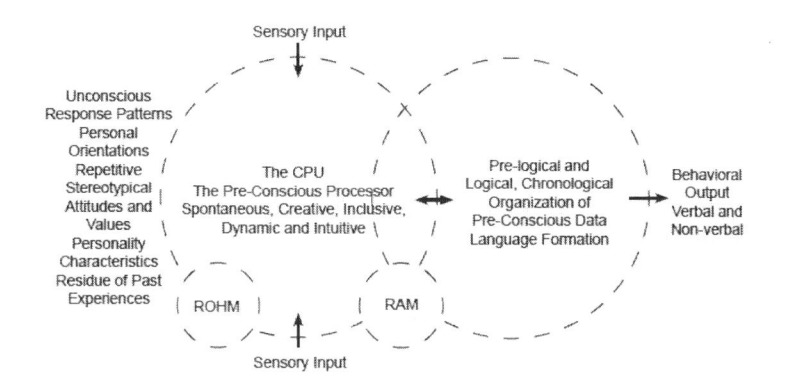

```
                          Sensory Input
                                ↓
      Unconscious
   Response Patterns
       Personal
     Orientations
      Repetitive          The CPU           Pre-logical and        Behavioral
     Stereotypical   The Pre-Conscious Processor  Logical, Chronological   Output
     Attitudes and   Spontaneous, Creative, Inclusive,  Organization of    Verbal and
        Values         Dynamic and Intuitive    Pre-Conscious Data    Non-verbal
     Personality                              Language Formation
    Characteristics
    Residue of Past
     Experiences      [ ROHM ]              [ RAM ]
                                ↑
                          Sensory Input
```

Change in the response patterns will occur as a result of reality-based experience, far more than from the manipulation of language forms and simulated experience. It requires changing and replacing the response patterns that reside at an unconscious level through self-reflection and actions taken to personally change the patterns. It requires first an awareness that a particular response pattern is getting in the way of living a more productive or enjoyable life and is in need of change, followed by a specific, focused effort to change the pattern of response.

Here is a simple example of changing a negative attitude toward a particular food. If there is an awareness that oysters may taste good and you want to develop a more positive attitude toward eating them, persistence will eventually change the pattern. Like other attitudes, the attitude toward oysters may have nothing to do with oysters themselves but perhaps due to other unrelated experiences such as early toilet training that implanted attitudes toward anything that is perceived as messy or slippery. The unconscious mind is full of patterns that remain long after the particular experiences that produced them occurred.

When the patterns of response are rigid/neurotic distortions of the creative process, they shape the language one uses to express those responses, they narrow the way one approaches problem solving, distorts and even eliminates important data that are the grist for the mill of a creative intellect.

The unconscious response patterns act like the computer's program. They tell the CPU what it will process and how it will process input; it shapes the output of the conscious processing unit and the ultimate manipulation of the products at a conscious level. Noteworthy is the fact that this process is unique to each person and must be worked out in a unique manner, most productively under the control of that person. When instruction is geared to forcing compliance with an imposed, rigid response that almost never reflects the internal processes of a unique person, this is a dominate source of destruction of the creative process, with pervasive negative consequences. Each individual, faced with this imposed process is continuously involved in compensating for the loss of individuality.

Particular response patterns that are composed of the reflections of an individual's unique experience will shape the activity of the central processing unit, the pre-conscious. Those orientations that are founded in fear will significantly modify the processing of experiential data or close it out altogether. Those that are open-ended will present a more open-minded orientation and a willingness to engage a wider world of experience with a minimum of distortion.

When distortions dominate the pursuit of meaning and become repetitive, they represent a state of mind described as being out of touch with reality. These distortions can become more than neurotic; they can become pathological, requiring intensive use of psychological interventions to help install more useful orientations that will free the creative capacities for constructing meaning based in reality.

Deprivation of positive experience and ineffective organizing strategies under the direction of educators often leads to the development of defense mechanisms and guilt feelings. These reside at the unconscious level, constantly shaping the day-to-day interactions as each new experience occurs. It shapes the language that is selected to communicate about those encounters.

Education must be focused upon removing the impediments that negatively influence the processing of experience at a pre-conscious level. A more open, less controlled pre-conscious will aid the development of effective cognition at the conscious level that will result in effective problem solving and personal satisfaction. To free this potential, neurotic, rigid, response patterns must be replaced with more open-ended response patterns that support a creative pre-conscious and a more dynamic and productive consciousness.

Learning is changing the unconscious response patterns and the conscious constructs and language forms that express them. Learning that lasts occurs when the preconscious processor generates a full complement of meanings arranged internally and expressed in language forms at a conscious level with a minimum of interference from negative elements of past patterns that reside in the unconscious. When these products of mentation challenge the current response patterns they will result in a change that reflects an updated version, thus learning has taken place.

Kubie's model illustrates the absolute uniqueness of every human being. It takes the mystery out of the processes of mentation so that educators can appreciate (a) the central role of our creative pre-conscious processes, (b) the critical role that past experiences play in any learning situation, (c) the need for active participation on the part of the learner in changing the learned response patterns that get in the way of openness to experience, and the reinforcing of those patterns that are constructive, and (d) the uses of language in the organization and communication of meanings processed from life's experiences.

Every individual has perceptual filters that are controlled by the nature of what has been learned from past experience, the details of which have long since been forgotten, but the results of which reside in attitudes and values that are projected onto each new experience. Changing these response patterns takes more than a substitution or acquisition of language; it requires active participation by the learner in re-processing the results of past experiences and ascribing new meanings to them.

Language forms, according to Susanne Langer, can be either signs or symbols. Signs are denotative, that is, they are limited to their specific meaning. Signs can be processed as a simple response to stimuli. Recognizing a stop sign, for instance, indicates that one must stop. This recognition requires little beyond the recognition itself.

Symbols, on the other hand, are vehicles for connotative meanings that reflect a wide range of reactions to pre-processed sensory data. Symbols, if generated out of one's pre-conscious processor, will reflect many variations of meaning, thus they are considered connotative—they are rich in meaning.

A most important object of schooling must be to eliminate the internal restrictions (both conscious and unconscious) that interfere with the full use of pre-conscious processing capabilities that every learner possesses. Creative processes must be encouraged making the arts as important as any other experience in the school's curriculum.

Professional educators, acting in a helping role, must grasp the full meaning and implications of this model to ensure against mismanagement of learning opportunities.

Today's schools focus primarily on the conscious cognitive mental processes as manifested in narrowly focused language composed mainly of limited signs. Students are subjected to endless repetition as an aid to recalling this language. What is presented may be a symbol to its author, but it acts as a sign to a learner who has not acquired the experiential background that would connect to those symbolic meanings. In the absence of experiences that provide a readiness for assimilating symbols as they are intended, learners are forced to memorize isolated, relatively meaningless information.

The schools ignore two aspects of mentation, the unconscious and pre-conscious, even though these two provide the foundation for any cognitive activity. This allows the school to accept as evidence of learning and mastery relatively superficial verbal language. Worse yet, the schools describe learning as being able to pass back to them the pre-determined forms of that language (signs) that they have arbitrarily declared to be important and essential.

The degree of accuracy in regurgitating the declared official language is viewed as evidence of learning. These degrees are stated as statistics that are published for purposes of communicating the extent of "learning" presumed to have occurred and the level of success of the school in which that "learning" occurred.

Lack of insight into the three forms of mentation and their interconnectedness, allows the school to place its highest priority on limited cognitive activity at the expense of the other two dimensions. The arts, as expressions of pre-conscious activity, are considered a frill to be cut first from the budget when finances are tight. (In truth, most of the so-called art classes for elementary students are not organized to produce graphic expressions of personal meanings; they are essentially crafts that are introduced in isolation from other school activities.) What is missing is the treatment of artistic expression of experience as a vital and accurate form of language that should be viewed just as essential as cognition, if not more so.

Evidence of the lack of connectedness between what is assumed to be art in the classroom and art as an expression of one's thoughts and feelings, is found in the results of "The Environmental Relationships Test" (discussed earlier). Most students cannot express three-dimensionality in their expressions of meaning in their lives, even though they developed that capability when they were seven, eight or ten years of age. Since the school has failed to recognize this, many students have been arrested at developmental levels of an earlier age.

When individual learners encounter the situation wherein the prescribed language required for passing the tests does not match his or her internal processes, they are left to deny their own ideas and replace them, however meaningful they may be, with the requirements of the school system. This process is destructive of mental health that leads to many human limitations and confusion in one's life.

The schools have institutionalized the near meaningless manipulation of shallow language as evidence of learning even though therapists have shown that the manipulation of language does not result in lasting changed behavior; it often compounds that behavior. The schools are guilty of planting the seeds for the many forms of aggression, depression, manipulation, greed, and human destructiveness that permeates our current society.

Fortunately, there are those who are motivated to seek personal meanings, to acquire compassionate orientations and to develop exceptional skills and insights. These motivations are often acquired in spite of what happens in schools and most are actualized outside of school.

Occasionally, learners encounter persons in school who serve as models or provide inspiration, but these examples amount to a small portion of the total population required to attend the typical educational programs. Erroneously, the uninformed often point to these limited examples of achievement as proof the school is doing its job. "Look at me, I didn't do that badly."

Robert Gagné, mentioned earlier, one of the foremost authorities on learning presented his version of learning in a book called *Conditions of Learning* that has been widely read and updated over the last fifty years. In place of the simple-minded versions of what constitutes learning as it is currently defined, Gagné's model is detailed and extensive. Eclectic in its viewpoint, his model accounts for dimensions that include behaviorist' beliefs of the important role of external stimuli and observable behavior, and the cognitive and humanist theories that account for internal mental processes that are generally referred to as higher thought processes.

Gagné's model begins with (1) the level of stimulus response that features automatic responses to experience. This is the initial and most elementary level of learning. Following the stimulus response level is a more elaborate level called (2) simple associations. Repetitions with certain stimuli (experience) create awareness of simple associations or connections, still at a very elementary level. These associations are combined into (3) motor-chains and later into (4) verbal-chains. This simply means that the individual first responds to the simple associations that have emerged by responding physically (motor) and later attaches language to those physical chains. Having achieved this level, (5) multiple discriminations can be made that begin to separate out variations in prior experience that lead to more elaborate recognitions of the more subtle elemental differences. This is pre-requisite to (6) concept formation. Concepts are mental images that contain the discriminations that have been developed at the prior level. Concepts are combined at a higher level called (7) rule formation. These more simple rules are then elaborated at a higher level called (8) principles and laws. The end result of this learning sequence is called (9) problem solving abilities.

Stimulus response, simple associations, motor and verbal chaining are progressively more complex automatic responses to experience. For young learners, verbal chaining marks the beginning of representational language. For older learners who are experiencing an event for the first time, these automatic responses are engaged in rapid succession and the potential for achieving higher levels of learning is more quickly within their grasp. For both young and adult learners, physical and psychological impairments can prevent the fulfillment of these cognitive potentialities. For example, a negative response pattern constructed out of past experiences, brain trauma or limited sensory apparatus can be impairments to learning.

Multiple discriminations mark the beginning of deliberate intellectual activity where concept formation, logical memory and the personally significant use of symbolic language is emerging.

The level of concept formation reflects qualitative differences regarding the number of discriminating dimensions that have been experienced. A limited concept contains fewer discriminating dimensions (fewer direct experiences) than a richer concept. Rich concepts emerge from direct experiences that add numerous dimensions or discriminations to what is known of an object, event, or process. The current practice of going on field trips to a museum only once and never returning is a perfect example of the violation of this important principle.

Concepts that form regular and predictable patterns emerge into statements of rules. These rules are shorthand for the many instances where regularities among concepts are readily perceived by the active learner. An active learner is one directly and creatively engaged in the subject matter, rather than one passively consuming the interpretations of others.

Seldom will passive consumption of the products of others reinforced with continuous repetitions result in the development of concepts that must be formed internally through direct engagement with the subject. A "correct" answer can be produced, but that does not guarantee that higher levels of learning have been achieved. For instance, correctly regurgitating a definition of Einstein's theory of relativity does not represent a rich concept of what constitutes this theory or what it pertains to in real life.

The rules developed from regularities among concepts are first limited in their usefulness. As they are tested-out in a wide range of situations, the rules become principles and laws that have a wider application, greater flexibility, and comprehensiveness in recognizing and solving problems.

Effective problem solving in a specific domain requires the completion of all levels in the learning sequence from stimulus response to the formulation of complex rules, principles, and laws. This activity presumes that appropriate language that facilitates the intra- and inter- communication requirements for learning have been acquired.

Learners at the earliest stages are limited biologically from achieving the higher levels of learning indicated by this model. When language emerges at the pre-logical levels, multiple discriminations begin to form, marked by imaginative and creative, representative expressions. When learners reach the logical stage of concrete operations, they are capable of concept formation (i.e. classification), rule formation (recognizing regularities among concepts), and the development of principles and laws based on and limited to concrete and direct experiences with life's objects and events.

Formal operational learners, (those capable of hypothetical deduction) can transcend the need for concrete or direct experiences in later stages of their development, although concrete and direct experience is necessary at the beginning of their learned responses to experience. At this stage, the learner is able to fully utilize his or her intellectual constructions that are necessary for problem solving.

Every new learning situation begins at the beginning. For those with formal operational capabilities, the time required to progress from stimulus response learning to principles and laws is relatively short, assuming appropriate, concrete experiences have been available at each succeeding level. For those below formal operational capabilities, the time required to fulfill the full range of possibilities is limited by the level of biological maturation achieved at the point of engagement in their experiences. No amount of contrived experience can significantly accelerate the maturational processes that are basically driven by the individual's genes. If you reject this notion, consider the absurdity of demanding puberty to emerge at the age of seven.

When this model of learning is contrasted with the current definition of learning, it is patently obvious that a concept of learning defined as passing back the conclusions of others is outrageous. This ignorance among educational personnel should be grounds for their dismissal, or at the very least, it demands exposure to a more effective educational process.

Periodically, I find reinforcement for the importance of the approach to learning geography and history that we developed in the late 1950s. About thirty years later, I was attending a conference and recognized a man who attended that class as a seventh grader. In conversation, he revealed that he had become a successful attorney. He asked if I was still working in the areas we had experienced years before. He stated that that experience was the most important experience he had in all of his education and he was using the principles he learned in his successful legal practice.

Developmental Theories

Unlike the absence of recognition of the dimensions of mental processes, educators claim to be familiar with developmental theories and their application. However, what they have extracted from developmental theory often represents a basic ignorance or perhaps a denial of the dynamics of development for each individual learner.

As a consequence, schools have adopted a distorted concept of development to justify organizing their lessons and texts to consistently match grade levels or ages of learners. In other words as an example, all fourth grade students are initially considered alike in their developmental capabilities, although age has no guarantee of developmental readiness for learning.

If fourth graders do not live up to this expectation, they are regarded as failing or at the very least they are behind and in need of remediation or further repetitions. If they excel in producing the evidence required of that grade, they are rewarded for "excellence."

Often, these rewards are for being unfaithful to one's internal formulations of meaning. In both cases, whether pegged as failure or excellence, this practice wreaks havoc on the creative capabilities of individuals searching for meaning in their lives in ways appropriate to their developmental capabilities. When inappropriate expectations have been internalized, that often requires a traumatic experience to shake loose those pre-defined, imposed orientations.

The work of Jean Piaget represents one of many constructs that can provide invaluable insights into human development and learning, giving direction to the teaching/learning transactions of the classroom. Piaget's model identified four major stages of development with sub-stages. The four stages, sensory-motor, pre-operations, concrete operations, and formal operations are viewed by some as arbitrary divisions. In Piaget's view, they represent levels (milestones) in an invariant continuum or sequence of biologically-based, maturational growth for each individual. Like with Erikson, this growth sequence is a matter of genetics. (Piaget, Jean and Inhelder, B. 1958)

Those stages represent consistent and distinguishable behaviors that can be observed. The sub-stages show the existence of the continuum or elaborations that occur as development proceeds. Each succeeding stage is dependent upon the full development of the prior stage.

Jean Piaget referred to his work as genetic epistemology. Epistemology is a branch of philosophy that investigates the origin, nature, methods, and limits of human knowledge. This definition generally refers to the most mature stages of human development.

Piaget's interest was in an expanded definition of epistemology, relating not just to the adult stage, but also to the multiple levels of intellectual capacities for knowing, programmed in the genes to develop from infancy to adulthood.

Since human growth and development are anchored in genetic codes, what can be known differs fundamentally at each developmental milestone in the life of the individual. What is known and what can be known is undeniably different for a person at a sensory motor stage for infants as compared to persons at each of the more mature, genetically-based stages–pre-operations, concrete operations and formal operations. Regardless of the level of development, learning and knowing are active processes that result in uniquely constructed orientations to life's experiences.

Experiences and learning can influence, both negatively and positively, the growth rate and the extent of elaboration of intellectual potential that emerges at each developmental level. The age at which a developed capacity is achieved varies with the biological program (the genes) and the experiential background of the individual—a combination of nature and nurture.

Age is not the determining factor of maturation. Increased capacities for processing one's personal experience emerge with achievement of each more mature developmental level; the amount and type of learning is shaped by the currently-developed and available capacities that exist at any point in time.

Individuals are presumed to strive for fulfillment of the potentialities available at each developmental milestone. Unfortunately, achievement of fulfilled potential is often stalled or driven off course by the use of developmentally inappropriate instruction and a preponderance of unfulfilling intellectual experiences.

To ensure that learners are engaged in developmentally appropriate experiences that foster success in learning, educators must have diagnostic skills for assessing and evaluating the varied dimensions of behavior exhibited by each learner. The developmental model of Piaget represents a core theory about the emerging intellectual capabilities for processing experience; its elements must be understood and utilized toward the end of maximizing learning and development.

Developmentally inappropriate instruction (instruction that does not match the capacities of the learner, or over-extends the challenges) can result in diminished capacity and motivation for learning currently and in the future. Examples of inappropriate experiences include out-of-context and direct instruction in phonics for pre-operational youngsters, as a pre-requisite to reading, and memorization of number facts for pre-operational youngsters, as a pre-requisite to mathematical literacy.

Further examples are the introduction of problems for concrete operational youngsters that require hypothetical deduction and presentation of problems for formal operational levels in the absence of sufficient, or quality experience needed to solve a required problem.

Mastery is defined by behaviors that are consistent with the biologically-based maturational capacities observable at each developmental level.

Pre-operational capacities are pre-logical and appropriate mastery behaviors are related to the creative and imaginative representations the learner attaches to life's experiences.

Concrete operational capacities allow logical constructions of experience, added to the prior creative and imaginative capacities developed at the earlier pre-operational level. If the pre-operational freedoms to creatively respond to experience are shortchanged, or formalized by instruction, the capacities of the concrete/logical phase will likely be diminished.

Formal operational capacities allow the learner to transcend the direct and concrete experiences required of the concrete operational level, and construct hypothetical propositions and abstract concepts. This level flourishes when the prior levels have flourished.

Piaget created what is called "conservation experiments" that reveal the essential and observable intellectual behaviors at each developmental level. These experiments address the capacity for logic and abstract reasoning.

A beginning, tactile exercise asks the learner to roll two balls of clay into round balls that are observed to be of equal size and amounts of clay. Once there is agreement that the balls are of the same size, having the same amount of clay in each, the learner is then asked to role one ball into a cigar shape. When this is completed, the learner is asked: "What about now, do the two lumps of clay contain the same amount of clay?"

The concrete operational youngster will answer, based on logic, that the two have the same amount of clay since no clay was lost. The pre-operational youngster will claim that the cigar shaped clay is bigger based on perception. Why, because it is longer. The difference between these answers illustrates the difference between logical and pre-logical capacities. In the presence of concrete experience, the concrete operational youngster applies logic while the pre-operational youngster operates with pre-logical perceptions without any logical test.

Consider the intellectual tasks expected of school children that require a capacity for logical reasoning, whether its arithmetic or baseball. In the above case, a logical task required an agreement of sameness that is retained (conserved) while the shape of the objects is altered, leading to the conclusion that the alterations did not change the original agreement. If this, then that, is a logical connection. The pre-operational youngster can appear to reach an agreement about an event or object but cannot retain or conserve that notion and apply it to the altered reality. Formal operational youngsters do not require the concrete objects to be present; they can complete the experiment in their heads, so to speak. They can retain and manipulate the hypothetical propositions without being distracted.

Other experiments are patterned after the one above. One such experiment uses two beakers of the same size with the same amount of water contained in each. The youngster is asked to agree that the beakers contain the same amount of water and if not make the necessary adjustments until there is an agreement. Then the water from one beaker is poured into a tall skinny beaker that shows the water at a higher level. The youngster is asked if there is the same amount of water in each beaker now or does one have more.

The concrete operational youngster will say there is the same amount since no water is lost. The pre-operational youngster will say the tall beaker has more water because it is taller.

The formal operational youngster can perform the experiment mentally and provide an answer reflecting logic and alternatively logical answers. For instance, this youngster will look into the beaker and see if it has a droplet of water left in it and claim then that there is a different amount of water since some was left behind.

The second experiment is more abstract than the first since the beaker has formed the shape rather than physical/tactile manipulation of the clay. A third experiment I have used many times features two green sheets of paper that are identical representing two hypothetical backyards, models of four identical imaginary dog houses, and four imaginary dogs of the same breed and size.

The youngster is said to have two dogs that play in the yards, each yard having two dog houses. The dog houses are placed side by side in the corner of one back yard, and the other two dog houses are placed in opposite corners of the other yard. The youngster being tested is asked if the two dogs in one backyard have more room in which to play than the dogs in the other backyard, or do they have the same amount of room.

Unless the concrete operational youngster is nearing the next level of intellectual capacity he or she will be unable to solve this problem even if he or she has developed beginning logic. This is due to the complexity of the exercise and the degree of hypothetical information that is presented. A formal operational youngster will be able to follow the hypothetical information, conserve that information and apply it in the solution to the problem and conclude that the dogs have the same amount of room since the areas are not altered by the different placement of the dog houses. A pre-operational youngster will fly away, if not physically, at least in terms of engagement with this problem.

Teachers can perform these conservation experiments with the individuals in their charge, if they see the importance of this information as it relates to appropriate developmental expectations. Without this kind of information, a teacher is apt to expect all students to perform at the same level; after all they are in the same grade. However, if this teacher were to perform these experiments with each of the learners in this grade, a revelation would be experienced. There would be a range of intellectual capacities discovered, even some in the same grade behaving at the pre-operational level, some at the concrete operational level and some perhaps even at the formal operational level. What then?

Can this teacher honestly teach this group as a class at the same grade level? And what happens if this information is ignored? What happens when the pre-operational youngsters cannot perform as expected of the grade level? How will these learners be treated, as failures in need of remediation? How about the rewards given to those who have reached a higher level of maturity, developmentally speaking? Are they being rewarded for the wrong reasons and are the failing learners left to nurse their inadequacies? The obvious pitfalls go on and on.

Viktor Lowenfeld contributed a very useful model for understanding the dimensions of development that extends the formulations of Piaget. (Lowenfeld, Viktor 1947) Lowenfeld's model deals with visual representation that correlates with each of the stages of intellectual maturation as defined by Piaget.

The first level of visual expression is called random scribbling. This occurs when the child is first able to grasp a marking instrument and applies it to a surface. Random scribbling is not considered to represent anything in particular, at least at a conscious level. They are just marks on a paper made by an individual at a sensory motor stage of development.

Random scribbles give way to more controlled scribbling as small muscle coordination develops and the neurological controls for those muscles matures. The markings are still not presumed to represent objects or experience—they are considered non-representational.

The next level of visual expression is pre-schematic drawing that does show the beginnings of representational forms that are somewhat recognizable by adults. This ability corresponds to other representational language that emerges at the pre-operational level. Although an adult would not readily recognize a shape appearing anywhere on the page as being a house, to the pre-schematic/pre-operational youngster, it is indeed a house.

Pre-schematic drawing gradually emerges into schematic representation which is distinguishable as a two dimensional view of objects anchored to the baseline or the bottom of the page. This drawing has limited detail; it lacks proportionality, and shows no depth.

Schematic drawings correspond to Piaget's early concrete operations where the youngster is neurologically unable to perceive hypothetical possibilities, that is, possibilities that have to be imagined. Learning is circumscribed by a need to relate concrete objects and events that are perceived in simple dimensions.

When the individual is able to perform more sophisticated meta-cognition, awareness of depth emerges even when direct or concrete evidence is unobservable. This marks the emerging level of realism, starting with dawning realism, moving to pseudo-realism and finally realism. Dawning realism is an in-between stage that shows in the same picture, both two-dimensionality and beginning three dimensionality.

At this level, a house may be represented in three dimensions in the near view and two dimensions in the more distant view. Look back at one of the drawings of a college student's response to the "Environmental Relationships Test" to see an example of this representation.

When full dimensionality, overlapping, proportionality, depth and detail are exhibited in the drawing, (realism) the individual is functioning at a level comparable to Piaget's level of formal operations. Abstract representation occurs when the individual is able to use skills of all prior levels with deliberate control for creating specific effects in a symbolic representation that may or may not resemble depicted objects or events.

Levels of maturation are points on a biological growth continuum that gradually emerge from one level to higher levels of sophistication and control, that is, if growth is not blocked or driven off course. Visual representations reflect this growth continuum. Pre-schematic drawing correlates with the emergence of representational language that is characterized by uniquely creative expressions of meaning.

These creative expressions are the grist for the mill inherent in concrete or logical operational capabilities when they emerge.

Rich pre-operational or pre-schematic expressions result in multiple variations of meaning, from which the individual will later abstract logical explanations and conceptual connections. Deprivation, with respect to experiences and creative expressions, leaves the individual learner with a limited repertoire to draw from when empirically-based conceptualization and logical connections are to be made at the next stage. Limited logic, exhibited at the schematic stage, limits each succeeding point on the continuum. When a complete three-dimensional image is represented, full capabilities for logical problem solving have developed.

The visual representations of familiar objects and events provide a snapshot of the current level of intellectual development achieved by an individual. These representations, when supported by additional data from testing and observation, can become a powerful diagnostic tool for use in the classroom.

The inability to represent a world view that matches an adult's is related to the individual's currently achieved developmental level. Once higher levels of maturation are reached, the inability to express realistic views (i.e. three-dimensionality) is not likely due to biology, but rather to a lack of appropriate experience. Instruction in how to draw is an appropriate strategy when performance does not match the more sophisticated maturational levels indicated by diagnostic data. But, instruction before the more sophisticated levels are reached will likely yield very limited skill development.

Any teacher can quickly determine a beginning notion of where an individual learner is functioning on these levels of visual expression by asking that a picture be drawn of the learner's own home and surroundings. Since this is a place concretely experienced on a day to day basis, it is concretely familiar to each person. The picture that is drawn will reflect the developmental stages described above.

The youngster who can hold a marking instrument will most likely draw random scribbles that have nothing to do with showing how his house looks. Those at a prior stage will just go back to sleep. Controlled scribbles, although more developed, will not be representational. When the pre-schematic stage is reached, the drawing is representational, that is, it is claimed by the artist to be a house even though an adult can only see curved lines located anywhere in the picture.

When schematic drawing emerges, the two dimensional house is placed at the bottom of the page (on a baseline) and if mother is in the picture, she might be taller than the house. If the youngster places a smiling sun in the upper corner of the picture, this undoubtedly results from some prior teaching about where to place the sun on the page. Discount these stereotypes that have been implanted by some well-meaning, but ignorant adults.

When dawning realism emerges, the house will be placed

back away from the baseline, on a base plain, but the house itself will have the front view appearing in three dimensions and the rear part of the house in two dimensions. For example, instead of the roof reflecting vanishing points of three-dimensionality, a straight line is drawn from the roof to the ground, a view that is not three-dimensional.

As the house becomes fully three-dimensional, all aspects of the house (or apartment building) are shown as they would appear to an adult who has seen a house and thought about its appearance. Trees will be in a correct proportion as will any people shown in the picture and the house will be shown on a base plain that features the lawn and shrubbery or sidewalk in the near view. Objects in the drawing will show overlapping where the legs of an animal block out the view of the picket fence that is behind the animal. When the individual is capable of deliberately representing aspects of any of the previous characteristics in a picture that is designed to convey a particular impression, then the level of abstract drawing has been reached.

This exercise, if repeated periodically, will reveal the current level of functioning and the changes that have occurred since the last picture was drawn. With this information, backed by other forms of analysis, the teacher will be able to intelligently respond to the developmental needs of each learner.

Lev Vygotsky developed a model to show how verbal language is developed and employed in the conscious transactions with life's experiences. Humans, programmed as we are to achieve a level of meta-cognition, or inner language, live in a social environment that fosters a need for communicating, and for developing the mechanisms of language that facilitate mental processes for organizing and communicating meanings with others.

There are five levels of language acquisition beginning with a pre-intellectual stage. Children at this stage of language development cannot consciously organize their own behavior through the use of signs or symbols. Their speech is essentially a form of contact with significant adults in a social setting. Pre-intellectual language consists mainly of mimicry.

The next stage is "intellectual: naively psychological." This stage involves essentially labeling of objects and events. The child at this level uses pictures in the form of direct representation, but the associations are not strong enough to guarantee recall at a later time.

The third stage is characterized as dominance of external signs. Youngsters at this level are first stimulated from the outside by language usage within the immediate environment. Speech simply accompanies the child's actions. Later, speech enables the child to direct his or her attention, to discriminate objects and events, and to organize and conceptualize the visual field. This is the beginning of problem solving activity where inner speech precedes an action.

The next level is called the in-growth or internalization stage. Here the individual begins to intellectually manipulate ideas using logic and logical memory. Limited egocentric speech now becomes inner speech which enables meta-cognition, logical analysis, and hypothetical deduction. In the previous stages, speech was limited to the use of signs.

Having reached the level of internal speech, it is then possible for an individual to readily assimilate and process another's language, provided there are no psychological, physical or personality barriers that seriously narrow his or her perceptual field. This is the stage when one can make maximum use of constructive social situations where language usage by others offers intellectual challenges to one's existing repertoire. Vygotsky called this the zone of proximal development; this zone exists at all levels of speech development, it is however, particularly potent to a learner at the stage of internal speech.

It is important to note that words (verbal language) can sound and look the same and yet be representative of significantly different meanings and uses. To the pre-intellectual youngster, babbling may sound like the language used in the environment, but it is assumed to be only mimicry, nevertheless important to the developmental maturational processes.

When the naively psychological stage is reached, words become more easily distinguished, and they serve a labeling function. Many words are used at this stage without the individual grasping the meaning, and through trial and error in a social setting, the individual gradually assigns the word to an accepted relationship with practical intelligence.

External speech is first used to accompany a child's actions; it is later used to synthesize events and plan problem-solving activities. External speech is first considered relatively meaningless utterances and later becomes focused signs. When narrowly focused signs are internalized, that is, synthesized as a vehicle for personal meanings, words then function as symbols.

Although the words sound or appear the same in usage, words used as signs denote something, while words used as symbols are connotative. This distinction is made by Vygotsky through his descriptions of external sign use and the internalization of meanings for which language becomes a vehicle for both intra and inter-communication.

Achieving an in-growth stage in language development is a desired goal for every learner; it opens up a wide variety of stimulating intellectual opportunities. If learners are simply introduced through instruction to external signs and required to duplicate their assigned definitions, that language will have very limited value, in fact, it may be harmful. This is what A.N. Whitehead described as "inert ideas" or words simply taken into the mind without having acted upon them or placed in fresh combinations. In contrast, internalized language emerges from experiences that have been symbolically and personally transformed into meaningful relationships. This is language that generates the creative manipulation of ideas and motivates sharing or communicating with others.

To make more concrete the relationship of these three models of individual development and possible consequences for disregarding the significance, consider the following example:

What's in a Picture?

Six year old Kathy, while sitting around the dining room table after supper, began to recite counting by twos. Her struggles to remember were greeted by encouragement from the adults who pounced on the opportunity to give positive feedback to this exercise. After all, having a first grader display her growth in mastering mathematics was an occasion worth crowing about. Right?

Even though I was churning inside about this accomplishment, I didn't say a word and hoped Kathy did not sense my disapproval. I would never discourage her from trying, but it was her teachers and her school that bore the brunt of my concern. What, you ask, could possibly be wrong with this display of presumed growth toward the mastery of mathematics and the ultimate capture of her share of the American Dream?

As an educational reformer, I have tried to encourage others to question the validity of many of the assumptions and beliefs held about the processes of education and their results. Unfortunately, not many, including teachers, seem to have a complete grasp of what was going on with Kathy's recital of counting by twos and how that can evolve into major problems in her adult mathematical life. Here are the sources of my assumptions and beliefs that underlie my concerns.

There are many related developmental models that resulted from extensive study of young children; models that can be validated in the lives of teachers, models I have found to be valid in my experience. I have studied the behavior of hundreds of first graders, 6 year olds, as well as others younger and older. Their behavior fits the descriptions provided by three prominent scholars, Jean Piaget, Lev Vygotsky, and Viktor Lowenfeld (as well as many others). As much as I can remember of my early developing years, their formulations seem to provide a valid description of my pattern of growth, as well. I have found as they did that age is not a determining factor as to when developmental capabilities emerge in each person's life.

These models are built on the assumption that a unique development for each individual proceeds along an invariant sequence, unless driven off course by well-meaning but ignorant educators and parents or by some physical or psychological malady. This sequence is biologically driven, being influenced for better or worse by experience.

Piaget's, Vygotsky's, and Lowenfeld's models rely on findings from observable behavior that can be described in general terms called levels or stages. Surely they knew that an attempt to describe a complex array of behavior in general terms would encourage the nitpickers to seize the opportunity for criticism. In many cases, these critics have questioned the validity of the findings of these two scholars, leading to a discounted opinion found today in the educational community. However, if educators and parents would deliberately test out the validity of these models, as I have done while participating directly in schools and colleges in the course of over five decades, I am sure they would find that the insights of these two scholars should take center stage in the understanding of young children's intellectual behavior—an understanding that will provide sound direction for creating productive learning situations not only in mathematics, but in all other areas of study as well.

To reiterate, Piaget's model identifies four levels in the development of logical thinking: sensory motor, pre-operations, concrete operations, and formal operations. Lowenfeld's model describes levels of children's drawings that correlate with those levels described by Piaget. His descriptions of children's drawings start with random scribbles then controlled scribbles, schematic drawing, dawning realism, and an eventual three dimensional realism. Abstract representations will emerge later. These two models correlate with Vygotsky's model of language development and Gagné's model of learning. Here is Kathy's schematic drawing.

Kathy's picture is a classic example of schematic drawing. As compared with other six year olds, her drawing is representative of the few who have matured to this level. Most of her peers, age wise, have not reached this level. Her recognizable house is two dimensional and is anchored to the bottom of the page, on a baseline. (Ignore the other doodles on the periphery for the moment; they are likely stereotypes copied from some source other than the child's authentic perceptions of reality.)

Kathy's previous drawings of a house would have been floating in the air, bearing little resemblance to an adult version of a house. Nevertheless, her picture would indeed have been a representation of a house in her mind. She would have insisted upon it. Prior to this current schematic representation of a house, Kathy would have been free to draw without any presumed reality check; making marks at random across the page and claiming them to be most anything she desired.

The picture of a house next to come after the schematic level will be called dawning realism. Kathy will then begin to see that a house is not just two dimensional. However, a fully three dimensional house is still beyond her developmental level. She will place the house back away from the baseline showing some awareness of depth in her picture but her house will be only three dimensional in the near view and still two dimensional farther into the picture. It is just beginning to dawn on Kathy that houses in their settings are fully three dimensional.

Notice the changes in Kathy's picture drawn ten months after her first drawing. Her house is still two dimensional. However, it is no longer placed on the baseline, it has been moved back in the picture behind a knoll that is covered with grass. She may be expressing overlapping where at the bottom of the right hand corner of the house is covered by the knoll. If this was intentional, she would have understood that the knoll blocks the view of the corner of the house. This requires an ability for logical reasoning. In Piaget's terminology she would have conserved in her mind a complete concept of the house and know that the knoll is covering that part of the house. This may have been a slip of the marker and not true overlapping which is what Lowenfeld would have described it. It bears further observation.

Look at the walkway entering the house. The walkway would clearly have blocked out that area from any view of grass. Likewise her father's lawn mower did not block out the grass. Since Kathy did not show it blocking out the grass she was not practicing logic. She was pre-logical. The house being set back away from the baseline shows the beginning of the ability to see and represent three dimensionality but she uses beginning logic only in her representation of the two dimensional house, viewed with some depth. Her house is still two dimensional, however. Kathy's mother is standing on the knoll where her feet are at the level of the first floor window and her head is above the second story window. Kathy is in the transition stage between pre-logic and logic or pre-operational and concrete operational intellect. She is not mature enough to logically deal with the realities of counting by twos.

It is interesting to note that Kathy appears to read with the fluidity of an adult and has read many children's books. Most parents and teachers, not being familiar with Piaget's or Lowenfeld's models, would typically view and interpret her reading from an adult perspective, rather than from the perspective of a pre-operational/concrete operational youngster. They would likely read into her behavior adult dimensions that do not exist.

How does it happen then that she appears to read so well when she doesn't think consistently at a logical level? This is where the work of Lev Vygotsky has relevance. Kathy would be described by Vygotsky as exhibiting mostly naively psychological language that is emerging to a level showing dominance of sign usage. She has developed what Gagné would describe as verbal chaining, just prior to multiple discrimination. She would not be able to describe the possible multiple meanings of events described in her books. Yet, she reads very well.

Words generally precede the full meaning of language at any level of development. Even adults will speak complete sentences that sound like they know what is being said, when in fact they are just voicing words. "Talk is cheap." Language that is used symbolically is internalized language that is full of connotative meanings, not a dominance of signs, or naively psychological patterns of thought. For Kathy, operating at a pre-logical level, she does not read at the connotative level, even if the adults around her assume that she does. This is a common error among adults and it leads them to mistakenly interpret children's intellectual behavior. Real meaning for the child would be revealed if a few questions are asked about what the child is thinking. This would surprise most adults.

Kathy's nine year old brother is also an avid reader, brought up in the same verbally oriented family. His teachers marvel at his presumed abilities. He drew a picture at the same time that Kathy drew hers. His picture showed a barn in two dimensions but there was a fence surrounding the barn and a horse was standing in front of the fence. The fence posts were not visible where the legs of the horse blocked the view. This is clearly deliberate overlapping. His drawing shows a transitional level between early concrete operations where the barn is two-dimensional and more fully developed concrete operations where the positioning of the horse is overlapping the fence posts. He is farther along in his intellectual development than his sister, given the logic of overlapping, even though he is still representing the barn in two dimensions.

How does this Happen and So What?

When I observed him practicing baseball with his peers, he would execute plays correctly on some occasions and in other situations when one would expect him to act on his logical reasoning, he would behave in less mature ways. His applications of logic in the game were inconsistent. He was partly in one phase and part in another. This normal behavior can be observed in other situations, especially in his schoolwork. This makes me wonder what his teachers interpret his behavior to mean.

Both Kathy's and her brother's language skills were acquired in a home atmosphere of verbal experiences. Growing up in a verbal atmosphere, where parents and grandparents or other significant adults frequently speak and read to these youngsters. This accounts for their language development. Gradually words become associated with objects and events. Words are first expressed as parts of sentences, then as phrases and later as complete sentences. These verbal sentences are associated with the printed word by being heard and later by being seen. This process evolves into every child's ability for recognizing the verbal chains that appear in the books, and reading back the language can occur at that point. Through trial and error, the reading becomes fluid, but the meanings derived from the printed words are tied to the developmental level of the learner. In the absence of logic, the ability to engage multiple discriminations is minimal, if it happens at all. If the adults are not familiar with the developmental levels, their interpretations are likely to be in error, at the very least, incomplete.

Eventually, Kathy and her brother will realize that the house has three dimensional qualities that show depth, proportionality, overlapping and detail so that any adult will recognize a three dimensional view with its surroundings as a "realistic" drawing. They will then be operating with logical and hypothetical thoughts that would not be available at Kathy's current age and level of maturity.

One needs to understand Piaget's model to see the correlations with Lowenfeld's and Vygotsky's models that lead to greater appreciation for the importance of children's drawings and what they might mean. Kathy is beginning to function at a level of early concrete operations with beginning logic. She is now able to represent in her drawings what she has experienced with houses and how she perceives of them.

She is only beginning to conceptualize that a house she has witnessed many times in her experience is more than two dimensional; she will gradually recognize that it has depth, overlapping, and proportionality. When she reaches the level of concrete operations, logical capabilities will be applied to the whole drawing, not just to the near view as depicted in the drawing when this ability was just "dawning" on her.

Before any logical, concrete operational abilities were available to Kathy, she was functioning mostly at a level of pre-operations, (pre-logical) free to act on whatever occurred to her at the time, whether or not it resembled reality as adults perceive it. Her creativity was relatively unencumbered. Left to explore with a minimum of external influence, she eventually would expand on each simple awareness with an additional ability, that of logical connections. This evolutionary process is natural and predictable if left to develop with a minimum of interference. Of course it can be facilitated, that is, if provided with constructive support.

Now, here she is, barely beginning to be capable of logic, being "taught" a process of counting by twos. Her verbal and non-verbal behavior indicated a struggle in this recital of information she had memorized, this nearly useless information probably attempted at the request of an uninformed teacher, consistent with the school curriculum, with applause from parents and other adults. The reward for reciting this exercise "correctly," even though Kathy has no use for this skill at this time and no comprehension of what it means in mathematical terms, she will dutifully try to perform just to get approval.

She will not only continue to practice counting by twos by rote until she can recite the counting correctly and efficiently, but she will expand her repertoire of what many adults think are the basics of mathematics; she will be willing to endure repetitions of other so-called skills just to receive the approval of adults. Adults will rationalize that memorizing this exercise will someday prove to be useful and therefore justified even though it is developmentally inappropriate and carries with it negative connotations/consequences.

One can more fully observe what Kathy can actually do with counting by twos by presenting her with a collection of blocks and asking her to count out loud by twos. Most likely she will be able to set out groups of two, but will fail to combine two groups of two to represent four, and three groups to represent six, etc. In short, she will fall far short of fully conceptualizing what it means to count by twos.

Had her teachers and her school understood the implications of the developmental level when logical capabilities become fully available, perhaps when she is eight, nine or ten, they would have deferred the assignment of counting by twos to avoid the possibility of damage regarding the mastery of mathematics. Had they waited, the exercise of counting with a personal reason for doing so would naturally have emerged when an appropriate level of development had been achieved. Instead, the cumulative consequence of this and continued exercises in memorization will most likely be devastating when she is enrolled in a course called calculus.

You see calculus requires a maximized creative mind, free to manipulate concepts of quantity and spatial relationships. Success with calculus requires a developmental level of formal operations, with a capability for relatively unencumbered hypothetical deduction and abstract thought. It features mathematics as a metaphorical manipulation of these aspects of reality. A learner who has been "trained" in repeating useless exercises during the most creative levels of functioning, (that is, at the pre-operations and early concrete operations levels, and when this exercise is compounded over the years by continuing repetitions of memorized information) will fail to grasp the intent of calculus. Without experiencing an intervention that will partially restore some, even if not all creative mathematical abilities, this learner will likely flunk out of engineering school.

I had the fortunate opportunity to discuss this in some depth with Dr. Robert Davis when he was at Rutgers University during his declining years. Coming from a scholar of his stature, it lends considerable credibility to my concerns about the likely results from pre-mature, developmentally inappropriate memorizations in arithmetic and their unfortunate effects on innocent children like Kathy. The same holds true unfortunately for many other areas of the conventional school curriculum as well (Davis, Robert, 1984).

My speculation was corroborated by Robert Davis, researcher and Director of the Madison Project in Mathematics of the 1950s that was conducted at Syracuse University. He stated that he and his colleagues from the University of Illinois found that engineering students, whose educational experience had resulted in the development of rigidly held algorithms that result from a practice of memorization and repetitions, will fail to function creatively at this more advanced level of mathematics; as many as 70% of otherwise capable students enrolled in calculus will likely flunk out of that course (Ranzan, David, 2006).

There are many today who believe that raising the standards for pre-kindergarten students will guarantee that more sophisticated mathematical principles can be embedded in the minds of learners.

What do parents and teachers know about the 2012 New York State Learning Standards for pre-kindergartners in mathematics and other core-curricular areas? Here are the academic performance guidelines for four year olds suggested to result from pre-kindergarten instruction in mathematics. "(1) Reason abstractly and quantitatively, (2) Construct viable arguments and critique the reasoning of others, (3) Model with mathematics, (4) Look for and express regularity in repeated reasoning, (5) Analyze, compare, and sort two-and three-dimensional shapes and objects, in different sizes, using informal language to describe their similarities, differences, and other attributes." There are thirty more just in math and more in the other so-called core subjects. It is expected that four year old pre-k students would sit, listen, and respond in a group.

How many four year olds do we know would grasp the meaning of these perfectly legitimate mathematical requirements? Nearly all four year olds are pre-operational/pre-logical due to their biological development. No amount of exposure to these suggested skills will produce anything other than damaged goods. Students will commit to memory adult versions of these dimensions of mathematics, with almost no comprehension of what they mean. When reading these suggested standards approved through official channels it is difficult to not be enraged. Are these people this ignorant about child development or do they have another agenda?

Correcting this situation will require a major overhaul of the conventional school which is overly satisfied with its current capabilities for enhancing the growth and development of its students. Systemic change is needed with dramatic changes especially in the way teachers are prepared to conduct constructive facilitation of the development of mature and functionally competent learners. Since there has been a plethora of criticism, much of it unfounded, about developmental models and their implications, a brief restated summary may be of value.

The nature of and the interrelationships between developmental models, drawn from the writings of Jean Piaget, Viktor Lowenfeld, Lev Vygotsky, Jerome Bruner, Lawrence Kohlberg, Albert Bandura, William Glasser, Howard Gardner and Eric Erikson, correlated with Robert Gagné's cumulative learning model are essential elements in an understanding of human development and learning that are missing from the dialogue about school reform.

As explained earlier, Lev Vygotsky developed a model to show how verbal language is developed and employed in the conscious transactions with life's experiences. Humans, programmed as we are to achieve a level of meta-cognition, or inner language, live in a social environment that fosters a need for communicating, and for developing the mechanisms of language that facilitate mental processes for organizing and communicating meanings with others.

The model includes a "zone of proximal development" and higher mental functions, including perception, logical memory, abstract thought, and voluntary self-regulated attention.

While Vygotsky's model was introduced earlier, since there is so much emphasis on language development in primary grades, it is important to restate this model in its entirety. Perhaps it will get the attention it deserves by repeating his message. Once this model is internalized, the process of learning to decode the written versions of spoken language (reading) becomes apparent.

There are five levels of language acquisition beginning with a pre-intellectual stage. Children at this stage of language development cannot consciously organize their own behavior through the use of signs or symbols. Their speech is essentially a form of contact with significant adults in a social setting. Pre-intellectual language consists mainly of mimicry.

The next stage is "intellectual: naively psychological." This stage involves essentially labeling of objects and events. The child at this level uses pictures in the form of direct representation, but the associations are not strong enough to guarantee recall at a later time.

The third stage is characterized as dominance of external signs. Youngsters at this level are first stimulated from the outside by language usage within the immediate environment. Speech simply accompanies the child's actions. Later, speech enables the child to direct his or her attention, to discriminate objects and events, and to organize and conceptualize the visual field. This is the beginning of problem solving activity where inner speech precedes an action.

The next level is called the in-growth or internalization stage. Here the individual begins to intellectually manipulate ideas using logic and logical memory. Limited egocentric speech now becomes inner speech which enables meta-cognition, logical analysis, and hypothetical deduction. In the previous stage, speech was limited to the use of signs.

Having reached the level of internal speech, it is then possible for an individual to readily assimilate and process another's language, provided there are no psychological, physical or personality barriers that seriously narrow his or her perceptual field. This is the stage when one can make maximum use of constructive social situations where language usage by others offers intellectual challenges to one's existing repertoire. Vygotsky called this the zone of proximal development; this zone exists at all levels of speech development, it is however, particularly potent to a learner at the stage of internal speech.

It is important to note that words (verbal language) can sound and look the same and yet be representative of significantly different meanings and uses. To the pre-intellectual youngster, babbling may sound like the language used in the environment, but it is assumed to be only mimicry, nevertheless important to the developmental maturational processes.

When the naively psychological stage is reached, words become more easily distinguished, and they serve a labeling function. Many words are used at this stage without the individual grasping the meaning, and through trial and error in a social setting, the individual gradually assigns the word to an accepted relationship with practical intelligence.

External speech is first used to accompany a child's actions; it is later used to synthesize events and plan problem-solving activities. External speech is first considered relatively meaningless utterances and later becomes focused signs. When narrowly focused signs are internalized, that is, synthesized as a vehicle for personal meanings, words then function as symbols.

Although the words sound or appear the same in usage, words used as signs denote something, while words used as symbols are connotative. This distinction is made by Vygotsky through his descriptions of external sign use and the internalization of meanings for which language becomes a vehicle for both intra and inter-communication.

Achieving an in-growth stage in language development is a desired goal for every learner; it opens up a wide variety of stimulating intellectual opportunities. If learners are simply introduced through instruction to external signs and required to duplicate their assigned definitions, that language will have very limited value, in fact, it may be harmful. This is what A.N. Whitehead described as "inert ideas" or words simply taken into the mind without having acted upon them or placed them in fresh combinations. In contrast, internalized language emerges from experiences that have been symbolically and personally transformed into meaningful relationships. This is language that generates the creative manipulation of ideas and motivates sharing or communicating with others.

When the roles of the teacher and the use of teaching materials challenge the students, it is often believed that the higher the standard, the better the challenge. This is the position accepted in the assessment programs of state and national programs. But, students exposed only to external use of signs will have great difficulty responding to assessments that require symbolic uses of language. A learner who is developmentally at a sign use level will fail, and a learner who is at the in-growth level will try to memorize the right answers for the test and acquire a strategy for succeeding without having internalized the language. The strategies for remembering the assigned meanings include cheating, cramming, and the use of rote learning techniques. This is a formula for disaster.

If the challenge is not too great, and the necessary time and experience is available for the external signs to become internal symbols, growth in the learner will be significantly enhanced.

If neither the time nor the opportunity to make the transfer from external sign use to internalization is available to the learner, the zone of proximal development will remain a chasm to be bridged; often with a span too great to be developed and therefore too challenging to be engaged. Overzealous educators who are bent on improving education are satisfied with the mere appearance of sign-based language as products of the school.

Albert Bandura proposed a social cognitive theory that

includes three interlocking components originally defined by Kurt Lewin. These components are behavior, environment, and internal events that influence perceptions and actions. These three factors account for the cognitive elaborations that result from the conscious, unconscious, and pre-conscious mental transactions with life's experiences. Bandura emphasized the significant socially encountered models that stimulate learning and language acquisition.

Bandura explains that behavior, cognitive, and other personal factors, and environmental influences all operate interactively in a system that shapes learning and development. A change in one component brings about changes in the pattern of the whole and in the effectiveness of the system in facilitating personal fulfillment. The personal factors in his model include unconscious response patterns learned from past experiences that screen the input from the environment, that shape the pre-conscious processing of sensory input, that result in the production of conscious constructs that are mediated through verbal and non-verbal language.

The behavior component relates to the results of personal processing of sensory data from the environment that activates other environmental contingencies that can be evaluated both independent of environmental feedback and in relation to that feedback.

The feedback from the environment, in conjunction with behavior, activates different environmental reactions including adjustments in an individual's self-perception. Since many of the environmental influences occur in a social context, other people provide models which stimulate the construction of meanings and internalized language, useful in intra and inter-communication.

Another way of stating the major concepts of Bandura's model is that learning is a function of the characteristics of the learner, the context in which learning takes place and the behavior that mediates the processes and expresses the personal meanings or output. The inter-connections of these factors are expressed through the individuality that each person possesses; a reality that educators should not fail to recognize. In addition, the actual dynamics of these interactions vary with each developmental milestone achieved by the individual.

Like Vygotsky, Bandura recognizes the importance of the challenges within the social environment that take the form of verbal and non-verbal models. A professional educator needs to evaluate the impact of these models on the learner and avoid situations that overly challenge the learner, resulting in disengagement and possible deterioration of one's self-concept. Since this engagement is enhanced through effective group dynamics that lead to consensual validation with respect to communication, the professional educator can best take advantage of Bandura's schematic when a mature group process is achieved and maintained.

William Glasser, MD has written about the realities of taking responsibility for personal choices that lead to both positive and negative consequences in our lives.(Glasser, William, 1998). Developed in the therapeutic arena, Glasser has applied his ideas extensively to an understanding of deficient processes of education. In his book, *Choice Theory: A New Psychology of Personal Freedom*, he illustrates the chasm between our technical progress and progress in improving matters of human concern. The choices that have been made resulted in a far higher priority for technical invention than for individual and community health, yet these need not be mutually exclusive conditions. Technical invention is financially more rewarding than many human relationships, however.

Glasser's theory is about the need for internal control of our individual and collective lives, and why coercive external control is so destructive. He points to a stagnated response to the needs of people to become productive and sensitive human beings in a world of exponential growth in technical know-how.

The freedom to enter into genuine relationships, whether in the classroom or the office, results from personal choices—all parties to a transaction can choose to continue to force others to conform to what each has determined to be right for them, or provide the necessary support for others to find their own way, to develop and share understanding of the consequences of behavior for themselves and for others. Choice theory represents a shift from a psychology of coercive external control to a positive psychology of personal freedom to make intelligent choices that result in greater personal happiness and personal competence.

Glasser's theory is based on the premise that our needs for survival, love and belonging, power, freedom, and fun are gene driven. When these needs are unfulfilled, there are serious consequences for each individual and for our society in general.

Glasser's descriptions of the devastating results of schooling are alarmingly clear to anyone who faces the evidences from a humanistic point of view. Many examples of both instructional procedures and institutional settings provide extensive data that show the destruction of the human spirit that routinely occurs in the name of education.

Choice theory represents a change in personal orientations from external control to internal control. This implies a change in personal orientations that involves many beliefs and attitudes deeply embedded in one's unconscious response patterns, resulting from a history of experiences that are based on external control.

Unless these fundamental orientations are changed and supported by a sound and validated rationale, there is little hope that manipulation and coercion will cease.

Glasser's concepts and procedures attempt to address these changes through intensive workshops that are designed to help each person face the responsibility for personal choices. If professional educators hope to create a more civilized society, they must not only understand and accept personally verified underlying assumptions and rationale for choice theory, but reflect the theory in their transactions with students, colleagues, and parents.

Choice theory does not address the issues that relate specifically to learning a science or mathematics, or history, but it is clear that if the substance of the theory is practiced, it would undoubtedly enhance learning in all areas of the curriculum.

Since moral and ethical decision-making are considered to be legitimate goals for education, understanding what this actually means is mandatory. Lawrence Kohlberg created a model for viewing moral decision-making at points along the developmental continuum described by Piaget. His model indicates three major levels and multiple sub-levels. The three major levels are pre-conventional, conventional, and post conventional.

The first level of pure expediency was added to Kohlberg's original schema. It refers to when the consequences of one's actions are not considered. An adult who throws garbage on the roadside, even though it is unlawful and damages everyone's environment, is one example. Infants, before they reach a level of neurological maturity that allows the processing of experience above the level of automatic responses, is another example.

Although adults, by choice can behave at any level of moral decision-making, young children cannot exhibit moral decisions above the level of biological maturation that offers limits to their use of intellect. The sequence of development reflects those levels of intellectual maturation that Piaget and others have understood.

Kohlberg's model for viewing moral decision-making begins with pre-conventional decisions that involve a punishment and obedience orientation and a personal reward orientation. Deciding what is right or wrong is governed by whether there is punishment or reward involved.

A punishment-obedience orientation is consistent with the biologically-based capabilities for automatic responses to sensory stimuli. The young child is able to process stimuli that relates to approval or disapproval from socially important adults. The behavior that represents this stage is based on the concept that feelings of disapproval, and resulting punishments, are to be avoided.

The personal reward orientation requires more sophistication than the simpler punishment-obedience level. This level requires recognition that a reward is more pleasurable than a punishment. In either case, decision making is pre-logical and essentially automatic. This is the level of decision making exhibited by Kathy in her example of counting by twos to receive the approval of adults, even though she has no real purpose beyond that for reciting this exercise.

The second level of decision-making is thought to be conventional. At this level there is a distinction made by others in the social situation that features a good boy and nice girl orientation. This conventional definition guides the morality at this level.

A law and order orientation follows this earlier conventional one. At this level, one makes a decision of right and wrong based on what the law requires (written or unwritten) or what traditions have been passed down that provide the necessary criteria for "appropriate" moral behavior. This level of decision-making is defined by what is viewed as acceptable behavior with punishments for non-adherence.

Conventional decisions require logical connections between personal needs and the existence of rules and regulations that exist outside oneself. Importantly, conventional decision-making often requires a denial of those personal needs, and conformity with that which has been established to make society behave appropriately (lawfully). Conventional decisions are dependent upon at least a concrete operational intelligence.

Post-conventional decision-making takes into account the conventions of society, but there is an added concern for the social and ethical consequences of decisions. In some cases, the social and ethical consequences of decisions can counter the conventional wisdom and rules of conduct.

Since the individual who acts on the awareness of possible social and ethical consequences can be in opposition to the conventions, there is a real potential for conflict and possible retaliation. Fortunately, in this country we have mechanisms to change the rules of conduct when decision making by convention is found wanting. The frustrations voiced in descent by the "Occupy Movement" represent the post-conventional morality for many and that position is often in opposition to the conventions that govern society. Conflict is inevitable until these differences are reconciled.

Young students who are pre-conventional are also pre-operational and therefore unable to process their experiences at a logical level. Pre-conventional youngsters will base their moral decision-making on perception rather than on verifiable concepts.

Adults who do not understand this reality will often misconstrue the pre-conventional decisions as conscious decision-making and inappropriate behavior that demands immediate measures of disapproval, when in fact the behavior is consistent with appropriate pre-logical developmental capacities.

It is not damaging, however, to point out the consequences of decisions, if in the process the child does not lose his or her sense of trust, autonomy, initiative, and industriousness.

While every person, young and old, needs to understand the conventions that make society lawful, there is a danger that only conventional decision-making can be accepted at the expense of independent and personally responsible behavior. Today's society is full of examples of moral decisions by adults that are like pre-conventional behavior of young children, or rigidly conventional, even in the face of overwhelming evidence that suggests the need for change.

While there is awareness that the ethics and morality in our society are in trouble, the decision to make changes that would improve the situation are in the hands of many who are themselves acting in ways more appropriately matched with biologically immature youth. Considering the importance of ethics and morality, they must become an integral part of the curricular experiences of schools and colleges, not as religious dogma, but as an awareness of the consequences of actions upon others.

Howard Gardner has written extensively about the multi-faceted nature of intelligence. He shows the types of talents that are possibly biologically selective, and certainly, experientially influenced (Gardner, H. 2011 edition. *Frames of Mind: The theory of multiple intelligences*. New York. Basic Books) His model serves as a reminder that intelligence is not a fixed and unchangeable characteristic of humans, it is dynamic and modifiable. Recent research on the plasticity of the brain lends credence to Gardner's propositions.

According to Gardner there are seven types of intelligence that begins with (1) verbal-spatial which refers to capacities to accurately perceive the visual-spatial world and to modify and manipulate those perceptions. (2) Bodily-kinesthetic refers to abilities to control body movements and handle objects skillfully. (3) Musical-rhythmical has to do with the abilities to produce and appreciate rhythm, pitch and timbre and the forms of musical expressiveness. (4) Interpersonal involves capacities to discern and appropriately respond to moods, temperaments, motivations and desires of other people. (5) Intra-personal involves knowledge of own feelings, strengths, weaknesses, desires, and the ability to use this knowledge to guide behavior. (6) Logical-mathematical refers to abilities to discern logical or numerical patterns and to handle chains of reasoning, and (7) Verbal-linguistic that involves sensitivity to sounds, rhythms, meanings of words and different functions of language.

Each learner has a biological blueprint and a history of experiences that influence the current selection of sensory input, the processing of that input, and the formulation and expression of all output behaviors. The uniqueness of this constellation of factors accounts for the individuality of every learner, and the preferences and aptitudes acquired by that individual through life's experiences.

These preferences and aptitudes for each learner are the keys to successful constructions of knowledge. They must become a legitimate part of the strategies used to determine the best ways to facilitate individual learning.

It would be a huge mistake if we simply focus on human development and behavior regarding school age children or adults and neglect the importance of infancy and toddlerhood. Piaget referred to this level of development as "sensory motor," meaning that a response to stimuli from both inside and outside the body is a physical or motor response. A loud noise, for instance, is reacted to by muscular contractions and startled behavior. Later this same response is accompanied with crying.

Random movement of arms and legs gradually become focused. The baby begins first to grasp objects, but has not yet developed the neurological controls that would allow the release of that object. As neurological maturity progresses, the baby begins to roll over in preparation for crawling and eventually creeping.

Creeping represents coordinated control mechanisms (a developing intellect) that are refined with practice. This coordination involves hands, arms, legs, torso, eyes, head etc.; a degree of complexity not available before. Mature creeping emerges into walking and eventually running with maximized coordination. To shorten the creeping stage by encouraging pre-mature walking is a serious problem that may limit coordination at older ages and stages and circumvent the natural progression in the development of neurological pathways important to intellectual problem solving.

At one point in the past, play pens were often used to contain the baby's movements. The limited space in which to creep encourages upright positions for walking. This happens before the youngster has mastered the coordinated movements of creeping. Today, babies at this stage are placed in canvas chairs where the feet are touching a flat surface or the floor, and they bounce up and down on the spring that suspends the chair. This takes the place of the play pen to occupy and confine the youngster's movements.

Both of these implementations encourage performance at a stage beyond that under development at the time. This practice of pushing the individual to perform at the next stage before the previous stage is fully developed is a practice repeated over and over throughout the childhood years. This practice is harmful when it occurs continuously at the expense of experiences based on the freedom to move and coordinate physical actions. Throw out a basketball and watch a group of nine year olds run. Clearly, one can distinguish those whose early development likely contained a short-circuited creeping process.

The foregoing presentations are my interpretations of models drawn from reputable scholars from different time periods and places of residence across the world. While I may have modified or omitted information as a result of studying and using these models in my work as a teacher of teachers, it is obvious that all of these experts are on the same page when it comes to understanding human nature. The evidence is extraordinary and must be considered seriously in shaping a changed and improved educational system.

During the six decades I spent working in primary, and secondary schools, in junior, senior colleges and universities, teaching in-service and pre-service teachers and conducting workshops with community members and educators across this land, I have found a disturbing situation that cries out for an explanation. Practices in most of our school systems are demonstrably inconsistent with the realities of (healthy) human development and behavior, including learning. These inconsistencies are at the roots (if not the cause) of many of the social, economic, and political ills we face today in this country.

It may be viewed by some to be heresy to offer harsh criticism of our educational system, but the facts cannot be avoided. The conventional school system is obsolete and ineffective; it is operated in the absence of a shared and validated foundational knowledge base. A knowledge base should contain what we know and can verify about individual human growth and development, both in our own experiences, and in the experiences of others, especially in the experience of those scholars who have studied human development in depth. This lack of an articulated, shared, and validated knowledge base is what's behind today's disconnected and sporadic attempts at improving the school.

The current solutions for improvement of the school are simply tinkering around the edges without changing the outmoded beliefs upon which the present system is based. These beliefs do not reflect our knowledge about how individuals learn and develop, alone and in groups and institutions. A few examples offered here illustrate the inconsistencies practiced in today's public school systems, and those proposed to bring about improvement. This reflects what I have come to believe as a professional educator.

It is accepted by everyone who has ever witnessed infants and toddlers that developmental sequences are as predictable as creeping before walking, and walking before running. However, we seem to have forgotten that individuals continue to progress through their developmental sequences at their own pace, both physically and intellectually. Youngsters at the same age function naturally and simultaneously at different levels of growth and maturity. This reality is violated in the practice of grouping students for instruction by age, assigned to grade levels on an assumption of commonality that does not exist.

Some places in the world have decided that schooling should begin at the age of seven rather than at the ages of three to five, as we are witnessing in this country. This decision rightly reflects the view that a larger percentage of children at age seven are able to utilize instruction due to advanced maturity over the three to six year olds. However, it is still the case that some five or six year olds are mature enough to profit from instruction and some seven year olds are not. Even some eight and nine year olds are not mature enough to fully profit from instruction due to developmental differences.

Centuries ago it was Rousseau who decided that the "age of reason" was achieved at age ten. Even his position failed to recognize that some eleven and twelve year olds are not at that level of development and some seven, eight or nine year olds are at that level.

Jean Piaget found that the "age of reason"—concrete operations—occurs between seven and ten years of age. Yet we see an insistence in a belief in this country that all three, four and five year olds are ready or can be made ready for formal instruction, particularly in the nature and use of the symbols of their language. This decision is fraught with peril.

We each elaborate our processes of maturing by interacting with our environment, which includes significant others, including parents and teachers. No two persons have the same DNA, and the experiences of each person are different; experience is processed independent of every other person.

We all live independently, but we learn to exchange/share our individuality (become interdependent) as we develop language and sensitivities to the variables of life that we each experience. We are dependent on social relationships for defining our unique identity. Groups that reach a mature level of "consensual validation" will aid this process immeasurably. The practice of departmentalizing and compartmentalizing instruction discourages growth in the development of identity and group/team development.

The examination and elaboration of life's personal experiences and validation from significant others is at the heart of our motivation to learn. Yet, the school is arranged to essentially ignore personal experiences, unique perceptions, and experientially-developed differences. These are predominately considered irrelevant in our systems for becoming "educated."

The goal of conventional education is to convey the pre-defined and pre-selected thoughts of others as the substance of curriculum and this is expected to be accomplished through the presentation of isolated bits of information and over-generalized conclusions. In this communication age, information sources that can be accessed electronically are far superior to most presentations by a poorly-prepared teacher of subject matter. This teacher-centered procedure leaves individual learners with a feeling of dependency on so-called experts; it denies them a personal sense of importance and a perceived-value in the scheme of things and leaves many in a relative state of ignorance.

Consider the inconsistencies of standardized tests described as "One-size-fits-all" designed to measure educational outcomes. How does this match up with the developmental sequences and unique variations ascribed to every individual as a natural process of maturing? Is there any justification for measuring so-called learning outcomes through the use of standardized tests that are narrowly focused on the most elementary levels of learning, that ignore developmental differences, that profile developmentally less-mature learners (mistakenly determined to need remediation), that segregates average learners from those who have been categorized by narrowly-defined criteria of exceptionality, all based on written tests that only sample what is recalled of the information taught in the school? Does it make sense to do this ignoring the many personal experiences every individual has available to potentially draw upon? After all, only eight hours of the day, five days of the week, roughly forty weeks of the year, for twelve to twenty years of one's life are dedicated to being instructed in our public schools. What happens during the rest of the time, during the remaining sixteen hours of the day, during the remaining twelve weeks of the year and the years of living beyond graduation? Is "homework" and grades all that is important during these times?

What is the justification for moving an emphasis on parsing our native language to the earliest levels of instruction—the pre-kindergarten? Is it to prepare students to read the pre-canned and corporate-promoted, expensive text materials that dominate the later grades? Young children have needs that do not include the repetitions of parsed language, learning the letters of the alphabet, or reciting the number facts. These are misplaced adult needs. It is clear that superficially-acceptable responses can be attained through repetition like with Pavlov's dogs, and young humans can likewise be trained to recite correctly, but at what cost?

Varied experiences in these earlier years will provide the foundation for creative responses to experience that become the grist for the mill at the more mature stages of intellectual development. When these imposed structured repetitions are the essential offerings of the early school experiences, they are not only an inordinate waste of the time required to teach the isolated bits of information (that would be mastered almost immediately at a later level of development) but they are harmful to the full development of abilities that can emerge at these later levels of maturity.

These imposed structured experiences offered at an early age and continued throughout the educational experience condition learners to adopt rigid psychological orientations that severely restrict the development of creativity and advanced intellectual capabilities. As explained earlier, Lawrence Kubie, a psychiatrist and critic of education, referred to this as contributing to neurotic distortions of the creative process, a state of mind he described in his book of this title.

Youngsters at these early levels need to experience as many aspects of the immediate environment as possible and have the opportunity to freely express their reactions through developmentally-appropriate language (whole language) and visually-constructed expressions of meaning. This is essential preparation for logical analysis and restructuring of experiences that appear at a later operational level. The structured experience offered to young children in our schools begins the development of rigid response patterns that deny flexibility and creativity in the life of the child. It encourages, if not forces, conformity.

Levels of maturity emerge at differing times for each individual. The school that is organized by grade levels does not accommodate these differences. Compounding this problem is the fact that what was experienced and processed to please adults is easily forgotten. Without a complete and organized record of experiences that reflects the personal translations of objects, events and processes encountered in living, kept for use at later levels in each individual's pursuit of meaning in his or her life, the value of these past experiences is lost. Memories of these experiences are difficult if not impossible to retrieve.

Organized recordkeeping using modern technological devices for input, storage and processing of the results of encounters with the world can aid the development of maturity that builds upon these past experiences. This is not happening in our schools. Most records of past experiences are recorded and stored in various repositories as assigned grades and test scores that are presumed to be reflective of the levels of acquired achievement. Performance in life, however, demonstrates that these grades are nearly meaningless.

A system oriented process has been developed and field tested—The Constructive Assessment, Recordkeeping, and Evaluation System (CARES). © Robert L. Arnold, 2010. This system has the capability to revolutionize and replace the mindless testing mentality that exists today.

The diminishing levels of enthusiasm about school work that emerges gradually and reaches its apex for many when individuals reach an ability level for logical analysis, is testimony to the negative impact this over-structuring and irrelevant instruction at the early levels of schooling has had. This is likely at the heart of the emerging problems of drop-outs and bullying, and various other social ills marked by over-aggressive behavior found in the school, in the home and on the gridiron.

Everyone has recognized that early childhood is usually characterized by an abundance of curiosity and enthusiasm. This enthusiasm for learning for most students is often lost by the fifth grade, resulting in prolonged unhealthy psycho-social development, often centered upon a misplaced sense of identity. Identity for many is manifested in identification with a group that overrides any internal sense of who one is and what one is capable of becoming. No wonder learners at the adolescent level present extraordinary problems that escape a solution, especially when we simply try to make more palatable what students have determined to be irrelevant in their lives; or worse, more restrictive and arbitrarily imposed by those in charge.

There is a widespread corporate investment in instructional materials and gadgets for use at the early levels of schooling coupled with an enduring faith that if only we can move instruction to these lower levels we will solve many of the problems that appear later. We have substituted inanimate objects (like Big Bird) to convey the alphabet and number facts through instructional media, at the expense of meaningful and developmentally-appropriate encounters with the realities of life and its surroundings in all its manifestations. Above all, there is a misplaced belief that we can meet and exceed more rigorous standards of performance by simply doing more and more of the same. This belief system will be hard to dislodge even though it is a formula for the destruction of our democratic society that is dependent upon an educated public.

While this brief analysis of the inconsistencies suggested between validated developmental concepts and instructional practices is focused on the early educational experience, there is a continuing inconsistency found throughout the school experience that warrants further analysis. These inconsistencies, among others, relate to a lack of understanding about the nature of communication, group processes, and group/team development, along with the nature of knowledge and the processes of coming to know. Incredibly, there is an almost total void in understanding and utilizing information about the nature, functions, and relationships among unconscious, pre-conscious, and conscious behavior.

The professional literature that deals with human development and behavior is often so involved and technical that it becomes nearly incomprehensible for the practitioners working in schools. They are overwhelmed with information that does not easily translate into practices they can use. As a result, teachers have become dependent upon prepared instructional materials and texts that seldom if ever reflect an accurate translation of the underlying principles of human development. At the risk of oversimplification, what follows is an effort to focus briefly on the essence of propositions taken from the writings of scholars in this area of study that I have found to relate directly to learning and instruction in schools.

In Conclusion:

The illustrations that follow are meant to show the interrelationships of five dimensions of human development of particular importance, worthy of being restated in different language that will connect with those who need this information. These five views of important developmental sequences are drawn from the scholarly works of Viktor Lowenfeld, Jean Piaget, Lev Vygotsky, Jerome Bruner, Lawrence Kohlberg and Robert Gagné. *Every teacher and parent should understand and apply these models, especially those with primary-school age children in their care, if we expect to change and improve their learning experiences.*

The relationships between each phase identified in these models are of particular importance to parents and teachers since evidence of the level of maturation achieved in one dimension reflects a corresponding level of maturation or lack of maturation exhibited in the others. These models provide the framework for diagnosing the levels of achievement accomplished to date and they shape realistic expectations important in the selection of fruitful, growth-producing teaching/learning transactions.

Viktor Lowenfeld's model deals with non-verbal, visual expressions that begin with scribbles, first occurring when the infant/toddler can grasp a marking instrument and apply it to a surface. There is a gradual, biologically-based maturational sequence that follows; pre-schematic drawings, schematic drawings, dawning realism and realism, culminating in the ability to utilize prior capabilities abstractly to communicate a particular message. This mode of visual expression is of utmost importance: (1) to the learner in organizing and communicating personal meanings, and (2) for those charged with assessment and evaluation of intellectual capabilities and intellectual achievements. Authentic drawings of familiar experiences reveal the levels of intellectual operations as defined in Piaget's model. Evidence of these developmental capabilities can be easily observed in children's drawings that follow this invariant developmental sequence.

Random Scribbles–Controlled Scribbles–Pre-Schematic Drawing–Schematic Drawing–Dawning Realism–Realism–Abstract Representation

Piaget's model begins with automatic motor/physical responses to sensory stimuli, the forerunner of deliberate operational intelligence. The subsequent phase, pre-operations, is characterized by an *inability* to deal logically with experiences, thus allowing a freedom of expression and creativity that does not require empirical validation (drawn from observations and experimentations). To insist that learners at this phase demonstrate logical solutions to problems is not only pre-mature; it is harmful to the developing intellect.

Concrete, logical capabilities emerging at the "age of reasoning" marks a pivotal point in the development of intellect with direct implications regarding the reception of meaningful instruction and for personal learning. Language that is the expression of realistic perceptions emerges at the concrete operations level of Piaget's model. It is seen to coincide with the phases in the development of verbal language.

Sensory–Motor Intelligence–Pre-Logical Operations–Concrete/Logical Operations–Formal Op.

Vygotsky's model of language development begins with a pre-intellectual phase that matures through usage to a phase of internalization and in-growth. This mature level represents an effective use of fully-developed language, its meanings and structure, and understood for its intrinsic value. Interference with the early creative phases of a natural process of language acquisition, by parsing the language, repetitious teaching of the alphabet and memorization of number facts destroys much of the spontaneity of this level of intellectual development. Those experiences negatively impact the full development of the later abilities of concrete and formal operational intelligence, and the development of language skills so important in the organization and communication of personalized meanings. Vygotsky's model is shown here.

Pre-Intellectual Language–Naively Psychological–External Signs Dominance–Internalization/In-Growth/ Symbolic Phase

Bruner described language development in three phases beginning with enactive language that contains both non-verbal and audible expressions that represent environmentally-influenced actions. This phase lays the foundation for the iconic language of imagery that marks the beginning of internal control of communication. It is here that reading skills become important to the developing youngsters, providing their language usage has not been poisoned by the imposition of phonetic analysis and parsing of language in their earlier years. The most mature level of language development is symbolic language, which is rich with connotative meanings drawn from the various experiences of the past, present and the imagined future. The full development of iconic expressions of meaning is prerequisite to full development of symbolic language; both are dependent upon the free development of earlier enactive forms of verbal expression.

Enactive Language–Iconic - Symbolic

Individual determinations of the kind of behavior that constitutes right or wrong are tied to the developmental phases as described by Lowenfeld, Piaget, Vygotsky, and Bruner. Lawrence Kohlberg described the phases in the development of moral decision making as pre-conventional, conventional, and post-conventional, with sub-phases. An initial level is expediency which is an automatic response to internal and environmental stimuli. This phase is followed by a punishment-reward orientation and a punishment-obedience orientation. The first level is essentially automatic and the subsequent phases are based on the recognition that a reward is pleasurable. This leads to a level referred to as a good boy/good girl orientation. At this level the social context dominates the youngster's decisions that are acquired through messages of right or wrong delivered by significant adults, and learned as a response to gain approval.

This more circumscribed, egocentrically-focused orientation of right or wrong gradually emerges into a wider context of conventional thinking for each individual. Consideration of the dimensions of law and order, or tradition, whether written or unwritten, becomes the controlling factor of moral decision-making at this phase. Conventional moral decision-making requires making a connection between personal experiences and the societal and family context. Making these connections requires at least early logical capabilities.

The post-conventional orientation takes into account the conventions of society but there is an added concern for social and ethical consequences of decisions. This most mature orientation embodies the potential for conflict with those who adhere predominately to the conventional wisdom as understood and often rigidly promoted by individuals and groups. Adherence by others to rigid interpretations of conventions often prevents those with an expanded view from actualizing their concerns about social and ethical matters.

Pre-conventional learners are pre-operational and therefore unable to process their experiences at a logical level. They base their moral decisions on what they perceive rather than what they have intellectually conceptualized. A parent or teacher who sees a child inventing the rules as they play, and assumes that to be cheating, has missed the point of pre-conventional decision-making. Cheating requires deliberate logical connections well beyond the capabilities of a pre-conventional learner. It is fine to remind these youngsters that this behavior does not follow the rules of the game, but we cannot expect them at this stage of development to understand that their actions constitute cheating as determined by an adult version.

Kohlberg's model provides a constructive view of moral decision making that can be related to other dimensions of intellectual maturation.

Automatic responses–Pre-Conventional moral decisions–Conventional decisions–Post-Conventional

When the five models briefly described above are juxtaposed with a comprehensive model of learning, such as that defined by Robert Gagné, the relationships become even clearer. Learning is an internal process of constructing meaning and modifying existing structures acquired through past experiences. The first level of learning in Gagné's model is labeled stimulus response. All learners function at this level unless they have physiological or psychological impairments. In time, this level emerges into simple associations, motor-chaining of associations and verbal-chaining which enables beginning language expressions of meaning that are dominated by external sign usage. Children at the pre-logical level of intellectual development can function at this level of learning.

Continued exposure leads to multiple discriminations wherein learners begin to recognize the objects and actions within their environment as having multiple dimensions. These multiple dimensions become the ingredients for concept formation. This capability is illustrated in children's logically-developed drawings at the schematic stage of development.

Pre-operational intelligence is not capable of dealing with concepts that evolve into simple rules, then into principles and laws. These are considered higher thought processes; concrete operational and formal operational intelligence is required to deal with these processes. The final stage of problem solving that begins at the level of concrete operations and later develops into formal operations is dependent upon the full development of all the previous stages. Gagné's model illustrated here shows a sequence that is comprehensive; it is a far cry from the oversimplified definition of learning that appears in the current discourse about education.

Stimulus response–Simple associations–Motor-chaining–Verbal chaining–Multiple discriminations–Concept formation–Rules formation–Principles–Laws–Problem solving

Achievement of maturity in this learning hierarchy is dependent upon the attainment of each of the capabilities found at developmental levels as described in Lowenfeld's, Piaget's, Vygotsky's, Bruner's, and Kohlberg's models. A teacher or parent, ignorant of these validated propositions, will unknowingly act in ways that often thwart the healthy development of innate capabilities. As a result, these capabilities may cease to be available in individuals throughout their lives; a problem that directly relates to aspects of incompetence we witness in life's current transactions.

Even those schools that are doing things consistent with human development would gain more lasting credibility if only they would tease out the relevant developmental and learning theories and relate them to the practices that work.

The interrelationships are illustrated below between developmental models, drawn from the writings of Lowenfeld, Piaget, Vygotsky, Bruner, Kohlberg, and Erikson, correlated with Gagné's cumulative learning model.

This next model should be read from left to right, consistent with the developmental maturational process. It should also be noted that the vertical relationships illustrated within each of the four developmental segments reveal the patterns of behavior that reflect all of the models shown here.

Auto-response to sensory stimuli	Pre-logical creativity	Beginning logical analysis	Advanced logic and creativity
Random Scribbles - Controlled Scribbles- Pre-Schematic Drawing -- Schematic Drawing- Dawning Realism- Realism – Abstract
Sensory-Motor Intelligence	Pre-Logical Operations	Concrete/Logical Operations	Formal Operations
Pre-Intellectual Language-Naive; Psychological- External Signs Dominance- Internalization/In-Growth/ Symbolic Phase
Babbling	Enactive Language	Iconic	Symbolic
Expediency	Pre-Conventional moral decisions	Conventional decisions	Post-Conventional
Early Childhood	Childhood	Pre-Adolescence Adolescence	Adulthood
Trust Autonomy	Initiative	Industry Identity Intimacy	Generativity Integrity

The illustration below shows the correlations between the five developmental models and Robert Gagné's "Cumulative Learning Model." (Read bottom to top and left to right)

Gagné Cumulative Learning Model				
	Developmental Capabilities			
Levels of Development	Auto-response	Pre-Logical	Logical	Advanced
Problem solving abilities				Advanced
Principles/Laws				Advanced
Complex rules				Advanced
Simple rules			Logical	Logical
Concept formation			Logical	Logical
Multiple discriminations		Pre-Logical/logical	Pre-Logical/logical	Pre-Logical/logical
Verbal Chaining		Pre-Logical	Pre-Logical	Pre-Logical
Motor Chaining		Pre-Logical	Pre-Logical	Pre-Logical
Simple Association	Auto-Response	Auto-Response	Auto-Response	Auto-Response
Stimulus Response	Auto-Response	Auto-Response	Auto-Response	Auto-Response

Debilitating dependency on others that diminishes one's personal identity and direction results from practices based on a lack of awareness and commitment to actualizing the dynamic dimensions of human development and behavior. Current standardized tests seldom contain questions beyond the level of verbal chaining; thus indications of achievement that represents the higher dimensions of cognitive development are left for speculation.

Intellectual capabilities result from biologically-based, internal constructions influenced by the external environment and often controlled by environmental influences when there is a weak self-concept. Subsequent levels beyond multiple discriminations are referred to as higher thought processes. These processes result in creative products constructed by unique individuals; these constructions are not standardized nor are they or can they be measured by current standardized tests.

The results of not putting into practice the messages derived from an understanding of the interrelated developmental processes are devastating to the fulfillment of human potential. What begins in the home environment, but most importantly continues in the school environment, deficiencies exist that result in many social, economic, and political problems in current America. Anything short of a systemic change in our school systems will not improve this situation and time is running out.

It is most important to heed what Bela Banathy wrote that is relevant to an understanding of the present standardized testing and standardized-core curriculum mentality. He stated: "Traditional econometric/statistical methods of performance measurement are unable to account for the complexity in educational systems. Oversimplified performance measures can lead to organizational pathologies. Performance measures that retain empirical grounding in systems-in-transition need to be developed" (Banathy, Bela, 1993).

Note: the CARES model described earlier contains performance measures with empirical grounding in systems-in-transition.

Chapter 4

Group Processes and the Public Schools

The consequence of the lack of understanding about the importance and practice of group development is a major deterrent to any improvement in public education and must be altered if we expect any breakthroughs in finding a better way to educate.

Ironically, most of our formal educational experiences occur within a group setting, yet educators and the public are either almost completely ignorant about group development or in denial about this aspect of life's experience.

The goal of group processes and group development is improved communication, leading to individual and collective productivity. To reach this goal, professional educators assigned to facilitate group experiences must be skilled in interventions that encourage and maintain healthy group (team) development. This is not happening in our conventional schools. Only on rare occasions do athletic teams achieve this status. How, you ask, can a collection of individuals become a fully functioning group that maximizes learning, encourages the development of problem solving abilities and critical thinking skills? What are the basic requirements for achievement of a fully functioning group?

Generally, the process of group development emerges through three distinguishable levels on its way to maturity. The first level is called "dependency." The second is "independency" and the third, "interdependency. When a group is first gathered together, the uncertainty of what to expect finds its members dependent upon an appointed leader to set the expectations and define the mission and parameters of the upcoming group experience. The make-up of groups at this level often contains at least two distinct factions; one part is made up of individuals who tend to prefer to make their own decisions, and the other contains those who prefer to have someone tell them what to do. These differences in orientation are initially suppressed, given the uncertainty of a new experience, but if allowed, these differences will emerge later in the group's experiences.

A group is maintained at the level of dependency by simply having the appointed-leader assert his or her authority over the group and arbitrarily establish the rules for conduct and penalties for violation. When there is little room for negotiation, the group will remain dependent upon the so-called leader.

The deeper feelings of personal needs that exist at the dependency level emerge at later levels of group development, provided the suppression of those needs is minimal. The underlying orientation for a furtherance of dependency by part of the group, and the orientation toward independence that was unexplored at the dependency level, must be dealt with at this level if the group is to move toward maturity. This emerging level is called, "independence." Its label represents a recognition of the need for the public assertion, a disclosure of authentic, independent needs and aspirations, necessary in order to confront and resolve the differences between individuals and discover the commonalities that also exist. Managing this level of expressed differences requires special skills in practice within our schools and colleges.

When and if the expression of these felt needs emerges in the conventional classroom, it is often ignored or openly rejected as irrelevant and disruptive. This is viewed as interfering with the "all-important" instruction, slowing down "progress" in the coverage of information. Often, the teacher who prefers to maintain dependency in the name of keeping order will discourage expressions of true feelings. When an individual's expression is persistent, he or she is often labeled a trouble maker and subjected to disciplinary actions. Reaction to the authority figure in this situation results in the suppression of one's true feelings. This often results in the expression of inauthentic outward behavior, displayed simply to avoid the reprimand of the adult in charge. This type of suppression, if not dealt with, will likely result in accumulated personal frustration that can lead to eventual hostility directed at others and perhaps at oneself.

When there is relative freedom to express individual points of view, inevitably, there will be potential conflict that must be resolved. To an outsider, this group might appear to be out of control, when in fact it may be engaging a necessary process that can lead to a fully functioning group characterized by mutual support and compassion for the uniqueness of each individual. Civility must be managed as the potentially conflictive orientations are openly expressed at this level of group functioning.

Unfortunately, authoritarian leaders will often view this level of group functioning as a breakdown in discipline and its leader/teacher as incompetent in asserting effective "leadership." In these days of standardization and high stakes testing, the pressure to assert authority has vastly increased to the detriment of any legitimate group process that might result in individual and collective maturity, relatively free of an unhealthy dependency. This trend can only exacerbate an already narrow practice of group dynamics as a means to improved learning and development in our public schools and colleges.

There are teachers, mainly of primary age children, who have intuitively and lovingly discovered the need for listening to the sincere expressions of feelings each learner will voice if given the opportunity. These teachers have found this experience leads to a vastly improved quality of communication with each individual. When sensitively shared, the quality of communication within the group as a whole will also be positively affected. When the system mandates formal instruction that does not reflect the developmental needs of these youngsters, the process of listening is seriously hampered.

Since most schools are organized hierarchically in an authoritarian rather than a democratic model, there is increasingly little opportunity for these teachers to actualize their discovery of the vital importance of this level of group process. With the current movement to arbitrarily demand the achievement of specific learning outcomes for all learners (much of it subject matter formally taught at later grade levels) makes actualization of these fundamental truths almost impossible.

Over the course of the elementary, middle and secondary school experiences, the accumulated results of suppression of one's individuality will be expressed somehow, often through aggressive sport, open rebellion and destructive hostility directed at others in the form of bullying and acts of violence against society, or dropping out—a withdrawal from the experience. The lack of conflict resolution within those years of schooling can also lead to the sorry state of affairs we are witnessing today with our representatives in government, those who exhibit few mature communication and group problem solving skills.

If a group of individuals is guided in their sensitive dealings with differing points of view and finds commonalities with others that exist at a fundamental level of living, these group members will emerge into the most mature level of group functioning called "interdependence" featuring "consensual validation" in its communications. The orientation found in this mature group level exists when the members strive to seek consensus in their communications, validated in their own experiences and in the experiences of others, including consideration of the propositions of scholars who have devoted a lifetime of study in topics of their interest. A group that functions at this mature level, and maintains this level through a concerted effort, will allow individuals to safely pursue independent needs and be eager to search the unknown using human capabilities for fulfillment of curiosity, adaptability, and inventiveness, accompanied by a tolerance for ambiguity.

These behaviors can predictably emerge for all members of any group when consensual validation is practiced and its results are felt. Leadership will shift with sanction from the group in response to perceived needs for matching individual competency with group needs, in the interest of effective problem solving activity. Such a dynamic group will collectively foster the development and utilization of individual members, developing and sustaining competence required of successful problem solving abilities. If this level of group functioning does not occur, its results will show that individual and group problem solving skills will remain untapped.

In a fully functioning group, engagement in the practice of creating knowledge in the disciplines, within what Philip Phenix postulated as all "realms of meaning," can be effectively actualized. Mastery of personal strategies for learning becomes the expected and desired outcome. This will lead to the development of a level of competency that has eluded many who remain dependent upon others.

The school is restricted in its job in its present form. The time to change is now. But inserting the practices of group dynamics into a system that discourages individual decision making, out of fear of disapproval from others or for other reasons, will not sustain the changes suggested by a sound theory of group dynamics.

Over the years, numerous reasoned practices have been inserted into the conventional system with the same outcome. The system appears to accept the changes, but experience shows the likelihood of survival of even sound innovations is very slim. Teachers are generally not involved in these decision-making practices. Billions of tax payer dollars have been injected into the conventional system through grants that have met with the same result, making little if any sustained improvements. Change must be systemic or the effectiveness of group development, as with other sound innovations, will be short lived.

Communication is enhanced with effective group relationships. When a group functions as just a collection of strangers who are brought together for purposes of tradition or authority, the level of communication is most often not very rewarding. In fact, as a result of such ineffective groups, individuals often develop survival techniques that are characterized by withdrawal, resigned boredom, or sabotage.

Group dynamics has a rich tradition and research base that is seldom understood by educators. Business and the military have been better able to translate group process theory into practice than those in education.

Attempts to ensure a higher level of productivity that yields more profits for business interests is their motivation. The need for development of cohesive and supportive group membership in the military that will ensure that "friendly fire" rarely happens and a team of soldiers can accomplish their missions is ample motivation to seek understanding of groups and practice interventions that encourage mature group development. However, even these examples are seriously lacking in their conceptual underpinning.

Few have attempted the translation of group process theory in education. Instead, their orientation about groups is conformed to the hardened categories of institutional conventions. Bits of theory appear in the school's institutional setting in the form of classroom management techniques, cooperative learning procedures, lesson and unit planning strategies, teaching models, assertive discipline, etc. None of these efforts truly reflect the theory of group processes and group development. They all have in common an attempt to improve the existing school system and they are all reactions to perceived unsatisfactory procedures of the school and poorly educated clientele. But this clientele is most often composed of individuals who have little investment in what takes place in the classroom group, and a realistic awareness that the activity there has little immediate personal payoff, beyond providing an opportunity to visit with a few selected friends.

R. and P. Schmuck (a husband and wife team) have translated group process theory for the classroom. They are well grounded in this theory and when they apply it to the classroom they do not try to bend the theory to conform to the conventional dynamics of the institution and its classrooms. They are true to their discipline (Schmuck, Richard, and Schmuck, Patricia, 2000).

Their model for small groups (ideally 20 or less) begins with the initial formation of the group. Students in the school find themselves together mainly by decisions of institutional authorities. They are placed in a group by grade levels and age that presumes a level of intellectual commonality that does not exist.

At the initial level of group functioning, individuals do not know what to expect of their teacher or the other authorities who have control over their lives. Warren Bennis defined this initial stage of group development as dependency. The Schmucks defined the earliest phases of dependency as an inclusion and membership stage. (Bennis, Warren et al., 1969).

Early in the life of a classroom group, students feel the need to find a niche for themselves among their peers. Since the teacher is the most prominent authority within the group, the students can be anxious to present a good image out of an intuitive concern for their own welfare. Everyone sizes up other members and the issues of inclusion and membership are of serious concern.

If the leader insists on asserting absolute authority with limited room for individual contributions from members of the group, the group will remain at the dependency level. Membership will be defined in a hierarchical relationship with control maintained at the top of the hierarchy. Important group decision making will be reserved for the leader at the top.

A leader who asks for suggestions and then does whatever he or she wants to do is the type of leadership Rensis Likert labeled consultative (Likert, R. (1967). This type of leadership gives the appearance of democratic processes and entices group members to feel their interests are being considered. In actuality, consultative leadership is basically authoritarian and there is no question about who controls the situation. Consultative leadership is practiced widely among administrators and some teachers in the conventional school. It is perhaps the most dishonest form of leadership among authoritarians. There are two other types of leadership identified by Likert, namely, "exploitative authoritarian" and "benevolent authoritarian." These two types do not mask their need for control.

If the leader genuinely provides opportunities for the membership to consider those areas where they have authority to make decisions, this conveys a sense that each member will be treated as a contributing and worthy person. This type of leadership was characterized by Likert as participative.

In the typical classroom setting, in the conventional school, even a minor shifting of authority from the teacher to the students is generally viewed as a lack of leadership. But even in the more progressive settings, this shift in authority is not always carefully managed so that members will learn to accept responsibility for their own actions.

Those who cling to an authoritarian orientation will view the shift in authority as a loss of control and perhaps a deficiency in the training of students to conform to society's established rules of conduct. Those with a participative orientation will engage the issues of inclusion and membership, knowing that if these issues are not resolved with recognition and respect for the individual members, the group will not progress to the next phase of growth on their way to group maturity.

As the group members become aware of being included in authentic decision-making, they begin to understand that the group can serve as a vehicle for achieving their personal as well as institutional goals. When authority relationships are resolved through discussions, members find it safe to express more of their true feelings and points of view, which in earlier stages were withheld out of fear or uncertainty. The result of this disclosure plays out in potential conflicts between those who want to be told what to do (the more dependent), and those who want to make decisions for themselves (the independent).

This struggle is between those who challenge authority and those who are more concerned with the peer group's pecking order even among group members who do not have any official right to make decisions. Tensions will exist between the students and the teacher and between students at this stage. If these tensions cannot be resolved and the power relationships balanced, the group will not move to a more mature level of functioning. In Bennis's terms, this stage is the beginning of independence, which is a difficult phase to move through.

Often those in authority within and outside the typical classroom will perceive expressions at this conflictive stage as a loss of control and will use their power to discourage its continuation. Such action is based on ignorance about the nature of group development, and it results in disrupting the sequence that is necessary for achievement of group maturity.

Disruption at this stage from authorities outside of the classroom has serious psychological consequences for individual members who may have been granted some authority and have a stake in the group's successes, only to have that authority taken away. This disruption has devastating consequences for the teacher/leader especially when that teacher is appropriately working with his or her group. Interference thwarts the achievement of high level individual and group productivity. The only exception is when actions are considered dangerous to the well-being of the individual. Defining what these actions are is considered in the nature of effective group processes.

The next stage is called individual and group goals by the Schmucks. At this stage individuals sense a degree of freedom to express their personal desires and where the teacher is free to consider with the membership the individual and group goals. Establishing these goals leads to the planning of activities to achieve them. Students at this stage can participate in setting goals and developing plans for accomplishing them through cooperative procedures. If time is not allowed for developing clarity about individual and institutional goals, and for formulating plans for achieving those goals, the future health of the group is jeopardized. Given time and support the group can enter its most mature stage.

The most mature stage is called interdependence by Bennis and self-renewal/adaptive change by the Schmucks. This stage is known for its supportive and consensually validated communication.

A high level of consensually validated communication and a problem solving orientation enables the group to achieve its institutional goals and yet preserve and protect the integrity of individual needs, aspirations, and personal styles.

Each level of group development is subject to regression when conditions change that are not conducive to growth. If the authority relationships are not resolved satisfactorily, if the struggles for defining and assuming responsibility for the group's actions are not reconciled against institutional demands, if the group is unable to finalize its plans for achieving goals, and new conditions are introduced in the form of imposed tasks, a change in membership or conflicts of any kind, these will diminish the group's productivity and the group must work its way back to higher levels of communication and group cooperation.

The message is essentially this: group productivity is dependent upon group maintenance; it is not something that automatically occurs and maintains itself. High levels of group functioning require constant effort, vigilance, and a tolerance for ambiguity.

Mutual trust, honesty, and openness are the building blocks of a personally satisfying group experience. These factors lead to cooperation among group members to identify and act upon the commonly shared goals of the group and the individual goals of its members, providing there is guaranteed safety in doing so.

A satisfying group experience translates to the larger context of family and community life.

Consensus building facilitates individual achievement for each member of the group. Becoming an effective group does not require a compromise of one's unique contribution or unique needs. On the contrary, in an effective group there is appreciation for the uniqueness and diversity of its members.

The first difficult obstacle to group development is found at the dependency stage where there is a need to resolve the issues surrounding authority relationships. Chief among these issues is the relationship of the group and its group leader, and to the requirements that are mandated as the responsibility of the institution. Determining what issues the group has the authority to act upon, and how far the group's authority extends, is pre-requisite to understanding the limitations for open discussion, goal setting, and decision making for each individual and for the group as a whole.

As the authority relationships are resolved, individual members will find it safe to assert their personal desires and points of view. This allows the membership to enter the stage of independency. Individual expressions are often at odds with other's points of view, and with the requirements of the institution and the appointed leader. This stage must be managed to maintain acceptance of differing points of view while information necessary for group planning is determined. Rules of conduct, that guarantee civility, are a requirement at this delicate stage of group development.

Once the desires of the membership and the requirements of the institution are thoroughly explored, group plans for action can emerge that are actualized through continuing a process of consensual validation. This interdependent activity results in satisfying communication and effective group decision making.

It is important to understand that consensus reached by a group is not the same as unanimity as Bennis has pointed out. "Rather it is a state of affairs where communications have been sufficiently open, and the group climate has been sufficiently supportive, to make all members of the group feel that they have had a fair chance to influence the decision. It is a psychological state that might be described as follows: I understand what most of you would like to do. I personally would not do that, but I feel that you understand what my alternative would be. I have had sufficient opportunity to sway you to my point of view, but clearly have not been able to do so. Therefore, I will gladly go along with what most of you wish to do, with the understanding that the decision is always open for further review if pertinent new information becomes available."

If only our U.S. Congress members understood the importance of this position, there would not be the gridlock and unresolved ideological conflicts that we see today. Most likely these members of Congress attended schools wherein the authoritarian model of group process was prevalent.

The school is a cooperative enterprise with groups of people of differing ages and interests, and personal orientations, pursuing institutional and individual goals and objectives. If professional educators are not skilled in diagnosing group problems and in using appropriate interventions that aid group maturity, we can expect to see a continuation of dysfunctional groups like our U.S. Congress.

While this model of group process and group development is generally applied to adults, the basic principles apply to group experience for any age or stage of personal development. Less mature individuals will require more time for responding to their dependent needs. They will predictably find it more difficult to transcend this stage.

As individuals mature, they can and will accept more responsibility for participating in the experiences that improve communication and individual productivity. The sensitive leader, with skills in the uses of appropriate interventions, will assist the group and all of its members in achieving consistently high levels of productivity and demonstrated competence. The length of time required to achieve mastery of any subject will occur much sooner and more likely when the tasks are engaged with enthusiasm and personal planning in a mature functioning group.

Since the level of group development referred to as independence is pre-requisite to achievement of interdependence, it is critical that leaders realize the necessity for group members to express potentially conflictive opinions, and equally critical that they have the capabilities for managing this stage so that a more mature level of functioning can be reached.

It is also critical that sufficient time is allotted to group development with the assurance that the time required for reaching decisions will result in greater efficiencies in learning as the group matures in its insight and skills.

Nothing should interfere with the work of a competent professional and his or her group, assuming that the goal of group development is improvement of communication that leads to greater personal and institutional productivity. The school must provide the time and support services that will make this growth possible.

As both Albert Bandura and Lev Vygotsky have indicated, learning and language development is, among other things, socially based (Bandura, A. 1977; Vygotsky, L.S. 1978).

Open communications with other human beings serve to provide models and challenges that lead to a stage of internalization of concepts and development of the vehicles for individualized expressions.

Although individuals at early developmental stages cannot fully grasp or articulate the values of participative group experience, the insightful professional will encourage independence and interdependence within the group, taking into account the existing intellectual and social limitations of each child. This strategy is in anticipation that a more mature and capable neurological system will eventually emerge in each child, provided psychological damage has not been inflicted in the interim.

When more mature intellectual stages are reached, the child is able to consciously participate in group experiences aimed at goal setting, planning for achievement of goals, successfully completing the tasks set forth in the plans and evaluating the outcomes.

There are those who view group processes as an invitation to permissiveness and anarchy. They rationalize the necessity for an authoritarian structure, with clear lines of authority, as the preferred organization. They believe erroneously that individuals need someone in charge of their lives. This orientation breeds dependency.

However, group processes do not absolve the teacher/facilitator of the responsibility to protect the members of the group from harm either from themselves, others, or the environment. The teacher/group leader must ensure civility within the group and strive for cooperative decision making based on the principles of team development.

When a teacher understands the principles of sound group/team development and acts on those principles, the group members will develop compassion for others and appreciation for the unique contribution each person can bring to the teaching/learning transactions. Questions of unacceptable behavior in this social context will be routinely dealt with. As a result of this effort, the group members develop a moral and ethical orientation that carries over into the community. The importance of the presence of an appointed leader is diminished as the group begins to assume responsibility for its collective actions with leadership changing in light of the needs of the group.

The competent teacher/facilitator must have clear authority to execute those interventions that can bring about mature group functioning. When "authorities" like principals, superintendents and other administrators, outside of the working group, control or interfere with its internal workings, the result is counterproductive. Those persons cannot possibly know what is happening within specific group settings.

This authority fosters an imposed dependency on members of learning groups that thwarts growth and healthy development and often leads to individual strategies of resistance, rebellion, and even outright sabotage. The price that is paid for this ignorance of group dynamics has devastated life in many communities and will continue until there is recognition of its origins and commitment to the principles that can productively deal with individual and group development.

Evidences of violence that emerge from groups that are stuck at the dependency level in the conventional school experiences are pervasive throughout today's society, both here in the USA and abroad. Today, violence is viewed with enthusiasm in video games, movies, over our cell phones and on the gridiron. It is acted out in aggressive behavior as bullying in the schools, as sexual assaults in and outside the home; it is revered in the military. Many seem not to be able to satisfy their appetite for violence as long as it does not affect them personally. Many have become observers of violent acts as part of our entertainment—we seem to get so much pleasure out of violence that it has become addictive.

Most solutions offered today aim to reduce violence by trying to control it. We have placed policemen within the school and seek legislation to limit exposure to violent episodes. Yet, at the same time we have changed the rules of sport to allow and encourage more aggressive behavior. Take the example of basketball, which once was a limited contact sport. Today, we witness the physical battles under the basket that would have prompted ejection only a few decades ago. These changes sell products for corporate interests.

As observers of violent acts, that are void of a personal

reality, we have become desensitized to the results of violence, the pain, and human suffering that results from those acts.

The origins of an increase in the need for viewing violent behavior seem to remain a mystery to many. Few recognize that the school system is contributing daily to the planting of seeds for this behavior. The schools and colleges see themselves as dispensers of information, most of which is irrelevant in the lives of students. Beyond the earliest levels of schooling, these institutions are organized with only sporadic regard for daily emerging human needs that are associated with interpersonal relationships that potentially can foster compassion and concern for others. There is ample evidence of a lack of understanding about the role and function of effective group/team development in the routines established for teaching and learning in our conventional schools.

Most educational experiences occur in groups that are just collections of individuals. These assemblies are usually organized more for financial reasons than for reasons of a perceived value in the learning process. In our elementary schools, groups of students are conventionally organized for instruction based on age and corresponding grade levels. Learners of variable developmental capabilities and variable backgrounds are grouped with others who are generally at the same age and placed within chronologically organized grades levels assuming a degree of commonality at each level that does not exist.

Fourth graders, for instance, are assumed to be capable of logical thinking, having reached a mythical level of reasoning. Performance at this grade is judged against that norm. If the learner happens to be developmentally pre-logical or lacks experience, he or she is deemed deficient and is targeted for remediation. If another student happens to be capable of dealing with hypothetical deduction and abstract reasoning and has a wider experiential repertoire, he or she is deemed to be exceptional and will be the recipient of frequent rewards given out by authorities. Those who are in between are at the average for their grade (at grade level) and are considered less bothersome within the system. Instruction for the average is commonplace with special provisions for the above or below average students.

The "Bell Curve" that illustrates a concept of central tendencies has been applied to describe such a phenomenon in statistical terms. Deviations from the mean have become the way to describe the performance of individuals within their groups. If performance is judged to be on the left of the mean (by pre-defined incremental deviations), that is considered below the grade level. If performance is judged as near or slightly above or below the mean, or at the mean, it is considered average for the grade level, or if performance is judged to be at the right of the mean (by pre-defined incremental deviations), it represents above average and superior performance.

Standardized test makers have employed this paradigm continuously throughout many years. They report the progress or lack thereof as measures of deviation from the mean, below, at, or above the mean. The public and the politicians have swallowed this paradigm, lock, stock, and barrel. In the interest of change, dislodging this paradigm will be very difficult.

Collecting and assembling individuals together, arbitrarily defined by age or defined by programs of instruction (classes or courses of study), establishes groups that exist at the lowest levels of development, as defined by the research and literature in this area of study. Warren Bennis and associates, well known and respected authorities in this field, described these groups as functioning at a stage of "dependency." This label is meant to convey that all members of this group at this beginning stage are naturally dependent upon the teacher or the appointed authority.

Appointed leaders can maintain this dependency simply by asserting their assumed authority that grants them institutionally sanctioned power to discipline, coerce, and evaluate. The power to pass, or fail, the power to withhold rewards, the power to control the content of instruction, all can be and are often employed to manage group behavior maintained at this stage of group development. Assertion of authority to maintain order keeps groups at this immature stage. Maintaining this use of authority accounts for much of the rebellion against authority we see played out in society today, especially in the rebellious behavior of teenage groups/gangs Students can only tolerate such a situation for so long before they resort to some sort of rebellion.

Having to "discipline" the learners in a dependent group becomes the dominating need in order to maintain control, before the group gets out of hand. When I was a student teacher, I was told that I must assert my authority right from the first day and maintain it until I could relax a little, but I was told never to let down my guard against a potential rebellion. Not knowing anything about group development, I did as I was told. However, I was uncomfortable with this advice and many years later found out the reasons why.

The alternative to maintaining power over the group, a power granted by the institution, is first to acknowledge the dependency needs of the group as the first stage of development along a continuum of dynamics that culminates at a level of maturity, a truly functioning group. This mature level was described by Bennis as practicing "consensual validation."

A group that functions at this level is a "team" that maintains open and honest communication, develops and implements shared and individual goals and objectives, solves problems and enjoys its own effectiveness and support from all its members. It is successful in its efforts to achieve its shared and individual goals. Occasionally a group will emerge at the level of consensual validation and teachers or coaches will not know how this happened, but will recognize it as something good. They can only hope it will happen again, but of course without insight into the dynamics of groups and the employment of interventions that bring about growth, the likelihood is very slim. Anyone who has ever experienced this level of group/team functioning will sense the value of these qualities. They will also recognize that group maturity is not guaranteed without effective procedures for maintenance. Unfortunately, functioning at this level of experience is seldom witnessed in the typical courses of study in our schools, colleges, and universities.

In a group that functions at a level of consensual validation, leadership roles shift to match the requirements of the group in its effort to accomplish its individual and collective goals. Leadership roles that are mandated by the institution become part of the group's consideration of the needs of the group in recognizing both the opportunities and restrictions regarding group decision-making. These authority roles must eventually be subordinated to the decision making processes of the team.

A current example of subordination can be found in the military. Groups of service personnel are assembled and hopefully developed into a successful team—functioning at the most mature levels of group development, motivated by life and death situations to do so. Even though there is a chain of command sanctioned by the military, rank becomes less important in a life and death situation and the team's orientation to problem solving is paramount to survival. The appointed leader must become an accepted member of the group in this situation. Had the assertion of rank, rather than group sanctioned leadership, been a predominant control- mechanism used in situations of combat there would be many more incidents of "friendly fire." This is not unrelated to the expressions of rebellion acted out in the authority-oriented classrooms of our schools, especially during the adolescent years.

In the classroom, a mature group would define what is to be accomplished and who within the group, if any, can constructively facilitate those experiences needed to accomplish its goals, whether those goals are mastery of the sanctioned curriculum, the requirements of a course of study or whatever. Learners in a fully functioning group will engage the issues of ethics and morality because this behavior becomes important to the establishment and maintenance of a satisfying group experience. A fully functioning group will accomplish its collective goals and at the same time recognize and appreciate the unique contributions each individual can make. In a fully functioning group the needs of each member of the group are considered; those individual needs are celebrated and sanctioned, not destroyed. Fostering a fully functioning group requires continuous maintenance to ensure its ability to function at a level of consensual validation.

An absolute requirement for success in team development is to provide the time needed for this collection of individuals, who are harboring felt and unidentified needs, to process through them as part of the establishment of a fully functioning group. Successful coaches will acknowledge that often it is the end of the season before a team develops to the point where it can accomplish even its more limited goal of winning.

Moving from class to class in a departmental situation negates nearly every aspect of successful team development. Team development cannot be turned on in one day or sustain itself over time with disconnected experiences. A consequence of departmentalization keeps individuals in a dependency state and assertion of the teacher's and the institution's authority becomes the predominate theme.

The teacher at this dependency stage becomes the main authority for what and how subject matter will be presented within a short period of time before the class moves on to the next class where the same procedure is maintained. Compared with what learners might gain from media sources today, the presentation of information made by a teacher during a forty-five minute period is clearly of limited value, perhaps as low as third class information. To be assigned to this task as a supposed authority in a field of study guarantees that few in the group will have the opportunity to maximize their learning and development, not the individual students nor their teacher.

Why then are middle schools, high schools, colleges, and universities using this departmentalized, organizational structure? The answer is simple, but its meaning is profoundly problematic. This organization is based on the assumption that individual learners will profit from the consumption of the pre-selected wisdom of those so called experts in their field, without question and even without personal relevance. Being educated has become synonymous with listening attentively and demonstrating the capacity to pass back to the authorities that which was conveyed during these brief episodes or presentations even when the evidence indicates that this process produces little insight or long-term retention. Of course, there is the matter of limiting expenditures of money.

This orientation is based on a limited definition of learning, a definition that indicates only the most immature, beginning levels. Mature learning requires internal elaborations from simple information or awareness, to translations, extrapolations, application, analysis, synthesis, and critical evaluation (using Bloom's Taxonomy of cognitive development). To accomplish the requirements of this learning sequence, sustained engagement is necessary over a timeframe unique to each individual.

Advanced, sustainable learning requires individual actions taken upon personally experienced information that will require time and extensive reflection. Standardized tests will not measure these higher thought processes since these thoughts are unique creations developed/constructed by each individual. Hence, those with mature insights are graded with individuals with far less maturity, using the same limited examinations. This accounts for the wide disparities in competency that are encountered in every day affairs in today's world. A passing test score does not differentiate between those who have real competency and those who have acquired enough short–term memory to answer the questions "correctly" or have been lucky enough to have guessed correctly when answering test questions.

Fortunately, individuals who have initiated expanded learning opportunities, on their own, can utilize the information presented as part of a much larger, personally-developed perceptual field. They can transform the presentations into meaningful and personally relevant uses. The same information that is presented, if considered within a fully functioning group, would likely be transformed into meaningful constructs in a shortened time frame and with maximized relevancy and utility. This is as true for young learners as it is for older adults.

If the learner has sufficient background to assimilate the messages presented by the teacher or college professor, and the environment for learning supports each individual's uniqueness, learning will occur by those who will combine the information with previously created constructions and formulate new and unique transformations. To assume that regurgitating the messages received, in a form that matches those of the presenter, is acceptable evidence of learning represents a serious error.

Messages received are always significantly different from the messages presented, due in part to the uniquely different experiential background of the receiver. To test for the exact interpretations of the presenter and make the judgment that this represents significant learning is pure folly. Learning is only begun with information. Learning occurs along a continuum that eventually emerges in time at the problem solving level. Individual initiative is required to reach this level and motivation to continue learning is its by-product.

To progress from the level of group dependency to the mature level of consensual validation, there is an interim level that is the most difficult to manage. Misinterpretation of the meaning of this level of group development results in groups remaining at the dependency stage. This interim level of "independence" is a necessary stage between dependency and interdependency. If this level is not allowed to progress, the most mature levels will remain an unattainable goal.

The hallmark of dependency is sublimation of personal

needs and aspirations and more or less acceptance of the pronouncements of an authority figure. The hallmark of independence is an open and honest revelation of heretofore undisclosed, perceived needs and aspirations. Since this revelation includes many differences of opinion, the opportunities for conflict are increased. These conflicts must be managed effectively by the group leader for the group to remain in existence and to progress to more mature levels of communication.

Opinions of individuals must not be eliminated or disregarded. On the contrary, they must be talked about and acted upon in a civil manner. These differences of opinion must be viewed as important to the person expressing them and worthy of respect. These differences are the honest expression of what is important to each person at the time and their expression provides an opportunity to recognize the uniqueness of each individual. Civil consideration of these differences leads to the resolution of potential conflicts by offering solutions and providing acceptance and respect for the value of each individual who has expressed them. Skills in conflict resolution result from this type of experience. Achievement of this level of maturity will vary with each group due to its unique make-up and procedures. Hence it requires a sustained experience until the goals are met, and this achievement does not lend itself to an arbitrary point on the calendar when school is over.

In the process of sharing differences there is also the opportunity to discover similarities in the experiences of individuals. This discussion begins to form an improved level of acceptance and appreciation of each person and establishes the basis for becoming more effective communicators. When refined, this orientation will progress to a level of interdependency marked by consensual validation in communication that carries over into other aspects of the lives of these individuals.

There is a temptation to view these conflictive situations as a breakdown in the authority and control within the group. In most conventional school settings, an authority figure will intercede and redirect or squelch the dialogue. I have witnessed many times, the efforts of uninformed administrators, within schools and colleges, the keepers of authority, to intercede from the outside of the group to micro-manage its internal affairs. They often do this out of ignorance of group development principles. By interceding, they destroy the opportunity for the group to take responsibility for its behavior, to mature and learn what it means to problem solve and join with the efforts of fellow members in actualizing the successful attainment of group and institutional goals and objectives. Of course, administrators cannot afford to allow uninformed teachers to mismanage the affairs of their groups, since parents and the public would likely object.

Unfortunately, most teachers are not fully conversant with group development research and interventions, and do not perform in the classroom with an adequate grasp of what is involved. Their teacher education programs are mostly void of an in-depth investigation into the theories and principles of group dynamics and in particular group development. An intensive in-service program would be needed to actualize these sound principles that were derived from extensive research and development at the National Training Laboratories back in the 1940s.

In a recent revision of the U.S. Air Force service manual, there is a chapter on group processes and decision making. While this translation leaves much to be desired, it demonstrates comparatively just how outmoded the organization of the conventional school is in regard to group development that has been allowed to continue.

If differences of opinion are revealed at the dependency level, the person in a conventional authority relationship to the group, whether a teacher or an administrator, will most likely take steps to squelch the discussion by asserting his or her power. Without the effective resolution of the potential conflicts of the group, the most mature levels will not be attained and the group will grudgingly disintegrate to the level of dependency for some, and outright rebellion for others.

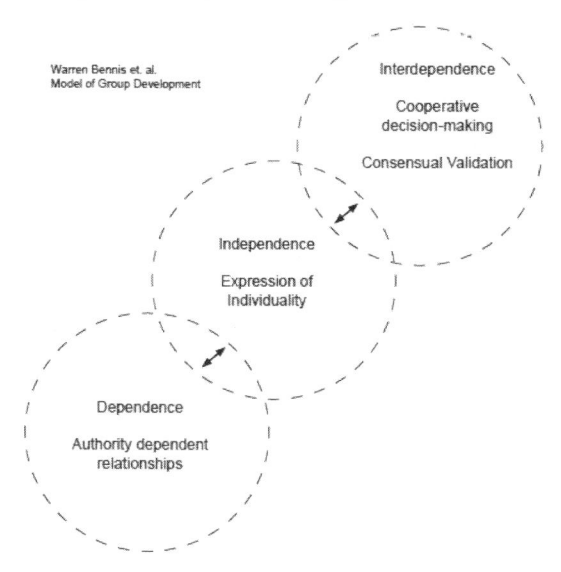

Warren Bennis et. al.
Model of Group Development

- Interdependence
  - Cooperative decision-making
  - Consensual Validation

- Independence
  - Expression of Individuality

- Dependence
  - Authority dependent relationships

In summary, the illustration that follows is a model of group development based on Bennis' research and writings.

There is an erroneous assumption that adult and young adult learners do not need a sustained small group experience. Nothing could be further from the truth. As a result of this assumption, most school and college experiences are organized for an efficient presentation of information that is more or less expected to be assimilated by each student. Consider the following once again:

Human beings are social beings who depend on effective communication with oneself and with one's friends, relatives, and associates for the achievement and maintenance of an intellectually productive, healthy personal orientation with life.

The first and most fundamental reality about communication between two or more human beings is that the meanings transferred through verbal and non-verbal communications are never identical in the mind of each participant.

The second reality is that we humans cannot, not communicate. Whether we want to or not, we communicate through our behavior both verbal and non-verbal. How that behavior is interpreted by others is dependent upon their internal structures. Even one's own internal interpretation of personal meanings is dependent upon the application of pre-developed, biased internal structures.

The interpretation of any communication is governed by the unique intellectual structures held by each participant.

Messages are assimilated into pre-organized structures; these structures impose their particular bias on the message and mold it to fit a pre-determined orientation. Thus, the message sent is never the identical message received. Acceptance of a correspondence of thought is achieved through repeated exchanges, yet its final conclusions are never, never identical. (Think about this in the context of classroom instruction.)

Acceptable validation between the senders and the receivers of the true meanings in the communication are sought by continuing the exchanges that lead to a mutual acceptance of the similarities of meanings held by each participant.

The intermediary conditions (outlined in the Introduction) that can impede or encourage validation of the exchanges between communicants are these: (1) The quality of the social context in which the communication takes place; this can be hostile or accepting, supportive or variously destructive, (2) The motivation for pursuing the communication, related to one's energy level, health status and need, (3) The level of maturation reached by each participant that exists at the time of the communication which allows or impedes messages. A child, for instance, who is at the level of pre-operations, with pre-logical capabilities, will not engage a logical argument in terms relevant in that instance. Instead, the pre-logical youngster will be free to define the messages in any way that occurs to him or her, a characteristic of the behavior of a youngster at this level of functioning, (4) The level, type, quality and quantity of experience encountered by each participant; a variable with importance that cannot be overstated. Often labeled "readiness" for learning and communicating, this requirement must be taken seriously and granted the time necessary for ensuring a reasonable match between the underlying meanings of the messages given and the messages received.

While there are many sources of information, including that presented by the school and supplemented by the media and communicated through a variety of electronic communications technologies, learning can be most effectively attained when it is developed within sustained group experiences that follow the principles of group development. While the "homeroom" concept in elementary schools comes close to a group experience, it is neither sustained nor an integral part of the processes of learning of academic concerns. It does not meet the criteria for sustaining effective group development.

If the school was organized for sustained small group development and the resources for learning opened for selection by the learners, a breakthrough could be happening in the learning outcomes of every individual. Coupled with a recordkeeping system that contains the learner's translations of experiences from wherever they originate, the needs of individuals can be met and the need to monitor institutional progress can be facilitated. The Constructive Assessment, Recordkeeping, and Evaluation System (CARES), discussed in detail elsewhere, would provide this opportunity.

Group development principles must be initiated at an early age. Once the tendency to behave aggressively occurs at the adolescent years, these attitudes have already been established. It becomes difficult, but not impossible, to change these aggressive attitudes after they have been established. A sustained therapeutic group experience can accomplish these changes in time.

To continue this early group experience, the schools and colleges must maintain and foster support groups that will promote awareness of the destructive nature of violence, competition and conflict so that individuals will be prepared to counter a potential obsession. These support groups must become the nexus for effective learning about life in all its manifestations, no matter where or when it occurs.

The opportunity to witness firsthand the results of our educational systems may well be played out in Washington. The behavior of party members in our government is likely evidence of the learning outcomes of some schools, both public and private. This is not a matter of placing blame; it is a matter of fact, recognizable if only most of the public would remove the blinders they may have developed.

The attitudes and values, beliefs and assumptions that direct behavior are developed gradually over time from past experiences, many of those experiences have occurred in our elementary, middle, and secondary schools. The school experiences are reinforced today by sound bites viewed daily in much of the media, reinforced by computer games, and displayed in trivial exchanges through social networks. The resultant attitudes and values developed through these experiences now-a-days often reflect rigid adherence to stereotypes and ideologies that remain unchallenged.

Once these orientations are established they are difficult to change, even in the face of overwhelming contrary evidence. Repetitious behavior is predominantly out of touch with the dynamic realities of the here and now in today's world. But challenging stereotypical behaviors during instruction unfortunately appears often to be considered off limits in this age of "political correctness."

Consider these questions. Is the inability to see the relationships of one set of ideas on another being fostered in our schools? Listen to the political rhetoric that often relates to the felt concerns of our citizenry and then consider the actual facts of the reality. Is this a prime example of the failure of our educational system to develop an awareness of the relationship of one set of ideas on another? Could an absence of this skill and insight be related to the isolated, disconnected, departmentalized experiences with abstract subjects taught but not learned?

Is the lack of recall related to the extent to which information has not been processed and internalized, but rather simply passed through the mind and never put into fresh combinations?

Can a dependence on authority result in demands that the President act like a king and direct the affairs of government? Is this a reflection of the hierarchical organization of the school and the lack of concrete knowledge of civics in our constitutionally run country? Does a "group-think" orientation come from practices that encourage standardization, grouping and judging all students on the basis of inflexible and limited criteria? Could this be related to the use of standardized tests, designed in a one-size-fits-all format? Is immature, ego-driven behavior developed in our schools and reinforced in the home, leading to those frames of mind that influence, if not direct, diminishing social behavior, individually and as a group?

How does it happen that our representatives seem not to communicate effectively and fail to function as a mature group? Is this related to the fact that our schools maintain a departmentalized structure where the sustained group experiences that are needed to develop the skills of communication and mature group behavior are limited—where matters of unethical and immoral behavior are disregarded? Have many of these representatives passed their standardized examinations and received the accolades of a system that rewards superficiality, disguised with grade point averages and graduation with honors? Why do so few exhibit observable skills for problem solving and behave with a scarcity of ethics to carry out their responsibilities? Have they been taught to ignore their sense of concern for fellow human beings?

Why is it that almost no one seems to recognize the connection between the structure of our school systems and the tragedy played out in Washington? How much longer can we sustain what we can only assume to be a democracy, when facing an inability to develop grown-ups who can act responsibly as citizens of a real democracy? When are we going to recognize that we desperately need systemic change in the way we educate and develop our youth, if we hope they will behave in a more mature fashion when they assume an active role in our democracy, if it still exists when they come of age?

Are those who think the results of standardized tests indicate anything related to the needs of our democracy wrong? Standardized tests do not differentiate between individuals who may have developed competency in the limited subject-matter they purport to take responsibility for and those who simply have enough short term memory to pass the test. Can we expect a change when charter schools mirror the same procedures that have shown to be gradually destroying our democratic way of life?

Very little formal education is conducted as independent study; instruction occurs mostly in groups of varying sizes. Yet, a review of teacher education programs and so called innovations introduced in our schools reveals a scarcity of emphasis on group dynamics, group development and group interventions, other than the usual disciplining and class management techniques and lesson planning, advocated by those who seem to know little about the theory and practice of small groups. It is disturbing to note that Wikipedia describes group dynamics as "Relevant to the field of psychology, sociology, and communications studies" and Education is not mentioned.

The researchers who initiated the serious study of group dynamics in the nineteen forties began their work at the National Training Laboratory founded by Kurt Lewin and Leland Bradford with headquarters in Bethel, Maine. Their work produced a plethora of literature about the theory and practice of groups. Familiar names like Kurt Lewin, Warren Bennis, Ronald Lippitt, Leland Bradford, Kenneth Benne, Douglas McGregor, Chris Argyris among others, including Richard and Patricia Schmuck and Carl Rogers of more recent times, have frequently appeared in the professional and popular literature with a special focus on the application of the theory of groups in education, apparently with little impact on the conduct of our schools.

These early researchers produced a superb series of handbooks that have served well many groups outside of education. An outstanding article that appeared in *The Adult Education Quarterly* in the Spring of 1958, written by Leland P. Bradford, entitled: "The Teaching-Learning Transaction" is just one of many that warrant resurrection in this age of turmoil in the seeking of change in public education. What will it take to get the policy makers and the public to read and reflect upon these works?

A group process-related emphasis on in-service training for teachers surfaced in the nineteen sixties, first as sensitivity training and later as encounter and marathon groups. Experiments with these innovations unfortunately were practiced without a full awareness of the potential for encouraging "over exposure" where participants were left with raw, unresolved feelings about their revealed personal dilemmas. This contributed to a short tenure for such concerns in education.

This was an emotional response to perceived irrelevancy in schools and colleges, as part of the counter revolution movement that swept this country. Its half-life was shortened by the resurgence of conservatism, in the "back to the basics" political changes that were a reaction to the openness being advocated by students and some adventurous adults. Architects picked up on this movement and designed schools as open architecture with lots of flexible space. Most of these buildings have since been re-constructed to conform to the more traditional egg crate structures that are more suited to formal instruction in isolated classrooms. Open architecture, open education, along with the rest of the movement, faded into the woodwork and has seldom been heard from since.

I had experience supervising student teachers in an open architecture school building that was converted to isolated classrooms. Temporary walls were constructed within previously designed open spaces and it would take me days to find all of my student teachers in this "rat maze."

So why should group process literature be resurrected as a part of the solution in re-directing today's failed public schools? To begin to understand the answer to this question, there is a need to examine what is being practiced with groups, as the mainstay of instruction at all levels of conventional education, contrasting this with what has been known about group processes and group development for at least the past sixty years.

It's important to restate the purpose of group development and the desired outcome of group development that is improved communication. Small groups of fifteen to twenty members provide an opportunity for dealing with the individual needs and aspirations of every member, encountering and resolving the impediments to communication and learning as they are happening. I found, even with the skills of group facilitation, a group of 22 members was the limit for fostering healthy and growth producing interactions. (Of course, large group instruction can be used to efficiently dispense information and this can be effective for those who are adequately prepared to use the information in their personal lives. Unfortunately, readiness to receive these messages is often overlooked.)

Becoming sensitive to the individual needs and unique perceptions and understanding of what Whitehead referred to as "life in all its manifestations" is a necessary and important part of group dynamics. When handled effectively, confronting life as it is occurring results in vastly improved communication and personal productiveness. If sound group processes are initiated in early years when there is an active curiosity and fewer rigid stereotypes, attitudes and values can be developed that do not just tolerate individuality, but celebrates its value in the formation of a productive society. These attitudes when sustained throughout the educational experience will result in more fully functioning groups composed of unique and more competent individuals, ready and willing to work together to solve problems in a mutually supportive environment.

When I began preparing for teaching several sections of a course entitled "Human Development and Behavior" for students in an elementary education program I studied the usual texts that others had used and passed on to me for use in my classes. The texts and their accompanying tests fit into the conventional model that most faculty used with their college students. This model was certainly not one that I could embrace, in fact, I had eliminated it from my repertoire many years before.

I was faced with the realization that I had to invent a way of handling a legitimate course in Human Development and Behavior in ways consistent with my creative orientation to history and geography. I concluded that relevant information was necessary for students to be able to create personal and institutional meanings in this subject matter, in ways consistent with treating this discipline as a way of knowing. I decided that each person's experience throughout life contained the raw data for making sense out of the development and behavior of human beings. I was confident that acting upon those data would produce a conceptual framework that would enable each student to identify with the language and concepts detailed by experts in this area of study and understand the dynamics of life for others.

I devised a procedure for assisting each student in resurrecting past events that had a bearing on current development and behavior. The first step in this procedure asked all students to create a listing of personal experiences that were regarded as contributing to who they had become. The list was to be kept confidential at this stage so that personal information could be included that the individual would not wish to divulge openly. The directions suggested that the listing be truthful and extensive, collected over several days and kept for later reference.

Students began building their lists and at a time when

they were felt to be complete, the next step was explained. Students were to examine their personalized listings and group these random entries in categories that were inclusive of all the information. For instance, those events that related to their school experience would be grouped in a category and labeled accordingly.

Likewise, information relating to experiences with religion, to social events, family ties, and family trauma were included as separate categories. Groupings were required to be inclusive of all the information entered in the original list and any other facts recalled in the process of studying the entries. The original lists numbered in some cases several hundred items. These random entries were reduced to a dozen or so categories.

After the categories were constructed and written down, the students were asked to determine how these categories related one to another. What was to be considered had to do with the relative importance and juxtaposition of categories. Some would identify family relationships as having the most influential bearing on their development, while others would list a devastating school experience or any number of other categories. Some of the categories would be closely related and others were viewed to be in opposition, one with the other.

Once this procedure was engaged, the students were asked to construct a visual model that illustrated the groupings and how they related one to another. These models consisted of pencil and paper drawings, diagrams, mobiles, three-dimensional illustrations, arts and crafts that were designed to aid communication of the essence of the relationships as seen through the eyes of its creator.

I constructed my model in the same way I prescribed for the students. These models were then shared with fellow class members so that comparisons could be made and ideas refined that would lead to important insights about human development and behavior.

It was important to remind these students that their

formulations would provide the foundation for understanding what often is viewed as a complex subject matter. This subject matter is conventionally viewed as the prerogative of professionals in a mysterious enterprise much of it conducted behind closed doors by psychologists and psychiatrists. It is often thought of as a topic that could possibly do harm if handled inappropriately by amateurs. Confidentiality is of utmost importance and in our procedure it was given that important status. Students were reminded that each contribution must be respected for its reflection of the view of another person, something to be learned from, not ridiculed.

With these important rules adhered to in the course of sharing the individual models, something astonishing happened. There was a level of appreciation for the similarities and differences in life's experiences that I had seldom witnessed before, especially among college students from a variety of backgrounds. Empathic communication resulted in productive discussions focused on personally relevant information that had enormous implications for understanding human development and behavior.

Like my previous experience with history and geography, the processes of coming to know resulted in vastly increased motivation to embrace the subject matter, knowing that it had the potential for making life more personally understandable and more productive.

This experience prompted me to investigate the literature on communication, group processes, and group development.

With this discovery of a working model each member of the class was then in a position to view the text materials from a more insightful and critical position than ordinarily experienced in the conventional class lectures and test-taking format.

The students were able to transfer their constructions of what human development and behavior involves, to the study of the technical language and abstract constructs found in text materials. They demonstrated their insights through successes on a limited use of typical tests.

One student from that class decided to use a mathematical construct to present his information. The application of this mathematical model was so sophisticated that a journal accepted his materials for publication. It had the effect of helping fellow students with their struggles to see relevancy in the study of mathematics. Most students felt lost with mathematics resulting from past instruction in that field—instruction that often starts with memorization and continues with that strategy long after that level of learning no longer has any utility. If you ever tried memorizing algorithms of trigonometry, you know what I mean.

Since the college expected the students to be tested at the end of the semester and a grade submitted for the record, I went about devising a testing procedure modeled after the Environmental Relationships Test. The content, of course, was not geology etc. but rather dimensions of human development and behavior. The students were instructed to piece together the patterns that revealed their concepts of important elements of human concerns and their abilities to translate the technical language and expert propositions that indicated a sophisticated level of mastery. The administration was impressed with our creativity and the products of learning illustrated by the tests.

The following year, I was asked to team teach with a visiting "distinguished professor" Alice Keliher, who was assigned a group of senior elementary teacher candidates. When the seminar began I was thoroughly impressed to see how this visiting personage related to her/our students. She knew their names and a great deal about them on the first day of class. She listened to them with sincere empathy. This experience reinforced my belief that it was appropriate to be personal in communication with and concerned about the individual needs and aspirations of young people. As a result of this experience

I made an extra effort to be myself in my communications, able to give encouragement to other members of any group.

In graduate school, I enrolled in a seminar that was conducted by two authorities in the field of psychology and human development. One of these instructors, Arthur Jersild, had written and revised numerous textbooks for use in teaching human development and behavior with a particular emphasis on child development. The other, Millie Almy, coordinated the U.S.A. replication studies designed to accurately reveal the essence of the theories and constructs developed by Jean Piaget.

The seminar was divided into two three week sessions and the child development specialist took over the first three weeks. Keep in mind that I came to this class having assisted my students in developing models of their personality dynamics and had developed my own as well.

As the instructor presented his vast knowledge and insights, much of it in a conversational mode, I assimilated into my model what he had to say. Everything he revealed fit into the structure I had brought with me to class.

My fellow students were always busy copying down bits of information they thought to be important. They took volumes of notes. I sat there drinking in what was being offered and occasionally would jot down something I wanted particularly to remember as it was said, or some thought that didn't fully integrate with what I had previously learned. I reorganized my model occasionally to take those changes into account.

This instructor was steeped in the testing movement of Thorndike so test items that were predominately multiple choice questions appeared on his final exam. He had identified about three hundred questions that covered nearly everything he had discussed throughout the three weeks. I felt I had little trouble answering the questions correctly even though I didn't spend much time preparing for the exam.

My colleagues spent the whole night before the exam cramming for the test.

When I attended the final session of that segment, this instructor asked that I meet him in his office at the conclusion of the class. This conjured up a long standing fear that I must have "bombed" the test.

He sat behind a pile of papers and books that he had been working on. When I entered his office, he said: "You are not a psychology major, are you?" His question reminded me that all the fellow students were psychology majors. He then proceeded to ask me how I would explain that I had the highest score in his class. Obviously he suspected that I had found an advanced copy of the exam and had memorized the answers.

To his amazement, I explained to him that I had brought with me a model of human development and behavior constructed with my students and validated through the use of standard texts. He told me that I had only missed two questions. I asked him which ones they were and we discussed what brought me to answer them the way I did. After this discussion, he admitted that the questions could have been answered differently if one assumes a different set of facts. This encounter led to an extended relationship involving assisting in his work with a Long Island school system that offered courses in human development for high school students.

The second three week session was directed by a leading authority on the work of Jean Piaget. I was familiar with Piaget's writings and the mystique that surrounded his work. He was often criticized by educators, researchers, and psychologists in this country since he was known to have begun development of his formulations by observing his own children. Certainly, in the eyes of those steeped in the "objectivity" methodologies of research in this country, observations of one's own children could not be taken seriously. Beyond this criticism, many objected to his stage theory as being too definitive and perhaps arbitrary.

I remember reading a speech Piaget delivered at Cornell

University translated by Eleanor Duckworth. She often translated his work for the English speaking world. Piaget took this opportunity to lament that psychologists and educators in the U.S. had misinterpreted his work in significant ways. He indicated that they prostituted his constructivist theory by trying to squeeze it into their behaviorist models.

Piaget particularly directed his comments toward the Harvard psychologist who reported the Woods Hole Conference on Math and Science and used his name to buttress claims for the appropriateness of teaching the structures of disciplines to youngsters of any age.

The instructor in this seminar segment had directed replication studies to determine if Piaget's stage theories and methodologies could be validated. Her studies indeed suggested that Piaget's framework and data gathering processes were not only valid but they had far reaching implications for teaching and learning in our schools.

Piaget's stages were labeled sensory motor, pre-operations, concrete operations, and formal operations, in that order. Although he labeled the stages, he viewed the developmental sequence as continuous wherein one stage blended into the next. The labels were seen as benchmarks rather than absolutes.

I found the class discussions to be very exciting. My experience with students of primary, intermediate and high school age provided a vast reservoir of direct observations that helped me to a better understanding of the application of Piaget's theory. His formulations made sense to me.

Everyone in this seminar had to prepare a lengthy paper for review, indicating our individual understanding of Piaget's schema and our thoughts about the application of this formulation in our schools. I chose to compare Piaget's work, as I understood it, with several popular authors who claimed to be indebted to him. These authors exemplified what Piaget had complained about in his speech at Cornell. They indeed were attributing their importance to Piaget while "squeezing" his constructivist formulations into behaviorist orientations that, upon close examination, were found to be incompatible.

The truth of this is best explained by the statements made in *The Process of Education* about how "the" structures of disciplines could be taught in some legitimate form to those of any age. What is required in grasping a sense of structure in any discipline requires intellectual capacity for logic. Piaget's conservation experiments reveal the emergence of logical thinking at the level of concrete operations. This stage on average is found to be about the age of seven, or later, give or take a year or two. The lack of developmental readiness to deal logically with a subject matter would preclude grasping any real meaning of the structure of a discipline. Furthermore, expecting that youngsters at the pre-operational stage could grasp this abstract notion is ludicrous.

The truth is that such an expectation would not only be unfulfilled, but probably harmful. This is because the hallmark of pre-operations is a freedom to invent creative responses to experience since youngsters at this level are not encumbered by having to logically test reality. Teaching "the structure of disciplines" would not produce conformity with the pre-ordained meanings they were expected to learn.

Piaget's constructivist position suggests that individuals construct their own meanings that are consistent with the level of their intellectual capabilities.

Individual development is biologically-based, and will mature if prior experiences have not thwarted or killed those capabilities before they have a chance to emerge.

Any practices in schools that ignore this reality are doing great harm to the potential capabilities of individual students. Take the example of reading instruction in our schools across this country. Students are introduced to isolated letters of the alphabet with the expectation that someday this will be transferred to the processes of learning to read. There is relative meaninglessness in the introduction of these letters.

Its relative because meaning is developed, but it is most

likely manifested for many students in a diminished respect and confidence in personal capabilities. When repeated enough times, within a punishment and rewards context, students will respond in ways that teachers view as validation of their work.

Instead of spending time tediously repeating the letters of the alphabet with pre-operational youngsters, the schools should be offering a wide variety of experiences in participative functioning groups that stimulate personal responses with all forms of language, verbal and non-verbal, including visual expression through art. Initial responses to experiences at this stage are holistic, not piece-by piece that seldom adds up to the whole. Verbal language comes naturally from being exposed to verbal language, whole words and sentences expressed in the context of communication. Reading to and speaking with learners develops a connection with words that are engaged in their entirety; only later are these words meaningfully connected to the written form.

When the youngster is approaching concrete operations, making connections between letters and language, the printed version of spoken language will naturally emerge, if there are no physical constraints or mental impediments that resulted from less than meaningful prior instruction. Like the acquisition of verbal language, reading comes naturally from being exposed to reading by first being read to, when those experiences are consistent with the developmental capacities of the individual. Independent reading comes gradually through trial and error with feedback from significant adults. The logical structures of language become meaningful to a learner at a late concrete operational stage.

My instructor read my treatise on Piaget with special interest. She asked if I was sure that Piaget held some of the beliefs that I had attributed to him. I had found numerous examples of discrepancies between translations and what I concluded were Piaget's positions. I used a film in my classes entitled *Piaget on Piaget*. The film was prepared under his supervision in hopes of clarifying his position.

However, the French language spoken by Piaget was translated into English sub-titles. There were differences that, to many, appeared to be subtle and therefore considered not too important. With a background that included an understanding of the patterns established between concepts in Piaget's formulations, I saw instances where concepts were misrepresented, that were incompatible with his pattern of thinking, or left out entirely. I came to that class with a strong belief in consistency within any pattern and if items were missing they could be reconstructed reliably to fit the pattern.

Many so-called authorities on Piaget exhibited less than inclusive interpretations of the scholarly work of this man. This is a probable byproduct of a school system and philosophy that deals almost exclusively with piecemeal instruction rather than promoting creative construction of structures, patterns, and interrelated conceptual frameworks.

This belief system has to change if improvement in our schools is to take place.

In the course of attending classes, teaching and learning, I also enjoyed frequent discussions with a friend, Frank Jennings, who at the time was the educational director of the New World Foundation, an author who wrote about Piaget and the processes of learning to read, and an editor-at-large of the *Saturday Review of Literature*.

Jennings introduced me to the book *Neurotic Distortions of the Creative Process*, by Lawrence Kubie, a psychiatrist who was particularly interested in the processes of education or miss-education. His book was published in the late 1950s.

Kubie introduced me to the roles of the unconscious, pre-conscious, and conscious dimensions of mind. His work spoke volumes about the role of rigid responses to life's experiences and the tendency to distort those experiences to fit preconditions that have resulted from the myriad experiences in one's past. The details of those experiences may have long since been forgotten but their residue remains in the form of fears, stereotypes, and orientations to life both positive and negative. Kubie's work provided me with plausible explanations for the widespread resistance to change I frequently encountered throughout my career.

Citing numerous examples drawn from clinical experiences and studies, Kubie developed a compelling story of how we have been damaged by the processes of education that form our neuroses—rigid response patterns that are seldom modified sufficiently even in so called normal life and in need of dramatic change in those whose lives have become unbearable.

Kubie's model was summarized in a diagram that illustrated the relationship of the unconscious, the pre-conscious, and the conscious mind. He showed the unconscious to be beneath the other two dimensions of mind projecting onto those dimensions whatever response patterns that had been developed over one's lifetime.

The pre-conscious was viewed as having the capacity for creative, spontaneous responses to experience provided it was not adversely affected by a rigid response pattern of the unconscious. The conscious mind was viewed as an extension of the pre-conscious, the aspect of mentation that originates the creative manipulations of life's input, shaped by those orientations that originate in the repertoire of the unconscious mind.

Consciousness involves language and logical analysis that reflects the other two dimensions in many ways, in our language and behavior

I have continued to study, think about, and expand Kubies's model since it explained so many things important to learning and development. Kubie did a masterful job showing how formalized, segmented education has helped to create the neurotic distortions that shape our responses to life's daily experiences and how educators have done little to correct this shortcoming. I have presented an expanded version of Kubie's construct, using the computer as a model that correlates with the dimensions of mind.

I have presented this expanded model with students who struggle to find meaning in their lives and make connections with the content of their course work in personal health, psychology, and human development. Testimony to the usefulness of this formulation has been generously received by every group who participated in defining this model. They were able to see the relationships between heretofore isolated and relatively meaningless concepts outlined in their texts.

The next experience discussed here may seem impossible to carry out. I proposed that I would work full time with a group of randomly selected freshman planning to enter teacher education. I explained in my proposal that I had an extensive background and experience with the proposition that students needed to engage in hands-on experiences with each discipline, at least until they constructed a conceptual framework that revealed the essence of that discipline, when they would become effective and critical consumers of other's propositions. I stated that my experience with history and geography and the classes with Phenix gave me confidence that this task would be successful. This type of experience would allow students to be more efficient and competent consumers of the subject matter required by the college.

I proposed that I assume responsibility for engaging a group of freshman in the official program offered to students entering elementary teacher education. The standard general education courses included among others, basic mathematics, science, which included biology, botany, zoology and astronomy, art and art history, English and literature, human development and behavior and American History. I proposed that I would demonstrate that these students would be able to show significant evidence of mastery and motivation in all of these areas and engage their studies with enthusiasm and self-confidence.

Twenty-two students appeared on the first Monday

morning, anxious to find out what they had been selected to endure. The group included two older married students, several young relatives of immigrants from the Caribbean, including Cuba, and a majority of graduates of the schools of nearby urban communities. It took a great deal of reassurance from the President of the College to reduce their anxieties about entering this experimental program.

One of the older students particularly was traumatized by the thought that she would be involved in experiences quite different from those she anticipated to be consistent with what she knew about schools. After considerable discussion, the group remained and our work began.

The traumatized student mentioned above, had a particularly difficult time breaking from the past when dealing with mathematics. She was struggling with conceptualizing bases other than ten. She would share her thoughts and I would simply encourage her to continue by responding to a few questions. One day she came to class, flying on cloud nine. She went to the board and began writing what had been revealed to her when she was awakening that morning. She had a breakthrough and she knew it. Not only did mathematics have a great deal more meaning, she had experienced a new and powerful sense of her abilities to figure things out on her own. This student never went back to her old ways of segmented thinking. She went on to graduate school and finished her doctorate. She taught at a university in Arizona.

I knew from past experiences with classes dealing with human development and behavior that the exercise in self-understanding that I described earlier would help these students begin to embrace the subject matter required by the college. I also knew that the process of sharing self-models would develop appreciation for the differences and similarities found in the life experiences of every member of the group.

I didn't understand fully the implications of what transpired when my group first shared themselves. It wasn't until much later that I discovered a rich literature that helped me understand what was happening in the context of group processes and group development. All I knew was that a group was forming that featured open communication, mutual respect, and shared responsibility. I didn't need to know the theory behind group processes at that point in time. I simply recognized that it was happening. Any teacher or coach recognizes this phenomenon when it happens even though they may not know or fully appreciate why it happened.

My study of groups has led me to a much more sophisticated understanding of group dynamics that allows me to shape predictable activities of group development leading to the achievement of group maturity. Every teacher must become conversant with the group process literature and test out the validity of the theories in their own experiences that will translate into interventions that work in the classroom.

None of my freshman group of students had ever experienced the out of doors as a camper or visitor of the wilderness. They were all raised in an urban setting. Even though it only cost 25 cents to cross the Hudson River to Manhattan, few had gone there. Here was a group that had little to rely upon but their past experience enduring their classes and passing the tests that allowed them to enter the college.

I knew that these students had missed out on many experiences that were available and they hadn't really examined what they had experienced in their relatively isolated lives. I set about to provide them with direct experiences that would introduce them to the fundamentals upon which much of the required subject matter was based. For instance, we went to a Staten Island beach and dug for clams and other specimens that were buried in the sand. We took the specimens back to the science laboratory for further examination. This investigation was part of the biological studies required in their program. It was then that I first encountered the resistance of fellow faculty at the college.

I discovered that the keys to the microscope cabinet were not available to us. The head of the science department took it upon himself to show his disdain for the project in the name of protecting "his" sensitive laboratory equipment. I reported this to the President and he immediately phoned the science department head. He instructed this person to unlock the cabinet and assist in any way he could to help the students and their teacher.

We referred to the standard text used in the biology course at the college, and found the part that dealt with specimens of living creatures that matched our discoveries. This provided an opportunity to organize that text so that it was more meaningful. We identified other experiences we needed to fill in areas of knowledge that we lacked. Other field trips were planned around our needs and interests. We crossed the Hudson and visited the Bronx Zoo, the Museum of Natural History, the Botanical gardens, and the wilderness areas of the state.

I'll never forget my reaction to the first visitation to the Natural History Museum when the students ran through the exhibits and were ready to go home in less than an hour. While this was disappointing, I knew that it meant this experience did not serve a real need as yet and I had much more work to do. Gradually, as we experienced more of the natural world, our return trips to that same museum were more rewarding. We visited many times for specific purposes and in the end spent hours studying the displays and were reluctant to leave at the end of the day.

Each of these experiences were recorded, backed up by the texts and visual aids, and gradually integrated into a model of the discipline that made sense and was validated by experts in those fields. We had access to involvement from other faculty members who were willing to share their insights and they entered into the dialogue and served to validate our constructions. These discussions were very rewarding for me and my students.

We attended many events in Manhattan such as Broadway plays, "An Evening With (Robert) Frost," etc. and visited the Metropolitan Museum of Art. We camped out with handicapped children and visited with students in elementary classes, helping out whenever we were needed.

One experience stands out in my mind. We visited the Willow Brook Institution before Robert Kennedy had called attention to its appalling conditions. We were greeted by a man who was labeled an "idiot savant." He asked each of us to share with him the date on which we were born. He would then proceed to tell us the correct day of the week on which that event took place. We all were amazed, but reminded about how little we knew about human development and behavior.

In the course of our day at Willow Brook we visited many areas of that institution's facility. We were exposed to the most unforgettable situations one can imagine. Dozens of infants were in an enclosed area, naked and living in their own feces; their cries still ring loudly in my ears.

We entered a so called recreation room for adults. There were probably fifty adults crammed into this small room, standing toe to toe, face to face. When they saw us they literally embraced us as they were completely starved for affection. They reached into our pockets and took our wallets and money. It took a great effort to retrieve our valuables before we left.

The whole experience was so devastating that we could not even eat the meal we were offered. Instead, we all went home with our thoughts and feelings that were beyond any words we could say. We left in complete silence.

We took the next day off to recover from the effects of that experience. When we reconvened we began to describe how we felt. There was an outpouring of expression that took the form of poetry, music, paintings, and stories. This level of creativity was never experienced by this group before. Through this experience all members of the group discovered something about themselves that almost never occurs in the context of school. They developed a much greater appreciation for the creative efforts of others, whether it comes in the form of a novel, a painting, a drama, or sculpture.

Another experience that was related to their course requirements took place on campus. There was a building constructed nearby the original structure that housed the President's office and numerous classrooms. This building was an ivy-covered, Victorian structure typical of college campuses. The new science and mathematics building next door was a stark, multicolored, building with metal window frames and doors. There was no shrubbery to be found at the foundation. The contrast between this "neo-nazi" structure, that was a modern structure, and the old Victorian structure that served the college for many years was striking.

We decided to add some aesthetics to the campus and further explore what we were studying in art and botany. We designed a landscaping plan to soften the harsh lines of this new building and make our planting a botanical garden. We drew plans with the help of art department members. The plan would use shrubbery in ways that would beautify the building.

The selection of the individual plant specimens considered the climate, rainfall, and soil conditions around the building. We selected shrubs of many varieties so that our botanical garden would be complete. We contacted several nurseries to determine availability and costs. We approached the city and the college administration to secure funding which actually was limited to several hundred dollars.

We found the city to be cooperative, much to the surprise of many, and they agreed to help us plant the shrubs when they arrived. On that day, the trucks from the nurseries came to the campus and unloaded their plants. The city workers had brought extra shovels so that students passing from class to class could plant their own shrub. We hoped this would help its continued maintenance since many students would have a personal stake in the project.

Each plant was placed according to the plans and the varieties were labeled with their common and Latin names. We furnished a small map so that students passing by could see just what we were up to. When finished, the project received much praise and it added much to the growth of our class members.

A graduate student at the college did a study of "Arnold's Group" and published her findings. She interviewed each student to ask for their perceptions of what happened in their group experience. She interviewed other students about their perceptions of "Arnold's Group" and how that experience compared with theirs. She concluded that the project was a great success and cited many examples to reinforce her conclusions. (Morgan, Barbara Ann, 1966)

At the end of the year, I had been offered a new position at another college closer to my family home in upstate New York. My parents were in their declining years and I wanted to be of assistance to them if they needed me. I agonized over my decision to leave this group and the institution that had provided me with such rich opportunities. After agreeing with my students that they would be involved in my new work, helping to spread the word, they agreed that I should go.

The President of the college was greatly disappointed that I decided to move to another college and he openly expressed this with tears in his eyes. I secured an assurance from the college administration that my students would register as a group during their remaining years at the college.

I knew that the level of group support that existed would provide a strong support system where individuals would be cared for and their successes would be facilitated. While these students sought out their areas of interest that involved other students, they did stick together throughout their undergraduate career. They were considered a privileged group on campus and that presented some problems. However, they all graduated with extraordinary grade-point averages.

Leaving graduate school and the doctoral program also presented problems. By this time I had completed all the course requirements for the degree of doctor of education, and had passed the comprehensive exams required to receive full entrance to the program that would lead to a doctorate in education. All that was left to finish was to complete a study and write a dissertation that would be reviewed by a committee of faculty and students.

I presented several outlines to my advisor, according to the protocols of the university. One of the outlines was directed at a validation study of the "E*nvironmental Relationships Test.*" My advisor urged me to abandon that idea and work on a topic more in keeping with his interests and expertise. I wasn't going to waste any time trying to persuade this individual to accept the project that I was interested in doing since I was on my way to some exciting experiences, or so I thought. I left the program to pursue these exciting possibilities and didn't return.

The project I developed at my new college as the instructional leader was heavily dependent upon the execution of effective group processes, especially group development. This project was labeled "The Open Curriculum." All of the elementary education majors in this college, about three hundred, were assigned to groups of twenty to be led by members of the teacher education department. These groups were also served by specialists in the disciplines representing their general education program. This curriculum was competence-based and students were expected to meet the standards developed for each discipline. When students demonstrated competency in a discipline, their record of completion was recorded in the registrar's office, as credit without a grade.

The students were allowed a great deal of freedom to select experiences that would assist them in mastery of the subject matter. The label of "Open Curriculum" indicated this openness that demanded personal responsibility for learning. The group leaders, called generalists, were expected to facilitate the work of each student within the group for which they were responsible.

Students could acquire as many areas of competency as their personal effort would allow. Some students earned many hours of credit, while others, the more dependent students, gained few if any credits. In spite of its endorsement by many established scholars, the project only lasted two and one half years, before it was phased-out, and the college returned to established traditions for preparing teachers.

Placing members of the education department in positions of leadership for learning groups, demonstrated the unfortunate reality that many of them could not conduct effective group development processes, in spite of their positions as teachers of teachers. They were ill-prepared to conduct productive learning groups.

Chapter 5

The Structure of Education From a Systems Point of View

A school that functions democratically under a written constitution teaches students an important lesson and provides professional educators with an environment for shared responsibility. A democratic system will ultimately cost much less since it eliminates a top heavy administrative hierarchy. It will be far more effective when it involves all the stakeholders in meaningful activity that encourages the fulfillment of personal and institutional goals.

There is widespread recognition that fundamental change is needed in education. "Fundamental change is systemic, in that a change in one aspect of the system requires changes in other aspects for it to be successful. This means that virtually all aspects of the current educational system are likely to be changed, *must be changed,* including the use of human resources (e.g. the roles of administrators, teachers, assistants, students), material resources (e.g. space/classrooms, instructional materials, and advanced technology), and time (e.g. grade levels, periods in the day, hours of operation, and days of operation)" (emphasis added) (Reigeluth, C., 1993).

Systemic change must begin with a proposed constitution and bylaws.

Given the present political scene, with its questionable ethical and moral standards, wrangling, deal-making and voter apathy/cynicism, if there were not a written constitution and bylaws that maintain stability in government we could expect utter chaos to develop. Fortunately, in spite of any imperfections it may have, our Constitution provides a framework for conducting business that remains in place throughout the years no matter what representatives of political parties have been elected to office.

Not so in education. Every time a new administration is installed, dramatic and pervasive shifts are seen in how business is conducted and what is considered of value in the management of the school. There are state and national-level laws and regulations that are supposed to maintain stability throughout the system, but without a validated and agreed-upon assumptive base against which these laws and regulations are tested, everyone is left to decide what is or is not effective education based primarily on what they have experienced by having gone to school. Fluctuations from one extreme position to another are commonplace; mandates can be in conflict with effective practices, research is narrowly focused, change involves tampering with the system and common sense and intelligent decision-making are missing. Frequent fluctuations are destructive of morale, resistant to sustained inquiry, and disruptive in the conduct of day to day problem solving activities.

Compounding the problem is the maintenance of a top-down organizational framework that features highly-touted and publically-supported administrative control, manifested by the elevation of an individual ("leader") as the highest paid person in the system. While these so-called leaders are supposedly serving the wishes of boards of education, these boards too are left to operate from their own biases and often limited experiences and insight. Without the necessary guidelines that address the mission of the school, these boards often relinquish their institutional authority to an authoritarian leader who takes charge and furthers the authoritarian model that flourishes in today's schools. In a limited number of schools, the appointed leader believes in participative decision-making and most often will demonstrate the validity of this organization. But, if conflicts arise with either of these leaders, they are usually replaced and a new cycle of disruption begins again.

I'm often asked what I propose to do about unions in my plan to change/improve public education. The implication is that unions are today's main obstacle to change.

Somehow the questioners fail to remember why teachers of the conventional school needed their unions. Think about it. The conventional school is organized like a corporation with a board of directors that hires a CEO to run the business. This person is granted "management confidential" powers over the underlings, the laborers, and exercises this power often with widespread support.

This organization makes perfect sense if one views education as a business. It's not surprising that the corporate profit making interests in today's reform efforts have zeroed in on the unions as the primary problem, charging them with holding at bay their grandiose plans for change

It is also no surprise that teachers considered as laborers are frustrated in their efforts to improve their standing and effectiveness as competent teacher/facilitating professionals. Compounding the problem are teacher preparation programs that are a farce when considering the complexities of effective facilitation of learning.

If it weren't for the right of collective bargaining granted through legislation, teachers would have no voice in determining their terms and conditions of employment. They would serve entirely at the behest of the administration, the "corporate" administrator, and staff. The CEO, with sanction from a board of directors, would be able to completely dictate the affairs of the school under directions from a higher up CEO and a board of directors (in New York State referred to as the Board of Regents) and a czar for education known as the Secretary of Education at the Federal level.

Unions were created to achieve a more equitable balance of power between labor and management. This organization allowed teachers to gain rewards for their work, but that move created an adversarial relationship between these two groups, labor, and management. This is often a destructive force within the school system, making genuine communication and constructive group decision making very difficult if not impossible to accomplish. It often has the effect of politicizing decision making.

Unfortunately, the teachers' unions appear to have taken on issues that deal primarily with salary and benefits while appearing to be less concerned about issues of curriculum and instruction. The CEOs and the wannabes have been relatively free to dictate the structures and processes of the school, even though they are usually remote from the activities of the classroom and often ignorant about the problems of teaching and learning that teachers and learners face on a daily basis. The elaborate bureaucracy unions have created, which seems to resemble that of the establishment they were organized to challenge, adds to the negative perceptions.

If we can change the dynamic that unions are necessary to protect the teachers from authoritarian leaders, we can expect to create real change in our public school systems. But if we remain incapable of visualizing an alternative that might have the effect of disrupting this long-standing organization, and fail to convince the public that change in this aspect of the conventional public school would not create a state of chaos, the possibilities for real change are limited. The public seems willing to go along with the current state of affairs in spite of its shortcomings and potential problems in the reform movement.

Here is a proposed plan that offers an alternative that everyone in this public has at least some background knowledge about. We all have some general knowledge about the organization of our democratically organized government that operates under a constitution and bylaws, featuring three branches—the legislative, the executive, and the judicial. These branches have specified roles and responsibilities that were designed to "operationalize" a real balance of power. These roles and responsibilities are spelled out in the constitution, its amendments, and bylaws. It is proposed that this organization can be adapted for governance of an effective public education system.

To avoid disruptive changes in the organization and mission of the school, the outline of a constitution and bylaws is proposed here as the supreme law of the system. This constitution, modeled after our national and state constitutions, has three branches—instructional, management, and quality assurance. Each of these branches has a defined set of responsibilities that feature a balance of power and ensures equitable resource distribution and shared responsibility.

One may be justified however in questioning whether modeling after our constitutional governing system would be a good idea given the present political scene, (characterized by its questionable ethical and moral standards, wrangling, deal-making and voter apathy/cynicism.) What we are experiencing today in government is the apparent result of a loss of commitment to the spirit of cooperation and concern for fellow humans that was once at least tacitly accepted by frontiersmen needing their neighbors for survival, not a defect in the system itself.

The underlying beliefs and assumptions held by our forefathers have now been displaced by the rewards of wealth based on the belief that aggressive and exploitive competition is the most important strategy for survival. Apparently, the documents of the founding fathers did not guarantee the sharing of the underlying assumptions and beliefs that place the welfare of each individual citizen above all other interests.

We can prevent this development from happening within a new school organization that is based on the same organizational structure by making sure that we have an approved, publicly shared set of assumptions and beliefs that is based on the latest information we have about individual development and learning. This document would need to be continuously updated as new discoveries about individual human beings are found. This information would be a constant reminder that human beings are each unique in their DNA, their experiences and what they have done with their experiences, and any violation of this premise would be understood as detrimental to the maintenance of a democratic and compassionate society.

As with the conventional school, without a constitution and bylaws, our government would be changing with each new personality that takes charge. Fortunately, in cases of dispute among members in our democratic system, our courts can decide whether we are operating within the constitution and bylaws. Without the judiciary, disputes would remain unresolved.

Ignoring provisions of the constitution and bylaws by any of the three branches of government, along with denial of the basic beliefs and values that guide the conduct of the organization, will potentially lead to chaos, inefficiency, and even corruption as we are witnessing today.

Since there is a built-in balance of power in our democratic governing organization, there is no need or provision for unions to guarantee the rights of one group against a powerful authoritarian leadership. The basic arbiter must be that which is governed by a commitment to the basic values that have antecedents in our foundational concepts as a democracy.

Real change in public education will only occur when the adversarial relationships between structural components of the system are eliminated. But, how can this be accomplished?

The establishment of a constitution and bylaws that is consistent with what is known and can be verified about how human development and learning occurs, alone and in groups and institutions is imperative. A constitution and bylaws must become the supreme law of the educational system, ratified by the stakeholders, by those who are knowledgeable about the educational system, are impacted by the system, and have an interest in refining its effectiveness. This constitution and bylaws will provide an orderly process of operations providing the methodology for systemic correction when needed.

Without an updated and clearly defined, written set of assumptions and beliefs, a statement of values that will undergird the operations of the system, and without a written constitution and bylaws, the rest of any plan for sustained change in our public schools is without promise. Since we do not have such documents, they must be created as the first step in the process of real change.

A proposed constitution here features three branches in the operation of public school systems—an instructional branch made up of the facilitators of learning (those who work directly with learners), a management branch that manages the financial accounting and legal responsibilities of running the school, and a quality assurance branch that is responsible for maintaining the constitution and its bylaws, and acting in judgment of the constitutionality of the activities of the other two branches.

This organizational structure guarantees a balance of power that provides for a more rational distribution of resources. It is a democratic organization rather than an authoritarian, hierarchical decision making structure.

Once this new form of governance is in place, the critical processes of examining and re-defining the content and processes required of learning can begin in earnest along with a reallocation of the existing resources directed in the service of the teacher/facilitators and their learners. All the components of the system must be addressed and brought into alignment so that the new system is cost effective and yet extraordinary in its productiveness. (See the "Solutions Generator" described on the website—remakingourschoolsforthe21stcentury.com and provided in this treatise)

A Proposed Constitution and Bylaws

(A broad-based framework within which specific details are to be worked out with all stakeholders)

Preamble:

We the people of Our Public School District #1, in order to form and maintain a responsive, dynamic, self-correcting educational system, that strives to meet the needs of each unique individual; that fosters collective ownership of the system, and concern and pro-

tection for fellow human beings in their pursuit of life, liberty and happiness; that supports professionals who can provide constructive, participative leadership throughout the enterprise; that enables each learner to develop his or her potentialities to the highest levels of achievement for functioning in everyday living, including skills involved in personal, interpersonal, group and institutional living, decision-making and participation as worker, dedicated members of family/community and world citizens, do ordain and establish this constitution for our school.

Article 1
Powers of the Instructional Branch

The Instructional Branch is composed of the professionals directly working with learners—teachers, aides, paraprofessionals, volunteers, resource consultants, human services personnel, counselors, the library/media/technology staff, students, and their parents.

Their responsibilities include:

Managing teaching/learning transactional strategies

Clarifying individual and collective goals and objectives

Assembling equipment and technology

Managing record-keeping and reporting procedures

Formulating and monitoring accountability criteria for staff and students

Recommending staff appointments subject to approval by all three branches

Managing diagnostic assessment and evaluation procedures

Assisting students in formulating plans and individualized learning programs

Providing in-service training for professionals and helpers

Continuing study of learning and development, individually and in groups

Conducting community workshops on fundamental concepts of learning, development and training

Assisting in the nomination of potential members of the Board of Trustees

Participating in the process of election of Board members

Article 2
Powers of the Management Branch

The Management Branch is composed of an elected Board of Trustees. An appointed business manager with financial and legal responsibilities for budget management and accounting, executive secretary, maintenance workers and contract services personnel, public relations, and promotional director and resource development specialists.

Their responsibilities include:

Budgeting, audit and control, facilities development and maintenance

Formulating and monitoring institutional policies and procedures regarding audit and control

Coordinating and facilitating resources development

Recommending staff appointments subject to approval of Instructional, Quality Assurance and Management Branches

Formulating and monitoring accountability criteria for management

Monitoring and upholding federal and state laws and regulations and seeking changes when required

Facilitating formulation of plans and program changes, and goal setting within the framework of the assumptive base

Supervising and training management staff

Administering to the needs of teachers and students in support of their efforts in maintaining a constructive climate for self-examination and self-correction

Providing needed services

Facilitating problem-solving and shared decision-making

Assisting in the processes of nomination of members for the Board of Directors

Participating in the process of election of Board members

Article 3
Powers of the Quality Assurance Branch

The Quality Assurance Branch is a representative body drawn from stakeholder groups within the school and the community. Its members are selected from those who are involved in, are impacted by and are knowledgeable about the enterprise.

Their responsibilities include:

Reviewing proposals for change

Monitoring activities within the system to determine consistency with the Constitution and Bill of Rights

Gathering data about the system's effectiveness and reporting the results to all Branches and to the Community

Monitoring learning and training procedures

Serving as liaison with the community regarding the Constitution and Bylaws

Arbitrating disputes

Participating in approving appointments of personnel

Establishing membership accountability criteria within the Assurance Branch

Assisting the process of nomination of members of the Board of Directors

Participating in the process of election of Board members

Article 4
Powers Reserved to the Learners

Each learner is guaranteed the least restrictive environment for receiving the full educational services that result in development of the unique potentialities for living in a global world. All persons within the jurisdiction of the school cannot be denied due process of law and equal protection, freedom of religion, speech, and press.

Article 5
Amendment of the Constitution

A proposed amendment to the Constitution can originate by a two thirds vote of all three Branches or by a two thirds vote by the parents of children within the school. Approval of a proposed amendment requires support by three fourths of the parents and the three branches with approval by the Board of Trustees.

Article 6
Supreme Law

This Constitution shall be the supreme law of the school. All members of the three branches shall be bound by affirmation to support this constitution; but no religious test shall be required as a qualification for any office or public trust within the school.

Article 7
Ratification

Ratification of this constitution requires approval by three fourths of the stakeholders within the school.

Article 8
Assumptive Base

Individual human beings develop and learn in accordance with biologically-based capacities that emerge in life through invariant sequences, influenced by the quantity and quality of experiences. What is learned is unique to each individual; all learning is conditioned by perceptual filters composed of personal meanings given to past experience. Learning and thinking originate at a pre-conscious subliminal level that can give rise to awareness that is organized and communicated at a conscious level. The unconscious response patterns each individual has acquired throughout life, shape and focus the perceptual filters, that is, the interpretations and importance one ascribes to specific objects, events and processes, and the verbal and non-verbal behavior one exhibits.

Individual interpretations of life are communicated through processes of interaction, interpersonal exchanges of viewpoints in language forms that are assimilated and processed in the unique mechanisms of other persons. The more validation that occurs between the intended message and what is actually heard, the better the consensus, and the more satisfying the communication will become.

Groups of individuals grow toward consensual validation in their communications by overcoming barriers to those transactions, by developing from a state of dependency to independence and eventually interdependence. Interdependence is the stage of group maturity marked by productive, therapeutic communication. These maturational stages are recognizable, and appropriate interventions will facilitate growth from one level to the next. Effective group processes do not require sublimation of diverse individual needs and goals; effective groups facilitate individual growth and development in an atmosphere of inclusion, mutual support and trust.

Each of the knowledge disciplines, practiced by scholars and artists, represents the most productive strategies for learning and communicating known to humans. They are themselves constantly being modified and improved/updated, and they reflect the best approaches to learning and understanding of our time. Each learner needs to acquire a sense of the underlying structures of these disciplines through active participation in order to make effective contact with these fields and with the accumulated products that have evolved from them over the centuries. All learners need to acquire these conceptual frameworks to efficiently process the vast amount of information generated through instant contact with the universe brought about by emerging technologies.

The school is a system that functions as any other system, made of parts that interrelate to form a whole; a change in one part of the system brings about a change in the relationships between the parts and a change in the nature and capabilities of the system. The school is a social system with a social responsibility that reaches deeply into the fabric of the community. While it has a mission to enhance the development of every individual and his or her capabilities, it also has a responsibility to reflect its values throughout the community and seek its understanding and commitment. All decisions that change the system must be examined for their implications for the whole system and each of the participants within it, seeking a supportive human enterprise that encourages personal growth and responsibility for fellow human beings.

Facilities Layout

All features of school facilities must reflect the assumptive base and support the activities of the three Branches of governance. Facilities must be designed to support learning, not simply to aid the dispensing of information through pre-canned instructional modules.

It must be recognized that the organization and maintenance of small support groups is central to the attainment of maximized-learning and development for every individual. The school building must house the resources to provide direction for inquiry by active learners in all six realms of meaning, supported by a technology hub that extends throughout the school and beyond.

In an effective school, members of each support group will be expected to draw upon the constructive resources of each realm of meaning within the context of emerging needs of individual learners—the empirical sciences, the synoptic disciplines (geography, history, and cultural anthropology), the esthetic arts, the symbolic languages, including mathematics, the concerns of ethics and morality, and the pursuit of self-knowledge. Resources will be made available in a school building that becomes a community center. In that setting, the wisdom and experience of all citizens will be included, especially those volunteers who have the time and energy to help.

The resources of the school building and its personnel must be available throughout the year, during evenings and on weekends. Learners cannot be restricted in their inquiry by arbitrary schedules that accommodate very little of the available resources for learning. Freedom from restrictive practices will be assisted by innovative communication technologies.

The school must be viewed from a systems point of view. Its system is made up of parts that are potentially interrelated. Any one of the parts can be identified as out of sync with the rest. Inconsistencies between the parts of a system prevent its full functioning and its products are diminished as a result. The model below represents a brief outline of the parts of the system that must have internal consistency to be effective. Attention must be focused on creating a fully functioning system with a minimum of internal inconsistencies. To accomplish this, all the parts must be tested against a shared assumptive base or set of beliefs about learning by individuals, alone and in groups and institutions.

The effectiveness of a new system of education will be judged by its ability to produce competent and compassionate individuals who can function ethically in a twenty-first century global environment. This system must be based on an ever-widening knowledge about how humans learn and develop, alone and in groups.

The model that follows illustrates ten components important for improvements in education.

There are also ten issues facing any efforts to change and improve the current educational system:

There is a lack of consensus about what is or is not effective educational practice, resulting in endless arguments, tinkering with the system, frequent shifting sands of change, and spiraling costs.

1. An effective plan will feature a written, shared, theory-based, internally consistent, personally-verified and continuously updated set of assumptions about how individuals learn and develop, alone, in groups and institutions. This written set of assumptions will help resolve arguments, sustain continuous inquiry, and generate intelligent solutions and appropriate actions in solving the problems of education. All decision-making within a new system must be guided by this written set of assumptions, thus minimizing the fragmentation of problem solving activity.

2. Curriculum and instructional decision-making in the conventional school, even with a committee structure, is heavily directed by administrators, leaving those professionals who work most closely with students, and parents, feeling powerless.

A new system will have an established governance mechanism that is modeled after our constitutional form of government, which balances the power and financial resources between management and instructional personnel, and places authority and responsibility for instruction with those who deliver it, provides a legitimate role for parents and students, and is guided by a written constitution and bylaws that reflect the assumptive base. This governance structure provides for a quality assurance body that monitors the constitutionality of decisions by both management and instructional staff. The constitution and bylaws, with a clearly defined assumptive base, maintains continuity within the system even with periodic changes in personnel.

3. Goals and objectives formulated by state and national agencies, however lofty, require resources for achieving them.

Central to a new system is a view that sound and officially-stated goals and objectives are achievable if appropriate learning experiences are adequately supported and focused upon clearly-articulated targets beginning on day one and continuing seamlessly throughout the school experience of each student. The experiences for students in a new school must be designed to develop a sense of structure and organization within each learner—an orientation that integrates and generalizes experience within and between areas of interest and inquiry. Mastery of systems is the goal for all learners and specific learning objectives must reflect strategies for its achievement.

4. There is a lack of consistency among school personnel regarding the implementation of higher standards for achievement. Implementation frequently resembles many elements of the conventional wisdom with few examples of a breakthrough in instructional design.

In this more effective school, curriculum and instruction is based on an internally consistent organization of six "realms of meaning" as defined by Philip Phenix in his book: *Realms of Meaning: A Philosophy of Curriculum for General Education*. This model subsumes all the conventional subjects of the current system, reorganized within a verifiable theory of knowledge (an epistemology). This framework reduces ambiguity, eliminates internal inconsistencies, and provides a dynamic target for constructive learning of legitimate content within each of the realms. Learners will be engaged in a developmentally appropriate way, in the creative processes of constructing knowledge aided by approaches defined by the disciplines within each realm. Once a sense of structure in disciplines within each realm of meaning is achieved, the learner becomes an effective, critical, and adaptive consumer of information from all other sources.

5. While the high-stakes tests currently in use are more performance based, the tests are perceived as coercive and threatening. The tests are not diagnostic, nor are they developmentally sensitive. Furthermore, they are not fully representative of the potential range of learning possibilities within each field of inquiry and communication.

The effective school will feature a student centered assessment, evaluation, record-keeping and reporting system. This system will track each learner's history of experiences and personal constructions of meaning that evolve from those experiences. The records will feature all forms of artistic and language/mathematical expressions modeled within a strategy for hands-on analysis, inquiry, and design in a systems-oriented constructive learning environment. Using modern technology, each learner will build personalized records that continuously document their learning experiences in all realms of meaning and the transformation of those experiences into higher and higher levels of cognition and expression, judged against rigorous standards of performance.

6. School facilities often dictate the type of curriculum and instruction that is possible. Patterns of architecture that reflect an egg-crate design often thwart a creative approach to curriculum and instruction. Flexible facilities for an effective school will be designed to respond to the needs of learners who are freed from the usual classroom restrictions. With this age of instant communication technologies, there is a reduced need for elaborate structures that were designed principally to accommodate rigid groupings in attendance five days of the week.

In larger school districts, the school population would be regrouped in manageable units—(250–300 students) in a community center. This plan calls for a school within a school concept. Multiple units will be grouped under a single office for business management.

This school model will feature a facility designed for twenty-first century communication requirements and curricular frameworks that encourage independent and collective inquiry and creative expressions of insight. The physical facility will be designed to the requirements for each realm of meaning and the needs of learners to transact their insights with others. Resources will include teachers, parents, retired experts, and other community persons. It will provide for connectivity with the worldwide network of information.

7. Resources of the community are now sporadically utilized within the school. The expertise of senior members of our society is often forgotten, and the welcome-mat for meaningful interchange with all stakeholders is not generally an integral part of the daily life of the school.

A systemic model school achieves a meaningful integration with the community. All resources of the community, especially retired volunteers are to be brought into the mainstream of school activity.

8. Support services are sporadic in the conventional school and they often lack focus for a timely response to a variety of needs when help is most required.

An effective school system provides support services with a purpose, that is, to respond to the need for removing as many impediments to leaning as is humanly possible. These impediments are both internal to the learner and within the social setting, the external environment where learning is taking place.

The learner's needs are diagnosed through the application of models that include physical/biological dimensions, developmental capacities, self-concepts and self-esteem, personal orientations, past experiences and learning or lack thereof, acquired personal learning strategies, the social context of home, community and school, and finally, teaching/learning transactional strategies available in the institution to positively bring about growth and change in every learner.

9. The conventional school, as a place to work and learn, is often intellectually stifling, unrewarding, frustrating, and repressive, and this is what is initiating the next generation of teachers into the profession. This situation is frustrating to many in the graduated class, preventing them from fulfilling their potentialities and chosen mission.

A new school establishes itself as a center of inquiry into teaching and learning as Robert Schaffer described in his book of this title. Everyone will be engaged, especially pre-service and in-service teachers, in self-study and group/team development supplemented with a study of the system in which they perform. This will ensure that the necessary skills to foster positive growth and development will be acquired for the at-risk students by tapping into the gifted potentialities of every learner.

This plan calls for full inclusion and a widening diversity in the student body, with credentialing requirements for professional educators that are flexible and rigorously accountable.

10. The information age has thrust upon the entire population a new era of exchange and learning only imagined a few short decades ago. The perceived complexity of technology combined with the lack of consensus about educational practices, commercialization of electronics equipment and software, and lack of resources, has led to uses and configurations of technology in schools that fail to tap the full potential of the medium.

A model school will feature information management and communication technologies designed to enhance self-sustaining learning. This element will become the hub that will serve all curricular realms and connect all learners and their teachers with the very best and timely learning resources available worldwide. Widespread use of real time telecommunications technology will link all learning areas within the school, the school to schools of our nation, and the school to other learning centers around the world.

The following twelve items listed below are drawn from the "Executive Summary" submitted in our rejected Charter School proposals. Our new school system is to be designed to achieve exceptional faculty and student performance through the implementation of all the following elements:

1. A written, continuously updated, and validated statement of beliefs/assumptions about how individuals learn, grow and develop, alone and in groups and in institutions,

that will guide decision making by all the stakeholders, including parents, students and professional staff.

2. A governance system modeled after our constitutional form of government, to guarantee checks, balances, and meaningful/orderly input by all stakeholders, that distributes responsibility, authority, and accountability to many members of the school community.

3. A central goal that focuses upon the most socially useful learning in the modern world—learning of the processes of learning that foster competence, an openness to experience, incorporation into oneself of the processes of change and the skills to organize and communicate one's thoughts and feelings.

4. A teaching/learning transactional strategy that features independent and collective student planning for learning, facilitated through supportive group processes, and the implementation of plans whereby individuals and groups are held accountable for accomplishing agreed-upon goals and objectives.

5. A competence-based curriculum that embraces all "realms of meaning" with a balanced and student-constructed integration of the arts, sciences, mathematics and other languages, career development, history/geography, religion, ethics, and morality.

6. An individualized, computer-based (student constructed and maintained) record of learning in all curricular areas with assessment techniques that honor different learning styles, interests, and individual capacities for learning, and evaluation criteria that allow for individual differences while maintaining the commonly-shared goal of mastery.

7. A diagnostic orientation directed to reduce impediments to learning for all individuals regardless of age, race, emotional, social, physical or intellectual capacities, with an acceptance of the values of ethical standards for dealing positively with diversity, pluralism, and inclusion.

8. A school building and other learning environments

designed to respond to the needs of a modern curriculum and active learners in this age of electronic communications and expanded learning opportunities.

9. A support system for learners that involves highly skilled professional educators, informed parents, trained leadership (including trustees), community input, selected outside professional resource agencies, higher education faculty and students, and volunteer retired experts from a variety of specialties.

10. A health and fitness program for all students, staff, and other stakeholders.

11. A laboratory for beginning teachers and an intellectually challenging environment for professional staff, parents, students, and volunteers.

12. A system that integrates information management systems and the appropriate uses of modern technology configured to maximize learning and developmental maturation.

All educational systems in this country must practice full inclusion without discrimination. They must hold all students accountable for their behavior and expect parents (however possible) to actively participate in their child's learning. The schools must be cost-effective, placing its resources in the service of student needs. Staffs must be held to a high level of professional competence and ethical behavior.

All students must be viewed as at-risk for failure in specific areas due to differences in the type and quality of experiences in the past, genetics, and many other variable factors. Students considered at-risk for failure in conventional schools must now be considered learners with unique needs that are to be understood and met with constructive and growth-enhancing experiences as a routine within the new school. The school must support an individualized, continuous progress, non-graded model, where all at-risk conditions can and will be significantly diminished.

To ensure that student needs are being met, a needs and accomplishments profile will be developed and continuously updated for and with each learner. This profile will illustrate individual achievements, including personal learning records and the results of diagnostic assessments that can indicate the unique areas of personal strength, along with indicators of currently-perceived impediments to learning and development.

Data from each profile will provide a basis for strategic planning for individualized, independent, and interdependent inquiry.

Each profile will include facts and informed judgments about an individual's characteristics such as (1) the learner's bio/genetic potential, health history and current state of being, (2) the current and past developmental maturation levels including physical, intellectual, social, emotional, language, moral and aesthetic dimensions, (3) the degree of self-confidence and self-esteem exhibited by each learner, (4) personal orientations and personality characteristics that have the potential to impede or enhance learning, (5) the social context in which the learner lives, (6) the quantity and quality of past experiences and achieved levels of learning regarding those experiences, (7) personal strategies acquired for learning and (8) instructional opportunities afforded each learner by the home and school.

Each dimension of these profiles will be interpreted through models drawn from the literature of known authorities that have proven value in interpreting human experiences. Such models are drawn from the writings of Piaget, Erikson, Maslow, Kubie, Kohlberg, Lowenfeld, Vygotsky, Bandura, Gagné, Schmuck, Bradford, and others.

Using systems concepts as an organizing framework for inquiry and record keeping, teachers will be presented with a workable strategy for assessment, record keeping, and evaluation of the unique products constructed by each learner. Students, who are determined through diagnostic assessments to be exhibiting pre-operational intelligence, will be afforded many opportunities to experience their world to develop the verbal and non-verbal language extensions that are the mark of the normally creative, spontaneous and inquisitive nature of this level of biological maturity.

Beginning with concrete operational youngsters with logical intelligence, strategies for learning will be guided by the creative processes of the academic disciplines ("realms of meaning") as practiced in those fields. All teachers and supportive staff in a home-base facility will foster student use of the materials and processes of these disciplines with the help of specialists in each "realm." Group development and team building strategies will play a central role in creating a supportive, yet challenging environment for individual learners with varied interests and abilities.

Individually accumulated records of experiences and achievements in a systems format will provide teachers with constructive diagnostic tools. These tools will provide students with continuity in their learning, wherever or whenever it occurs. This kind of evidence reduces reliance on purely subjective or assumed to be objective judgments when determining the value of independent, uniquely formulated constructions, and provides the basis for planning new experiences aimed at the achievement of personal and societal goals. This plan places primary emphasis on learners and learning—teaching is the process of facilitating that learning.

In this school, every student will belong to a supportive peer group that encourages learning, led by a skilled teacher/facilitator—a home base teacher.

Research in group dynamics shows that when there is a clear and empathic communication within a group, a supportive social climate emerges that provides each individual with expanded learning opportunities. Group development, team building, and participative decision making will be a continuing responsibility for the home base teacher and his or her group.

Sometime during each day, all students who are not already on special assignment will assemble with their home base teacher. A review of accomplishments and formulation of plans will dominate the meetings. Those who are on assignment will be required to report in periodically via available communications technology. Open discussion at the home base meeting will reveal individual needs and desires and provide the teacher/facilitator with a continuing opportunity to place before the group important institutional goals and objectives.

Each teacher will be aware of the nature of expected exit outcomes in six curricular areas based on the six "realms of meaning," These expectations will become a focus for long range planning processes occurring at all levels. As clarity is reached and connections are made between institutional requirements and personal interests, individualized plans will be formulated with the help of peer interaction and adult facilitation.

Utilizing the completed plans, individuals will pursue their independent and/or team interests for the day or for longer periods as indicated within their projected procedures and timelines. Dependent, less mature individuals will likely remain in the relative security of the home base setting, but as responsible independence is achieved, those students will take advantage of expanded opportunities for learning in other locations within or outside the school facility.

In the course of daily group transactions, special needs will be identified that will be served by specialists within the school and by resources connected to the school such as local experts and remote learning opportunities. These connections will take many forms from providing and interpreting essential information, to demonstrating processes of inquiry, facilitating the design of strategies for learning and monitoring student progress. There will be specialists on staff representing each realm of meaning with expertise in the processes and structuring within each contributing discipline.

Multi-age learners with similar needs and interests will be grouped to receive assistance in fulfilling the tasks outlined in their plans. These instructional sessions will evolve out of a process of diagnostic decision making and scheduled to accommodate to the needs of the students. The home base and specialist teacher/facilitators will place particular emphasis on developing self-insight and self-confidence. By engaging the students directly in the planning process and holding them accountable for fulfillment of their agreed-upon plans, they are experiencing the importance of responsibility that is transferable to all aspects of life.

The school curriculum will be organized around the six "realms of meaning" and a technology network that will provide each learner with vital resources for learning. This organization is based on a book written by the late Philip Phenix, a noted educational-philosopher, entitled *Realms of Meaning: A Philosophy of Curriculum for General Education* (McGraw Hill, 1964.) Curriculum centers in the school will be organized to represent each of the "realms." (1) Empirics will include all the sciences including social science, (2) Symbolics will include mathematics and all other languages, (3) Aesthetics will contain all the arts, (4) Ethics will include the moral sphere, (5) Synoptics will include history geography and cultural anthropology, and (6) Synnoetics will legitimize one's self-knowledge.

The science resource specialists will help shape the empirical investigations into all aspects of the universe, beginning with in-depth study of the immediate surroundings. The specialists in history and geography will provide learners with primary sources of information and knowledge of the methodology for constructing meaning in these integrative (synoptic) fields. The languages and mathematics specialists will provide insight and practice in how the learners can organize and communicate their ideas using conventional symbol systems that have evolved for that purpose. The specialists in the arts will facilitate each individual's development of the skills and values of artistic expression and intuitive/insightful interpretations.

The ethics center will provide students with the opportunity to debate ethical considerations that are important in the conduct of human transactions where respect and interpersonal acceptance is encouraged.

The technology hub will serve all the learning centers of the school and each of the learners within the school, including professional staff and parents. Specialists and the home base teachers, with their own areas of expertise, will monitor each student's progress in acquiring the intellectual tools of learning and engaging in the construction and communication of knowledge in developmentally appropriate ways.

With the advent of modern communications technologies, it is unnecessary for learners to be continuously bound to classroom instructional tasks, but instead they will be encouraged to pursue learning whenever and wherever it can be facilitated. Provided, of course, their inquiry is, or can become, part of an agreed-upon plan for both short and long range requirements.

We all know that much of our "real" learning develops outside of the classroom, often in spite of what happens in school. In this school, the outside is the inside for learners who are connected electronically to the home base and to each other, whether they are near home or overseas; whether they are watching NOVA, the History Channel, or a Discovery program.

The home base is a place to plan, to practice the strategies for learning and for communicating face to face. The universe is the laboratory. All available tools for observing and connecting with its vast, but manageable, complexities will be utilized.

Every student will maintain a computerized record of experiences that aids the individual in making sense out of the booming, buzzing universe. This record will represent the results of learning experiences in ways that serve the processes of accountability, constructive assessment, evaluation, and reporting of student achievements.

The accumulated representations of experiences found in the record feature models especially valuable to the learners since they have constructed them. Learners need to periodically revisit past experiences and personal constructions in order to maximize their value. It is also important for professional facilitators as a tool for assessment, evaluation, and planning, and to employers who are interested in knowing just what potential employees have experienced and what, in their own words, was actually accomplished with those experiences.

Of course, we will find time for relaxation, exercise, sport, and physical fitness.

Coordination of home base activities will require a high degree of sophistication and skill in group development along with a general knowledge of the nature and relationships of the six realms of meaning. Group processing expertise will be applied in diagnosing student potential for learning, constructing developmentally appropriate plans, conducting formative and summative assessments, gathering and directing learners to resources required by individuals and groups of learners. Group experiences will be guided by the work of Richard and Patricia Schmuck (Schmuck, Richard, and Schmuck, Patricia, 2000).

The teacher specialists will be primarily responsible for assisting learners in achieving constructive results through legitimate inquiry within their realm of expertise. For instance, the specialists in the "empirics" center will assist learners in scientific inquiry in an array of disciplines, including social sciences. Likewise, in the areas of synoptic disciplines, the specialist will assist students in historical and geographical inquiry. Specialists from all other realms will guide the students in practicing the ways of knowing and communicating that which has been developed to date.

The conventional school is based on a hierarchical model where power and direction rests essentially with the person at the top, designated to "lead." This model has been expanded to include department heads, other administrative officials such as guidance counselors and director of athletics. This model removes other staff members, lower on the totem pole, from taking personal responsibility for the school system. Taking responsibility will be a necessary ingredient in creating and sustaining a workable, successful systemic model for education.

Administrators, directors, and heads of departments are paid significantly higher salaries than teachers and teacher's aides. Spiraling costs and a breakdown in communication, unhealthy competition, and aspirations based on a potential for personal gain are the result of this type of school organization. It teaches children that democratic processes are only words to be recited, not processes to be engaged.

The hierarchical model legitimizes the existence of tyranny in the classroom that is rewarded by those who have an authoritarian point of view.

We must take seriously the symptoms of a dysfunctional system when students mark the days till vacation, drop out for an imagined meaningful life, seek an escape through drugs, take out their hostility on others, and yes, even contemplate suicide or worse, commit it? The current school system can and often is a breeding place for these serious social ills. If it is not completely changed it will continue to show the same results.

The more authoritarian a school system becomes, the more likely it will develop the kinds of social ills that are mentioned here.

There are four distinctive elements in an effective governance structure for an effective school that would create a place that respects all the participants and does not foster a top heavy hierarchical governance plan.

First, there would be a written constitution and bylaws based on a verified assumptive base. This constitution, like the U.S. Constitution, will serve as the guideline for decision making.

Secondly, there would be three branches designed to achieve a relative balance of power and responsibility. The management branch will be composed of all formally designated administrative personnel (people who do not ordinarily have direct responsibility for facilitating student learning) and the board of trustees. Trustees are legally responsible for the school's mission within the written constitution and bylaws.

The instructional branch will be composed of all instructional staff, the students, and their parents. Leadership within the instructional staff (as with other branches) will shift as talents are matched with specific tasks as identified through group consensus.

The quality assurance branch will serve as a watchdog committee to ensure the constitutionality of decisions made by either the management or the instructional branch.

This branch will conduct research to ensure that the new system is fully functional, and will identify any impediments that can be corrected. The quality assurance group will be composed of elected representatives of stakeholders—parents, instructional staff, students, trustees, management staff and support personnel.

It is expected that decisions will be reached by consensus whenever possible. In cases where deadlines or legal matters require immediate decisions, a simple majority of the trustees will prevail. However, these issues must be open for further discussion and possible consensus or alternative solutions at a later time.

To reach consensus, time must be considered paramount so that all members can state their position and state it fully enough to get the feeling that others really do understand. This condition is essential to free individuals from a lingering feeling that they could have succeeded in getting their way if others had only understood what they had in mind. Only by careful listening to the opposing views can such feelings be forestalled, and effective group decisions reached. In cases where legal or policy-based procedures pertain, the group must adhere to those requirements. This provides protection for those held legally responsible within the system.

In every case, the decisions of management and instruction must be consistent with the constitution and its assumptive base. If consistency cannot be achieved, the inconsistent items in the constitution's assumptive base must be reviewed and altered if necessary by a prescribed procedure.

Chapter 6

Teacher Education for the Twenty-First Century

Most people, when asked about the teachers they remember, invariably describe the behavior of those who took the time to relate personally with them, giving them support, understanding, and encouragement.

Teachers are also frequently described as not supportive, in fact, were rigid, unrelenting persons who often degraded their students, resulting in feelings of failure and humiliation. The vast differences in the personality characteristics of such teachers were likely observable when they were attending college, on their way to becoming a licensed teacher. However, due to a view that these differences in personality are either insignificant or off limits, the persons with detrimental characteristics are allowed to slip through the system and end up in the classroom to impose their will upon their students.

Teacher education is a key to improved education. Teachers of childhood age students, including early adolescence, hold the key to change that will take a generation or two to be fully realized in the larger field of education at all levels. What happens with students at these younger ages will shape the needs for educational experience at later levels, in the middle school, high school, junior college, college, graduate school and throughout life.

I have often introduced my students to an overview of what teaching entails using an article published in *Adult Education*, in the spring of 1958. This article was entitled, "The Teaching-Learning Transactions" by Leland P. Bradford. Bradford's insights about the requirements for successful teaching in a teaching learning transaction are so profound and clear that it is reprinted here in its entirety with permission from Sage Publications, with some minor editorial changes and additional emphases. This article is as relevant today as it was in 1958, perhaps more so.

Bradford wrote his treatise on *The Teaching-Learning Transactions* in 1958, nearly 55 years ago. You can decide how many of his ideas have been implemented.

He stated: "A reexamination of the teaching-learning process is long overdue. Explorations into the many complex motivational, perceptual, and emotional forces in learning are needed even more than studies of procedures for presenting knowledge or methods of measuring recall. *Analysis of the conditions which must be present before the individual can learn and change need to be made.* An effective teaching-learning process should include two basic assumptions based on validated research and experience with processes of learning and changing.

First, that the teaching-learning process is a human transaction involving the teacher, learner and learning group in a set of dynamic interrelationships. Teacher and learners engage together in a complex process of exploration and diagnosis of needs for and resistances to learning and change; of experimentation and fact-finding; of testing and planning for utilization of learning and change in the life of the individual. The relationships among learners and between teacher and learners have much to do with the ultimate learning.

Second, that the target of education is change and growth in the individual and his or her behavior; and this, in his or her worlds. This is a deeper and broader goal than cognitive learning alone.

These two assumptions lay a basis for a reexamination of a teaching-learning theory. They indicate the need to combine teacher interventions and understandings of the motivational, emotional, and cognitive characteristics of the teacher and learners, with skills of working with learners and a learning group in creating conditions for learning and change.

The following seven areas are some of those which must be examined in developing an effective teaching-learning theory.

1. What the learner brings to the transaction (in addition to ignorance and abilities).

2. What the teacher (helper) brings to the transaction (in addition to subject knowledge).

3. The setting in which learning and change take place.

4. The interaction process.

5. The conditions necessary for learning and change.

6. The maintenance of change and utilization of learning in the life of the learner.

7. The establishment of the processes of continued learning.

What the Leaner Brings to the Teaching-Learning Transaction

What, for example, are the learner's perceptions about the need for learning and change? How deep is his or her dissatisfaction with the present situation? How acutely, to use an analogy, does he or she feel pain? Are external pressures to learn and change reacted to but not really accepted internally? Where is the balance between desire for and resistance to learning and change?

What implicit theory about learning drawn from a variety of past experiences does the learner bring? If his or her concept is built around hearing lectures, reading, being quizzed, he or she will feel uneasy with and resist a learning process which is more deeply involving. If his or her concept of learning keeps him or her a passive recipient he or she will fail to enter into an effective learning transaction.

One of the first major tasks of the teaching-learning transaction is to help the learner learn different ways of learning.

What are the learner's perceptions about the potentials for learning in him or herself, the teacher and learning situation? Does he or she perceive the learning as abstract and irrelevant to personal needs? Does he or she perceive the teacher as capable of understanding and helping him or her? To what extent does he or she even recognize the kinds of help they would most appreciate as well as most need? Does he or she feel acceptance or rejection from the teacher and group? Does he or she have security in the learning situation and the learning group?

Inevitably each person enters a change situation with actual or latent concerns and anxieties. To learn poses unknown possibilities. To change raises images of potential failure, discomfort, or pain. What threats to self-image are present as the individual opens him or herself up to consideration of present inadequacies in knowledge or behavior?

We all recall what fears and anxieties we can have in learning a new language or a difficult course in mathematics.

Each person has a perceptual screen filtering out or distorting communication to him or her. Information too threatening to accept because it attacks his or her self-image is blocked out or interpreted in such a way as to pose less of a threat. Adults, particularly, have self-images more resistant to the subordinating role of accepting knowledge from others. What information about personal performance does the learner accept or reject? How much does he or she pigeon-hole knowledge, or turn it into abstraction, thus removing or modifying its threat to self-image? To what extent does he or she maintain the ability of verbal recall, but reject internalization into being or behaving? Does he or she have sufficient acceptance of him or herself as he or she is, that he or she can accept need for improvement?

Motivation, perceptions, anxieties all influence and affect the teaching-learning transaction. Self-perceived threats to the learner as a person become real blocks to learning.

Venturing into the unknown means leaving the tried and

sure and safe, unsatisfactory as it may be. Resistance to leaving the safe, but at the same time wanting the new, frequently causes the learner to prefer the kind of presentation of knowledge that can be copied and recalled but never internalized, rather than a deeper process of learning involved in a program of change. *Students frequently encourage more passive, but less effective methods of learning and, by their satisfaction in being protected from important learning, reward teachers for ineffective teaching and thus perpetuate poor teaching.*

Each learner brings to the learning situation his or her skills, or lack of skills, in group membership. If he or she lacks the ability to work effectively with others in a group situation, it is difficult for him or her to enter into the human transaction of learning. Inadequate ability to listen and interact with others makes it less possible for him or her to learn from the learning group, thus increasing tensions and anxieties about him or herself, decreasing satisfaction with the learning transaction and very likely increasing resistance to learning.

Because the learner is one part of the human transaction of teaching-learning, his or her motivational, perceptual, emotional, and attitudinal systems are very important factors in how learning and change are approached and how open he or she is to them. *It is the total individual, not just his or her mind, that comes to the learning experience.* When only part of him or her is understood and approached, all of him or her is not reached, and learning does not get very deeply into him or her and their actions.

The field of social science contributes much to our total understanding of the processes of learning and changing. From psychiatry and clinical psychology come knowledge of individual anxieties and concerns.

From social psychology and sociology comes knowledge about resistance to change and the process of changing. From psychology comes knowledge in broadening and improving understanding of human behavior. From education must come insightful decision-making, implementing valid concepts of the teaching-learning transactional processes.

What the Teacher Brings to the Teaching-Learning Transaction

The teacher, like the learner, brings far more to the teaching-learning situation than a knowledge of the subject, skill in organizing and presenting material, or ability to test for recall.

First, he or she brings a certain degree of awareness, or lack of awareness, that the teaching-learning process is basically a delicate human transaction requiring skill and sensitivity in human relations.

The effective teacher's role is that of engaging in a relationship with the learner and the learning group in which the learners and the teacher go through the process of diagnosis of change needs and blocks together, of seeking and analyzing relevant information from outside sources and from the interaction of the learning group, or experimenting in new pathways of thought and behavior, and of planning for use of new behavior.

The teacher's role of helping in the complex process of learning and change, however, is based upon a set of human relationships precariously established with the learner and the learning group. These relationships are always precarious because of the anxieties of the learner, the threat of the teacher as a judge and expert, and the mixed feeling held by the learner about his or her dependency on the teacher. The teacher needs to be aware of the importance of these human relationships, sensitive to changes in them, and adept at repairing them.

Second, the teacher as a partner in the transaction of learning needs to be aware of his or her own needs and motivations and of their consequences to the learning process. To what extent do his or her needs to control people, to maintain dependency upon him or herself, or to seek love and affection, distort and disturb his or her helper function and the learning transaction?

(This does not mean the other extreme of having to make him or herself love the learner. Rather it means the ability to enter fully into a human transaction without need for either rejection or over acceptance.) Knowing one's own motivations and their possible consequences on others better enables one to keep motivation under direction and control.

Third, the teacher brings an ability, or lack of ability, to accept the learner as a person. Acceptance means ability to respect and listen to the other and to separate the person from un-liked parts of his or her behavior. The physician who, hating disease, also hates and rejects the person who has the disease, is not an effective doctor.

Yet, teachers frequently are not aware that they reject learners because of lack of knowledge, abilities, or effectiveness in relating to them. Acceptance does not mean approval of the present status of being and behaving of the learner. Rather it marks the basic point from which the teacher tries to enter into a helping relationship.

The teacher works with a learning group. Good teacher-group relations are certainly as important as good individual teacher-student relations. The degree of ability in group leadership and membership skills on the part of the teacher has much to do with learning of the individuals in the class group.

The teacher is a second part of the teaching-learning transaction. His or her emotional, motivational, perceptual, and attitudinal systems, and his or her awareness of them and their consequences for learning and change are important forces in effective teaching-learning. Social science again has much to contribute in understanding the teacher.

Setting of the The Teacher-Learner Transaction

Most education takes place in group situations. Thus the teaching-learning transaction includes teacher, learner and learn-

ing group. Each has its forces and impact on the learning outcome for the individuals. The class group is not merely an economical way of teaching. It should be at the heart of the learning process. Group impact and influences on its members can be a powerful force toward learning or toward supporting the learning process.

Research into the dynamics of group behavior indicates how powerful group forces are in group and individual productivity. Some groups have the task of making machine parts, others of reaching decisions, and still others of increasing the learning of their members. In all instances for the group to be successful, attention must be given to helping the group form, organize, grow, and keep in good repair. *Just as the leaders in work groups should assume responsibility for encouraging the growth and maintenance of the work group, so should the teacher of the learning group.* As teachers recognize emotional aspects of group behavior, individual anxieties and hidden motives, interpersonal threats and competition, problems of relations to leadership and authority, factors of individual involvement in groups, they will be better able to help classes become groups where the group task is individual learning and where group forces of cohesion are exerted on the learning of each individual.

As it is, group forces, inevitably present in all group situations, often work against the teacher and against learning. The class group bands against the teacher to reduce learning if the teacher does not know how to develop an effective learning group where members help members and where morale is high.

How many teachers fail to encourage, or even allow, learners to help educate each other? If teachers were able to create learning groups in which member influenced and helped member, learning results would be far greater.

The learning group is the third part of the teaching-learning transaction. Educators must realize the powerful forces present in groups which could measurably increase individual learning and change. Research in group dynamics in many university centers and experimentation with applied group dynamics carried out by the National Training Laboratories and subsequent basic research in group theory has much to offer an expanding teaching-learning theory.

The Interaction Process

The interaction process is basically a network of interactions taking place in a group setting. Teacher interaction with one student may be heard in many different ways and with different consequences by others. Praise or regard to one student may be heard as punishment to another because he or she was not selected for reward. To the learner, interactions of support and reaction from the group may be more valuable or more readily acceptable than from the teacher.

The teacher needs to be aware of the consequences of any interaction on all members of the learning group and on the group itself. Does an interaction designed to give needed knowledge to one learner create greater unhealthy dependency on the teacher by other group members?

The interaction process has two basic purposes: first, to establish and maintain relationships that reduce anxieties and defensiveness in the learner and help him or her open up for learning, and second, to bring about learning and change.

It is a false assumption, more common in secondary and higher than in elementary education, that the mature person doesn't need sensitive teacher-student relationships or group support. Educators must discover the fallacies in this assumption and the importance of developing a supportive climate reducing resistance to learning.

With the interaction process basic in learning, the actual interventions of teachers and learners, and the way they are responded to, are of critical importance. What are the consequences, for example, of action or lack of action by the teacher on shifting the balance of motivation of the learner? What are the consequences in increasing or decreasing a feeling of support or of changing the perceptions of the learner? What are the consequences for the helping relationship between teacher and learner? Does any particular action create over-dependency on the teacher? Is the teacher sensitive to the stages of group development, the goal being improved communication? *Groups mature from a dependent state, to expression of independent perceptions, to a recognition of the value of interdependent relationships that support each member's pursuit of personal and group goals.*

It is unfortunate that studies dealing with the effects of teacher interventions on the learning process are not well grounded in the basic research on groups. In the fields of consultation and therapy, much more has been done to train for sensitivity to the interaction process. In these fields, as well as in the field of medicine the interaction process is recognized as basic in diagnosis and treatment.

If the interaction process is basic to learning, then experience in the area of consultation and therapy, and research in the social science fields of social and clinical psychology are important to a full development of a learning theory.

Work on human relations training carried on by various group development laboratories has been exploring the area of teacher intervention in the interaction process. Experience in clinical psychology is highly relevant to this area. Finally, studies in social psychology on the process of change and the function of helping with change have importance.

Conditions Necessary for Learning and Change

Learning and change take place most effectively only when certain conditions are present making it possible for the learner to enter into a process of diagnosis, experimentation, information finding, generalization, practice and application leading toward learning, growth and change. These conditions discussed by the author are merely outlined here.

Revealing Thought, Feelings, Behavior

Until the thoughts, feelings and behavior needing change are brought to the surface for the individual and made public to those helping him or her (in formal learning situations, the teacher and other members of the learning group) there is little likelihood of learning or change. Buried, they are blurred and indistinct for the learner, covered by misperceptions of adequacy, anxieties, and defensiveness. Surfaced, they can be examined by the learner, teacher, and learning group in the light of greater reality.

Until thoughts and behavior are revealed and exposed there is little that the learner or helpers can take hold of, to bring about improvement or change.

Learning is not a matter of filling a void with information. It is a process of internal reorganization of complex thought patterns, perceptions, assumptions, attitudes, feelings and skills, and of successfully testing out this reorganization in relation to problems of living.

The basis of reorganization, and thus for learning, is diagnosis of inadequacy. Such diagnosis should be made collaboratively by the learner and those helping the learner. It is ineffectual for someone else to make a diagnosis for the learner—a frequent fault in education.

The diagnosis is never simply of general inadequacy. It should include motivations, desires, anxieties, defensiveness, insecurities, perceptions. In combination, they created the normal ambivalences found in learning and change.

Diagnosis depends on having adequate data. Surfacing or revealing the thought, feeling, and behavior patterns of the learner provides a common experience for learner, teacher, and the learning group to make possible collaborative diagnosis.

Seeking Reactions to Revealed Ideas and Behavior

Revealing inner thoughts, attitudes, behavior without securing accurate and acceptable reactions from teacher and learning group, from additional sources of information, or from self would be without much value. We do not learn by doing only. We learn by doing under conditions in which relevant, accurate and acceptable reactions that we are able to use, get through to us.

Increasingly it is clear that the concept of feedback has important meaning for the educational process. Information following exposure which recognizes the individual's perceptual system and which has for its purpose development rather than destruction is the heart of learning. *Feedback must be clearly and completely heard.* Here is where the human relationship aspect of teaching-learning perhaps has greatest importance.

In an executive development program, one member told the group in various ways that he saw himself as a warm-hearted person who liked people and who was a democratic executive. His recital of his problems of apathy, irresponsibility, and lack of creativity in his immediate subordinates revealed him as fearful and hostile toward people and certainly autocratic in his management. Lectures of discussions about good executive behavior would have been heard by this man as referring to himself. Only as his behavior was revealed to himself and to other members of the learning group, and as he gradually received helpful feedback reactions enabling him to correct his perceptions of himself and ultimately some of his behavior, did real learning and change take place.

Climate

Revealing thoughts and behavior and accepting reactions about them take place effectively only when the atmosphere of climate in the learning group and the teaching-learning transaction is one which reduces threat and defensiveness and which also provides emotional support while the learner is undergoing the difficult process of changing patterns of thought and behavior.

The teacher has the important responsibility of helping to create a climate conducive to learning. It is crucial that the teacher help the group create this climate. The temptation to the teacher is to attempt to supply all the necessary understanding and support necessary for each learner. This keeps the learner in the bondage of emotional dependency on the teacher. If the climate is built up by the group, with encouragement and assistance from the teacher, the individual learner can accept emotional support interdependently, rather than dependently, because he is contributing to the group support given to other members.

Information Seeking and Receiving

Knowledge from a variety of sources is vital to the learning process. Some comes from the analysis of the learning situation, some from immediate reactions of teacher and peers, some from experimentation and research results, some from past experiences of the individual and others, and some from the wide wisdom and vast experiences of the past.

Knowledge giving as a factor of learning, however, has attributes and consequences, all of which need much further exploration. The first is timing.

Like a road map that is useless to the person who has made no decision to take a trip, information is often presented in teaching situations before the individual has made any personal decision about learning and change. *Teachers need constantly to realize that attendance in a learning group does not necessarily mean commitment to the process of learning and change.*

Experimentation and Practice with New Ways of Thinking and Doing

Knowledge that remains basically outside the being and doing of the individual is likely to become compartmentalized. Learning tends not to become a basic part of being and doing of the individual until one has the opportunity to try out in practice situations that which reveals new possibilities for thinking and doing. Experimentation and practice are important conditions in the total process of teaching-learning.

Application of Change into the Learning Situation of the Individual

Application of learning and change in the life of the individual is a far more difficult task than initial learning and change in a protected learning situation. Unless the teacher and the learning group give time and attention to individual problems of internalizing and using learning, regression and loss of learning is likely.

These conditions need much further exploration and research in terms of completeness, relative importance, and integration. In various sections of the social sciences, some exploration is present.

New research on feedback, or information theory, has immediate value for an enlarged concept of teaching-learning. Modern systems concepts have a great deal to offer, as well.

The various approaches to counseling and therapy have developed experiences in the area of establishing receptive climates. Research in human relations training has stressed the integration of these conditions and methods of training for application. Social psychology and sociology has worked on the problem of helping to apply and maintain change.

The Maintenance of Change and Utilization of Learning in the Life of the Learner

Education has long recognized the importance of transfer of learning. Too frequently such transfer has meant only the application of principles to new situations. This has ignored many of the problems of resistance to putting change into practice in the individual and his or her external worlds.

The problem of maintenance of change and utilization of learning have both emotional and cognitive aspects. The learner's motivations to maintain change in thought and behavior must be sufficiently strong to overcome one's own hesitations and the forces in the environment pushing against change.

Many a summer school program has inspired teachers to want to improve practice, only to find resistance among colleagues, students, and parents in their school system. Change, to be maintained, must be well rooted in the individual and well supported by forces in his or her external worlds.

If maintenance of change and utilization of learning is a necessary part of a theory of teaching-learning then efforts must be made during the process of formal teaching-learning to prepare for the problem of maintenance. A number of helping steps can be taken at that time.

(1) Help needs to be given to the learner in diagnosing forces of resistance to change, and support for change likely to be found in him or her and the environment. Basically, he or she needs help in locating and building supports in internal and external worlds to maintain new learning and change.

(2) Help needs to be given the learner in assessing potential strengths and weaknesses in terms of support for change.

(3) Help should be given the learner in planning how to reestablish him or herself in outside worlds (after leaving the teaching-learning situation). ...Each person needs a foundation from which to encourage change in himself or herself and situa-

tions. Learning which totally removes such a foundation will not lead to continuing change.

(4) Help needs to be given the individual to develop a continuing system of learning. Methods of experimentation and analysis can be taught which will encourage the person to continue to learn from a variety of experiences.

Learning to Learn

The teaching-learning process should endeavor to help the learner learn how to learn more effectively so that more of his or her experiences can lead toward learning and change.

As individuals learn to use scientific methods of experimentation, observation, and analysis in daily decision-making and problem-solving, instead of stereotypes, perceptual distortions, and closed eyes and ears, learning and changing from experiences can more likely become a continual process.

As individual learners become more aware, through an effective teacher-learner transaction, of their own anxieties and resistances to learning, they may be able to reduce them more frequently and thus enhance learning and change.

As individual learners become more accepting of himself or herself and gain more internal security, they will become less defensive and more able to perceive accurately and to use reactions to their thought and behavior patterns.

Conclusion

An effective teaching-learning transactional process should include, in addition to the seven areas discussed above, strategies for facilitating learning and experiencing, and methods of testing their learning and change.

As this broadened picture of teaching-learning is developed, it is obvious it has major implications for the entire field of teacher training, both in-service and pre-service. It will not be enough merely to add social science subject knowledge to what the prospective and in-service teacher is expected to "know." Engaging in the complex human transaction of teaching-learning requires more than knowing about human behavior, although that knowledge is essential. It calls for sensitivity and awareness to on-going relationships and for skills of interacting with the learner and the learning group."

Teacher education, especially for childhood levels, has a reputation for being "easy ed." This reputation is partly due to the tendency of teachers at these levels to be more concerned with the individual needs of their students over concern for subject matter. However, they have recently had to abandon much of their primary concerns in lieu of raising standards and responding to high stakes tests.

Teachers of subject matter in the conventional middle and high schools are primarily concerned with conveying selective "truths" and insisting upon adherence to what they consider to be high standards of performance. An attitude of superiority held by the so-called secondary pre-service teachers is prevalent in many teacher education programs; it was true during the fifty years I spent working with elementary pre-service teachers. The subject matter teachers claim they have more depth in their subject and therefore are better prepared to convey important information to their students.

In the early seventies, I met with the social studies editorial board of a major textbook publisher of materials for use with elementary students. This board was composed of young, energetic folks with a subject matter orientation. They were showing me some materials that listed the major crops grown in various parts of our country. I paid particular attention to the information that pertained to an area of my state with which I had familiarity.

The information stated that the major agricultural crop of this area in the 1970s was oats. I explained to them that oats went out with the horses when other forms of transportation emerged on the scene, beginning around the turn of the century. Their response was revealing. "That doesn't matter because the teachers will not know the difference." They, of course, were correct about the elementary teachers but the truth of the matter was, the secondary subject matter teachers would not know the difference either.

The way subject matter is thought about and dispensed/acquired is one of the major problems of teacher education and education in general. The so-called liberal arts faculty members of teacher education programs often maintain a mystique about their "superior" knowledge and they look down upon the education faculty and students, but not completely without merit.

The concerns for child centered advocates cannot be sustained in isolation from those of the subject centered priorities. There is a vital need to find a way of integrating the competing concerns between subject matter and child development, and reducing the conflict that helps keep change at a stalemate. The turf wars that have resulted from this situation have kept at bay the improvement of teacher education and education in general.

When my great uncle, Roswell, became a teacher in 1850, he had to demonstrate exceptional achievement in the subjects of his earlier education.

When my Aunt Adelaide became a teacher in the 1920's she reflected the emerging philosophy of John Dewey and she brought to her work an integration of subjects and skills development along with a strong belief in the worth of each individual child.

When two of my sisters and one brother were becoming teachers of elementary students in the mid 1930s they attended a normal school. Students who had excelled in their earlier studies were introduced there to subject matter in the context of teaching with a strong emphasis on skills development in the three Rs, civics, and geography. I suspect that faculty of the universities, even then, felt the same way as the secondary teachers I have known. They would have viewed teacher education at the normal school as a watered down version of "real" education.

When I attended college to become a teacher in 1949, it was called a teachers college. Methods of teaching were taught in conjunction with teaching the important aspects of a given subject. The mathematics instructors, for instance, would teach their subject in a way that would directly apply to the work of the teacher in the classroom with students. Other members of the mathematics department, those who taught the "real" scholars, viewed the teachers of teachers to be watering down their subject.

A few subject matter teachers were directly assigned to the teacher education programs, while other members of the department taught their subject to students in "more rigorous" programs.

When I went back to that college in 1956, as a faculty member, it was becoming a "college of arts and science." There was a teacher education program, but it was separated from the academic "liberal studies" departments. The so-called liberal arts faculty assumed responsibility for teaching subjects for general education offered to all students and liberal arts concentrations that were thought to provide in-depth exposure in specific fields of study.

The faculties of the teacher education department were left with the task of teaching methods of teaching with some background courses such as the history and philosophy of education. They supervised and certified "student teachers." The major, narrowly conceived thrust of teacher education has now become learning to write lesson plans followed by a demonstration in carrying out lessons in the classroom, and the students are usually not involved in the planning.

The chasm between the subject-centered people and the child-centered has prompted the introduction of outside evaluators to study teacher education programs. They attempt to see how they have integrated their offerings and how they determine their effectiveness. The work of the National Council for Accreditation of Teacher Education (NCATE) is an example of this effort.

Accreditation has been linked to effectiveness and it is NCATE's job to engage faculties connected with teacher education in an examination of what they claim to be doing, how they are doing it, and how effective their programs are in achieving their goals. Agencies of state government have adopted this effort to improve teacher education with the threat of closing down programs if they do not live up to the standards expected of them.

At the arts and science institution where I spent forty years, teacher education programs formulated after I left that institution in the early 2000s were rejected by NCATE for accreditation, several times. The college turned to an arm of the Board of Regents of the New York State Education Department, called the "Teacher Education Accreditation Council" (TEAC). The Board of Regents, in conjunction with SUNY, were faced with the real possibility that one or more of their traditional teacher education institutions would no longer be accredited and would be compelled to close. TEAC was formulated to derail that possibility, possibly to avoid embarrassment.

The SUNY unit where I worked was quick to reject the program that had been developed and field tested over the forty years that I had worked there. New administrators arrived who were determined to make their special mark. A series of reports were submitted to the administration, including the new president of the college, detailing what was needed to achieve accreditation, and these fell on deaf ears. In fact, it was after nearly a year of frustration in dealing with a lack of response from the new president that a FedEx communication was delivered to his office and a response was received on "Public Relations" stationary, stating that he had referred the matter to appropriate members of his management team. Nothing occurred as a result.

A model of the then existing comprehensive teacher education design that was the product of development since 1966, was presented to the new dean in charge of teacher education.

This model is included here providing witness to the efforts to build a program for teacher education that was based on years of research and development and a rationale drawn from the necessary assumptions that are discussed in the contents of this book.

The dean in charge of teacher education was presented with this model in an attempt to continue the work of the decades that preceded his arrival. He responded to the presentation with: "This is a very comprehensive program." Nothing further came of this discussion until a vote was taken at the so-called faculty senate that a new direction was needed. It was apparent that the last forty years were dismissed probably since the new administration had not originated the plan.

There was no effort to interview faculty who had been involved and only one person testified at the senate meeting, one who knew that institutional accreditation with NCATE evaluation was doomed to failure. This faculty member was dismissed under an evaluation plan at the college that is directly influenced by administrative authority.

A model of the teacher education plan that had been developed over many years of experimentation and research is included here for review.

The model designed for effective teacher education has eight levels of engagement beginning with the establishment of foundational concepts and ending with advanced study.

The first year is to be devoted to an in-depth experience in the creation of knowledge in the geography and history of a personally familiar place, preferably one's home town or city, along with a study of its cultural anthropology. An objective of these creative experiences is to assist students in learning how to learn and to establish a vital frame of reference that will begin to transfer to the understanding of other places and times. Most importantly, this experience is designed to bring out a heightened awareness of one's place in the real world.

These three disciplines were identified as having a *synoptic* role in the creation and communication of knowledge that has the effect of maintaining "an eye for the whole chessboard, for the bearing of one set of ideas on another." (Whitehead) Having this orientation, learners will be ever cognizant of the relationships between variables of the universe while they choose and pursue a specialty in one area.

In addition to these in-depth studies in these selected academic disciplines, each teacher education candidate would be engaged in frequent visits to schools to become familiar with the existing approaches to learning in these areas of inquiry. All candidates would be introduced to an individualized assessment, recordkeeping, and evaluation system (CARES) to be used throughout their careers for their own enhancement and for the enhancement of experiences for their students.

They will be introduced to systems concepts particularly as applied to the systemic model of teacher education that becomes an ever present goal to be used for guidance throughout their studies. In-depth studies will be made of learners at varying levels of development, (including self-analysis) and the nature of learning, along with the nature of communication and group processes, the nature of knowledge and how we come to know, and the nature of the school as it currently exists. These foundational concepts are to be continuously refined throughout all levels of study in becoming a competent professional educator.

The second year of studies for teacher education candidates involves in-depth engagement in the other five realms of meaning beyond synoptics as defined by Phenix, namely, symbolics that encompasses all languages including mathematics, esthetics encompassing the arts, empirics which includes all sciences including social sciences, ethics that includes the moral sphere, and synnoetics or self-knowledge. Each of these remaining five realms contains approaches to learning and sharing of meanings that are treated with equal importance. Again, frequent visitations to classrooms will encourage familiarity with the existing treatment of these disciplines in elementary and secondary schools.

The third year will be devoted to the translation of the creative processes of disciplines adapted to uses in a developmentally sensitive curriculum based on validated assumptions and beliefs about how humans learn and develop. Throughout this process will be a refinement of understanding of the nature and roles of the disciplines in all six realms of meaning.

The fourth year is devoted to a supervised internship that focuses on the translation of all creative processes in the classrooms, consistent with the foundations concepts of human development and behavior, the structural nature of disciplines and the development of effective learning groups that behave at a mature level of functioning. At the end of successful completion of this year, a bachelor's degree is granted. Competency will be determined through an analysis of the complete record of experiences along with the completion of an inventory that reveals what each candidate knows and is capable of doing (See Appendix A).

The fifth year would be devoted to validation studies that extend and refine the concepts of the foundations knowledge base and the translations of those assumptions into effective transactional-strategies with learners. A master's degree is granted upon completion of this year of study and practice.

The sixth year focuses on job refinements under the guidance of mentors who have been schooled in the systemic dimensions of the program.

The seventh year is devoted to continued study while on the job with emphasis on renewal of requirements for licensure.

The eighth year focuses on research leading to advanced degrees from institutions of higher learning.

This plan does not require significant changes in the organization of the colleges of education; it requires a change in personal orientations among instructors and an acceptance of the implications of those changes in re-structuring the program for teachers.

This plan is guided by systems theory and its components have support from numerous scholars. Its future depends upon initiation of a dialogue required to demonstrate its value and its difficulties. The levels of research required would first assure that the system is fully functional and then through comparative studies demonstrate its projected superiority over the existing approaches to teacher education.

Most importantly, it must clarify the significant changes in the conventional schools this teacher education program will be designed to bring about.

Teacher Education Design Model

Basic to the lack of significant improvements in teacher education is a lack of a comprehensive, validated set of assumptions about how individuals learn and develop, alone and in groups, and a reluctance to engage in a substantive examination of existing points of view. This deficiency results in a piecemeal approach to change; actions based on invalid assumptions and stagnated improvement. A vision for what is possible is needed.

Childhood education is the place to start. When current practices are examined from a comprehensive, validated set of assumptions, it is clear that education for children and adolescents has serious shortcomings. Simulated experiences are substituted for direct experience with life's many manifestations.

To make this criticism more believable, consider a schematic developed by Edgar Dale in the 1950s. He tried to convey a framework for determining the relative effectiveness of different types of experience from concrete to abstract. He labeled his formulation, the "cone of experience."

At the base of his cone was *direct, purposeful experience*. He claimed, and rightly so, that direct experience coupled with the motivation to pursue the tasks, is the most fruitful type of experience. That is, it has the most potential for generating insight and skill development.

In the absence of an awareness of the immediate purpose, direct experience can be contrived that will provide the opportunity to see the importance of an experience and encourage engagement that also has great potential for generating insight and skill development.

The next level of experience is dramatized, life-like engagement, while perhaps not as generative as direct experience; it has the potential for stirring the emotions and intellect that will generate insight and skill development.

Still photos and recordings of life's events and objects is the next best experience, provided these representations are tied to the direct experiences, or dramatized experiences within the learner's background.

The next experience is found in visual representations that look like the objects and processes they represent. Visualizing three dimensional representations of areas of the world is an example of this type of experience.

Following this type of experience on the way from concrete toward abstract, is common language. Experience with common language, while understandable, has the potential for a variety of interpretations, some of which may not have a basis in reality.

The next level after common language is simulations. This type of experience is fraught with peril, especially when it is pre-packaged by commercial entities and broadcast over media on a daily basis, designed for the "education of young children."

When cartoon characters are significant conveyors of the information that is pre-selected by adults (regardless of their expertise) with the intention of influencing youngsters to "learn" things like the letters of the alphabet or "acceptable" behavior, this comes as close to promotion of insanity as one can imagine. By definition, insanity is being out of touch with reality. These simulations encourage fantasy over reality. While this criticism is extreme, it is a reminder that a steady diet of simulations and cartoon Big Bird characters allows the learner to live in a fantasy world, one that does not generate competence in understanding real life in all its manifestations.

Experience is more out of touch with reality if it does not have a direct experiential background. This includes the presentation of visual symbols, followed by written language and finally verbal symbols. Verbal symbols, when developed through the efforts of individual learners, open up many possibilities for learning and development. However, verbal symbols offered to learners without the necessary background for an effective translation, results in memorization of nearly meaningless terminology that is not only useless, it is psychologically damaging.

Dale's message was clear and compelling. Direct experience and all other experiences tied to direct experience, will bring about the learning we all have great hopes of affecting. Simulated experiences alone do not take the place of direct experience, no matter what the motivations are for presenting them.

When the young were on the farm they experienced life directly and learned many lessons without the help of organized instruction. When the population left the farm to join the industrial centers, schooling remained as it had been traditionally practiced. Nothing took the place of the direct farm experience. The direct experience on the farm with the physical world had compensated for the formalized learning of the school, but after the migration, education continued to be practiced mainly as manipulation of abstractions. The results of the "Environmental Relationships Test" have indicated direct experience with the environment has been seriously limited. Now through colorful appearances in textbooks and cartoon-interpreted reality, the educational establishment is trying to recoup its losses. This has to stop, or at the very least, limited in its use.

The relative ineffectiveness of education at these early levels has caused later attempts at instruction to be predominately reiteration, regurgitation and remediation, since the foundation for learning has not been developed early on. This accounts for topics of American History being taught repeatedly with slightly more sophistication at various points on the instructional continuum. I used to joke with my students about how many times in the course of education we land the Pilgrims. I hoped sometime they would be allowed to walk ashore.

Had these topics been grounded in a process of in-depth inquiry into the local community using the materials and methods of History and Geography as disciplines, within the realm or spirit of synoptics, later investigations would build upon those well-established conceptual frameworks. It would be unnecessary to repeat these topics, a process that has not shown to result in lasting recall or constructive problem-solving.

The same is true of mathematics and other disciplines that underlay the six realms of meaning identified by Phenix. Memorization of number facts as an introduction to mathematical insights leaves the learner with little understanding of the potential power of these symbol systems, and it generates a real fear of this language, viewed as an abstract and meaningless enterprise.

The arts are relegated to a class, often on Friday, where students are presented with the techniques of so-called arts and crafts that fail to teach the central lessons of art as modes of communication and insight, useful and essential in everyday life and every aspect of the curriculum.

The joys of reading are reduced by an incessant analysis of parsed words and phrases, along with pre-mature analyses of the structures of one's own and other's language.

Physical fitness is relegated to a weekly hour or two of activity in the gym or on the playground or participation in a competitive sport designed for winning that is supposed to teach the ups and downs of life.

If the foundations for learning were established properly at the early levels through early adolescence, the later levels of education would change dramatically, that is, if there isn't continued resistance to change. This could mean that the university might actually flourish as a center for research and development without the need to offer remedial courses for those whose backgrounds are lacking in the fundamentals of learning.

When the students of early ages, through beginning adolescence, reach the high school with a background wrought out of effective group and individual engagement, there will need to be serious adjustments made in those later programs. Students will bring a sophistication that allows critical analysis of both the programs and the personnel offering them. And if the personnel are educated in the creative processes of a full range of disciplines, and insightful about the individual students with whom they work, the programs that follow the childhood and early adolescent levels will be dramatically changed. This will be true in regard to every level of education attempted beyond those initial levels as well.

The question remains: What is needed now in teacher education to get the change initiated and what must it become as changes occur when a new generation of students gradually emerge through the system?

The first proposition to consider is that the preparation required to teach at any level of education is the same. There are fundamental assumptions that can and must be validated that provide direction for teaching-learning at all levels, including the university.

The current situation finds the elementary teachers having to deal with a wide variety of factors in their daily work with groups of young students. This includes helping in learning to tie shoes, toilet training, and establishment of social graces.

The middle and secondary teachers are most interested in the acquisition of their canned subject matter rather than engaging students in the creation of knowledge that can stand scrutiny from experts in academic disciplines. This enterprise is generally separate from the learning needs of students.

Junior college teachers, some of whom are offshoots of the elementary and secondary classroom, bring a mixture of concerns that form an undercurrent on the faculty.

The college liberal arts faculties are mostly concerned with transferring their interpretations of knowledge to students in ways they feel are important in their discipline.

The university faculties are generally engaged in their own research or experimentation and the relationships they develop with students is often one-on-one. When group instruction is warranted, at this level, teaching assistants are enlisted to offer the courses and test for recall.

Whether teachers at the higher levels of education utilize group instruction, laboratory research, or other interventions, they must all be required to develop a validated set of assumptions about all aspects of the teaching-learning process and practice appropriate interventions. Much of the most inconsistent and ineffective methodology found in education is practiced in the classrooms of higher education.

There are five components in an effective teacher education program. (See model previously displayed) The first component addresses what is known and can be validated in one's own experience about human development and behavior, including learning. The sub-components address all the dimensions of individual development including physical/neurological, intellectual, social/emotional, moral, and aesthetic dimensions.

The second component addresses interpersonal dynamics that includes communication, group processes and group development and applications in the institutional setting.

The third component deals with the disciplines as ways of constructing and communicating meaning within the six realms of meaning.

The fourth component addresses the dimensions, dynamics, and historical evolution of the educational enterprise in its entirety.

The fifth and final component addresses the personal characteristics of the individual entering into a helping relationship with learners at all levels of maturity, acknowledging all dimensions of uniqueness.

Since there is no shared knowledge base for teaching-learning processes, the education of teachers must begin with establishing such a conceptual framework within peer groups of no larger than twenty-five and preferably, eighteen to twenty members. Since long term memory is limited for all of us, a complete record of experiences and learning that occurs must be maintained and continually updated by each learner and validated through open communication within their group.

This record is the central vehicle for assessing learning outcomes that indicate the competencies essential to one's efforts in becoming a competent teacher.

In my experience in the education of teachers, the record is maintained as an educator's handbook that contains the complete and comprehensive record of all that is acquired to develop competency in this complex profession.

Each individual candidate must maintain this handbook and update its contents as new insights emerge within the profession. In this way, change will be built into the routines of education at all levels and dialogue will be directed productively to the end of maintaining relevance and effectiveness.

Procedurally, the first and most pervasive component is self-insight. It is assumed that one's personal orientation to the world, unique perceptions, identification, and definitions of problems, strategies for coping with concerns, and all other aspects of personal decision-making are conditioned, if not directed by the beliefs one holds, the attitudes one assumes, and the values one has acquired in the course of life's experiences.

Such personal characteristics are essential subject matter for in-depth experiences throughout the teacher education program. Presumably these individualized characteristics shape interpretations of the other four components; each component is therefore examined and validated through personal experiences and with introductions to the experiences of others, especially those of other members of the group and experts in relevant fields of inquiry.

Included in the personal investigations is an analysis of personality characteristics, prior experience, experiential and social context, self-awareness, evolution of levels of maturation, biological potential, and acquired techniques and strategies for learning and coping with life. Consideration of these personal factors will reveal the possible impediments and aptitudes that affect the development of a high level of self-actualization and personal well-being, essential in any teaching/learning transaction.

Many instruments and strategies for revealing personal characteristics can be used to aid self-analysis. The results would be interpreted using models drawn from relevant literature that summarizes findings of research. These models can serve as "advance organizers" as described by David Ausabel (Ausubel, D.P, 1960).

"The Personal Orientation Inventory" authored by Shostrum and similar inventories are useful tools to help teachers identify elements in one's personal orientation that can interfere with fully-functioning life styles. Models drawn from the work of Lawrence Kubie, MD and others introduce dimensions of mind that account for conscious, pre-conscious and unconscious elements directly related to mental health, learning, personal uniqueness and diversity. These analyses of individual characteristics using models from literature call upon all the elements of the second and subsequent components of the foundation experience.

The second component, interpersonal dynamics, includes investigations into the nature of communication, group processes, and group development along with various institutional organizations that support sound principles of communication and group development. The group experience is conducted with full awareness of the need to understand the dimensions of communication that get in the way of fulfillment of both individual and group potential, and the full realization that communication is improved when groups achieve and sustain a level of consensual validation, the most mature level of group development.

The group experience becomes the laboratory for testing-out propositions about communication and group process, and institutional dynamics. Attention is directed toward any interferences that are prevalent in any group setting, institutional or otherwise, and these interferences are acted upon through development of alternative strategies and modified orientations to problems.

Without sufficient time to develop mature group decision-making, with opportunity to validate the essence of models drawn from the literature in these fields, and the utilization of verified interventions that promote growth and development, individual achievements would be greatly limited. Sustained group decision-making is critical to lay a foundation that is presumed to be expanded and further reinforced or modified as each candidate engages the content and processes of other components in the program.

Relevant models pertaining to this component are to be entered into the teacher's handbook along with the evidence of having recognized and internalized how important mature group processes are in aiding and maintaining individual growth and development.

The third component or focus of the foundation experience involves the interrelated dimensions of individual development and behavior, including learning. Each dimension, initially considered separately, is later integrated and validated by members of the group. Validation involves testing out the propositions through library research and hands-on investigations with fellow group members and learners of all ages.

For instance, each candidate would validate Piaget's model by performing a series of "conservation" tests with school age children at various levels of maturation, share their findings with other group members. These tests reveal the sequence of the development of logical capabilities and the variations in performance by children that is not age or grade related. From these exercises, it will be seen that children of the same age perform at different levels of biological maturity, thus furthering the proposition of the uniqueness of individuals.

Similarly, the models revealed in literature that describe other dimensions of individual development and behavior, including learning, are investigated within the group and relevance to their personal lives is clarified and tested-out through hands-on experiences. This series of investigations culminates in the achievement of a synthesis among all the dimensions represented in models constructed by each developing teacher/facilitator.

Each model is accurately represented in an appropriate file in the record (the educator's handbook) along with an analysis of the impact such information has on the candidate's ability to internalize his or her expanded and modified belief system. When the candidates can represent the synthesis achieved among all the dimensions of individual development and behavior, can critically evaluate the consistencies or inconsistencies among the positions of the authors, and can construct a model that includes all the relevant elements, then it is assumed that competency has been achieved in this component to be integrated with all the other components as they are developed and validated.

Once validation occurs, it is possible for implemented practices to follow that are consistent with the foundation concepts.

Competency can be achieved by all candidates in varying timeframes. More mature, experienced individuals will grasp the concepts quickly and move to implementation. Others will need to spend more time. Flexibility with respect to the achievement of synthesizing capabilities and critical evaluation must be honored if lasting, internalized competencies are to be developed and maintained as part of a belief system that will guide decision-making in the acts of teaching.

The fourth component involves a consideration of the academic disciplines as ways of constructing and communicating personal meanings. This component is adapted from the work of Philip Phenix. In an effort to establish a comprehensive and consistent basis for the organization of disciplines/subjects currently included in the curriculum of primary to post-graduate education, Phenix determined that there are six realms of meaning inclusive of all disciplines. His schematic establishes categories from structures disciplines have in common, based essentially on their ways of constructing and communicating meaning. He placed mathematics within the category of symbolics with other languages.

Phenix placed the social sciences within the "empirics" category along with other sciences. He defined a place for ethics/morality and for self-knowledge, along with esthetics, and synoptics. His schema evolved from an extensive study of the nature of individual disciplines and their relationships, one to another.

During group experience, organized experiences leading to a sense of the processes of constructing meaning using tools of inquiry inherent within selective disciplines is only the beginning. It is to be expected that the general education and liberal arts concentrations throughout the college experience will reinforce, modify, and extend this schema (an epistemology). In this manner, candidates will not only achieve a lasting grasp of structure within each realm and between realms, but the experience will lay the groundwork for meaningful instruction within the elementary, secondary school, and in higher education.

The methods of inquiry established in the candidate's construction of meanings will transfer from the college experience to the acts of teaching and living and will yield significant results among the learners.

Hands-on activities are to be organized that involve the history and geography of each candidate's hometown, in selective years where extensive data is available for constructing a complete picture of life in time and place. This step is essential for developing a frame of reference that is grounded in the reality of familiar surroundings and one that provides an overview that will keep individual specializations in perspective.

Data must be available that relates to all dimensions of the social, economic, political and geographical scene for various periods in time. Candidates will engage these materials and develop a verifiable model of the nature of each dimension of the region under investigation and the interrelationships between each of these dimensions. This synoptic experience demonstrates, in stark contrast, that history and geography are unique ways of knowing that integrate and summarize the findings of other disciplines that fall within other realms of meaning. This integration aids retention of facts and principles with lasting significance.

The fifth component includes an analysis of the dimensions and historical evolution of the school as a social institution. Exploration in this component requires the cooperation of local schools and colleges. Without a clear understanding of the existing educational system, there is little chance to significantly alter its structures to reflect a clearly defined foundation knowledge base.

Each and every dimension of the school must be investigated through first-hand observation, selective interviews, and selective readings. Given earlier developed understandings of self-development, group dynamics and development, individual development and behavior, and disciplines as ways of constructing meaning, each individual will become far more critical of the existing system than is now the case.

With the background or foundation that is developed by candidates, and documented within their records, a lively and engaging dialogue is expected that will advance the level of discourse within the profession and throughout society.

While the treatment of the content and processes of the five components of the foundation's knowledge base establishes some of the highlights of the effective teacher education program, it is understood that the ultimate goal is further investigation leading to integration of all components into a personally constructed and coherent theory and philosophy of education required of all competent teachers/professional educators. It is also presumed that the record of those experiences must be kept and made accessible as evidence of achievement of learning outcomes that go well beyond what a standardized examination can reveal.

These sensitivities and skills are not gained from traditional methods of teacher-training. They will require a process of experiential learning in which the prospective and in-service teacher is helped to gain self-awareness, understanding of how others perceive his or her behavior (the consequences of his or her behavior on others), practice in diagnosing human relations and group problems, experiences in sharpening sensitivity to what others are feeling and trying to communicate. These awarenesses and sensitivities are primary and teaching procedure secondary.

A healthy expansion of our knowledge of the teaching-learning process thus needs to be followed by an equally long overdue reexamination of methods of teacher training."

It is incredible that such insights as those written by Bradford and others were published over fifty years ago and still there is an abundance of ignorance and a resistance to change that is nearly unmovable. When the listing of items addressing what an educator should know and be able to do is juxtaposed against a current profile for teachers and school administrators, the picture is alarming.

I have found less than 5% of the teachers and administrators who exhibit what is considered necessary competencies for being a professional educator. These persons within the 5% were undoubtedly influenced by a culture that accounts for their orientations, not the direct result of the quality of their educational experience. The others have passed through the hoops and received a license to teach.

Bradford's insights and mine grew out of the creative struggles of the late fifties, the sixties, and early seventies. School architecture changed to project openness. Teachers underwent training workshops in human relations. Curricular content underwent an examination by those who were supposed to know. There was hope for change when the mood of the country abruptly shifted to a more conservative mode probably out of the fear of change. The dialogue that focused on the real issues of school improvement faded into the rhetoric of patriotism and the need to conform to higher and more arbitrary standards.

To conclude this chapter I will outline a strategy that is consistent with Bradford's treatise that was developed with the help of a few graduate students at the institution where I worked for forty years. We labeled this strategy "Constructive Learning and Instructional Planning With A Systems Orientation (CLIPSO). There are five steps in this strategy that will be recognized from the content of previous chapters.

The first is defining/redefining components of the system to be mastered. The teacher and the learners cooperatively develop a listing of the parts that will ultimately make up the system to be uniquely constructed and validated by each learner. The listing of parts (the record's table of contents—each part represents a file for the computerized record) becomes the basis for goals which take into account what is required by the curriculum, what is presently known about the subject as drawn from within the group and from others. The listing is subject to change as inquiry proceeds. New parts may be added or some listed initially may be removed as more insight is developed. The agreed-upon listing of parts is then translated into learning objectives that provide structure for building toward mastery that is continuously tracked in the record.

The second step is accumulating experiences that assist

in the translation and conceptualization of each component/part of the system and inserting evidences into the record. The performance objectives for this step include: first experiencing, and then translating those experiences into personal language forms, followed by interpreting and personally connecting the new experiences with related ones from the past, analyzing the experiences and finally inserting all of the results (concepts) into the record under each appropriate file. This process is continued for each file or part of the system being constructed. It is of utmost importance at this step to have access to a rich bank of information from all types of media and an opportunity to experience directly as much as is possible.

The more direct and life-like the experiences, the richer the concepts will become. Richer concepts will lead to greater possibilities for making connections that build toward the construction of a meaningful system. It is the teacher's responsibility to provide information-rich experiences for each of the parts in the table of contents. It is the learner's responsibility to translate those experiences into personalized language forms and insert the results into their records.

The third step involves model building that organizes and reorganizes the findings from the previous step. The records of experiences contained within each file will accumulate over time. When the evidences are sufficient, integration or syntheses will occur within each file. These integrations will be represented by models that summarize the meanings derived by the learner. These models will take the iconic form so that there is a conceptual backing for the words used in any symbolic models. When models are constructed that represent a synthesis of ideas, the accumulated evidences that led to the model are then removed to a permanent file and catalogued for future reference.

The fourth step is synthesis and critical/creative evaluation that serves to formulate communication of the levels of mastery achieved to date. As models within files are constructed, logical connections between concepts of multiple files develop which result in even higher levels of integration (interfile constructions).

These higher level integrations result in more elaborate models that show the relationships of discrete experiences to a completed synthesis—the development of a system. This synthesis gives rise to critical evaluation and creative manipulation that takes the form of a completed formulation designed to communicate the results to others. These communications take many different language forms, including narrative, demonstration, artistic representation, or performance.

Step five is verification that involves comparing and contrasting one's models with those of others. Once the system is constructed and communicated to others, the process of comparing and contrasting the individual constructions that are generated by each learner proceeds. This input from others serves to validate the content of the record and challenges the author to support and perhaps change the contents to reflect new information. In this way the record provides the evidences that support the learner's constructions of meaning. This facilitates retention, examination, and validation of the evidences.

Since the learner has constructed the record from personal experiences, the defense of the record is not difficult. Since the record provides a snapshot of the current understandings, it can easily be modified and updated as new evidences present themselves. Once constructed, the structures of meaning are in place that will not be lost and new information will be assimilated into those new structures.

This five step process can be easily implemented if given the chance and its underpinnings can be found to reflect verifiable foundational concepts for effective education.

Chapter 7

How Can Change Be Accomplished?

Having spent the last fifty years trying to change/improve education, I can personally attest to the difficulties of achieving success. My experiential background illustrates clearly many of the roadblocks to change that can and will occur when the status quo is challenged, regardless of importance or vision. In fairness, no one can anticipate the extent of anxiety that will emerge when school and college staffs are faced with a change in their traditional roles and procedures.

In 1966, I had great hopes that not only would I be able to move forward on what was a mission for me, but I could be closer to my roots and my aging parents by changing my place of employment. We bought a house in a rural village, 25 miles from my new college campus. Our children began the process of integrating into their new community in the spring of 1966.

I knew a member of the administration at the new college I was to serve that was located near my homestead in upstate New York, near the Canadian border. We had attended the same university (Teachers College, Columbia University) during our master's program. We had kept in touch so he was familiar with "Arnold's Group" conducted at Jersey City State College. He reported the successes of this effort to his boss at the college, a former school superintendent and ex-football coach who ascended to the position of vice-president for academic affairs, second in command at the college.

Speaking on behalf of the administration, my friend

asked me to enter into discussions regarding the feasibility of restructuring teacher education at that college, moving from a lock-step, traditional program to a more dynamic one built around the vision I was developing for general education and teacher education. I was invited to come on board to spearhead such an effort.

Based on the experience with "Arnold's Group" I knew there were significant benefits to be gained by creating groups of students working together over extended periods of time, each group with an experienced faculty leader serving as its mentor. This model would need to become a central focus of a more dynamic teacher education program that could bring out the capabilities of each member while engaging in experience that would resemble the way teachers of elementary students would be expected to teach.

Consistent with the Jersey City State experience, these learning groups would be assisted, as needed, by specialists who represented the academic disciplines required of the general education program. The academic disciplines would be offered as ways of knowing, using their methods and materials to achieve a real sense of their structures, thus meeting the goal of making these students more critical consumers of important information, whether from a lecture, a canned instructional program or any other source.

These experiences would begin in the freshman year. Mastery in each discipline would be defined in ways that recognized the uniqueness of individual constructions. I had field tested new ways of assessing and evaluating student-developed products and planned to install in my new college a competence- based program utilizing these procedures.

The first clue that should have signaled difficulties ahead came when it was decided that I must scale back my plans and work with a single group of students who were already enrolled in their traditional teacher education program. These students were beginning their junior year. Typically they would have been enrolled in two courses that included educational methods, materials, philosophy, and history. These courses totaled eleven semester hours. These two course requirements were lumped together and a group was identified to be led by me in a room located next door to a first grade classroom in the college's laboratory school.

The students who were slated to be my guinea pigs were all in some academic difficulty. If their grade-point average did not improve they were in danger of being dismissed or placed on probation. The challenge of working with such a group did not deter me from anticipating success. I was confident that these students would help in gaining the support of the college at large and keeping the administration in line to support a much larger plan down the road. My prior experiences had taught me the lessons needed to proceed.

I began with the procedures that helped these students dig deeply into their life experiences and share their insights with their fellow students. High levels of empathic communication and group resolve to work cooperatively in pursuit of the college's requirements developed quickly.

Success became apparent to these members and attracted attention from others outside this group. A visitor, who had been attending the first grade class as a volunteer next door, came by frequently to see what was happening.

This person was a gifted writer and could be relied upon to take careful notes. Having such a person ready and willing to put into prose what was occurring on a day to day basis was important for helping group members see how their activities were being perceived by an outsider. The written products were also invaluable in communications with administrators and the college community.

This person was the product of a difficult childhood, personally connected to Hollywood through her brother, a regular 1960s TV personality who conducted science experiments on the air aimed at school children. She gained the respect of our group and became "addicted" to what was transpiring.

When our writer/guest observed the sharing of personal

histories, in the context of education, it appeared to her to be a form of therapy and she became very worried. She was aware of the potential for such information to be used inappropriately, possibly harmfully.

Even though I had stressed the importance of confidentiality and respect for the uniqueness of each individual, she was very concerned about what she observed as it related to personal experience in a safe environment. She became so concerned that she called a psychiatrist friend and described her concerns.

His response was reassuring. He said in essence, one can't do something to others that they are not ready to do for themselves. She continued to watch the progress our group members were making toward accepting responsibility for developing their unique abilities, which included finding their way in a career as a teacher of young children.

Our group became known throughout the education department by other students and faculty who were enmeshed in their traditional courses. Students across the college campus became curious and interrogated the members of our group; often times arguing that such experience would not prepare them to be "real" teachers. Close proximity to the first grade classroom right next door, in fact in the same room only separated by a folding partition, gave us a decided advantage in being able to interact with children whenever we wanted to try out our wings with real kids

Our members were not intimidated by outsiders because we had developed a high degree of confidence in our abilities to find meaning in our studies. We were not covering the texts; we were engaging the subject matter in ways that made sense to us, unafraid of challenging assumptions that had shaped traditional education. We believed that if a proposition could not be supported in our own experiences and in the experiences of sensible authorities, it probably was in need of revision or perhaps abandonment altogether. We planted the seeds of reform with students who were not being rewarded by their institution. We created another "Arnold's Group."

When the fall semester ended, another group was assembled for the spring semester. By this time, the first group could and did assume a significant role in the orientation of the second group. Both groups were involved in spreading their impressions across the college community.

By this time, there had developed a mission to change the way teacher education would be conducted for upcoming groups.

A dinner meeting, organized by the students and I, involving administrators and faculty members, was designed to communicate how a dramatic change was on its way. Students from these two groups acted as ambassadors, each discussing education with faculty and administrators in ways that even I was impressed to see. Their maturity did not go unnoticed.

Faculty had evaluated many of these students and they were amazed at the change they witnessed in the levels of insight and motivation these same students displayed. Keep in mind, these were the same students that faculty thought were deficient and expressed that disapproval with a failing or nearly failing grade when they last saw them.

One very articulate student adopted the college president as her target to impress upon him what had happened and what could happen if the college would get behind a change in teacher education. She was so successful that the president asked all of the administrators and faculty in attendance to remain after the students went back to their dorms. The dinner meeting was held in a college-owned conference center where the comfort of its living room offered a relaxing setting for a follow-up meeting.

By this time, the administrators of the education department and I had developed a skeleton proposal for the change that we hoped would be approved by the college. We presented the major aspects of this plan using visual aids we had developed for that purpose. We proposed that the freshman class of elementary education majors (approximately 300 students) would be divided into groups of twenty. Each of these groups would be led by a member of the education department and representatives of each course offered in the general education program would be assigned to the program. The group leaders were labeled, generalists, and the representatives of academic disciplines, specialists.

The groups were to engage the academic program within their groups with the help of the specialists. Specialists and generalists were expected to clearly define competence levels that were worthy of credit. All faculty members were supposed to guide experiences that would help the students achieve the required levels of competence. Students would be granted credit for completion of their liberal arts/general education coursework certified by the specialists.

Exposure to elementary classrooms was to begin early to help students connect children's development and behavior especially with the assigned psychology course required in the general education program. Credits in professional education were to be granted by the generalists. Nothing would appear on the registrar's records except the credits earned by each student.

The after-dinner group convened with the president of the college. There was much discussion and after consuming a liberal amount of bourbon, at three in the morning, a decision was made to install what became known as *"The Open Curriculum."* I was considered to be the director/curriculum leader of the project, although no formal declaration to that affect was ever committed to paper.

This meeting took place at the end of the spring semester so the summer months were available as preparation time. The project was to be housed in the campus laboratory school so that our college students would have easy access to elementary students for observation and participation.

We had resources to hire consultants to assist in the preparation of a formal proposal, complete a statement of rationale and a review of relevant literature, and design a research plan featuring operations research to determine if the program was actually functioning as proposed.

The plan included subsequent comparative studies to determine how this program would stack up against other more traditional programs.

We brought in the members of "Arnold's Group" from the prior college who engaged the generalists in discussions about the conduct of a productive group experience focused on the mastery of the general education program. These student consultants had great reservations about whether some of the generalists would be able to lead a group experience in productive ways.

During that summer, several new faculty members were hired as generalists and the specialists were assigned by their department chairs. As it turned out, most of the specialists assigned to the project were viewed as problematic by their department heads.

Two of the generalists were selected that I had worked with in graduate school or as a fellow faculty member from the former college. A third generalist was hired after a short meeting that occurred in the college parking lot. There was a chance meeting with a former teacher and principal of a California school who was accompanying his wife who had taken a job in the nursing department at the college. Based on what I learned about this person, I recommended that he be employed. The remaining generalists were selected from a pool of volunteers from within the education department, some more reluctant than others.

A decision was made that the "campus school" would also become an example of "open" education modeled after the propositions outlined in the rationale and literature of the project. This involved over twenty faculty members who conducted their classes from nursery school through the ninth grade. Their students were expected to continue their education beyond the ninth grade in the public and private high schools of the area. This represented a source of great concern about whether an "open" education would prepare students to be successful in a more traditional high school program. As it turned out, these campus school students adjusted easily to the traditional courses of the high school.

The use of the term "open" connoted to many a kind of laissez-faire approach characterized by traditionalists as an outgrowth of Dewey's philosophy for progressive education. Many remembered the criticism that got much publicity about how students would come to school and be asked what they wanted to do today and they would answer: "Nothing."

Such a criticism was born out of ignorance about what the progressive activities were actually accomplishing, and even with the advent of longitudinal studies such as "the eight year study," that proved the positive results of the progressive education experience, many still clung to their biased beliefs.

In retrospect, the use of the label "open" did not accurately reflect the real nature of the "Open Curriculum Project." Openness in this project referred to the existence of many opportunities for adult students to make choices about their own progress toward a defined goal. That defined goal involved engaging in the methods and materials of disciplines and mastery of fundamental concepts and organizing principles inherent in these disciplines.

It was anticipated that students would define the elements of structure in unique ways that would be judged on their individual merits.

This concept grew out of the work of Phenix and the subject matter commissions of the 1960s, thirty years after Dewey's efforts with the "progressive education movement." Nonetheless, the traditionalists continued to perceive this project as just another "hair-brained" scheme to improve education.

I was expected to conduct intensive workshops with the faculty assigned to this project, beginning during the summer of 1967 and continuing throughout 67 and 1968. There were fifteen generalists, twenty two specialists and twenty more faculty members who worked in the campus laboratory school.

Many of these workshops brought out the deep-seated reservations held by some more traditionalist faculty members. There were many opportunities for an open expression of these feelings which was frightening to them. Masking these feelings in the conduct of their jobs was the way many of them had conducted their lives in the past. They were now being asked to confront those feelings and determine the supporting assumptions that underlay their orientations.

Emotions ran high throughout early stages of these workshops. In one case, two of the faculty of the campus school, who held opposite views of what constituted "good" education, actually engaged in a physical conflict that featured hair pulling. While this example was an isolated incident, it illustrates the prevalence of living with conflictive feelings without ever getting them resolved. Such repression often leads to physical and mental disabilities that are prevalent in the way schools are run, diminishing the effectiveness of educators in significant ways.

The upshot of this altercation resulted in finding common ground that led to mutual acceptance and continued dialogue; positive outgrowth from a stressful situation.

Another episode that is worth mentioning occurred when faculty were attending workshops that included their student teachers. When faculty openly expressed their feelings about critical matters, some traditional faculty became visibly upset. One such member went directly to the dean of the education division and complained about the inappropriateness of student teachers witnessing these discussions. The dean, out of an apparent ignorance about group development and group communication, ordered student teachers to be disallowed from attendance at these workshops.

As happened in this group experience, whenever the membership is arbitrarily disrupted, the group reverts to a lower level of functioning. They recognize that authorities outside the group have veto power over their deliberations. This can destroy the progress of a group that is working toward its levels of maturity and additional time is required to re-establish a productive atmosphere.

Generalists in the college level program who conducted their groups had similar internal conflicts about the legitimacy of these more open procedures. In many cases they conducted their group leadership in ways that reflected their well-entrenched views and preferred procedures.

One generalist retreated to his office and worked on his own projects and let his students flounder, all in the name of his concept of "open education." Another, a specialist in reading instruction, taught her class as a typical instructor with words of wisdom to pass on to her charges. Another generalist was working on a favorite project in gathering data on classroom interactions and he taught the methodology of his project.

Only two of the fifteen generalists fully understood their role as leaders of groups that were to become teams engaged in mutual support and mutual acceptance of the task of engaging the subject matter of the college's requirements. The warnings of members of "Arnold's Group" proved to be true.

Ironically, several of the "specialists" understood this new role and could have been far more consistent with the intent of the project, had they not been previously designated as a "specialist."

One uncooperative specialist in biology actually refused to make his video tapes available to students in the open curriculum even though these tapes were the property of the college.

The students who were assembled in the auditorium on the first day of class were anxious for some answers about their future. After considerable discussion about the organization and intent of the open curriculum project, one student commented that this is like a greased pig, just when you think you have it captured, it slips through your fingers.

Some students recognized an opportunity to earn many credits if their efforts were directed at achieving evidence of competency in numerous subjects. In fact, it turns out that some students proved their competence in the equivalent of ninety semester hours of credit in one year, while others didn't show competence in any areas of the curriculum. This, of course, did not sit well with the parents of those who had little to show for their year's work, except their recognition that achievement requires effort.

When the semester ended, and the registrar was to record the results of student efforts, all she had was a record of those credits earned and no grades. She panicked from the realization that not only were "grades" unavailable, but her system of assigning such labels as a member of the "dean's list," and summa or magna cum laude, no longer had any place in the scheme of things. Instead of finding ways to approach this dilemma, she became greatly stressed and took a leave from her position.

This is an example of how a far-reaching project, such as this, impacts aspects of the total system. Coping with these challenges is often overwhelming, requiring empathic support while alternatives are being worked out.

Empathic support is seldom available in a traditional, authoritarian system that is oriented to "stability" that comes from the execution of routines that often do not require or allow any fundamental re-evaluation requiring more than superficial changes.

There were likely widespread complaints made to the inner circle of the administration and they were not grounded sufficiently in the underlying assumptions of the project to defend their value. This internal whisper campaign resulted in the president calling in an expert with impeccable credentials to evaluate the project.

This person was considered internationally as the "Dean" of social science as it applied to educational research. This person (Dr. Ralph Tyler) worked at Syracuse University when the president of this college was working on his doctorate. The president reportedly held him in high regard. This consultant came to the college and spent an entire week interviewing faculty and students, studying the written documents that described the plan and its future, and he prepared to report his findings to the president and his executive committee.

The president convened a meeting and sat down at the piano in his living room and began playing some familiar tunes that everyone recognized and could sing. After this interlude, he convened the business part of the meeting to discuss the future of the "Open Curriculum Project." He opened the session by stating that this project was in trouble and he had invited a consultant to study and evaluate the project to help in a decision about its future.

The consultant began by stating that this was the most significant project in teacher education that he had ever witnessed. He said its rationale matched anything he had found in his extensive career.

He stated that the project was being carefully implemented, but it would take a ten year commitment to bring it to its full realization. He recommended highly that the project was worthy of its continuance.

Keep in mind, that person was known internationally as an expert in educational research, who spearheaded the "eight year study" of the progressive education movement, and was currently directing an effort to compare our educational products with those of many other countries around the world. His judgments were considered to be of the highest quality.

At the conclusion of the presentation, the president of the college said, "When can we phase out this project?" This response brought back the memory of my former boss at my prior employment when he warned me that this president would not stand firmly in my corner when reforms are challenged, regardless of his promises to the contrary.

During the following semester, twelve of the specialists were dismissed from the college through a system of "peer review" that relies upon the judgment of fellow faculty members who had little or no connection with the project, nor interest in its continuance, but understood how valuable support for the positions of the chief school administrator could be.

An outside administrator was hired to take over the project and modify it to placate the disgruntled. This person became the principal of the campus laboratory school. He was steeped in the "sensitivity movement" that was then beginning to penetrate the school settings as a panacea for improving education.

When he began to set in motion sensitivity training sessions with campus school faculty, without consideration for the personal characteristics of individual members, I strenuously objected. This led to an open conflict with administrators, the middle management, who had previously supported my efforts and the open curriculum project. I came to work one morning and found my office desk moved out into the hall. I occupied this desk for several days and continued the work I had begun.

One of the specialists in the project contacted a nationally known expert in group development who had been hired to consult with the faculty during its implementation phase. He wanted this consultant from the University of Chicago to intercede on his behalf with the local administration to help him secure the new director's position.

The vice president for academic affairs called me into his office and informed me that the executive committee would probably not grant me tenure. He suggested that in order for him to "protect" me he would assign me to an official administrative position.

What he likely didn't consider is the fact that I was aware of the authority any high level administrator has over decisions of hiring and firing fellow administrators—especially firing. I rejected his suggestion and asked to be considered for tenure in the usual manner.

What he didn't anticipate was a relationship I had developed with the chairman of the college council, appointed by the governor. We had worked together in business and professional matters outside of the college and he was supportive of my efforts. Knowing the possible political consequences of rejecting my tenure appointment, they reluctantly granted it.

The open curriculum project was phased out after two and one half years with little regard for those students and faculty who were involved. I was reassigned to a typical role as an instructor in the department of curriculum and teaching for elementary education students. I came in to the institution at the rank of an associate professor and remained at that rank for twenty-six years until I decided to retire.

The transition back to the traditional course offerings occurred swiftly and administrators were content to declare stability once more. Yet there was an underlying problem. This maverick was now positioned amongst the rank and file faculty who had seen the power of administrators at work. The college hired a new administrator for the education department, a storm trooper type who didn't wear high top boots but rather spit-polished shoes matching an array of fine suits and ties. This new administrator immediately began to assert his authority by calling in to his office each member of his department and grilling them about their roles and performance within the department.

One seasoned female faculty member was overheard to say that she was so frightened that she wet her under garments.

When it became my turn, I was summoned to his office and confronted with this question, "You are not viewed as a member of this department, are you?" He said that my fellow faculty members held that viewpoint. I responded, "What department do they think I'm in, the history department or what?" His continued efforts to threaten and undermine me and my work were responded to in a similar manner. He became so frustrated that he literally pushed me out the door of his office and slammed it shut behind me.

During his tenure, I was involved as a member of the

executive committee of the faculty union. In my role as the chair of the terms and conditions of employment committee, I frequently found myself assisting faculty with their grievances against administrators. Adding this effort to my reputation as a trouble maker gave adequate incentive to escalate a pattern of harassment.

One example occurred when rooms were being assigned for leaders of groups in which they were to conduct seminars. I was assigned to a language laboratory that featured thirty "carrels" in rows bolted to the floor.

A request for a telephone to be installed in my office was denied. This incident marked the end of my patience and I filed a human rights complaint, claiming retaliation for conducting my official roles in the college community.

With the help of an assigned attorney from the Human Rights Commission, an investigation was conducted and a hearing was scheduled before an administrative judge. The college was represented by an attorney paid for by the state who had never lost a human rights case.

The judge ruled against me so I filed an appeal. At the appeal, I represented myself and won. When the results were communicated to the college president he emphatically declared that he would take the matter to court. Of course, the state would cover his costs, but I would be left with covering my expenses.

After considerable thought, I decided that the effect of having lost at the appeals level would diminish incidents of harassment and it turned out to be true. Incidentally, the attorney for the state was removed from his position and elevated to the governor's office. The president was promoted to become the academic leader (the Provost) of the entire SUNY system.

Attempts to squelch any activity that appears to be getting out of control, middle management will often employ strategies or threat to employ strategies of intimidation as they did in my case. Rory O'Day wrote a brilliant article about these rituals of intimidation that exist in our schools and colleges. (This article is re-printed in its entirety in appendix C.)

Dr. O'Day published his article entitled "Intimidation Rituals: Reactions to Reform" in the *Journal of Applied Behavioral Science* in 1974. Shortly after publication, a colleague and I organized an invitational conference with a grant for the sharing of incidents of perceived intimidation experienced by faculty members at our institution. The conference was immediately fully subscribed and Rory O'Day was the featured speaker.

Prior to the scheduled conference, we circulated a brief survey of opinion about the presence of intimidation at that institution. The response was overwhelming. One faculty member relayed a critical message that he was so distraught with the treatment he had received that he was considering suicide. We immediately went to his aid to help him through this crisis.

Now, over thirty-five years later, an effort to press for reform in teacher education and general education throughout the public educational systems is underway and Dr. O'Day's treatise offers a vital link for understanding the reasons why reforms in the public school systems have not been easy.

Having worked with both pre-service and in-service teachers for over fifty years I seldom encountered teachers who were resistant to ideas they could relate to that made sense to them. Pre-service teachers were distinguished for their enthusiasm for teaching with an expectation of being able to improve the lives of children.

Once in the system, these same enthusiastic teachers were frequently found to be disheartened, disillusioned, and stuck with unfulfilled expectations. They were encountering a "tough" hierarchical structure where administrators above them controlled their professional lives.

Most teachers are aware of the inconsistencies between imposed policies and procedures such as standardized tests and a standard core curriculum and what they intuitively sense are important matters of individual human development and behavior. Those who remain employed, hope for change and improvement; even though they often encounter the "intimidation rituals." Many who survive have either left the profession or succumbed to the forces of intimidation. No wonder we have seen widespread resistance to innovation and change in the way we educate our youth.

Keep in mind that those who practice intimidation rituals are part of a system that creates a need for the employment of survival techniques even if their results are hurtful. These participants are seldom "bad" people; they are members of a system that encourages this behavior.

The reaction of authority in social systems to the reform initiatives of a subordinate, viewed as a series of intimidation rituals, was explored in O'Day's article. "These rituals divide into two major phases, each involving two distinct steps. The first phase, Indirect Intimidation, includes the rituals of nullification and isolation; the second, Direct Intimidation, rituals of defamation and expulsion. Why these rituals for protest-suppression in organizations are powerful tools in the hands of the middle manager is discussed. Attention is also given to various images projected by the organizational reformer and reasons for resistance to reform from within an organization.

This paper characterizes the reactions of superiors in social systems to a reform-minded subordinate as a series of intimidation rituals. Each successive "ritual of control" represents an escalation in the effects of authority to discourage an individual (and those who may support him or her) from continuing to seek reform.

Middle Management's Mechanism of Control

The rituals of intimidation satisfy the two primary concerns of authorities confronted by a subordinate who appears not only able to articulate the grievances of a significant number of other system members but also capable of proposing solutions to them. Their first concern is, of course, to control the reformer so that he (or she) does not succeed in recruiting support. Their other concern is to exercise this control in ways that absolve them of any wrongdoing in the matter.

The individual in question must be controlled in such a way that he or she neither continues to be an effective spokesman nor becomes a martyr. When superiors are confronted with a reform minded subordinate, they want his (or her) silence or his (or her) absence, whichever is easier to achieve, The "authorities" must also preserve their carefully managed image of reasonableness, and would prefer that the reformer leave voluntarily rather than be removed officially.

For purposes of illustration, this presentation will describe intimidation rituals used by various organizations in the service of protest-suppression, for organizational authorities prefer to intimidate a reform-minded individual rather than commit organizational energy to the structural and personal changes required to transform a "nonconforming enclave" into a legitimate subunit. It is further suggested that an organization undergoes major changes that incorporate and accommodate a group of dissidents only when the intimidation rituals do not succeed in silencing the individuals who constitute the "leading edges" of the reform movement.

The full text of O'Day's article is found in Appendix C.

In the midst of establishing absolute authority within the curriculum and teaching department of my college, after the death of the Open Curriculum Project, the dean of the education division declared that a new, revised program had to be developed by a specified deadline in order to be included in the upcoming program descriptions for the subsequent fall semester. He appointed committees to begin deliberation to produce a new program for students of elementary and secondary education.

I set about planning a response to that mandate, but did not share it with fellow faculty members, since I understood the risks of convoluted involvement of faculty and the threat of intimidation by middle management if the proposals were viewed as a threat to the status-quo. I knew that a program that resembled the "Open Curriculum" would not fly but a modification might be installed if the circumstances were handled with care.

Since this new mandate was initiated within the education faculty, it removed from deliberation any involvement of the liberal arts specialists who offered courses for education majors. I focused on an attempt to secure some of the remains of the prior project, such as that embodied in group experiences that would give ample time to develop personal theories of education with each of the teacher education candidates.

Early involvement in schools was proposed for the purpose of validating the positions that would grow out of a more intense exposure with the underlying assumptions that direct decision making. My proposal restructured the professional education sequence into three 12 semester hour blocks of time that provided for unfettered activity involving frequent visitations to schools.

The first block would be dedicated to the foundations of education—its philosophical, historical, and psychological dimensions. The second block was to deal with the methods and materials of teaching that I hoped would build upon a verified set of assumptions about teaching and learning expected to be the product of the first block. The third block involved the student teaching phase wherein each student would be required to demonstrate an ability to work productively with young students, consistent with the orientations of blocks one and two.

I developed projector overlays to be used for a future presentation of a new organization and framework for teacher education. I knew that the deadline for a proposal was rapidly approaching, and the faculty committees were in various stages of disarray. The day for consideration of the products of these committees finally arrived.

A lively discussion centered upon resistance to change and it became apparent that the committees assigned the task to produce proposals for consideration by the whole department had failed. The hour for a decision was fast approaching in response to the dean's mandate.

At five o'clock on a Friday afternoon, I decided that was the time to present my suggestion for a new program. I labeled this program, "The Block Program." Using those previously developed visual overlays, the program's basic structure was delivered to an impatient faculty, interested in splitting with utterances of TGIF.(Thank God Its Friday) The majority of the group responded in favor of adopting this block program and they were finally free to go their own separate ways.

As I left the meeting, I was accosted by several faculty members who accurately accused me of a secret plot to re-instate parts of the "Open Curriculum Project." (Incidentally, these same faculty members found that the block of time provided in my plan for instruction gave them much flexibility to interact with actual classrooms of students and they were so impressed that they later publicly asserted that they were the founders of this innovative program.)

This block organization became a model for sister institutions and it received accolades from many quarters across the state. In fact, the program received a national award for "excellence" granted by a national professional organization.

My assignment was with the foundations block—Block One. This block provided an extended period of uninterrupted time to work with a group of students in an effort to get them to examine fundamental assumptions that influence decision making in schools. Extensive involvement with elementary classrooms became routine as part of the block experience, linking theory with practice. The pattern of group experiences from the past portended exceptional progress in developing a much higher level of competence than had been accustomed to happen in the past.

Our students turned in consistently high scores on state wide teacher exams. This assignment gave fellow faculty many opportunities as well to examine their assumptions and beliefs and find validation for them or find good reasons to abandon those positions. A vibrant group of block one instructors resulted from this interaction.

My block one group participated in the exercises I had experienced many times in the past. We delved more deeply into the personal histories of each member than occurred in other blocks.

There was one incident that comes to mind that warrants entry in this treatise. This incident illustrates the inner conflicts that many people have that are seldom resolved and compensations are manufactured to allow life to go on.

This incident involved a student whose mother was white and his father was black. His mother raised him alone by working and sacrificing for his welfare. John was enrolled in my block during the intense and aggressive activities of the black community to gain respect. There was intense pressure for him to declare his identity with the blacks and deny the whites. He perceived that he was being asked to abandon his loving mother who was white and assert his blackness along with his community brothers and sisters.

In the course of sharing personal histories, this student revealed aspects of his past that he had never shared before with anyone. During the course of the discussion he realized how much self-disclosure had occurred and how vulnerable he had become if this information were to be used without regard for confidentiality.

He sat motionless in his chair and gradually slumped like a bag of potatoes. He was temporarily unable to talk or move. Realizing the severity of this occurrence, I asked his closest friends to stand close by while others in the group silently retreated to their dorms. I sent one student to telephone a friend in the nursing department who specialized in psychiatric nursing. When she arrived we were able to move John to the comfort of a friend's apartment.

As one whom John trusted, I remained with him, reassuring him, and encouraging him to breathe with me. I spent the night at his side. John got some sleep during the night and in the morning we were able to travel to where he could get professional help in understanding what had happened and why. His close friends, brothers and sisters, rode with us and provided support and encouragement.

Upon admission to a state run mental institution, I walked arm and arm with John until he felt adjusted to this new environment. We all left him in the hands of the professional staff. We visited him for the next several days.

Gradually John became more like himself and he was on his way to becoming a different, more confident individual. After a week, he was released with a positive bill of health. He returned to his class and was greeted with genuine empathy and renewed support.

All the students in our block were asked to write about their experiences and John did his part. The first half of his paper was written in the "king's" English; it showed his unusual skills for analysis and communication. In the middle of his paper he stopped abruptly and wrote: "Fuck it." Then he launched into a similar analysis of his experience but this time in the language of his brothers and sisters of the Bronx.

In spite of his use of an unfamiliar lexicon for whites like me, he left no doubt about his message. It was in this section that he decided to offer his definition of me as his mentor. Speaking for himself and his fellow classmates, he wrote: "You came on like a virgin pussy, and you slipped it to us like a sly old fox." To many this would sound vulgar but to me it represented a major step for John in facing and accepting his identity and yet maintaining the values of his experiences with whites and especially with his white mother. John went on to become a professional in a government agency and never looked back.

While John did not choose to go into the teaching profession, his white classmates did. This incident served to make them examine and shed many of their stereotypes and prejudices.

It is not an afterthought that many of those in training to be psychiatrists are asked to engage in analysis. Self-understanding is absolutely required for all those who are expected to relate to others in need, with empathy and compassion. Just think how little of this adventure happens in the preparation of teachers who are placed in charge of the lives of many, many youngsters whether in their formative years or beyond. There are few experiences in the typical teacher education programs that would deal with problems of personality. Specifically, authoritarian personality characteristics remain unrecognized and they do not preclude a teacher candidate from entry into the teaching profession. No wonder some of these teachers are practicing "terrorists" as described in Manny Bernstein's book, *The Secret Revolution: A Psychologist's Adventures in Education.*

Block Two was unfortunately filled with faculty who had traditionally offered their preferred methods and materials for teaching subject matter and the skills of reading and communication. They were seldom committed to seek consistency with the assumptions about learning and development that were explored during "Block One." As a consequence, "Block Two" was not well coordinated with the block one experience and this led to frequent conflict. "Block Three" likewise ignored the efforts of block one faculty and determined that the ability to write and implement a lesson plan would be sufficient to guarantee that teachers would be able to teach effectively.

This position has always ignored the fact that these lesson plans, were and are, organized and presented in the absence of students during the planning stages. As a consequence of this fact, it forces teachers to seek ways to develop motivation for getting their students to listen to the presentations and demonstrations, since these students were not involved in the planning and usually had little commitment to seeing the lesson's purpose or value. Motivating techniques and discipline strategies were necessarily required, even if they only dealt superficially with the problem.

Without genuine student motivation, this places the student teacher in a precarious position since in the present setting attentiveness on the part of students is paramount to success. This is still a central thrust in the effort to improve education, only in these modern times, the lesson plans are packaged by outside companies and presented through the electronic media for teachers to use in their classrooms. This not only further distances the students from the processes of planning; it does the same to the teachers.

This practice has become so prevalent that state and federal funding of projects aimed at improvement speak of the need for developing "teacher proof" directions by mandating "better" lessons that are required of the classroom teachers. This has the effect of making teachers mindless robots that carry out the mandates of some "experts" who have decided how education is to be conducted. Interestingly, teachers have now discovered a new way of making money by selling their lesson plans to other teachers. While this can be useful, it still represents the same practice promoted by corporate interests – that of designing teacher proof directions for teaching.

Of course, there is always the possibility that teachers are not prepared to use their own intelligence and need to be told what to do, even if what they are told cannot be supported by any rational examination from a valid position about what constitutes productive human development and behavior.

In the midst of the attempts to phase out any remnants of the open curriculum project at my college, members of the faculty of the campus school were informed that they no longer would have a job. The college administration decided to close the campus school and transfer the twenty positions to a newly formed business department.

The faculty and parents decided to protest and they lobbied the state legislature to stop this move. With the help of local legislators and chairs of important legislative committees, a proposed law was brought to a vote by both houses. The law passed overwhelmingly, but was vetoed by the governor.

His position was that his approval would open the doors to undermining the authority of the local college presidents.

Only two members of the education department participated in this effort. Most of the department members were against "open education" and cared little about the lives of these innovative faculty members. Incidentally, it became apparent as campus school faculty traveled together to the state legislature to lobby for a decision to keep the campus school open, these faculty members suddenly realized there were two political parties whose members sat on opposite sides of the chambers of the two houses. Their educational experience with government was so limited this was where they were at that point.

Ironically, a new principal had been hired to help close the campus school, but he became committed to keeping it open after witnessing the qualities exhibited by faculty and their programs.

This principal was the first one to hold that position who actually had a vision of what education could be. I suspect that his resume contained a few key words that other administrators like to see, but they were obviously unaware of what this person was really all about. Having worked with seven different administrators in ten years, I was most impressed by this one. He lasted three years.

There was continuing conflict between the views of the traditionalists and progressive members of the faculty. This situation led me and others to seek more rewarding possibilities and activities while still struggling for some rationality in the block program. These activities, while appearing to be diversionary, were in actuality extended opportunities to test out and expand the application of the basic principles of learning and development in other venues.

I was at the time actively involved in a community service organization. I often presented programs to the club members as if they were students engaged in trying to make sense out of life. I was elected president of this active club seven times. During those years, there developed a need in our community for recruitment of a resident doctor to offer primary health care for the local population. I read an ad in the *New York Times* that announced the efforts of a major foundation to help rural communities to recruit doctors.

When I read the article, I knew that a viable proposal could be written that would be attractive to this foundation. I recruited fellow club members to work as a committee to pursue this possibility. We began to organize the community in response to the widely perceived need.

A local philanthropist donated a building to house a primary health care clinic that would respond to the requirements for recruiting doctors and retaining those doctors in an isolated rural community. The proposal was written that featured a centrally located clinic equipped with laboratory and x-ray facilities with several satellite offices and an affiliation with a local hospital.

Our proposal received a grant of $450,000 to cover the renovations of the clinic, purchasing of equipment and furniture and start-up capital. In addition, we had raised several hundred thousand dollars locally through fund raising events. This foundation-supported project was to be coordinated by a well-known university in North Carolina. This university was authorized to help recruit physicians to work on the project. They identified three family practice, board certified, physicians who were assumed to be a team eager to work on an innovative project. Our project was one of nine funded across the U.S.

It became apparent that these physicians did not operate as a team, in fact, they were often in conflict. The thing they had in common was the culture of the post-Vietnam Era. They exhibited a troublesome level of ignorance about the ways and means of developing a team oriented staff at the clinic, in spite of their training as certified family physicians having graduated from a university known to be the center of family practice in the United States.

These physicians refused to abide by the provisions of the project as outlined in the funded proposal. They viewed the satellite offices to be detractions from their perceptions of their preferred clinical practice. This behavior led to a serious shortfall in gross income compounded by questionable accounting procedures conducted by an employee who was alleged to have cooperated with professional staff for personal gain.

The clinic and its satellites were to be governed by a consensus model that was well-documented in group process literature. Since I was the designated administrator, on leave from the college, it was my responsibility to oversee the conduct of the center under the scrutiny of various government agencies. When decisions had to be made that had not been arrived at by consensus, or could not be arrived at in time to respond to mandated requirements, my decision to respond to those situations was viewed as a deliberate departure from the group decision making activity. In fact, I was personally viewed in time by the doctors as a traitor.

The doctors recruited community political types to plead their case against me and I decided to step aside. Before resigning, I reorganized the clinic so that it would conform to the usual legal procedures of a corporation with a board of directors. In spite of efforts to disrupt this process by some community members whose political aspirations were reflected in their behavior, the reorganization occurred without delay and a new board of directors was put in place to direct the project and supervise the staff.

While I was away celebrating an anniversary, some members of the clinic's staff organized a kangaroo court proceeding that took place at the local bank on a Saturday, run by a politician and his supporters. Community dignitaries voiced the position that we should tend to our own business and abandon the idea of serving other communities.

This experience taught me a valuable lesson that I will not easily forget. To substitute a consensus model as a replacement for the line and staff organization of a corporation, there needs to be clear provisions for decision-making that requires immediate action. Those instances, when occurring, need to be discussed at a later time to develop a clear understanding of the perceived need for the decision and perhaps find a better response that can be developed and supported by consensus. Clarity about this provision is paramount to avoid conflict over required decision-making processes.

The primary health care clinic, minus the original planned satellites, is still functioning in spite of the turmoil that plagued its formative years.

Among other diversions that fit into my mission was a series of consultant jobs in North Carolina schools and federally funded projects aimed at school improvement. In one such project, there was an interest in developing local history studies modeled after the *Discovery Approach to the Teaching of Social Studies*. Noting that local documents were needed to allow teachers to implement this approach, we set about finding a technology that would store historical and geographical documents and display those documents when needed in the classroom.

We experimented with microfilm and automated viewing equipment. We improved this type of media as we discovered its shortcomings by photographing documents on thirty-five millimeter color film, mounting these images on aperture cards that were organized and punched for retrieval, and displaying the images by projection.

We experienced a degree of success over previous technologies that included printing reproductions of documents by offset press, photographing on microfilm and black and white microfiche. All of these approaches, however, had serious shortcomings from the perspective of image quality, display equipment, and cost. Like experiences in the past, as long as we could provide usable visual documents for the classroom, the teachers could implement the Discovery Approach. Our attempts to supply data failed and so did implementation of the Discovery Approach.

A more elaborate project was attempted in Ohio where I was asked to workshop with a newly hired staff to be installed in classrooms in a newly constructed elementary school. These workshops employed many of the approaches to improvement I had attempted in other settings and earlier times. After several weeks of workshops, the staff gave their enthusiastic endorsement to the possibilities they were introduced to, and agreed to work to install a newly designed program in their classrooms. I was much encouraged with their response.

I visited their school approximately a month after the conclusion of the workshops, and what I found was most discouraging. These teachers were performing almost exactly the way they had experienced their own education and had adopted those approaches as the way to teach.

In discussion with these teachers, I learned they did not receive support from the administration to innovate; they were not given the resources to implement any new plans, so they abandoned them and returned to that in which they felt secure when conducting their teaching activities.

Having become familiar with the Carolinas, I participated in what was called a "Jobs 70" program, a federally sponsored plan to employ the under-employed members of the community, mostly Afro-Americans. I was designated as a consultant in a large textile factory that produced denim for the more affluent markets.

My job was to conduct seminars with first line supervisors within the textile mill. These supervisors were white males who had grown up in the mill. Their fathers and grandfathers had worked there and passed on the traditions and skills needed to be successful in that plant. The thought of bringing underemployed, Afro-Americans into their workforce was most troublesome. They viewed these people as lazy louts who would rather hang out on the street corner than work.

I was asked to conduct group seminars with these supervisors during their shifts to prepare them to integrate these underemployed low-life's (as they referred to them) that would be thrust upon them by the government. There were three shifts, the first one began at seven A.M., the second at three P.M. and the last one at eleven in the evening. After an hour lapsed during which the supervisors had finished organizing their shift workers, they appeared at the seminars.

I introduced them to exercises that were designed to establish a basis for open and honest communication about their work and the problems they were encountering. Production was their most important concern. If their shift did not meet its quota, they would be held responsible. This concern was foremost in their discussions about taking into the production line, individuals who were not motivated to produce, at least as they perceived the situation.

I introduced them to developmental theories that would help explain how motivation to succeed could be diverted or destroyed. Their understanding of human development and behavior was primitive and what they did understand from life's experiences didn't seem to translate into a plan to solve their dilemma.

I introduced them to Piaget's theory of the development of cognitive capabilities, Maslow's hierarchy of human needs, Erikson's model of personality development etc. Each of these models were considered as explanations for how and why human beings behave as they do and what might be done to improve their lives.

In the course of the seminars, a problem developed within the plant involving the quality of the denim that was being shipped to its largest customer. There was a defect described as a variation in shade from side to side on the bolts of cloth. Each shift was aware of this problem and outside engineers were peering over their shoulders to determine the cause.

This problem provided an opportunity for me to introduce the concept of model building that would aid problem solving. I suggested that these supervisors take me through the production sequence and explain to me how each machine worked and what it was supposed to do as part of the production sequence. I asked the supervisors to draw a diagram of the sequence, labeling and sketching the machines and their importance in creating a perfect product. I suggested that this exercise in gaining an integrated concept of the whole production sequence would work wonders with any new recruits.

As we proceeded to diagram the production sequence, members of the group pointed to the potential areas where the side shading problem could be found. The night shift looked at this problem and said emphatically, there is a problem with the adjustment of the "sand roller." Since they were so convincing, I decided to meet with the plant manager the following morning to tell him of our discovery.

I had met before with the manager frequently to explain what was happening in our seminars. He had heard of Piaget's theory from prior discussions and he was somewhat skeptical about any new theory we might have concocted. When I explained the model building exercise and the conclusion that the problem rested with an adjustment of the "sand roller" he scoffed at it and shouted, "Don't you think the engineers we have researching this problem would have found that if that was the problem?"

With that admonition, I continued my work with each seminar, waiting to see what the engineers found out. After about a week, a memo came down to the supervisors, ordering them to change the adjustment on the "sand roller." No mention was made of where that idea originated. This angered the supervisors, but it led to a much greater appreciation for how they were being treated that related to the way they were treating these new workers who were thrust upon them.

In another project, I was hired to consult with cell biologists who were designing instructional materials and programs for use in medical schools. A group of this country's leading cell biologists were assembled to define what they considered essential in understanding their discipline. They came from Harvard, Cal Tech, the University of Vermont, and other institutions engaged in medical education. They met under my leadership to identify and define the content of cell biology and the relationships between its parts.

After several days of intense discussion within this group of experts in their chosen fields of inquiry, a model of the human cell was developed in the form of a series of expanding circles surrounding the core, the human cell. Within the first circle the fundamental parts of the cell were displayed. The next outer circle contained elaborations of the parts identified in the first circle surrounding the core, the human cell. This exercise was determined to be the first step in improving instruction in cell biology offered to medical students.

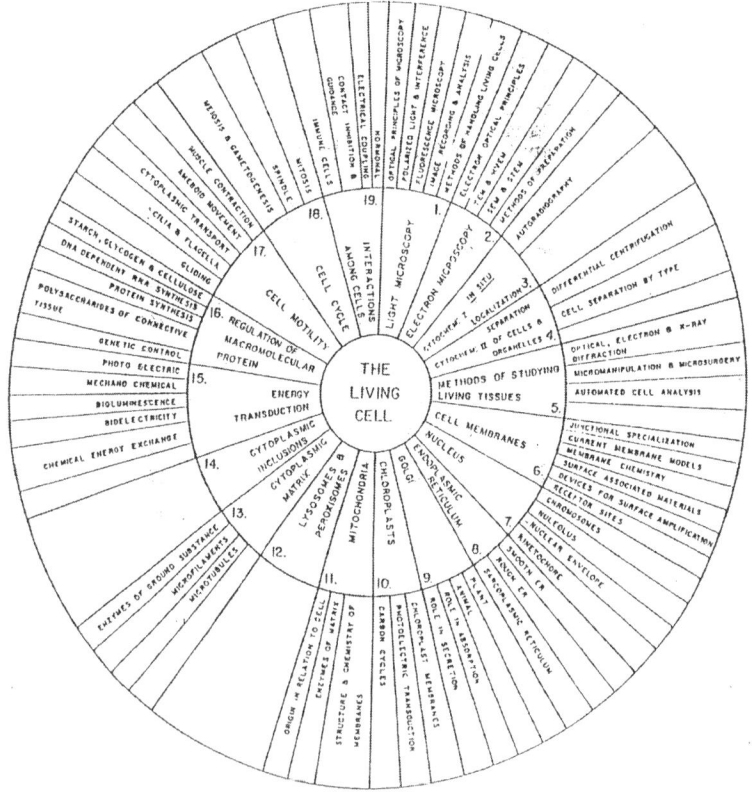

Cell Biology Study Program
(Content and Process Matrix)

I transferred each of the items contained within the model to a set of playing cards. On the front of each card was displayed a part of the human cell that these experts placed within the conceptual framework for their discipline. That framework contained a listing of the content and discoveries known at that time and the relationships that were known to exist. This represented what was considered to reflect mastery of cell biology, important for the education of doctors who would be prescribing medications etc. for patients.

It was believed that doctors needed to recognize the possible consequences that would likely occur with the insertion of foreign substances into the human cell.

In an effort to determine the nature of instruction in cell biology that was happening in the medical schools across North America, a questionnaire was prepared to report what was in their curricular offerings. The results indicated that medical students were introduced to cell biology about at the level of the content offered to sixth graders in our public schools.

To further gather data about cell biology instruction I took my deck of cards containing information of what the experts felt was essential to understanding cells and sat in the lobby of a Miami Hotel and interviewed over one hundred teachers of cell science from medical schools who were attending their annual conference.

Each interviewee was asked to examine the cards and arrange them in a pattern that would illustrate the relationships they recognized among the parts that had been identified by the panel of experts. The results were troublesome to say the least. Only a hand full of teachers of cell science could build a pattern of the relationships of the parts of the human cell in ways that resembled that which the experts had developed.

With this information, we set about the task of designing instructional modules that would engage medical students in activities that would enable them to formulate their own models that could be verified by comparison with those of the experts in that field. These modules included visual aids and instructions for experimentation that were designed to derive real insight and retention of important information needed in the practice of medicine.

Unfortunately, the directors of this project resided in California and western Canada, and were impressed with what educators were promoting at that time, the use of "behavioral objectives" to ensure a common definition of the desired instructional outcomes.

Representatives of this "innovation" came into the group and tried to restructure the modules to conform to their propositions. This turned off the cell biology experts who had been working on the creative instructional modules that they believed would result in the development of real competence. Once these education types entered the scene, the project began to deteriorate and only a few packaged instructional units were ever produced for distribution to medical schools.

I was convinced that implementation of approaches to learning that required easy access to information, other than texts, was a key to attaining a degree of improvement in our schools. Apart from my college teaching, I entered into the development of what in the 1980s was an innovation in the storage and access of visual information. I was introduced to color microfiche and computer controlled display equipment.

We believed these potential innovations could be refined if sufficient capital could be raised to launch a research and development enterprise with the hope of becoming a viable business for marketing these products to schools and universities. I spearheaded an effort to raise capital through Small Business Agencies and found $450,000 dollars that was made available for this purpose. We organized a corporation and were able to set up a research facility equipped with machinery and components needed to refine the technology for color microfiche and computer controlled projection equipment. We launched our project in the mid-1980s.

This technology was being introduced at the same time that digital imaging was on the minds of everyone. In spite of numerous attempts to show that color microfiche exhibited qualities for the storage and access of information that was unmatched for archival storage and pixel resolution at that time, the promises of digital imaging over those of analog images on film kept potential buyers from investing in this technology.

We produced hundreds of ultra-high resolution images on 105mm color film stocks that were tested to last over one hundred years. We were contracted by Kodak to produce images on this film that were used to compare with digital images in their early stage of refinement. We entered into discussions with professional associations that maintained a vast archive of slides and were considering converting them to other media that would make them archival and more accessible.

The Dermatology profession maintained such a collection of hundreds of 35mm slides, frozen in their archives, to be duplicated and distributed to medical schools for training physicians to recognize a variety of skin conditions. We had designed and built a prototype of an automated viewer/projector that would select specific images and project them on a screen. This package attracted much attention at expositions, but there were very few takers.

We decided to reproduce full color maps of every area of the world, depicting geographical and historical data that would make it possible for teachers to access this information in their classrooms. With this technology we believed that teachers would finally be able to fully implement a discovery approach using the latest information produced by our federal agencies, the CIA, the Department of Agriculture, the UN, and *National Geographic*.

We developed the necessary computer programs to search and display these full color images on demand. Only a hand full of customers ordered our products and they mostly sat on their shelves and collected dust.

Eventually the inevitable happened. We filed for Chapter 11, and ultimately Chapter 7 and closed our doors. I wrote an article for an international association that had an interest in promoting film technologies. In this article, I argued that using color microfiche as a storage medium was extremely important since the visual images would be a more valuable record than images stored digitally on a disc that had a limited archival quality, eight to ten years, as opposed to over a hundred years for film.

This fell on deaf ears since the digital mania had arrived with its promise to solve all the problems of storage and accessibility through computer technologies. I'm happy to find that the digital technologies today have reached a level of excellence that was only dreamed about in 1993, when our business went under.

Recently I experienced, first hand, a validating experience for my contention that a visual, film-based record is necessary for storage of important information. I had raised doubts about the appropriateness of storing information only in digital form but no one seemed to care.

During a move of my residence, I lost my discharge papers and needed them in order to apply for relief with land tax for veterans. I decided to contact the local veteran's office and they filled out a form that was transported to the central archives for veteran's records.

After two months delay, I received a letter stating that the veteran's records for the period in which I had served, were destroyed by a hacker. They replied that if an additional form is submitted, that gave them all the information I had available about my record, perhaps they would be able to respond to my request.

This form was submitted with documentation from the Veteran's Administration. Several weeks passed and the archives communicated by letter that my file had been removed in response to a prior inquiry and a search had been unable to find it.

Now, had these archives not relied entirely on a digital record, without backup by a visual record, they would not have had that problem. Multiply this incident by thousands and the future does not look good. Just another example of how the latest fade will cloud any rational intelligence that may or may not have developed.

Faced with a disastrous experience in business and continuing frustration with decision makers within the college community, I decided to retire, after twenty-six years. I then formulated a plan to establish an Institute on campus dedicated to furthering the work that had been ongoing in teacher education and assisting schools in teacher training and grants development.

The Institute was approved by the department where I worked, (provided that it was not represented as the opinion of the department) and approved by the dean and the president of the college. I was given an office space to continue my work and entered into part time employment as an adjunct, teaching the same courses I taught when I was employed full time.

The advantage of this move was that I essentially removed myself from the direct influence of college decision-makers and found a level of independence that allowed me to work on projects of my choosing, on my time table. For the college, hiring an adjunct is much cheaper than hiring a full time faculty member.

I continued to refine the block program since I was able to work with all three blocks as an adjunct. This allowed me to find ways of developing continuity between the blocks that resulted in the discovery of extraordinary talents in students and comprehensive plans for aneffective teacher education program. Formulations that define improvements in education, found in chapters of this treatise, came from the studies occurring during the years since 1993.

I organized a team of professionals that developed and submitted a comprehensive response for proposals to change education advocated by the senior President Bush in his "New American Schools" project. I attended meetings prior to building this team that were organized under this Bush initiative, conducted by knowledgeable and dedicated educators. I was convinced that they were serious about searching for better ways to educate our youth.

The project was predicated on the assumption that huge sums of money would be forthcoming from private donors to underwrite grants for selected proposals from across the country. The guideline for preparation of these grant proposals was well written and it contained forward looking objectives, sufficient to warrant the investment of time and money required by our team's efforts.

We submitted a proposal with high hopes that it would be read by competent reviewers and approved for implementation. We anxiously awaited word from their deliberations. They ranked our proposal as 17th among over six hundred proposals submitted. Shortly thereafter, an announcement was distributed stating that the ambitious fund raising goals were not met and the project was being scaled back.

By the time the few finalists were announced, none of the original participants who were involved in the project at its inception had remained on the project. An announcement of the finalists was made by the commissioner of the national football league. So much for Bush becoming the "Education President." The funded projects are little known today and for good reasons.

There is never a shortage of labels used to identify the latest thrust to improve schools. Goals 2000 is just another example. The state education departments with federal money launched this project and sent out an RFP to all schools. The local centralized school entered into discussions with me concerning submitting a proposal.

Knowing that a single school would not likely receive funding, I wrote a proposal that included a consortium of schools in this rural area with this district serving as its administrator.

The proposal was constructed around many prior efforts, using the appropriate language of the times. The grant proposal was based on a five year plan. It was funded for $350,000 for the first and second year.

There were six districts involved, slated to engage in workshops for teacher education. The budget covered a purchase of specialized equipment and in the interest of documenting the activities of the project and doing some data gathering about the impact of the project in bringing about changes a small staff was hired for this purpose. A transcript of every workshop was to be published along with the results of questionnaires that provided feed-back from the participants. I was hired to conduct the workshops. This feature was required based upon the demonstrated experiences in my resume. It didn't hurt that a former student of mine from Block One had become the associate commissioner of education at the state level.

To encourage serious participation, a stipend was included to be paid to all teachers who participated during the summer months. The workshops rotated to different locations in consortium schools.

The grant paid for consultants with specializations in academic subjects, each spent time helping to describe their disciplines in ways that would translate easily to classroom applications. High school specialists in subject matter were asked to do the same.

Using the model of the human cell that specialists in cell biology had developed some years before, these high school specialists developed and published models of their disciplines. These models were analyzed to determine a developmental sequence of experiences that would allow students to develop and validate their own formulations over time. A member of the school board, a local physician, publicly derided the products of these efforts as just a bunch of useless diagrams.

Much workshop time was spent establishing a set of validated beliefs/assumptions based on what is known and could be supported in one's own experience about human development and behavior, group dynamics and communication, the nature of knowledge, the nature and evolution of the school system and most importantly, the importance of self-understanding in developing a supportive relationship with students of all ages and stages. The project used a well-established approach to the assessment of change.

To illustrate how difficult it is to change fundamental beliefs, a questionnaire was distributed, designed to gain insight into the actual progress or lack thereof attributed to this project. A leader of the faculty came to me and asked if she should try to provide answers that she thought would make the state happy or should she tell the truth. Unfortunately there were too many who shared this orientation to give much encouragement to the possibility of bringing about real change.

Midway in the second year, an outside consultant was brought in to evaluate the project, and instead of focusing on the goals and objectives as stated in the proposal he decided to evaluate using traditional criteria that he felt the board of education and other administrators would recognize. This led to heated discussion that never did get resolved. Due to political maneuvers, the project only received two years of funding of a five year plan.

During a series of summer workshops, consideration was given to creating a re-designed school building, proposed to be built. One faculty member produced an elaborate design for a community center that featured the integration of many community activities as part of the legitimate operations of the school. Her design was outstanding. The project budget allowed for ten thousand dollars to be used to secure the services of an architectural firm to be commissioned to propose a new school building. We submitted the faculty's design. The architects simply ignored this design and proposed a more traditional structure that could be found in most school districts across this country. Of course, since the school board was most impressed with the "wisdom" of this architectural firm, they went along with their plan.

The project produced extensive documents of all the workshops. These faculty productions have undoubtedly been relegated to the administrative offices collecting dust along with the other projects that have had little long range impact on the improvement of schools.

A copy of the project's process recordings is included in Appendix C.

Undaunted by more disappointment, I decided to develop a charter school proposal which in my state would be managed by the State University's central office or the State Education Department. A team of educators was assembled and a proposal was prepared according to the published guidelines.

Consider this published document that was supposed to reflect the intent of the charter school law.
1. To improve student learning and achievement.
2. To increase learning opportunities for all students, with special emphasis on expanded learning experiences for students who are at-risk of academic failure.
3. To encourage the use of different and innovative teaching methods.
4. To create new professional opportunities for teachers, school administrators and other school personnel.
5. To provide parents and students with expanded choices in the types of educational opportunities that are available within the public school system.
6. To provide schools with a method to change from rule-based to performance-based accountability systems by holding the schools established under this article accountable for meeting measurable student achievement results."

Surely, this sounded like some of the higher-ups were serious about genuine change in the programs of the schools. Don't believe it; this is just another example of words, words that sound good but actually represent a limited objective such as that of privatizing education.

Our first charter school proposal was submitted through channels established within the State University. They had set up an office on a downstate campus to receive and coordinate the review of the proposed projects. Having communicated frequently with this office, they asked us to accelerate our timeline for submission to accommodate to their lack of response from others.

Our proposal was voluminous, complete with relevant appendices that included the entire history of projects in support of this new effort. I hastily hand-carried our proposal to the downstate coordinator's office, arriving a few minutes before the deadline. As I recall, numbers of copies of the proposal were required, one for each of the reviewers and some for the university officials. Several boxes were lugged up to the second floor office and deposited in a storage room.

Consistent with the established timeframe for the review process, a decision was finally communicated to all participants. Our project had been reviewed by a selected group whose expertise was oriented exclusively toward traditional approaches to change in existing institutions.

Of course, our proposal was aimed at a comprehensive reform that included the establishment of a validated set of assumptions about how individuals learn and develop, alone and in groups, a far cry from what was apparently expected by the reviewers and their directives.

The total costs projected for our new approach were based on elimination of many high paying administrative salaries that would be diverted to the requirements for learning.

The reviewers panned the project in every conceivable way including a personal attack on its authors. This so enraged me that I contacted the *New York Times* and brought to their attention the treatment we had received in this much publicized attempt to improve education. As a result the university officials did eventually remove or reassign the coordinator but they replaced him with another similar type.

By this time, our disillusionment, led to a more aggressive attempt to submit our proposal, but this time through the State Education Department. We renamed the project, using the name of the then current governor in its title. We had previously written the governor for his permission to use his name. We included the statement that if we did not hear from him we would assume that his permission had been granted.

We had obtained the cooperation of the redevelopment enterprise that was then working to convert the local SAC air base to civilian uses. A building on that base had been found especially suitable for our new, demonstration school. We proposed to make this a regional center for rural education with provision for local college students and schools to participate in the formulation of a laboratory for remaking our schools.

The review process reflected similar makeup of the review panel and procedures as was used by the state university. The state board of education and its chairperson, and members of the staff at the state education department led by the commissioner, were steeped in a new wave of efforts to raise standards. This effort included renewed efforts to expand the use of "high stakes testing" as the way to improve the schools.

Attending the meetings of the state board of education revealed the unlikelihood of our proposal receiving a positive hearing. However, our enthusiasm for our plan motivated us to pursue this avenue, regardless of the outcome.

On the day of the final decision to reject our proposal, I traveled across the state to attend the meeting. The Board of Regents members, one by one, voted to reject the plan, without ever having read the plan or discussing its contents with its authors. Ironically, one of the board members was and is a member of the faculty of the state university campus in the town where the plan was to be implemented. He especially took that opportunity to assert his objection.

The board relied on the recommendations of the staff of the education department, most of whom had not read the proposal and they apparently relied on the negative opinions of the reviewers. The only comment that came from the then chairperson of the board was in a threatening tone, calling into question whether the governor knew his name was being used in this project.

Everyone interested in educational reform should attend meetings of the state board of education. Here you will witness the effects of an authoritarian structure that has its sights focused on manipulating its system to sustain its biased views. It has mastered the art.

Incidentally, the administration of the local college decided not to support charter schools, without ever reading our proposal or interviewing its authors, in spite of our long term affiliation with that college.

I continued to work out of my office on campus dedicated to the activities of my Institute. In that capacity, the threat of being removed from that office and from the campus was ever present. Volumes of letters were exchanged with administrators determined to succeed in not only closing the Institute, but removing its director from the campus community.

Finally, while I was temporarily off campus assisting a school district in preparation of a grant proposal, my office was closed, the lock was changed, the signage was removed, my phone was disconnected and my files and personal belongings were moved out into the hallway in a pile.

Without my knowledge, the college had finally succeeded by vote of the deans to rid the campus of this "problem" and restore loyalty to its established procedures. I was denied employment as an adjunct. I filed an age discrimination complaint that was denied as well, claiming that my replacement was more qualified than me, the person who wrote the plan for the program that was in place. The chancellor of the state university is required to respond to an appeal of this case, but he never responded.

A new administrator was hired to seek accreditation for the professional education programs. He received an outline for a new, comprehensive program designed to achieve accreditation from national accreditation agencies based on the historical evolution of innovations that spanned the period that began in 1966. This administrator rejected any continuance of this plan and set about establishing "his" plan.

After three tries, the college did not receive accreditation for its teacher education programs from NCATE. It continued to offer their uncertified programs to unsuspecting students and parents. However, finally the college received accreditation by an arm of the State Board of Regents, the Teacher Education Accreditation Council (TEAC).

Calling attention to this apparent unethical practice, I prepared a lengthy statement for the local newspaper, quoting liberally from its pages about how "progress" was being made.

I received a nasty response from its editor accusing me of holding a grudge against the college.

Acting as the public relations arm of the college does not produce any real investigative reporting as witnessed by the many upbeat statements reporting the wonderful gains made by this local institution.

I was in attendance at a so called "faculty senate" meeting and witnessed the actions that led to the demise of any remnants of prior efforts to improve teacher education. One faculty member with experience in the college over a nine year period was the only spokesman allowed to object to the proposed new dean's plan. This faculty member has since been fired as the college claimed that he lacked "scholarly" evidence in his personnel folder.

The faculty senate meeting began with the inner circle of administrators and wannabe administrators exchanging their usual jocular communications. The vast majority of faculty, representing each department of the college, sat through this ordeal with resigned boredom.

They knew all too well that the administrators who decide matters of hiring and firing are seated at the senate and in charge. To object to their plans is tantamount to dismissal. Of course, this representative senate is proudly defended as democracy in action. To me it is so corrupt that to stomach its charade is only tolerated with an ample supply of martinis.

I still haven't lost hope that something substantial can yet be accomplished. After a period of nearly total disillusionment where I sought out more hands-on productive projects, then, with the advent of the call for change in the 2008 national election, I thought, perhaps the time is ripe for someone to pay attention to what is required, other than simply spending more money or hiring new people to run the schools.

Unfortunately, those placed in charge of educational improvement since 2008 have not only adopted the standardization mentality of the prior administration but have expanded its influence beyond what any rational educator or parent could have envisioned.

It will take a decade or more in the best of times to change/improve our schools—an institution that our grandparents would recognize, in spite of its glitter and Sesame Street mentality that is its orientation in these modern times. Textbooks, workbooks, tests, lesson plans, and presentations sound very familiar to us all, whether they are delivered in person or in texts or on the air or over internet channels. The products of this institution, former and current students, are everywhere.

Our crowded health caring institutions reflect recent generations experienced in seeking the direction of others who are considered wiser and more important than their subordinates. The adage that says, we must recognize that if we want to find "top notch" people for executive positions of power, we have to pay them highly.

It's strange that the most intelligent and caring people I have had the privilege of working with would work for little or nothing if only they could see some light at the end of the tunnel.

Only in an authoritarian organization, can this higher paying premise be supported, especially in one that masquerades as a democracy. Incompetence and poor mental health is pervasive in our world; education and educators must assume much of the blame along with corrupted politicians and greedy business persons.

Step one:

In spite of the difficulties and frustrations that accompany real change and improvement in education, there are three steps in the process of reform that will lead to the development of a much improved system of education for all levels of engagement.

The first step of change can be affected immediately without huge expenditures and without extensive teacher training.

This change involves the assessment, record-keeping, evaluation and reporting procedures. This change will set in motion a process that will build, with each generation, a readiness to accept the broader premises of an effective educational system for the twenty-first century.

The CARES model (Constructive Assessment, Record-keeping, and Evaluation System) discussed at length in earlier chapters will provide the structure for this change. Today, our assessment and evaluation system revolves around testing. A heightened anxiety about the effectiveness of education has increased emphasis on testing with "high stakes" consequences for the students, parents, teachers and school systems.

This effort to achieve higher standards (higher test scores), has not produced significant improvements, in fact, it has exacerbated the levels of anxiety and frustration experienced by teachers, their students and their parents. Only incremental changes have occurred in test scores.

Even if these tests were reflective of all that is to be learned, which they are not, they would fall short of improving the outcomes of a system that is in disrepair. Changing the assessment and evaluation system will ultimately change the educational procedures and will result in increased competency and improved mental health within our society.

The heart of the CARES model is an individualized electronic record of the experiences encountered by each learner along a developmental continuum. This record will contain the translation of an individual's experiences, wherever they occur, into personalized language forms, the eventual construction of models that integrate the results of observation, experimentations, and reflection, and evaluation/validation of the products of each individual's searches for meaning. Having a record of the continuing experiences of the learner, allows the opportunity to revisit those activities and formulations. This will lead to refinement and increased sophistication in the skills and insights of the learner.

A beginning record of experience will document the current experiences in the immediate surroundings of the learner, the home, neighborhood, the town, and perhaps the county. This focus enables first hand observation and verification that ultimately leads to the formation of the foundation for transfer to more remote places and times. It will also contribute to the development of competencies that translate to genuine efforts to improve the life of the local community, skills now in short supply.

The table of contents of the record identifies the files to be contained within the computer. The files will house pictures, graphic illustrations, descriptive language and individually constructed interpretations.

The following file names provide the broad categories to be investigated first in the local surroundings and later in other areas throughout the world.

The first category of files relate to the local natural/physical characteristics and manmade constructions, alterations of the landscape.

1. Rocks and minerals
2. Soils
3. Relief features
4. Vegetation
5. Animal life
6. Water and drainage patterns
7. Weather and climate
8. Location
9. Manmade objects, buildings, equipment, machines, communications networks, transportation routes, electricity grid, etc.
10. Other

The second category of files contains the social/cultural, economic, and political realities.

1. Customs, manners, philosophy and personal orientations
2. Religion

3. Recreation
4. Heritage and ancestry
5. Social and service organizations
6. Education
7. Community architecture
8. Art and architecture
9. Any other social/cultural factors
10. Trade and commerce
11. Banking and money
12. Agriculture
13. Industry
14. Transportation
15. Employment opportunities and requirements
16. Profit and loss
17. Purchasing/shopping
18. Retail and wholesale
19. Any other economic factors
20. Boundaries–Village, City Town, County, State, Nation
21. Laws and courts
22. Constitution
23. Government
24. Political organizations
25. Voting
26. Agencies
27. Any other political factors

Each of the above file names will be used to suggest activities that will be offered to the learners and as they experience these topics their experiences are recorded in the record. Over time, the record will present opportunities for revisiting past events and reconstructing the responses to reflect up-to-date interpretations. The completed files will interrelate as more and more experiences are recorded and connections between files are discovered.

The ultimate model that will be constructed includes all the above files, and more. It will provide a structure for more fully understanding the systemic parts and their relationship to the whole.

This structure will help enormously in recall of information and in bringing to bear the important conclusions in the tasks of problem-solving. The construction of these relationships and their implications will be the hallmark of competence.

The experiences required in each category are, wherever possible, direct, and purposeful or at least direct experience that is carefully contrived to aid in gaining important exposure to the variables of any region. Any media and experimentation that shows graphically the nature of objects and events of the area will be essential.

The foundation for mathematics as a language for dealing with quantity and spatial relationships and other spoken and written language is experienced in the context of investigations and the recording of the reactions to those investigations. Counting and correspondence between objects and number is routinely expressed. Computation and computer/system's language are needed skills as data are sorted through and recorded.

The spoken language is first translated verbatim for entry into the record. The tendency to edit the language has to be avoided keeping in mind that learning is something that takes place from the inside out. The learner will eventually modify his or her own language structures as the need to communicate is developed from having developed genuinely thought about ideas and propositions, and models are offered by adults that will be recognized by the learner. Whole words and phrases are the natural language of younger learners, not parsed words and alphabet letters. The letters will be recognized in due course as the youngster matures toward logical capabilities.

What now occupies most of the instructional time in early education is a repetitious presentation of parsed words and separate letters, an inefficient process at best and a harmful process at worst. Be confident that maturing youngsters will eventually find and need language forms including mathematics, to communicate their personal discoveries. When this level of maturity arrives, what now occupies several years of effort in schools will be accomplished in a very short time. Vital experience that yields exciting results will bring about a growing need to communicate with others.

Maintaining the record of experience prior to the learner assuming that responsibility will require assistance from the classroom teacher. Perhaps once or twice weekly, older students in the school can be enlisted to assist the process with each individual's recordings of experience. In this way a vital aspect of implementation of constructive assessment and evaluation is accomplished without cost and with extraordinary personal gains for both the younger and the older students.

The record travels with the individual learner, and is accessible to each teacher who engages the students as they mature. The record will show what experiences have been engaged and what the learner has made of those experiences.

This will provide the basis for planning additional experiences to modify and update what already exists in the record and to add new material to the record to expand the content of its files.

Returning to previous opportunities for experience will become routine in order for each learner to reflect upon the earlier reactions and expand and refine those reactions at a higher level of insight. The use of hand held computer/camera instruments (cell phones) will be used extensively to aid the process of collecting and recording details that enhance the development of concepts all displayed in the files of the individual's computer-stored record. As individuals take over the recording process at a later stage of maturity, they will use the cell phone and other computer technologies extensively to assist their memory and provide concrete/personalized data to be used in the analyses of their experiences.

Transportation will be necessary to bring learners in contact with the events and processes of the community and beyond. Much of the time spent for instruction will be needed to visit each of the topics for the file, outside the classroom. With the aid of the electronic media, the outside can be brought back to the classroom for analysis and discussion whenever necessary.

This recordkeeping process provides the basis for assessment and evaluation.

The record is evaluated using criteria applied to the student-generated constructions. It includes:

1. Clarity and organization within the record. This is a goal that will not be fully attained early on since the learners are not mature enough to engage it. Achieving this goal will require assistance from adults until the individual at a later time can assume the task. Emphasis during this phase of the process will be placed on the development of the skills of communication, grammar, and spelling in the day-to-day context of experiencing and keeping records.

2. Accuracy of the information entered in the files. This too is a criterion that will be met with the help of adults during early stages of development. Accurate information is essential for generating useful conclusions.

3. Comprehensiveness of the record. At any point in time, each of the files will contain more or less information. The goal is to include as much data as possible, thus it will be comprehensive.

4. Support from personal experiences and the experiences of others. In the process of recording experiences, individuals within and outside the group will share their findings and shape their interpretations.

5. Internal consistency within and between files. This activity will not occur much before individuals reach the level of maturity that allows logical analysis and testing out in reality. This level will emerge as biological maturity occurs and not before. To insist on logic before this ability emerges is counter-productive and likely harmful.

6. Generativity or identification of questions unanswered or hypotheses untested is the next phase. This too will require logical abilities that will emerge as the individual matures.

It is plain to see that the CARES model can be implemented with little additional cost and with a minimum of training. It simply requires a decision to pursue its approach and have patience enough to allow it to demonstrate its superiority over existing assessment and evaluation strategies. This approach does not preclude the use of standardized tests but it must be understood that the results of current tests are suspect since they do not reflect developmental differences and they only include a small sample of possible information available to the learners.

Schools have computer capabilities for storing the records of each individual or at least they can upgrade to accommodate those requirements. Safeguards will need to be established to protect the individual's privacy along with policies to define access.

Step two:

The second step in the process of change to a more effective system of education involves the identification and organization of information to be made available to the learning groups. As noted earlier, local historical and geographical data have not been made available to schools since their reproduction costs cannot be supported by limited market potential.

This need will require a national effort to enlist local historians and geographers in identifying and publishing raw data about all the elements of the local setting for the current period and for periods that date back to its origins. This effort can be completed with funding that enlists the help of the local experts and makes available the recording instruments that will transfer these data to computer files accessible to individuals in the school.

Connections to museums and historical restorations

must also be made readily available so that individuals can process their information on their way to making sense out of their lives and those of their ancestors.

In a Goals 2000 Project, a company developed color micro images that expanded an effort to make available to students a large data bank of primary information about the geography and history of the world, starting at the local level, then the state, national and international regions.

Thousands of maps and charts of data about all the elements of the physical/geographic, the social, economic, and political aspects of life around the world were photographed in full color on ultra-high definition films and organized for computer retrieval.

The cooperation of local historians, local geographers, regional repositories, museums, libraries, and government agencies were enlisted. The bugs were worked out of a system to deliver these raw data to the classroom to be used by students who are mature enough to logically construct models that would demonstrate their ability to identify and integrate a large volume of data depicting life in all its manifestations throughout the world.

This photographic library is available to supplement the vastly expanded data sources of Google-like entities.

Without primary information, organized for easy retrieval, the constructive learning process cannot go forward. This will require government subsidies aimed at local town and county levels to entice local resource experts to compile and reproduce the needed primary information. **This effort would put many to work at the grass roots level and make a major contribution to the development of an effective educational system.**

Just imagine if every individual has the opportunity to access primary information that will support the development of conceptual frameworks for understanding the interrelationships between all the variables of local regions, throughout their evolution, across the United States. Historical and geographic literacy would be elevated above anything we have ever experienced through education. It will lay the ground work for a far greater capacity for understanding the regions of the world.

Further, imagine individual students able to integrate the contributions of the knowledge disciplines as they occur. For instance, when a discovery in science provides a new and different view of the events and processes of our past, the patterns of history and geography are modified to accommodate to that change.

An example occurred when the process of carbon dating emerged that more accurately identified the origins of artifacts. This caused a major modification in historical knowledge that had been based on different assumptions. The discoveries of genetic codes have led to a different dynamic in the conduct of our democratic processes. These and other examples challenge our stereotypes and create a more dynamic interaction with all the realms of meaning available to our citizens.

Step three:

The third step in the process of reform will involve intensive workshops aimed at current educational elementary, middle, and secondary personnel, pre-service educators, parents and higher education faculty. The purpose of these workshops will be to establish the foundations knowledge base—the development of shared assumptions about how individuals learn and develop alone and in groups.

Preparation for the conduct of these workshops will require a trained cadre of persons willing and able to grasp the significant concepts of the knowledge base with the skills to conduct learning groups within each of the entities identified above. These workshops will be made available through regional higher education institutions that will perhaps receive funding through the Federal Office of Education or major foundations.

This process will require several years of effort followed by intensive implementation. At this point, the efforts of the first generation of newly skilled and insightful students will be emerging into upper levels of education. They will bring with them a new and more sophisticated level of educational needs that will require accommodations to build upon their skills and insights in ways consistent with the foundation base and continuous with the processes of learning that have been already established in this emerging population.

These workshops will further refine the procedures for implementation of the constructive learning modes in the disciplines within each of the six realms of meaning. This process was begun with prior experiences with cell biology and elaborated in the Goals 2000 Project noted above. Models were developed that defined the parts of systems to be constructed within each discipline. These models are available for review along with extensive descriptions (process recordings) of the workshops that assisted in their development. The model developed in the early eighties by experts in the field of cell biology illustrates one example of what is required to move forward.

The following model is designed to provide an overview that defines the goals for general education with an emphasis on community evolution and the developmental realities for engaging these dimensions.

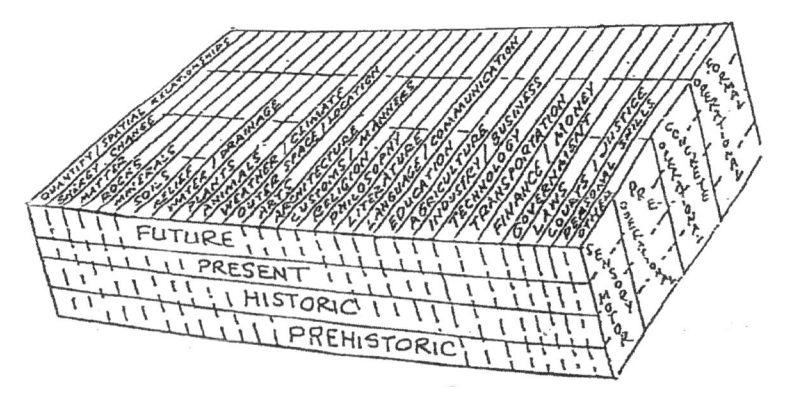

Chapter 8

A Solutions Generator

An exploration of the problems of education has been provided in the preceding chapters that includes:

The introduction of a new and improved way of assessing and evaluating learning outcomes, based on a valid set of assumptions and beliefs about how individuals learn, alone and in groups,

What constitutes individual human growth and development and how it occurs.

How learning groups develop into highly productive teams,

How the subject matter of the curriculum can be re-organized to include academic disciplines as ways of creating and communicating knowledge.

What structural changes in decision-making procedures will be required,

What components will be found in a systems oriented school system.

How teachers can be prepared to fully implement the transactional processes that will enhance the learning of each and every individual,

An overview of the long range requirements for change and improvement in our public schools.

Now is the time to initiate the dialogue that must occur within each school district as the first step in the change process. To begin to understand the status of each school district there needs to be a recognition that change is needed, now. The following "Solutions Generator" is designed to help.

We all use the word "system" in our daily vocabulary as if we know what we are talking about. We refer to the digestive system, the solar system, the braking system, the accounting system, the heating system and on and on. We speak of these systems, as with the school system, using words that contain little factually validated content. These words are used denotatively, that is, limited in their meaning, referring to a single dimension—like the place where I went to school—rather than words full of connotative meanings based on an analysis of the systemic parts of the school system.

The words "school system," with connotative meanings—meanings based on in-depth analyses of the systemic parts and the interrelationships between parts—are missing in today's conversations about school reform. To help with a common sense analysis of the school system, that provides a sound basis for school reform, a "solutions generator" is presented here for your use.

The illustrated "Systemic Design Model" below provides a view of the component parts of the school system as most of us have experienced it, though seldom fully understood. (Systemic Design Model) Illustration by Sid Couchey

These ten parts of the school system are identified in the illustration above.
- Philosophical/theoretical assumptions and beliefs
- Finance, administrative decision making and accountability procedures
- Goals and objectives for the system and the learners.
- Curriculum and instructional/learning transactional strategies
- Assessment, evaluation, record-keeping and reporting procedures
- Facilities and utilization patterns
- Community involvement
- Support services
- In-service and pre-service demonstration sites
- Information and management technologies

Experience with effective systems tells us that all the parts must be functioning effectively and interactively with all the other parts. A system that contains weak or defective parts will cause the system to malfunction. Injecting new parts into a system of old parts will invariably cause problems with the old parts and their ability to function interactively.

A school system that features inconsistencies between its parts will not function effectively and will fail to achieve its desired outcomes. A school system that is poorly designed, regardless of consistency between its interactive parts, when based on invalid assumptions and beliefs, will also fail to produce acceptable outcomes.

A systemic overhaul is required, based on valid assumptions and beliefs, with parts that are in sync with other parts designed to meet the desired goal as stated at the center of the foregoing "Systemic Design Model" – "To Design a Learning and Training System That Produces Competent and Informed Citizens of the US, Ready to Meet the Challenges of the 21st Century." Using this model as the focus of a "Solutions Generator," all ten parts of the school system are to be visited in a study of the state of education in each school system. This study is necessary to help create a functioning system with a minimum of internal inconsistencies, required to meet the goals of this century.

In illustration of the consequences of tinkering with the system, if you know something about the systems of your car you will identify with my experience, tinkering with the exhaust system of my 1956 Ford that I bought new. At about 100,000 miles, it developed a leak in the exhaust tube that was connected to the automatic choke. Heat was conducted through this tube to activate a spring thermostat that opened and closed the choke. Broken, it made an annoying whistle so I decided to do something about the problem. I plugged the hole in the exhaust manifold through which heat was designed (engineered) to escape. This was a point of interface between the exhaust system and the fuel system. The whistle was no longer annoying me after I plugged the hole. What do you think happened?

My ingenious solution to stop the whistle increased the temperature inside the engine and caused valves to overheat. Burned, the valves could not maintain sufficient pressure in the combustion chamber making efficient ignition impossible and the engine began to spit and sputter.

I headed for the nearest repair shop and presented my case. A mechanical "expert" looked me in the eye and said: "I can repair the engine for a fee." Trusting in his expertise, I allowed him to work on the engine. He replaced parts that had no relationship to the problem and at the time I didn't know the difference. I ended up paying through the nose for my ignorance. It appeared he had fixed some problems but he created others in the process that affected the total functioning of the car. Frustrated, I bought a new car.

This experience taught me to stop before I started tinkering with the parts of a system when I didn't fully understand the consequences of my actions. Consequences in this instance went well beyond the exhaust (sub) system to all the other sub-systems that make up the total system, the car.

Tinkering with the school system can have the same results.

Remember, each part must be designed to function in a predictable fashion and become a working member of the system in which it is placed. A change in one part brings about changes in the system as a whole, changes that may result in improving or diminishing the functioning and effectiveness of the system.

The Goals 2000 initiatives featured a forward looking, participative model for grassroots decision making. The states set up locally-based shared decision-making committees whose work was supposed to transform the school system into a more dynamic and effective system. However, in illustration of parts of the system in conflict, consider the fact that this participative model was injected into a strictly hierarchical system that would only allow limited decision-making power to local school districts. Ultimately, this restriction doomed to failure the Goals 2000 efforts.

Little wonder teachers view attempts to change the schools as just another fad that will disappear if they wait a year or two. They have plenty of historical evidence to support this position. Apparently, teachers view the current efforts, the imposed common core and increased emphasis on standardization, as just another fad that will fade away in time. Otherwise they might be protesting in the streets.

Starting with the part called philosophical/theoretical assumptions and beliefs. Assume that this part is based on the reality of individual differences; that no two people anywhere throughout this world are identical, not their DNA, not their experiences, nor what they have done with their experiences.

Assume that individuals develop their intellectual abilities as they emerge along an invariant sequence that is directed by a unique genetic code influenced for better or worse by the experiences encountered in day to day living. Consider learning as a creative process developing over time with a gradual accumulation of holistic insights that eventually are formulated in the mind as useful principles and laws found to apply in the solution of problems.

Assert your belief that individuals are best assisted in learning within groups where learners are operating at a level of consensual validation, regardless of age or social/economic standing?

Look at part number four called the "curriculum and instructional/learning transactional strategies." Take the position that this part is based on a concept of standardization, meaning the curriculum and instructional strategies are designed to be appropriate for all learners, regardless of their developmental or experiential differences. Assume also that appropriate subject matter can be determined apart from the learners and be successfully delivered to learners through various teaching techniques and instructional media in compartmentalized classrooms.

Which of these propositions do you endorse? If you endorse proposition one, how do you reconcile the differences with proposition four identified on the design model? If you endorse proposition four as requiring standardization, how do you deal with the realities of proposition one that asserts the principles of individual learning and development?

Up to this point, having looked briefly at only two dimensions of the school system, we find these parts to be incompatible and we have eight other parts to consider before we can determine the system's total functionality.

How about a comparison of parts one and five? Part number five is defined in today's rhetoric about educational reform as standardization, the savior of a failing educational system where the lofty statements of goals and objectives for the system and the learners have not been met. Is this type of standardization arbitrary and rigidly imposed? How is this type of standardization reconciled with principles of individual development and learning?

What happens to individuality in the world of standardization? Does this inhibit creativity, the entrepreneurial spirit, the ability and the will required to solve problems?

Going further, consider number five, strategies of assessment, evaluation, record-keeping and reporting. Is standardized testing compatible with number one? What if individuals do not fit the pre-defined definitions of success, as measured by standardized tests? Do you favor segregating the students into categories of average, above average or below average? What effect does this have on healthy personality development?

If there are assessment and evaluation alternatives that are compatible with number one, that identify accurately the dimensions and extent of learning each individual has achieved at any point in time, would you consider them or reject them if they challenge your long held positions?

Let's suppose there are teachers who buy into the propositions of part number one and attempt to install procedures that match those assumptions and beliefs. Most school systems exist under hierarchical, authoritarian structures with an appointed leader who has nearly ultimate authority. What chance does an individual teacher have when trying to implement the propositions drawn from number one if the administrative organization or the administrator does not allow it?

What roles do the propositions of parts number one through five have on the design and maintenance of facilities? Is the egg crate building design compatible with a compartmentalized/departmentalized design? Does a compartmental/departmentalized instructional design facilitate the development of holistic insights and connected knowledge required of intelligent problem solving? Would a flexible community center that invites-in all of its members better serve the learners of all ages?

Do utilization patterns of a school that operates consistently with compartmentalized instructional designs allow learners the time to internalize experiences and form their own patterns of meaning, or does it encourage an unhealthy dependency on so called experts?

Why are education decision-makers eager to move instruction into the earliest levels of development? Is it because they feel the later experiences within the system are ineffective because instruction starts too late? Do the advocates of this point of view understand the principles of learning and individual development?

Consider systemic part number seven. What kind of support services are required to assist learners with impediments that may be found interfering with learning? How are these services obtained and distributed within an authoritarian structure?

Can the contents of part number nine be ignored? What kinds of pre-service and in-service experiences will assist educators, teachers and others, in developing validated assumptions and beliefs that will guide the development of effective strategies for individual learning and development?

Are these validated assumptions and beliefs as important to learning at the college and university levels as they are for early, middle and secondary education?

What is the role of modern communications technologies (part number ten) in facilitating learning at all levels of education? Can the cell phone and the social networks be harnessed to facilitate the development of insights into reality, or will they continue to languish in the mire of social trivia and vulgar, often hostile uses, and be restricted by the school?

Without a serious investigation into the nature and roles of each and every part of the educational system, will we continue to tinker around the edges and waste more human and financial resources? Will we likely encounter further difficulty in gaining support for a non-functional system?

What choices do we have when we find parts that are not functioning well? We can send the problematic parts back to the drawing board and decide which position holds more credibility and validity, verified first in our own experiences and then in the experiences of others, especially those of reputable scholars in this field. Or, we can rely on a position of conventional wisdom handed down through the ages, seldom subjected to a rigorous analysis.

Can the future of this country function in a democratic mode when an alarming number of the products of our schools can't function as productive members of a democratic and capitalistic society in this twenty-first century?

The answer is obvious, but the solution is difficult. Change is inhibited by the reluctance to abandon the traditions that possibly served us well sometime in the past but are woefully deficient in today's world community.

Systemic change is needed, but not just changes for change sake, but change that is based on a rigorous examination of the parts of the system and their interrelationships, viewed from a validated set of assumptions and beliefs about how individual learners can best fulfill their needs for themselves and for their country.

Good luck in your investigation.

BIBLIOGRAPHY

Almy, M. C. (1979) *The impact of Piagetian theory on education, philosophy, psychiatry, and psychology.* Baltimore: University Park Press.

Argyris, C. 1990. *Overcoming Organizational Defenses: Facilitating Organizational Learning.* Boston: Allyn and Bacon

Arnold, Robert and Lahey, Charles (1965) *Inquiry, A Source Book for the Discovery Approach to Social Studies.* New York. Selected Academic Readings.

Arnold, R. (1967) *The Open Curriculum Project.* The Educational Research and Demonstration Center (Preliminary Proposal) for the State University College of Arts and Sciences, Plattsburgh, NY.)

Arnold, Robert (1987) *"An Inquiry Teacher Education Program" in Faculty Forum, Volume XII, Number II*, New York. SUNY Plattsburgh.

Ausubel, D.P. (1960). *The use of advance organizers in the learning and retention of meaningful verbal material.* Journal of Educational Psychology

Banathy, B. (1993) "Systems Design: A Current Educational Predicament." In Reigeluth, C. *Comprehensive Systems Design: A New Educational Technology.* NY: Springer-Verlag.

Bandura, A. (1977). *Social Learning Theory.* New York. General Learning Press.

Bennis, Warren et al. (1969) *The Planning of Change.* New York. Holt, Rinehart and Winston

Bernstein, Emmanuel. (2007) *THE SECRET REVOLUTION: A Psychologist's Adventures in Education.* Canada. Trafford Publishing.

Billington, Ray Allen and Ridge, Martin (1949) *Westward Expansion: A History of the American Frontier.*

Bloom, B et al. (1956) *Taxonomy of Educational Objectives: The Classification of Educational Goals, Handbook I: Cognitive Domain.* New York. David McKay Co Inc.

Bradford, L. P., Gibb, J. R., Benn, K. D. (1964). *T Group theory and laboratory method,* New York. John Wiley.

Bradford, Leland (1958). "*The Teaching-Learning Transaction*" Adult Education Quarterly. Spring, 1958.

Brady, Marion (2011). "Unanswered Questions about Standardized Tests" *Washington Post.* April 27, 2011

Bruner, Jerome. (1960) *The Process of Education,* Cambridge. Harvard University Press

Bruner, Jerome (1968) "*The Course of Cognitive Growth.*" Cambridge. in American Psychologist

Dale, E. (1969). *Audiovisual methods in teaching.* New York. Holt, Rinehart and Winston, Inc.

Dewey, John (1998) *Experience and Education.* Kappa Delta Pi

Davis, Robert, (1984). *Learning Mathematics: The Cognitive Science Approach to Mathematics Education,* London. Croom Helm).

Dwarkin, Martin (1968). *Dewey Education.* New York. Teachers College Press

Elliott, David (1963). *Curriculum Development and History as a Discipline.* New York. Teachers College Columbia Unversity. Unpublished doctoral thesis.

Erikson, Erik H. (1993). Childhood and Society. New York. WW Norton

Flavell, John (1963). *The developmental psychology of Jean Piaget*: New York. Van Nostrand.

Gagné, R. (1985). *The Conditions of Learning (4th.).* New York. Holt, Rinehart & Winston.

Gardner, H. (2011) *Frames of Mind: The theory of multiple intelligences.* New York. Basic Books

Glasser, William (1998). *Choice Theory: A New Psychology of Personal Freedom.* New York. HarperCollins

Harrison, Charles (1966). *Arnold's Group Tackles Freshman Curriculum*. Newark. The Bergin Record

Hord, S. et al (1987). *Taking Charge of Change*. ASCD

Jennings, Frank. (1982). *This is Reading*. New York. Springer

Jersild, Arthur. (1933). *Child Psychology*. New York: Prentice-Hall Inc., 1933.

Kilpatrick,William (1918). *"The Project Method,"* New York. Teachers College Record

Kohlberg, Lawrence (1981). *Essays on Moral Development, Vol. I: The Philosophy of Moral Development*. San Francisco, CA. Harper & Row

Kramer, Rita (1991). *ED SCHOOL FOLLIES – The Miseducation of Americas Teachers*. New York. The Free Press.

Kubie, Lawrence S. (1967). *Neurotic Distortion of the Creative Process*, Farrar Straus Giroux

Lahey, W. Charles (1966). *THE POTSDAM TRADITION – A History and a Challenge*. New York. Appleton-Century-Crofts.

Langer, Susanne. (1957). *Philosophy in a New Key: A Study in the Symbolism of Reason, Rite, and Art* 3 edition. Cambridge. Harvard University Press.

Likert, R. (1967). *The Human Organization: Its Management and Value*. New York. McGraw Hill.

Lowenfeld, Viktor (1947). *CREATIVE AND MENTAL GROWTH,* New York. Macmillan Co

Mager, R. (1962). *Preparing Instructional Objectives*. Palo Alto, CA: Fearon Publishers.

Maslow, Abraham (1954). *Motivation and Personality*. New York. Harper.

McGregor, Douglas (2006). *The Human Side of Enterprise*: New York, McGraw Hill

Morgan, Barbara Ann (1966). *"ARNOLD'S GROUP – AN EDUCATIONAL SUCCESS?: AN EVALUATIVE STUDY OF AN EXPERIMENTAL PROGRAM AT JERSEY CITY STATE COLLEGE UTILIZING ONE TEACHER FOR ALL COLLEGE SUBJECTS."* Jersey City. An unpublished "Term Paper for Professional Writing and Research."

Muller, Robert (1989). *A World Core Curriculum* In Social Education. Silver Spring, Maryland. National Council for the Social Studies.

O'Day, Rory (1974). *"Rituals of Intimidation – Resistance to Change"* in Journal of Applied Behavioral Science, Bethel. NTL

Phenix, Philip (1964). *Realms of Meaning – A Philosophy of Curriculum for General Education.* New York, Mc Graw Hill Book Co.

Piaget, Jean and Inhelder, B. (1958). *The Growth of Logical Thinking from Childhood to Adolescence.* New York. Basic Books

Powell, Thomas F. (1969). *Humanities and the Social Studies*, Washington, D.C. The National Council for the Social Studies.

Ranzan, David. (August 2006).*Guide to the Robert B. Davis Papers, 1957-1997:* New Brunswick. Rutgers University

Reigeluth, C.M., Banathy, B.H., & Olson, J.R. (Eds.) (1993). *Comprehensive Systems Design: A New Educational Technology.* New York: Springer-Verlag.

Rogers, Carl and Freiberg (1994). *Freedom to Learn.* Columbus. Charles Merrill

Ronald Reagan's National Commission on Excellence in Education (1983) *A Nation at Risk: The Imperative For Educational Reform*

Schmuck, Richard and Schmuck, Patricia. (2000). *Group Processes in the Classroom 8th edition.* New York. McGraw Hill Book Co.

Skinner, B.F. (1968). *The Technology of Teaching*, New York. Appleton-Century-Crofts

Vygotsky, L.S. (1978). *Mind and society: The development of higher mental processes.* Cambridge, MA. Harvard University Press.

Whitehead, Alfred North (1985). *The Aims of Education and Other Essays.* New York. Free Press.

Appendix A

What should a teacher education candidate and a graduated professional educator know and be able to do that must become an integral part of their education and training?

Objective #1

A teacher education candidate will be able to articulate in writing and other forms of communication, a conception of self, mental processes and mental health that is:

(a) clear,*

(b) comprehensive, **

(c) internally consistent,

(d) supported by research in literature,

(e) supported by personal research and observation, and

(f) generative of hypotheses.

*Being clear means the materials reflect an organized presentation, judged for clarity by the appropriate uses of language such as grammar, spelling and structural matters.

** The conception of self, mental health and mental processes should include at least the following dimensions:

1. The origin of attitudes, values, and personal knowledge.

2. The nature and role of personal knowledge and skills.

3. The role of conscious, pre-conscious, and unconscious behavior.

4. The self-concept and self-understanding.

5. Motivation and personal goals.

6. Personal needs and personal self-actualization.

7. High level wellness

Objective #1 a

The candidate will demonstrate an ability to accurately recognize, within oneself and in those with whom they work, the essential elements included in Objective #1.

Objective #2

The candidate will be able to articulate in writing and other forms of communication, a conception of individual development and behavior that is:
  (a) clear,*
  (b) comprehensive, **
  (c) internally consistent,
  (d) supported by research in literature,
  (e) supported by personal research and observation,
  (f) generative of hypotheses.

*Being clear means the materials reflect an organized presentation, judged for clarity by the appropriate uses of language such as grammar, spelling and structural matters.

** The conception of individual development should include at least the following dimensions:
  1. Social
  2. Emotional
  3. Physical
  4. Intellectual—cognitive/affective and psycho-motor
  5. Morality/ethics
  6. Aesthetic/creative
  7. Language
  8. Learning

Objective # 2a

The candidate will accurately recognize, in oneself and in those with whom they work, the essential elements included in Objective #2.

Objective #3

The candidate will be able to articulate in writing and other forms of communication, a conception of interpersonal dynamics, small group processes, and institutional development that is:

(a) clear,*
(b) comprehensive, **
(c) internally consistent,
(d) supported by research in literature,
(e) supported by personal research an observation,
(f) generative of hypotheses.

*Being clear means the materials reflect an organized presentation, judged for clarity by the appropriate uses of language such as grammar, spelling and structural matters.

** The conception of communication, interpersonal dynamics, small group processes, and institutional development should include at least the following dimensions:

1. The nature of communication processes and problems.
2. Small group development including stages, leadership roles, interventions, decision making procedures, conflict resolution, and problem-solving.
3. The school as a social institution, including its history and development, its components and changes.

Objective #3a

The candidate will demonstrate the necessary leadership skills that are consistent with the essential elements included in Objective #3.

Objective #4

The candidate will be able to articulate in writing and other forms of communication, a conception of knowledge and knowing that is:

(a) clear,*

(b) comprehensive, **

(c) internally consistent,

(d) supported by research in literature,

(e) supported by personal research and observation,

(f) generative of hypotheses.

*Being clear means the materials reflect an organized presentation, judged for clarity by the appropriate uses of language such as grammar, spelling and structural matters.

** The conception of knowledge and knowing should include at least the following dimensions:

1. The nature of knowledge and what it means to know.

2. The nature of disciplines as ways of creating meaning, including sciences and social science, mathematics, arts, extra-sensory phenomena, and self-knowledge.

3. The integration of knowledge disciplines that differentiate; disciplines that synthesize, organizing principles, key concepts, and theories.

4. Inquiry modes, model building, and the concept of structure from a dynamic point of view.

5. The language of disciplines within six realms of meaning.

Objective #4a

The candidate will demonstrate the necessary interventions that allow and encourage the individual student's pursuit of meaning in all six realms of meaning.

Objective #5

The candidate will be able to articulate in writing and other forms of communication, an integrated conception of how individuals learn, grow and develop, alone and in groups and institutions, drawing upon all previous foundation objectives.

This conception must be:

(a) clear,*

(b) comprehensive, **

(c) internally consistent,

(d) supported in literature,

(e) supported in personal observations and experimentation,

(f) generative of hypotheses.

*Being clear means the materials reflect an organized presentation, judged for clarity by the appropriate uses of language such as grammar, spelling and structural matters.

** This conception must include all five dimensions outlined in the previous objectives, based on the following:

1. An intensive child study.

2. Effort to implement change strategies in institutional settings.

3. Creation and refinement of personalized teaching models.

4. Validation of assessment, evaluation, record-keeping and reporting procedures

designed to assist the learner and provide evidence of developed and developing competencies.

5. Personal and professional change strategies.

Objective #6

The candidate will be able to articulate in writing and other forms of communication a conception of the nature and organization of the school, both today and throughout history, that is:

(a) clear,*

(b) comprehensive, **

(c) supported in literature,

(d) supported in personal observations.

*Being clear means the materials reflect an organized presentation, judged for clarity by the appropriate uses of language such as grammar, spelling and structural matters.

** This conception of the school should include at least the following dimensions:

1. The scope and sequence of all curricular areas.
2. Instructional materials for all areas of the curriculum.
3. The nature of support services.
4. Roles of staff and students.
5. Assessment, evaluation, record-keeping and reporting procedures.
6. Community involvement.
7. Administrative organization and decision making procedures.
8. Goals and objective of education.
9. Philosophy.
10. Teaching strategies,
11. Building design and utilization patterns.
12. Educational laws,
13. School finance.

Objective #6a

Teacher candidates will demonstrate an awareness of the elements and dynamics of the conventional school and will formulate strategies for improvement based on the elements described in Objectives 1,2,3,4 and 5.

Dimensions of Competency

Given the outline of what childhood education teacher candidates and other educators should know and be able to do there are four categories suggested for viewing the dimensions of competency of professional teachers and other educators. First among these is *personal orientation*, followed by a *foundations knowledge base, content and process requirements*, and *professional characteristics*.

There are terms included in this competence profile that are defined as follows:

1. Model: a representation of any subject of inquiry–a theory, process, object or system.

2. Models can be expressed in these forms–enactive, iconic, symbolic and analogic.

3. Conceptual framework: A synthesis of concepts that represents the individual components and their interrelationships within the whole–as with a system or discipline.

4. Validated model: Determined to match personal experience and the experiences of others, especially those who have studied the matter in depth.

5. Strategic plans: Cooperatively derived plans for learning that take into account the purposes, rationale, goals, objectives, experiential requirements, timelines, and evaluation criteria.

6. Realms of meaning: Empirics, synoptics, symbolics, aesthetics, ethics and synnoetics or Self-knowledge.

Items listed in these initial characteristics are adaptations drawn from the work of Maslow and Shostrum.

Personal Orientations

1. Lives in the present with consideration of the past, with realistic goals for the future vs. lives essentially in the past or in the imagined future at the exclusion of the present.

2. Motivated essentially out of own convictions with consideration for the views of others vs. primarily outer-directed, lacking trust in own decisions.

3. Flexible and adaptive vs. rigid and inflexible.

4. Open to experience vs. closed minded.

5. Expresses feelings easily vs. reluctant to express feelings.

6. Has positive self concept vs. has a negative self-concept.

7. Has a capacity for warm interpersonal relationships vs. has difficulty showing affection.

8. Sees opposites of life as meaningfully related vs. sees opposites in life as antagonistic.

9. Flexible in the application of values vs. rigid in the application of values.

10. Can articulate ideas clearly in writing vs. writing is sub-standard.

11. Can articulate ideas clearly in speech vs. speech patterns interfere with communication.

12. Recognizes relationships between non-verbal and verbal communication vs. ignores relationships of non-verbal and verbal communication.

13. Communicates for understanding and support vs. communicates to impose own views.

14. Is tuned in to own thinking vs. ignores or downgrades the importance of own thoughts.

15. Recognizes meanings expressed in non-verbal communication vs. unable to read meanings in non-verbal communication.

16. Communicates non-judgmentally vs. communication is often judgmental.

17. Exhibits goal-directed behavior vs. servitude to whatever life presents.

18. Evaluates impact on personal actions vs. fails to consider impact on others.

19. Sensitive to feedback from others vs. ignores or discounts feedback

20. Acts consistently on validated principles and standards vs. acts inconsistently with little regard for principles and standards.

21. Sensitive to feelings of others vs. ignores feelings of others.

22. Demonstrates maturity of judgments vs. a lack of awareness of consequences.

23. Is dependable vs. fails to consistently meet obligations.

24. Shows initiative and professional commitment vs. lethargy and lack of commitment.

25. Shows continuous growth in the profession's knowledge base vs. maintains status-quo, even in the face of contrary evidence.

26. Has tolerance for ambiguity vs. has an intolerance for ambiguity.

27. Is systematically reflective about education and the work of a professional educator vs. spends little time or effort in thought about the profession.

28. Is respected by members of the professional community vs. is not respected by colleagues.

29. Is respected by students vs. lack of respect demonstrated by students.

30. Sees change as a natural process for improving the system and its effectiveness vs. avoids change.

31. Demonstrates leadership consistent with validated models of group dynamics vs. sees leadership as directives to control individuals and groups.

32. Demonstrates constructive interpersonal skills vs. fails to empathize with the thoughts and feelings of others.

33. Contributes to group maintenance vs. obstructs processes required to achieve consensual validation.

34. Strives to identify and achieve group goals vs. focuses essentially on personal goals without revealing them to members of one's group.

35. Sees change and innovation as model-based practices vs. sees change and innovation as disruptive and troublesome.

36. Has acquired knowledge of ecological consequences of choices vs. fails to acknowledge systemic interrelationships and the consequences of choices within systems.

37. Has developed a commitment to lifelong learning vs. avoids continued learning after reaching a threshold such as an academic degree or award.

38. Analyzes personal and professional effectiveness and seeks improvement vs. avoids questioning oneself.

39. Accepts students as unique persons, with individual patterns of growth and development vs. ignores individual differences and promotes conformity to pre-defined goals.

40. Recognizes what the teacher brings to transactions with students besides subject knowledge vs. considers teacher's personal attributes as irrelevant to teaching/learning transactions.

41. Has mastered communication and computation skills required of a competent teacher vs. cannot demonstrate sufficient mastery of communication and computation skills.

42. Demonstrates the interpersonal, organizational and personal skills needed to work as a productive group member vs. exhibits stereotypical response patterns in group work.

43. Demonstrates skills of decision making, problem solving, and resource management vs. limited tolerance for the evolution of decision making required for solving problems with existing resources.

44. Exhibits ethical behavior and understands the importance of values based on human needs vs. is willing to sacrifice ethical considerations when situations impact one's own personal objectives and values.

45. Exhibit's the ability to acquire and use knowledge and skills to manage and lead a satisfying life and contribute to the common good vs. is often experiencing personal crises.

46. Acquires and evaluates information using a wide variety of sources and technologies vs. seldom relies on available technology for acquiring information and is limited in ability to evaluate the information that is accessed.

47. Manages, organizes and communicates information for different purposes vs.views information from repetitive stereotypes rather than part of open-ended discourse.

48. Accesses and processes information acquired from data bases, computer networks, and other emerging informa-

tion systems vs. avoids using emerging technologies for accessing and processing information.

49. Appreciates and gains understanding of new developments in information technology vs. shows distain for new technologies and avoids their use.

50. Demonstrates knowledge, skills, and attitudes that enhance personal life management vs. lives by rigidly-held stereotypes.

51. Practices basic values of democratic self-government vs. does not participate in civic affairs.

52. Understands, accepts and acts on values of justice, honesty, self-discipline, due process, equality and property rights vs. sacrifices values of justice, honesty etc. in lieu of personal gain.

53. Regards oneself with esteem and others with respect for cultural differences, different abilities, styles and preferences vs. is distrustful of self and sees differences in others as a problem.

54. Adjusts, adapts and improvises in response to cues and restraints imposed by one-self, others and the environs vs. is rigid and un-adaptive.

55. Makes connections, understands complex relationships and interrelationships vs. seldom makes connections or understands complex relationships.

56. Views concepts and situations from multiple perspectives in order to take into account all relevant evidence vs. is unable to view ideas and events from multiple perspectives.

57. Synthesizes, generates, evaluates and applies knowledge to diverse, new and unfamiliar situations vs. is reticent to act on data of personal experience.

58. Applies reasoned action to practical life situations vs. is impulsive in everyday decision making.

59. Imagines role not yet experienced vs. seldom exhibits a vision of the future.

60. Meets and accepts challenges vs. avoids challenges.

61. Responsibly challenges conventions and existing pro-

cedures or policies vs. goes along accepting conventions regardless of the consequences.

62. Makes considered and informed assertions, makes commitments to personal visions vs. fails to acknowledge implications of personal assertions.

63. Originates, innovates, invents and combines ideas, productions, performances and or objects vs. avoids creative extensions of personal experience.

Foundations Knowledge Base

1. Can articulate validated models of individual development and behavior including learning and motivation vs. cannot articulate validated models of individual development and behavior including learning and motivation.

2. Can articulate validated models of small group dynamics, development and communication vs. cannot articulate validated models of small group dynamics, development and communication.

3. Can articulate validated models of academic disciplines and realms of meaning vs. cannot articulate validated models of academic disciplines and realms of meaning.

4. Can articulate validated models of the dynamics and evolution of the school system vs. unable to articulate validated models of the workings and evolution of the school system.

5. Can articulate a validated model of self and mental health vs. cannot articulate a validated model of self and mental health.

6. Can articulate a model of the interrelationships between all elements of the foundations knowledge base vs. cannot articulate a validated model of the interrelationships between elements in the foundations knowledge base.

7. Recognizes differences between strategies evolved from different models vs. does not recognize differences between strategies drawn from different models.

Content and Process Requirements

1. Can articulate a validated conceptual framework for disciplines within each realm of meaning vs. unable to adequately articulate a conceptual framework within each realm of meaning.

2. Can articulate validated content and process models for sciences including social sciences vs. an inability to articulate content and process models for sciences including social sciences.

3. Can articulate validated content and process models for mathematics as language vs. cannot articulate content and process models for mathematics as language.

4. Demonstrates insight/skills in language including those other than English vs. an inability to exhibit insight/skills in own language or languages other than English.

5. Can articulate models of the nature of history and geography as synoptic disciplines vs. articulating models of history and geography as arbitrary subjects to be consumed by the students.

6. Demonstrates self-understanding and awareness of personal impediments to learning and communication vs. does not demonstrate sufficient self-understanding to recognize personal impediments to learning and communication.

7. Can articulate an evaluative framework appropriate to each realm of meaning or way of knowing and communicating vs. an inability to articulate an evaluative framework appropriate to each realm of meaning or way of knowing and communicating.

8. Can recognize content-appropriate assessment strategies and instruments in each and all realms of meaning vs. does not recognize appropriate evaluation strategies for each realm of meaning.

9. Demonstrates insight and skill in content and processes of the arts vs. lacks insight and skill in the processes and content of the arts.

10. Demonstrates an ethical framework for judgment vs. makes unethical judgments for sake of expediency or personal gain.

11. Can articulate a validated model of self-knowledge vs. lacks a validated model of self-knowledge.

12. Recognizes that academic disciplines are effective ways of knowing and creating knowledge about all aspects of life in time and place vs. fails to appreciate and practice the constructive nature of academic disciplines.

13. Views theories as explanations that provide focus to decision making and informed prediction of events vs. views theory as untested assertions that are useless until proven true.

14. Recognizes that knowledge is the product of our actions upon personal experience vs. a view that knowledge is pre-existing to be assimilated as presented.

15. Recognizes that students develop understanding about themselves, others, and the world around them through observation, interactions with people, objects and events vs. a view that learning is a passive activity involving acceptance of truths.

16. Has acquired the insight to apply knowledge about political, economic, and social institutions and procedures in this and other countries vs. a failure to recognize and apply insights concerning the nature of political, economic and social institutions in this and other countries.

17. Has acquired the knowledge, understanding and appreciation of the artistic, cultural and intellectual accomplishments of civilizations and developed skills to express personal artistic talents vs. has not integrated the arts with other forms of meaning and communication of personal experience.

18. Has developed a broad background in a full range of ways of knowing and realms of meaning, and demonstrates in-depth knowledge in at least one of these disciplines vs. has limited background in a range of ways of knowing and lacks depth in one area.

Professional Characteristics

1. Can identify each learner's emotional, social, physical and intellectual needs based on validated concepts and theories about human development and behavior including learning.
2. Establishes a culture for continued learning after class and graduation.
3. Encourages maintenance of change and utilization of learning in the life of the learner.
4. Recognizes the complex forces affecting learning and strives to eliminate impediments to learning.
5. Uses assessment and evaluation strategies as tools for learning.
6. Can accurately identify levels of development and learning in each student utilizing known models drawn from the literature.
7. Can diagnose learning problems using validated evaluation models.
8. Can articulate models appropriate to developmental characteristics and each way of knowing.
9. Is able to conduct formative assessment and evaluation in relation to learning plans.
10. Can articulate the essence of mandated standards.
11. Is able to structure and conduct summative evaluation that identifies levels of

achievement, areas of need and future directions.
12. Recognizes cognitive, affective and psycho-motor dimensions important to the teaching/learning transactions.
13. Recognizes and establishes flexible procedures that maximize learning and change for each individual.
14. Plans instruction appropriate to individual development.
15. Recognizes and values individual learning styles.
16. Works effectively with members of a professional team.

17. Uses suggestions constructively toward self-development.

18. Inspires students and colleagues through active leadership.

19. Establishes and maintains productive group environments that support individual learning.

20. Facilitates construction of strategic plans with and for students.

21. Engages students in goal setting.

22. Responds to individual needs, including setting boundaries and establishing consequences for inappropriate behavior.

23. Views deadlines and distractions as often unavoidable.

24. Builds on students' natural curiosity and desire to make sense out of life.

25. Recognizes and accepts a full range of modes of communication as legitimate evidence of learning and development.

26. Recognizes the range of purposes for writing–to inform, persuade, clarify or obscure, explain, sell etc.

27. Encourages a wide range of purposeful writing.

28. Exhibits openness and flexibility in the application of values, listens and appreciates ideas, and is open to suggestions and bases decisions on the best available data.

29. Can implement instruction consistent with cooperatively-developed plans.

30. Identifies and reacts with informed sensitivity to the needs and feelings of learners, co-workers, and parents.

31. Designs and implements instructional activities that address the need for learners to learn about themselves, their environment, and the work roles played by individuals in a global setting.

32. Promotes effective communication among all group members–verbally and non-verbally.

33. Can design and implement evaluation of instructional effectiveness.

34. Recognizes strategies of teaching/learning consistent with foundation models.

35. Demonstrates coherent instruction to facilitate learning to meet identified needs.

36. Uses strategies appropriate to student needs and areas of study.

37. Uses probing questions to encourage active student engagement.

38. Provides timely feedback regarding evaluation of outcomes.

39. Demonstrates awareness of resource requirements for learning including technology, space, equipment, information and time.

40. Provides concrete learning activities with materials and people relevant to personal life experiences.

41. Designs interventions and activities that develop self-esteem and positive feelings toward learning.

42. Provides the learning environment for active exploration and authentic interaction with adults, other students and materials.

43. Encourages daily aesthetic expression and appreciation for art forms as aids to improved communication.

44. Provides stimulating experiences in physical, social, emotional and intellectual dimensions.

45. Deliberately and systematically engages students in personal record-keeping, self-assessment, and honest reporting.

46. Responsibly manages routines including administrative requirements.

47. Engages stakeholders in constructive dialogue.

48. Works in partnership with parents, communicating regularly to build mutual understandings.

49. Moves among the group to facilitate involvement with materials and activities.

50. Utilizes local setting as a laboratory for constructing relevant conceptual frameworks.

51. Provides opportunities for in-depth inquiry that leads to the transfer of insights.

52. Engages students in processes of creating knowledge using methods and materials of disciplines within all realms of meaning.

53. Specifies instructional goals and objectives which respond to needs of learners in concert with those of the institution.

54. Uses resources of the school and community appropriate to instructional objectives, including computers, media and software.

55. Demonstrates organizational and managerial skills to maximize learning.

56. Integrates the cultural environment of the learner, enabling personalization of content, processes and expected outcomes.

57. Demonstrates a repertoire of transactional strategies that reflect stages of group and individual development.

58. Designs curriculum and instructional activities that promote achievement of learning outcomes.

59. Facilitates the development of self-control in students through guidelines, modeling, setting clear limits, etc.

60. Bases decisions regarding remediation and other important matters on information gathered from observations in conjunction with test data.

61. Provides students with many opportunities to develop social skills such as cooperating, helping, negotiating, and problem solving.

62. Modifies instruction based on learners' verbal and non-verbal responses as indicators of need.

63. Provides opportunities for reading, writing and listening as pre-requisites to language analysis.

64. Encourages students to be responsible, sociable,

self-managing, and resourceful, acting with integrity and honesty.

65. Applies methods of inquiry and expression drawn from disciplines and uses methods and knowledge in inter-disciplinary applications.

Appendix B

Goals 2000 Educate America

Rural School Consortium for New Standards Implementation

Project Coordinator: Robert Arnold

First meeting of the Planning Team

Hand House, Elizabethtown, May 11, 1995, 4-7 p.m.

The Coordinator opened the meeting by identifying the four groups comprising the Planning Team:

1. Superintendent and teachers from Willsboro Central-School. AsGoals 2000 lead Agency, the Willsboro district will have an obligation to initiate in Fall 1995 the installation of a schoolwide assessment, record keeping. and evaluation system in keeping with the foundation concepts of the project.

2. Administrators and teachers representing other Consortium school districts: AuSableValley, Elizabethtown, Keene, Moriah, and Westport. The roles of these participants are to serve as liaisons between the project and their schools and to begin preparing for a long-range goal: development of a video/pc-based electronic networking system to enable all the Consortium schools to share and more effectively utilize information resources.

3. Representatives of the Compact for Learning Team and Willsboro School Board, in order to facilitate progress toward mutual goals.

4. Recorder, whose summaries of the proceedings will be

distributed to the Planning Team and will serve as a public record.

Funds for "Goals 2000 Educate America" were authorized by the Educate America Act and channeled to eligible states through the federal Office of Education.

To put the Consortium project in context, the coordinator described the three areas for which funds were available for New York State Goals 2000: Professional Development, Pre-service Education, and Local Improvement Planning and Initiatives-the Consortium project is funded under this category. 25%of the funds are to be used for planning; 75% for specific improvement initiatives.

The initial project period for Phase I is 3/15-8/31/95, with funds expected to be available for an additional 4 years. A primary goal of Phase I is to lay a foundation for what will occur after the initial project period, so that the Consortium can take advantage of subsequent funding.

The Consortium project's approach to achieving this goal will be guided by the learning modes named in Standards 1, 2, and 3 of the NYS Education Department's 1994 *Framework for Mathematics, Science, and Technology: Curriculum. Instruction and Assessment.* To begin, the group will engage in a comprehensive *inquiry* into the education system and its components, guided by five foundation categories (see p.3): This will provide a frame of reference from which to view problems in the current system, which is essential to an *analysis* of the system. Each participant's analysis will result from application of the clearly articulated framework. Finally, the Consortium participants will utilize the analysis *to design* the changes it implies. The specific content will be determined by the project participants, according to what they deem appropriate.

The Coordinator introduced the "Professional Educator's Handbook" provided for each participant. It's prepared, but tentative, Table of Contents (attached) outlines the suggested organization of the component files for the completed project portfolio, which will serve as both a personal record of the project and as a prototype for the assessment, record keeping, and evaluation processes that reflect the Framework's constructivist/systems point-of-view. .

The Coordinator discussed answers to the question: Why reform? To formulate desired exit outcomes for students and to plan effectively to achieve them, it's essential to take into consideration recent societal trends and changes: accelerating new knowledge, new technology, ever-faster communications. Increasing international interdependence, changes in the economy from industrial- to service based, shift from specialization to a generalist orientation, increasing societal diversity, new roles for individuals in their personal and work lives, and an increasing focus on health, wellness, and environmental issues.

To place the project in an historical context, the Coordinator reviewed the pattern of "pendulum swings" in educational thinking and practice during this century. The shifts, and their concomitant manifestations in schools, were between learning centered on and guided by content, and learning centered on the needs of individual students:

Early 1900s: content-centered

1920s-30s: "Progressive Education," based on the ideas of John Dewey, was widely discussed but had little impact except in a few elite schools.

1950s: The "unit" method was a partial compromise between content- and learner-centered education, because students made some decisions about their own learning.

1957: With the launch of Sputnik, there was a rapid shift to a content-centered orientation. guided by several major attempts, such as: 1–the federally funded Madison Project and the "NewMath," to redefine math; and 2–science projects such as the Biological Sciences Curriculum Study aimed at and reconstructing curricula'- for more effective teaching.

1960s: "Open Education" sidetracked these efforts in response to social unrest.

1970s-80s: "Back to Basics"
1990s: an attempt to combine the two approaches

What can be learned from the education pendulum of the twentieth century? To improve the quality of education, compatibility is needed between what is known about the needs and levels of development of each individual learner and the way students work with content.

The New York State Education Department has undertaken such a restatement of content in its Framework document, which proposes a new integration of math, science, and technology that will enable students to solve problems and make use of classroom learning experiences in the "real" world–outside the classroom and after graduation. .

According to Standard 1 of the framework, "Analysis, Inquiry, and Design," in order for students to attain these abilities, they need to be actively involved and at the center of their learning experiences. According to Standard 2, "Systems," a systems, or constructivist, view of content is also essential. Students need to be able to construct relationships in a meaningful way, at a higher than "knowledge of..." level of learning (see Bloom's Taxonomy below). Using the example of a car's braking system, the Coordinator demonstrated the importance of understanding the parts of a system and their interdependent relationships and the system as a whole. Students who achieve a thorough understanding of a system will also be able to explain the effects of change on any part of the system.

According to Standard 3, "Information Resources," real-rime access to a full range of information resources, through state-of-the-art networking systems, is vital £0 the learning processes outlined in Standards 1 and 2. The systems view clarifies the project's purposes as well. In order to make informed decisions about education, to continue to progress without getting hung up in opinions and arguments, the participants will need to establish a shared, mutually agreed-upon foundation of knowledge of the component parts (tentatively listed in the Handbook's Table of Contents) of the educational *system* and how it operates as a whole. As the group constructs this shared knowledge base, if any part appears inconsistent, either that part must be rethought, or modifications made to the already existing concepts. .

To illustrate the value and power of a theory, the Coordinator conducted a two-part activity. He distributed folders containing age-grouped drawings of "My House" by children ages 5, 6, 7, 8, 9, and 10. He asked the Planning Team members to name criteria to evaluate the quality of the drawings. The list contained subjective terms such as awareness, details, form, and skill. In sharp contrast, he introduced, with samples, Lowenfeld's theory of children's stages of artistic development (attached), which instantly objectified the evaluation process. Participants could now confidently sort the drawings according to the criteria of each level: random scribbles, controlled scribbles, pre-schematic, schematic (planned), dawning realism (a beginning grasp of dimensionality), and realism. Planning Team members copied and labeled the illustrations of Lowenfeld's theory under "Individual Development" in their Handbooks for future reference, as they will with other underlying assumptions about all aspects of education they will examine and verify. The theory provided not only a focus for evaluating drawings, but also access to other insights and extrapolations:

— Children of the same age are at different levels of performance.

— Each drawing can be placed in a context: where in this domain each child has been and where he or she is heading.

— Lowenfeld's stages of development parallel development in other areas and subjects.

— The schematic level is the start of the cognitive ability for logic-the beginning of meaningfully linking parts of a whole together.

— It's essential for teachers, whose job it is to guide students to where they will next be heading, to be aware of their "Current levels of development. Frustration and failure and their whole related syndrome of serious problems will result from insistence on children doing what they are not yet capable of.

—Children's growth results from a match between their abilities and the appropriateness of the teacher's expectations and the learning experiences he or she provides.

Other theories offering similar clarity and insights can provide information and explanations for topics I-V in the Handbook table of contents: the educator as a person and a professional; individual behavior and development, including learning; the nature of communication and group process/organizational dynamics; the nature and evolution of the school system; and the nature of knowledge and the disciplines as ways of knowing. These theories, if validated by the participants, can provide guidance to the Consortium as it develops its shared knowledge base.

The Coordinator reviewed Bloom's Taxonomy of Educational Objectives for the Cognitive Domain, which was developed from a review of thousands of teacher written test items in an attempt to ascertain teachers' testing objectives. It's a hierarchy of levels of objectives, listed from most sophisticated to simplest:

Critical Evaluation: The learner has developed a larger context in which he/she can solve problems. .

Synthesis; The learner can put his/her understandings together into an integrated statement, creating a new whole from the pans.

Analysis: The learner can break down objects or ideas into simpler parts and see how they relate and are organized. the planning team engaged in analysis when they returned to the children's pictures after being Introduced to Lowenfeld's theory. They Were now able to scrutinize particular features of the drawings. such as use of baseline and dimensionality, which they previously did not have enough information and understanding to do. \

Application: The learner can apply knowledge to actual situations and connect it to his/her experience. \

Interpretation: The learner can explain the information, define it in his/her own words, and describe what he means Ito him/her.

Translation: The learner writes it down. .

Knowledge of: The learner has simple awareness of information/facts.

Students rarely achieve a level of learning higher than Interpretation, with the result that the information is usually [forgotten in a short period of time. Educators now recognize that in order for students to internalize and retain concepts and details, they need to attain higher levels of learning in a context where the concepts and information have vivid meaning to them.

Typically, school curricula introduce the same information every year or every few years. (The landing of the Pilgrims is a common example.) There is repetition of verbal information with no elaboration to higher levels of thinking.

Ideally, using a constructivist (systems building) record keeping system, students' prior learning can be accumulated in a paper or computer portfolio through the years and built upon. They tan continually pick up where they left off before. building systems over time by gradually reaching the level of synthesis for each part and ultimately for the system as a whole. Computer portfolios enable the learner to most easily add, rearrange, res rate, etc. Graphics capability will further enhance the portfolios' value. The portfolio is both a learning tool for students and a continuous record of their thinking and development, although lower levels of thought can eventually be purged as .mature formulations emerge.

The Coordinator reviewed the objectives of this year's project, and a tentative organizational and scheduling framework:

1: The Planning Group will help shape the direction of the project and communicate it to their constituents. I

2: The project participants will begin the process of formulating a shared knowledge base. which will provide the foundation concepts needed to evaluate the education system and underlie all of their [decisions as the project moves forward. Realms #I-Vin the Handbook table of contents will provide structure for this inquiry process. These 2-day sessions will be organized by grade level: elementary, middle, and high school. \

3: During three-day sessions organized by discipline across instructional levels, participants will focus on the connections between the disciplines and Framework's first three Standards (see p. 2). This will prepare them to develop optimal approaches to learning for each discipline, including experiential requirements for students, exit outcomes, and information management systems.

4. The participants will create a portfolio (the Educator's Handbook) that will serve as a model for the constructive assessment; record keeping, and evaluation system to be introduced this fall in the Willsboro District and considered by all Consortium schools.

The value of this model portfolio is three-fold:
— Its contents are the findings of the group's inquiry into education undertaken in objective #2.
— The participants will acquire first-hand experience' in compiling a systems oriented learning record as they work together to reach high levels of cognition for each part of the education system and the system as a whole, and to reach consensus on the portfolio's contents. They'll become familiar with the process of creating a portfolio as they make judgments and adjust for internal consistency, decide what to include and exclude by distinguishing valid assumptions from invalid, revise as new knowledge is incorporated, etc. (They'll also engage in meta-

cognition, becoming aware of their own thought processes. Understanding the process of mentation is essential for teaching.)
— The evolving portfolios will help keep group discussions focused on the issues, serving as a reference for clarification and a means for backing up and evaluating suggestions.

5: The project participants will identify specific information and resources needed for study in each discipline, including where and it what form it is stored. They will develop a plan for accessing the information and making it available to classrooms on demand. After researching what is available and what is still needed, funding can be requested from communication businesses to begin creation of the Consortium districts' information accessing and sharing network.

Primary sources (original documents) of local historical information is a need that has already been identified. As learners productively construct a high-level understanding of local history and geography, they develop concepts that make possible transfer of insights to other locations and time periods, and a high-level understanding of them as well. (Information of interest primarily to local areas is not available commercially, because the market for it is too small.)

The project's evaluation tool is the Levels of Use of the Innovation (LoU) scale, developed at the University of Texas. Because the LoU recognizes that change, especially in education, is not an event or occurrence, but a process that develops over time, it utilizes a developmental sequence to monitor the degree to which innovations are used. The LoU can also identify causes of a lack of significant change in participants' behavior.

The Request for Proposals for Goals 2000 Phase II grants will be published in mid-summer. Another responsibility of the project participants will be to identify ideas for inclusion in the proposal. For example, the fact that an Internet course offered at PSUC during the summer session was oversubscribed suggests a valid need.

Goals 2000 Educate America

Rural School Consortium for New Standards Implementation

Project Coordinator: Robert Arnold

Second Meeting of the Planning Team

Hand House, Elizabethtown, May 18, 1995, 4-8 p.m.

The coordinator opened the meeting by asking the Planning Team members to reply in writing to the question, "When you think about the "project, what are you concerned about?" The responses were later read and discussed (see p. 6).

The team members had previously received draft copies of the summary of the May 11 meeting. They were asked to comment on it so that revisions could be made before it is placed in the public record. The consensus was that the summary was satisfactory.

The coordinator clarified one point in the summary, regarding the proposed "inquiry... analysis...design" approach to achieving the project's goals. The inquiry stage is a unique feature of this project. Participants will first engage in an inquiry into the components of the current education system, guided by five foundation categories:

the educator as a person and a professional;

individual behavior and development, including learning;

the nature of communication and group process/organizational dynamics;

the nature and evolution of the school system;

and the nature of knowledge and the disciplines as ways of knowing.

As the group investigates concepts and theories in these realms (such as Lowenfeld's theory on artistic development), they will be compiling a validated, shared knowledge base. The inquiry will provide a valuable frame of reference from which to view problems in the current education system, which is essential to an *analysis* of the system. Each participant's analysis will result from application of this clearly articulated framework. Finally, the Consortium participants will utilize the inquiry and analysis to *design* changes that are consistent with the basic premises and implied by the analysis.

Each team member received an illustration showing the relationships among the components of this assumptive base (attached).

The Coordinator returned to the previous meeting's illustration of the swings of the educational pendulum between individual- and content-centered phases of educational thinking and practice in this century. He asked, "Why has there been ongoing incompatibility between these two approaches? Why have they been viewed as extremes that cannot be joined together effectively?"

There were several responses from team members:

— Because the goal of schools has been to educate the group, a content-based curriculum has taken precedence.

— The orientation of teachers' training, which has shifted as the pendulum continued to swing, and the personal biases engendered by both training and "fads" teachers have experienced, have necessarily perpetuated the prevalent either/or dichotomy between content and individual.

— No one has yet broken down content for reorganization in a way that can unite content and learner. (The Coordinator noted that the 1994 state Framework for Mathematics, Science, and Technology recommends an integration of these subject areas, but because of its greater emphasis on content, doesn't take the next step toward optimal compatibility between content/instruction and individual learners' needs and levels of development.

- The current trend is a focus on the individual. Students are now more responsible for their own learning, and the teacher is more of a facilitator.

A rethinking of the definition of "content" illuminated a comprehensive answer to the question of the apparent incompatibility between content- and learner-based education. The Coordinator contrasted an extreme content orientation with a constructivist orientation. The content orientation is exemplified by a biology professor who filled numerous 4' by 12' chalkboards during each class session, actively generating information himself but failing to communicate it to the passive students. In this context, content is regarded as the same for everyone. It's an entity that individuals acquire in the form in which it's given to them.

In reality, though, content varies among individuals. Whatever we know is the product of our own personal construction. Each person perceives and filters content through his or her own experiences and senses. Individuals build meaning themselves and define the world according to their own constructs. Therefore content is actually unique to each individual. The Planning Team itself, and all project participants, should be aware that each person in the group translates the proceedings in a way that makes sense to him or herself.

This redefining of content, which helps resolve the traditional conflict between content- and learner-based education, underlies the grant proposal. The constructivist orientation written into the grant is part of the NYS Education Department's new Framework: Standard 1 calls for the learner to be actively involved in the learning process. Standard 2 recommends that learners be introduced to the systems concept, because a grasp of relationships among isolated pieces of information will enable them to make effective use of classroom learning to solve problems in the real world.

The current impetus for the constructivist orientation-just as Sputnik prompted a shift in orientation in the late 1950s-is the need for a new educational orientation that will help the United States succeed in an era of increasing global economic competition. (To date, a constructivist approach in education has been implemented most frequently in mathematics.) A long-range objective of this project is to understand both the individual and content sufficiently to develop techniques to bring about a felicitous meshing of the two in educational settings.

As a preliminary to future work on the grant project, each participant should develop a clear image of the concepts comprising each component of the assumptive base for education. The group has already been introduced to some of the concepts in the illustration. For example, Lowenfeld's theory on aesthetic development belongs in category #2: "Individual Development and Behavior" (which encompasses a comprehensive view of all developmental dimensions, including aesthetic, emotional, intellectual, moral, physical, and social). The information on the "pendulum swings" of twentieth century educational thinking belong in #4, "The Nature and Evolution of the School." Bloom's Taxonomy of Educational Objectives-Cognitive Domain would fall under #5, "The Nature of Knowledge and the Creative Disciplines."

The Coordinator introduced some of the research and resulting theories that belong in #3, "The Nature of Communication and Group Process/Organizational Dynamics." Most research in this area, beginning in the 1930s at the National Training Lab in Bethel, Maine, has been in the realm of business and industry. As part of his work.at the National Training Lab, Likert developed a formulation on leadership that identified four categories of leadership style:

Exploitative authoritarian: These people are working for their own purposes. They're intent on reaching the top of the organization, exploit anyone in the way, and consequently harm their subordinates.

Benevolent authoritarian: They're also in charge, but nice about it. They judge behavior and give rewards and punishments, including increases and decreases in their subordinates' freedom to act independently.

Consultative: These leaders ask their subordinates' opinions, but usually act only on advice that supports their own intentions and disregard advice that conflicts. Consultative leadership can be viewed as authoritarianism in disguise. The decision making process in institutions of higher education frequently exemplifies this style. Committees are requested to make recommendations after decisions have been made.

Participative: This style is characterized by open communication, mutual support, appreciation of individuals and what they have to offer, and revolving leadership. Work is a productive and rewarding team experience.

The research on organizational dynamics in business and industry conducted over the past half-century in the United States has culminated in advocacy of this management style and led to implementation of participative approaches such as Demming's Total Quality Management. Competition from Japan, believed to be at least in part due to their success with participative management, has been an additional impetus to a more universal recognition of its value in the U.S.

However, in certain situations, including this project, there are serious obstacles to full implementation of participative leadership. The Rural Schools Consortium grant project has been undertaken in a complex hierarchical and legal context:

On the state level, these parts function interdependently:
The Governor and Legislature report to the voters.
The Board of Regents reports to the governor and legislature.
The Commissioner of Education, Associate Commissioner, and staff report to the Board of Regents.
Within each school system, these parts function interdependently:
The school board reports to the Commissioner.

The principals reports to the superintendent, who reports to the school board.

The teachers and department heads report to the principal.

The students and parents ordinarily report to the teacher.

The person or group at each level is legally responsible and accountable for whatever occurs at lower levels, and each has a person or group above to whom they must respond.

This arrangement necessitates restraints on participative organizations such as the Compact for Learning Team and the Rural Schools Consortium. The project members, as they attempt to function in a participative framework, have to be aware of the existence of the hierarchical context and the fact that people at each level have needs and requirements that must be taken into consideration before any decisions are made. Every action must be taken with each participant's legal responsibilities in mind.

For example, the Coordinator has to respond first to the superintendent, and also to the other levels of the hierarchy and to the granting agency. These are givens that cannot be disregarded.

Disillusionment among participants will arise if conflicts occur between someone's intentions Within the group and responsibilities within the education system's hierarchy. For example, an imposed deadline outside of the project's context may force an individual to make a decision before the group has reached consensus. Problems such as these are unfortunately built into the current system. The state Department of Education is now requesting that more people be involved in decision making, yet it is operating under the same authoritarian hierarchy as before.

Furthermore, as a funded grant, the Consortium project has other limitations set by its funding sources. The United States Department of Education authorized funds filed for by the New York State Board of Regents for specific activities. The Board of Regents will necessarily monitor the project, and the federal Department of Education in turn will monitor the Board of Regents.

Both of these realities may necessitate occasional reversion in this group's functioning from participative to authoritarian. Members need to be sensitive to the fact that the reason for any unwanted reversion is imposed from outside the Consortium project.

In response to a Team Member's comment, the Coordinator said that it's the intent of this grant to utilize local resources and talent to create a system that will work here. Since 1992, State regulations allow school systems to petition for exemption from certain regulations and implement workable ideas if there is a supportable rationale.

Returning to the discussion of organizational dynamics, the Coordinator outlined stages of group development, noting that for any group to attain its optimal productivity, it must move through all three stages.

1. Dependency: Groups begin at this stage and remain here until each member not only understands the ground rules for the group, the purposes it intends to achieve, and the probable direction for achieving its goals, but also acknowledges that the purposes and direction are significant and appropriate for him or herself.

Issues of authority are confronted and resolved at this stage. How much authority does each member have in the context of the group and in the context of the larger hierarchy of accountability, needs, and requirements outlined above.

Subgroups may form at this stage: those who want to be given direction and told what to do, and those who want to formulate some of the direction themselves. It's the leader's role to utilize his or her authority to facilitate everyone's advance to the next stage.

2. Independence: Members realize it's not only their right but their responsibility to make their views known and to respect each others' point of view. Procedures for civility are being established to accompany each member's freedom to

speak. It's essential for all to feel comfortable about expressing themselves. If not, they'll either stop talking or stop coming.

3. Interdependence: Conflicts at the previous stage are resolved. The group routinely stays focused on its issues and tasks in spite of diverse ideas. For optimal productivity and achievement of its goals, the group should strive to move to interdependence as quickly as possible and then maintain this stage.

The Coordinator then specified the manifestations of several dimensions of group work within this framework of group development:

	Dependence	Independence	Interdependence
Goal setting	Goals are set for members	Members are given the opportunity to set goals	Goals are agreed on by the group.
Communication	One way; leader to group	A lot of discussion	More listening
Rewards	Given from the top down; leader to other members.	Rewards come from expressing your opinions.	Rewards come from feeling comfortable with group decision.

One major role of the Planning Team is to serve a liaison between the project and the schools they represent. The Coordinator asked what colleagues are saying about the project and what some potential communication problems may be.

Team members' responses were:

— Many people have worked to a point where they don't want to make any changes. They want to function by rote, without thinking. They're satisfied where they are.

— Other teachers at the same level have been positive and supportive.

— Some are saying it's just the latest change that will fade like the others, so there's no need to get involved.

Other remarks and the Coordinator's responses were:

— There's been no interaction among the Planning team members and there is no clear idea of what the team is planning to do.

He summarized the steps stated in the grant proposal for Phase I;

Acquire and document a common foundation knowledge base (p.1) so that the participants have shared language and concepts to build from.

Investigate each discipline and define the essentials of each in the way that will be most effective for students.

Develop a long-range plan for sharing resources, including human, curricular, and experiential.

Define anticipated projects for Phase II and for other funding opportunities. The frameworks defined in these steps will related to and support every decision made by the Consortium project in succeeding phases: standards, content, teaching-learning transactions; assessment, record keeping, and evaluation; and required information and technology.

Are we empowered to set up a common curriculum for the County? What is the County's standing in relation to the State Education Department? If this group endeavors to foster consistency among schools and produces, for example, a high school reading list and a description of what students will learn at each level, will the state allow its implementation? It's true that poor vocabulary and reading skills are nationwide problems, but we now have a grant to do something about it here. In order to do this, we need to know what's going on in other classrooms in our schools and in other districts. Electronic communication may assist here. Perhaps teachers should meet by grade levels and subject areas to share, plan, and act.

The Coordinator commented that these ideas will fit in with Phase II, which begins in September. He distributed a summary of the objectives of the current phase of the project. Phase I (attached). One objective is to create a long-range plan for sharing resources, so that what is needed can be included in Phase II proposal. Another objective is to investigate each essential academic area—science; math; history; and geography; and English, language arts, and the humanities and, with guidance from specialists in each ares, lay out a structure for defining them so that the project participants can create substantive and worthy standard for curriculum and instruction.

The concerns written down at the start of the meeting were read aloud:

— How can we get other teachers involved? Will they regard it as just one more thing to do?

— Is there enough interest and ambition to make it work?

— Will we have a choice about using the assessment, record keeping, and evaluation system and other innovations? (See below.)

— Is there enough time to do everything that needs to be done? (The Coordinator noted that the group will set its own schedule.)

— Electronic innovations may lead to depersonalization of education.

— Will we be expected to create a file on each category and to make presentations at our schools?

— What will happen if group members change?

— It's difficult to do your job and work on examining and redesigning it at the same time. (The coordinator agreed that keeping afloat in ones job while engaged in the process of taking it apart and putting it back together is tricky, yet eventually the two will be brought together.)

— Is there a stipend for people who attend in the summer? (Yes, it's $80 plus retirement per day, and the possibility of graduate credit will be looked into.)

— What are the purposes of the project beyond the portfolio assessment?

There's a gap between the Table of Contents in the Educator's Handbook and the assessment system. (The Coordinator responded that according to the grant, which is funded under local improvement planning and initiatives, the Willsboro district, as Lead Agency, has a responsibility to implement a portfolio assessment system based on a systems point of view. Although the proposed CARES model is consistent with this point of view, it is not the Coordinator's intent to force its adoption, but to develop a sound rationale to support it. The participants can modify the model or design another-in accordance with their shared underlying assumptions about the education system. Implementation will be at the discretion of each teacher.)

Tom McGrath gave an introduction to the project's evaluation tool, the Levels of Use of the Innovation (LoU) scale. Mr. McGrath is a certified LoU evaluator, and is currently working with the Public Broadcasting System on evaluating a new project based on its program, "Math Talk."

Mr. McGrath provided each Planning Team member with a "Project Evaluation Packet- (attached). He briefly reviewed some of the material, making these points:

— The LoU was selected for this project because it's descriptive, not judgmental. It provides precise data on what has been accomplished. The LoU utilizes focused interviews and observations to determine an individual's stage of implementation of an innovation (from 0 to VI) in reference to various categories: knowledge of the innovation, acquiring information (e.g., visiting sites, soliciting more information), sharing (discussing plans, ideas, resources, and problems with others), assessing (mentally or can involve actual explanation and analysis of data), planning (steps for adoption in both the short and long term); status reporting (teachers' personal descriptions of their stand on and use of the innovation at different stages of implementation), and performing (carries out the actions and activities entailed in operationalizing the innovation) .

— The use of the label "routine" for one of the levels should not be viewed as having a negative connotation. Rather, it may imply effective use of an innovation.

— The LoU is based on principles of developmental levels and a systems perspective similar to those guiding the entire project.

— The LoU is one application of the Concerns Based

Adoption Model (CBAM). (See the Evaluation Packet for a description of the implicit assumptions of this model.) The ·Stages of Concern" application of the CBAM model will not be prominent for this project.

— The evaluation of the project is separate from the project itself. It's valuable for mating mid-course corrections in the project and for reporting progress.

— The excerpt from an interview with a teacher implies that the interview helped her clarify in her own mind the effectiveness of her use of a new innovation and will assist her in making improvements in future lessons with this innovation.

— Change occurs slowly. The intent of the LoU evaluation is to follow this project over 3-5 years. Typically, in a multi-faceted project such as the rural Schools Consortium, 3040% of the participants are stable at level IIIa after three cycles. Implementation at stage IVa or higher takes 3-5 years. It would be impossible to measure students' gains until then.

To help the group members become familiar with the scoring procedure on their own" he provided the Levels of Use in the scenarios described in the "Scoring Exercise" and he encouraged everyone to read all of the material before the next meeting.

A Planning Team member asked, "How can we evaluate the policy makers' standards–what they want?"

The Coordinator reemphasized the importance of communication. Other related individuals and groups should be present at project meetings and workshops. Participants in this project, as they move forward, need to balance their actions with the concerns of others with mutual goals, and avoid treading on their toes. Cooperation through building on one another's experiences is the ideal.

He will meet with the Willsboro Board of Education so they will understand what the grant is about and help shape its development. Policy makers need to realize, for example, that effects of the innovations on students' progress won't be evident for several years.

In reference to a question about the difference between the Lead Agency and he other districts, the Coordinator explained that he had been given the go-ahead by Willsboro teachers in attendance at a meeting last year to pursue this grant with the Willsboro district as lead agency. The fundamental role of the representatives of the other schools is two-way communication for the accurate sharing of information. They will report Consortium proceedings to people in their districts, clarifying the aspects that will apply to them-that they can build from to develop their own projects. And they will bring back to the Consortium ideas from their districts that others can use and needs that the Consortium can try to meet. The "Rural Schools Consortium" concept will be significantly applicable to sharing resources.

The meeting concluded with a discussion of scheduling. A four-hour meeting of the Planning Team was tentatively scheduled for Wednesday, June 21. Scheduling of the estimated nine summer meetings for all participants will be based on the preferences of the Planning Team. The locations are not settled. Before leaving, team members were asked to complete a "Post-Meeting Reaction Form" (attached).

Goals 2000 Educate America

Rural School ConsQrtium for New Standards Implementation

Project Coordinator: Robert Arnold

Third Meeting of the Planning Team

United Methodist Church, Willsboro, June 22, 1995, 12-4 p.m.

Items for today's agenda were listed by the Coordinator as Planning Team
members generated them. The items were:
— summer workshop activities;
— outcomes of the workshops vis a vis the State Education Department;
— implications of workshop outcomes for implementation in all subjects and grades, and establishment of procedures for teachers under the parameters to be developed. In other words, what will 'workshop outcomes mean in terms of the curriculum?
— preplanning for the second grant; and
— overview of the project, especially relationships among content, record keeping/assessment, and student outcomes.

Before proceeding with the agenda issues, the Coordinator brought the group up to date with recent information from the State Education Department:

$20 million is allocated for Phase II; 6.9 million was allocated for Phase 1.

The outcome of Phase 1 work should be plans for the next 2-5 years. The pian for Phase II should contain specific action steps for continuing where Phase I ended; plans for succeeding years will necessarily be long-range and skeletal.

The Associate Commissioner of Education, who is in charge of Goals 2000 for New York, expressed keen interest in the Consortium project because of its uniqueness and its promise.

The project's goals and objectives, desert bed on pp. 4-6 of the April 1994 Working Paper (attached), should be aligned not only with the goals and objectives of the group and of each individual participant, but also with those of the State Education Department. For example, achievement of Goal #1, the documentation and verification of a shared knowledge base for 21st century education, will be evidenced by each participant's Professional Educator's Handbook. Participants will complete the portfolios as much as possible during the summer workshops and, afterward, continue to add information in identified areas of need. Goal #2, analysis of each academic area from the perspective of the Math, Science, and Technology "Framework" Standards 1, 2, and 3, and the elements of the shared knowledge base, is necessarily aligned with the goals of the State Education Department, since the Framework standards are based on constructivist learning theory. The outcome of the workshops will be implications for instruction, e.g., appropriate materials and experiential requirements for students to be actively involved in learning and mastery.

The Coordinator suggested that Planning Team members familiarize themselves with Math, Science, and Technology Standards 1, 2, and 3 on p. 6 of the "Framework" document. These Standards provide a general framework for educational change, and serve as the foundation of the Consortium project. Although in the context of the document, the Standards are intended to be applied to Math, Science, and Technology, they are in fact generic. These areas may be a starting point and eventually the Standards can be applied to each area of the curriculum.

The Coordinator referred to a monograph published by

the National Council of Teachers of Mathematics on the validity of the constructivist approach to teaching math, One of the articles in the series, "Teacher Development in Mathematics in a Constructivist Framework," was written by two educators currently at Rutgers University who will lead one of the project's summer workshops. If his health permits, they may be accompanied by another contributor to the monograph, Bob Davis, a leader in constructivist theory who headed the Madison Project, wrote instructional materials, and trained 17,000 teachers in New York City alone. The fundamental questions guiding the work of Davis and his colleagues are, "What is it about math that we want students to master?" and "What are the implications, from a constructivist point of view, for the teacher's role, students' experiences, and student evaluation?" Their focus is on trying to ascertain and recognize what is happening **in** children's minds when they are thinking mathematically. At the workshop, they will explain through discussion and videotapes how teachers can best observe students, ask questions that are most helpful for learning, etc. All of this is at the core of Goal #2-analyzing each academic area from the perspective of the Standards-and is applicable to all areas of the curriculum. Also, since it can be tied in with an assessment and record keeping system that supports the constructivist approach and provides a manageable way of organizing and looking at outcomes, implementation will be more likely.

Week 1 Workshops

Days 1 and 2: A large amount of information will be processed and documented in the portfolios, to lay the foundation 'which addresses Goal #l-the shared knowledge base. Participants will continue to reflect upon this information between the two week-long sets of workshops, and to add to their portfolios as time goes on. The consultant for these workshops will be someone whose area of expertise is language acquisition and usage,

Days 3, 4, and 5: History and geography will be used as an example of learning content areas through a focus on first-hand understanding of the world. The purpose of education should be to understand the world in which we live, yet students ordinarily study someone else's perceptions of the world through pre-created knowledge in textbooks and other works. Toward the end of the first week a consul rant who is a writer of poetry and short stories wi ll direct a consideration of the creative processes of language and their implications for teaching at all age levels, through a stimulating and involving experience of language from a creative standpoint.

Week 2 Workshops—investigating content areas and implications for teaching

Day 1: Week 1 will finish with a consideration of language; week two will begin with a consideration of another language: the language of mathematics and its implications for teaching. The consultants from Rutgers and Don Blais from Plattsburgh State College will guide the discussions.

Day 2 and 3: The focus will be on the same issues in the sciences, particularly earth science, and translations for chemistry, physics, and biology. Consultants from different areas of science will guide the discussions.

Day 4 and 5: At this point, the group will have a clearer idea of what the project's next steps require, and will be ready to begin identifying and structuring its needs for the long-range plan. They will be assisted by consultants who are adept at long-range planning. Plan writing will continue after the workshops are finished.

Although the workshops are intended to be sequential, information about them will be available to absentees: the written record, selective video tapings, portfolios, and evaluations. Assessment of the workshops will be incorporated each day.

In response to a question about the record keeping system, the Coordinator utilized a concrete example to illustrate its rationale and how it works. He asked Planning Team members to draw a system with which they are familiar: their local environment. These were the instructions:

"For the area where you live, draw a three dimensional picture of a chunk of earth viewed from the side, with these elements in it. [lists of names of rocks, minerals, ores, relief features, soils, water sources, flora, and fauna were provided.] Conceptualize and label each of the physical parts."

When everyone was finished, he told the group that this exercise is his "Environmental Relationships Test. He asked, "How would you define competence on this test?" Someone said that all elements are incorporated in a way that's accurate and makes sense to others.

The Coordinator elaborated on this definition. First, an understanding of the concepts relating to each of the parts needs to be demonstrated. For example, for rocks, a complete concept would include where they are located, how they are formed, what they look like, and other features, such as fossils, softness or hardness and the effects of water, smoothness or roughness, etc. The clearer and richer the concept, the more dimensions it will have and the more detailed the picture. In this group, one person knew that limestone and shale formed in layers, another knew their color, and another knew that limestone could be tested for with acid. This is typical: many individuals have just a few isolated bits of knowledge about rocks that may or may not relate to the real world. The next step is indicating which minerals are associated with the rocks, then relating relief features to the rocks and minerals, adding vegetation and relating that to growing season, annual rainfall, etc.

In the real world, these parts exist in an interrelated system. Therefore, there should be no contradictions in the drawing.

Someone who can differentiate each part and show the relationships among all the parts will also be able to describe the effects of change to anyone part on the rest of the system. In sum, competence consists in the ability to (1) conceptualize each pan, (2) relate them in a representation, and (3) anticipate the consequences of change to anyone part.

The Coordinator distributed copies of a student's drawing for the Environmental Relationships Test (attached). It was obvious there was total deficiency. How could this be remedied? A participant suggested a field trip to a road cut or quarry, where the characteristics of rocks can be observed and studied and data can be collected. For example, hardness can be tested for by scratching or rubbing. A good map showing rocks and minerals of the region will aid in identification of the rocks.

The group agreed that this drawing is at Lowenfeld's schematic or dawning realism level, and the student is probably a fourth grader, 8 or 10 years old. They were astonished to learn that the drawing had been done by a college senior, an honor student who had studied science. This proves that one can succeed in the current educational system with only surface knowledge, by merely accumulating and remembering isolated bits of information. If rated according to Bloom's Taxonomy, this student's and most people's drawings indicate they have not gone beyond the first objective, "knowledge of...":

What happened to this student? His understanding of content is extremely limited and superficial. He never had to visualize or draw the concepts he was learning. He only had to memorize words and recite them. But direct experience with the system to be mastered and practice in drawing would have enabled him to master real content. Most children stop drawing in the early grades, believe they can't draw, and have no practice in constructing and representing their knowledge. Even children who have not yet achieved realism in their drawing could represent a three-dimensional system adequately if they had direct and purposeful experience with it.

This is not to say that narrative should be excluded. Students should be able to describe a system in words-a symbolic representation, as well as in a drawing-an iconic representation. But the structure of language imposes limitations. It doesn't match the structure of the real world. Language is linear, and books necessarily are split up into chapters and smaller sections. That's why it's true that a picture is worth a thousand words. Also, because it's easier to produce something plausible in writing than in drawing, the pictorial representation is more authentic. One cannot bluff on the Environmental Relationships Test: you can't draw something if you don't have a concept of it. A labeled picture accompanied by a narrative is even more valuable for demonstrating total competence. And understanding that comes from direct experience and is crystallized in one's mind can also be represented in poetry, music, dance, and other forms of communication.

The construction of this system of relationships is a process geographers attempt to do. It may appear piecemeal because of the limitations of language: the components of geography can't be written down all at once. They have to be categorized—geology, relief features, vegetation, climate, etc., and it's up to the reader to put it together. Geography is descriptive. It's the study and description of what exists, where it exists, how it is distributed, and how it is related. Geology is not descriptive. It's the in-depth study of a specific part of the system in great detail from the standpoint of empirical science: observe, experiment, generalize, and develop a theory.

Like geography, the Environmental Relationships Test exercise is synoptic, not empirical. It's not about taking things apart and studying them in depth. Instead, it forces you to integrate isolated bits of information and to summarize relationships in a meaningful pattern.

Every discipline has identifiable characteristics: its domain, specialized language, structure, and rules. There is an essential difference between someone who actually studies a system, for example, a meteorologist, who studies the system of weather, and someone who describes the results of someone else's study, for example, the TV weather reporter.

The Coordinator distributed his Curriculum Matrix (attached) to demonstrate that as disciplines, history and geography are similar. Focusing on the physical environment of Essex and Willsboro in 1836, the group agreed that between then and now there would have been little change in the region's rocks, slightly more in the soils, and much larger changes in quantity and type of vegetation. The Coordinator shared some data on the amount of "cleared an improved" land in Essex and Willsboro in 1836 (which could be compared with current aerial photographs), and on population, schools, industry, and livestock. At that time, Willsboro had sawmills, a gristmill, iron works, an ashery, and a tannery.

In 1836, Willsboro also had the different] mills necessary for processing wool: fulling, carding, spinning, and weaving. Conceptually, understanding this process is like understanding geography. If you have a concept of the entire sheep-to-sweater system, you can transfer this concept to related systems.

At that time, Essex had a cotton mill. To the surprise of some, cotton was grown here. (It would have been impractical to transport it here from the South.) If we want to grow something today that is not native this area, we shelter and nurture it, and the same was done then. Why would cotton be preferred to wool? It was mixed with wool to reduce itching, as in linsey-woolsey, made from a mixture of linen (from flax) and wool. The fact that linen was and is still thought of as a more prestigious commodity says something about our social-cultural orientation and the value system we apply.

To create a clear picture of the historical-geographical dynamic at any point in time, we need to analyze and synthesize the complete set of relationships, as we did in geography. All social, cultural, economic, political activity at any time and location occur in an environmental context. In this case the context included mountains, water, 100 feet of glacial till, and a 5-6 month growing season. The geographical context and the economic potential of an area's resources determine land use, industry, architecture, customs and manners, literature, philosophy, communication, technology, etc. If we piece together the entire puzzle of life in this region in 1836, we'd have in our mind's eye a conceptualization of the system.

Therefore, history in general (and its specializations, such as economic history, political history, and historical geography) is, like geography, a synoptic discipline. It describes many different factors and their relationships. If the processes of history as a discipline became an integral part of students' experiences, they would be able to construct a system based on the facts and assumptions of their investigation, just as historians do.

They would also be able to understand the effects of change to one part of the system on the system as a whole. For example, at that time there could not have been a gristmill, sawmill, or fulling mill without a source of water power. After the advent of steam, these mills could be located near any water source.

And once students construct a system for one region and time period, they could more easily construct it for any other. The set of factors and the structure are the same, and when the different pieces are substituted, a new pattern emerges. As students put together the geographical-historical picture, they will find things they don't understand. In order to continue, they'll be forced to experiment and study further in order to fully conceptualize all the parts and fit them into the whole.

This is true for any level. In kindergarten, for example, children can prepare for an experience, do the exploration, then return to draw and tell about it.

Typically, these drawings are sent home, posted on the refrigerator for a few days, and end up in the trash. The graphic representation is lost and with it the short term memory of the experience and the concepts it elucidated.

The proposed record keeping system, whereby records of relevant experiences are accumulated and accessible, will make it possible to keep track of each student's experiences and development within the conceptual frameworks under study. On a field trip to the fire department, for example, kindergartners will gain beginning understandings in architecture, government, and technology. They can draw these concepts and include them in their portfolios. As the children grow and develop, they'll add to their understandings: differentiate the parts more fully, realize new relationships and logical connections, and be able to transfer to other situations. Their learning process over time will be facilitated by going back to their older drawings and building upon prior knowledge. The portfolio also provides evidence of students' degrees of competence. So it's of value to the student, the teacher, and anyone else who needs to know about the student's progress.

The "Constructive Assessment, Record Keeping, and Evaluation System" document (attached) from the Plattsburgh Research Institute for Defining Education provides guidelines for constructing a record of mastery. The categories and subcategories into which a system can be broken down (for example: the natural environment, economics and politics, social and cultural) become the portfolio's table of contents.

New constructs representing current understandings are integrated as a student keeps exploring at an appropriate level that is meaningful to him or her. As time goes on, older pieces are no longer needed because more elaborate connections supersede them

Although the specific structure, focus, language, and learning outcome of the portfolio is determined by the teacher and individual-what best matches and encourages his or her intellectual processes, there are general criteria for evaluating a student's work:

1) organization and clarity: Your own scheme of categories should make sense and you should be able to defend it. It should also be flexible and able to be reorganized as new learning is incorporated.

2) comprehensiveness: Experiences should have been provided that will result in a complete record, with no gaps.

3) accuracy: The information you put into the record should reflect your experiences as accurately as possible. The

record should include both your perceptions and reinforcement and support from others' experiences and perceptions. (Although it's possible that your position is accurate even if it's not confirmed by others.)

4) internal consistency: Contradictions among files indicate that relationships are not understood.

5) generarivity: It's important for the learner to be aware of what he or she doesn't know-to identify unanswered questions and untested hypotheses. This awareness also aids in planning for succeeding learning experiences.

These criteria allow for production of individualized records that can be evaluated objectively, even quantifiably, even though each student's is different. For courses where a textbook is the main source of students' information, the chapters taken together represent the system, and each chapter is a part. Competence is evidenced by conceptualization of the information in a drawing, diagram, model, or other visual (iconic) form. In the primary grades, aides can assist in the compilation of portfolios. After that, students keep it themselves.

Participants' questions and Coordinator's answers about the portfolio system;

Q: Does a system like this have to be undertaken school wide?

A: Goal III of this project is in fact to establish a school-wide assessment, record keeping, and evaluation system that is consistent with the Math, Science, and Technology Framework Standards 1, 2, and 3. Standard 2 calls for involvement of students in the construction of systems.

Q; What about students who won't cooperate with the portfolio process?

A: Compiling the portfolio has to become for students a valued activity with a personal payoff.

Q: Is the portfolio system computer compatible?

A: Yes; that's one of its advantages. Word processing and

graphics programs support it. Each part of a system can be a file on a disk. .

Logic ("if x, then y") is required to synthesize knowledge and construct a system. How and when do children develop the ability to think logically about elements in their environment and to put things together into a relationship? In one of his experiments with children's logic, Piaget showed children two identical glasses with equal amounts of water. He poured the contents of one into a tall, thin glass and the contents of the other into a short, wide glass. When children can realize that the amount of water in the tall, thin glass and the short, wide glass is the same, it means they are capable of "conservation" and have reached the level of concrete operations, which is the beginning of logical thought. Until then, they cannot be requested or expected to think logical1y. .

Although the sequence of development is constant for everyone, children reach this stage at varying ages, and once they do they are capable of the same level of cognition and conceptualization in all areas. Now experience, not biological maturation, is the variable that affects intellectual growth. Lack of experiences, or inappropriate experiences, in a particular area will result in an inability to think about it logically, even though developmentally the potential is there. The more experiences someone has, the richer his or concepts. With repeated experiences and review of previous understandings in the portfolio, continuity is built and nothing important is lost from beginning conceptualization to mastery.

If students are capable of understanding the logic of a system, they can produce representations of logical relationships for their portfolios. If they are prelogical in their thinking, the teacher can assist them in organizing their records.

Since every area of study has its own characteristics and essential student outcomes, portfolio evaluation should take both the structure of each discipline and developmental differences among children into consideration.

The theories we will be introduced to as we develop the

foundation knowledge base during the summer workshops will clarify other aspects of the development of logic and its manifestations in children's behaviors, and will assist the group in developing an appropriate curriculum.

In response to a question by a social studies teacher, the Coordinator discussed the constructivist approach and assessment model in terms of its use in different content areas taught in high school. This teacher's classroom mandate is social, cultural. economic, and political domains, but the natural physical environment is interwoven with these. Once the system is in place, cooperation among teachers will result in far more integration among disciplines. Students of social studies will have studied the environmental context in which history unfolds and which is essential for understanding the total pattern. They will bring that insight to *their* social studies class, and previously mastered patterns will transfer to the new content and facilitate its mastery.

The Regents exams are an impediment to the systems approach. They perpetuate the cram -> memorize -> take test -> forget syndrome that's been the teaching model for years and has resulted in very low quantity and quality of learning. The Regents exams are currently under review, and schools may waive Regents testing (and other state regulations) if they can show that an alternative is better. Some districts are rewriting the Regents to correlate with the way students are learning under the New Compact for Learning.

A participant mentioned the integration of content being undertaken with two groups of 90 seventh and eighth graders at Plattsburgh Middle School. Various content areas, including math, science, technology, social studies, and language, are brought in as the students work together on a project, for example, the rainforest, several times a week. There's a computer linkup to a camera in the rainforest.

The Coordinator commented that the project doesn't take into consideration how learning occurs-from the concrete to the abstract and from the immediate to the more distant. For an in-depth study of a remote area to have maximum benefit to children's learning, they first need an immersion in their own local area. Once they comprehend the pattern, they can transfer it elsewhere, using their insight to fill in the gaps they find. Attempts at learning in reverse order, omitting study of the local area first and beginning with the abstract, is at the root of the inability of most people to grasp basic relationships in their immediate surroundings. This is evidenced by almost universal lack of success on the Environmental Relationships Test. The deficiency is caused not by a lack of capability, but by inadequate experiences=exposure only to bit5 and pieces of the total picture, not enough to develop relationships and build a comprehensive structure over the long term.

A participant expressed a concern that there seems to be too much to accomplish in the 180-day school year. The Coordinator replied that with the systems approach, there is a shift from focus on teaching to focus on learning. When students start constructing ways of creating relationships and generating structures that make sense to them, they can assimilate vast amounts of information. Learning this way is completely different from being given information by a teacher. This information makes sense to the teacher, but it may not to the student, and it certainly doesn't enable students to develop structures and learn on their own.

Once a transition to the systems approach has occurred, students begin to routinely process new data and generate constructs, and the teacher's job becomes easier. In the Coordinator's own experience with junior high students, it took a long time for them, as seventh graders, to achieve competence in the system of the local environment. But once they had, the same process for a neighboring community was much more rapid. Their mastery continued to accelerate as they moved from the local level, to regional, national, and finally world economic geography in ninth grade. With the structures for assimilation firmly in place, they could process far more information than students lacking thorough grounding at the local level. Isolated information made sense, and they could devour the chapters of a textbook, completing a one-year course in 10 weeks. This phenomenon is predictable from what is known about communication and learning.

The Phase II proposal is due on August 15, and funds will be allocated on October 1. We have a good chance of utilizing significant capital to continue the project. The two weeks of summer workshops will provide essential background to most effectively build on what we're doing and write our needs into the proposal. Participants suggested we include field trips to the real world outside the classroom and make use of Willsboro's 1812 Homestead and adjacent outdoor education facilities. Equipment is fundable, and a computer camera could bring full-color photographs from remote sites directly to computer monitors in the classroom. Other suggestions were for computers and training in their use for the specific purposes of the project, and for a device that projects a computer screen onto an overhead projector.

The Coordinator mentioned that we may want to file the Phase II proposal under Professional Development instead of Local Initiatives and Planning, because there is a possibility of greater funding.

During the summer workshops, the consultants will help us define each discipline in terms of expected outcomes. Insights in math, for example, will enable us to avoid the common pitfalls-problems, blocks, and fears-of math education. Aversion and failure is created right from the start by trying to force logic on youngsters too soon.

An interesting experiment would have been to give the Environmental Relationships Test to the students who took the Earth Science Regents. It's unlikely that they would have been able to express the relationships satisfactorily. Yet given the appropriate experiences. they would succeed extraordinarily on both tests.

The participation of representatives of the Consortium districts will be essential as the long-range plan for the project continues. They will facilitate resource sharing for more isolated districts and elsewhere. They will be go-betweens between the project and their districts, informing the other project participants of the needs of their districts and informing their colleagues of the project's progress. And they will be catalysts for improved communication among teachers in their districts. Coordination, which is time-intensive, can be built into the schedule. Schools in Rochester and Syracuse, for example, gained 42 days through a new system of block scheduling.

While coordination among districts could benefit students who change schools, a uniform curriculum and chronology preclude local control, autonomy, and freedom in planning. A better approach to solving continuity problems is to utilize the permanent record keeping system. Teachers at the student's new school would know exactly how to proceed. Also, the absurd syndrome of repetition of the same curriculum would be eliminated.

Several aspects of project evaluation were discussed. Some teachers may be unwilling to change, for reasons that are legitimate to them. If the new approach is intriguing enough, perhaps they will participate. If not, their decision has to be accepted and adapted to.

Regarding student outcomes, Tom McGrath, the project's Levels of Use of the Innovation evaluator, explained that the project's built-in evaluation model, which is based on expectations for and outcomes of the project, takes into consideration the fact that evaluating students is premature until after 3 or 4 phases, when the project is in operation and all participating teachers have reached level 3 of implementation (mechanical use) or higher. Before student outcomes can be evaluated, factors such as organization, scheduling, equipment, and materials have to be in place, and other aspects of the project, such as familiarization with the innovations and problems in mechanical use, still have to be resolved. The complexity of the Consortium project means a lot of time will be needed to work out the "bugs," get beyond routine use, and reach a phase of further refinement. Until then, innovations will not have a significant impact, and any student outcome data will be invalid.

The Coordinator read the six "Stages of Concern About the Innovation" from Mr. McGrath's Project Evaluation Packet, and participants realized that right now they are at Stage 0, 1, or 2.

The Coordinator and the participants were satisfied that all agenda items had been adequately addressed, and the Coordinator adjourned the meeting.

Participants received copies of the results of the previous meeting's evaluations and completed evaluations of today's meeting.

The Planning Team will next meet on Friday, July 14, at 9 a.m. This meeting and the workshops will take place at the Elizabethtown School Library.

Appendix C

"Intimidation Rituals: Reactions to Reform"

By: Rory O'Day–With permission from Sage Publications

"Intimidation Rituals: Reactions to Reform"

By Rory O'Day

Dr. Rory O'Day published an article entitled "Intimidation Rituals: Reactions to Reform" in the Journal of Applied Behavioral Science in 1974. Shortly after publication, a colleague and I organized an invitational conference with a grant for the sharing of incidents of perceived intimidation experienced by faculty members at our institution. The conference was immediately fully subscribed and Rory O'Day was the featured speaker.

Prior to the scheduled conference, we circulated a brief survey of opinion about the presence of intimidation at that institution. The response was overwhelming. Now, over thirty five years later, an effort to press for reform in teacher education and general education throughout the public educational systems is underway. Dr. O'Day's treatise offers a vital link for understanding the reasons why reforms in the public school systems have not been easy.

Having worked with both pre-service and in-service teachers for over fifty years I never encountered teachers who were resistant to ideas they could relate to that made sense to them. Pre-service teachers were distinguished for their enthusiasm for teaching with an expectation of being able to improve the lives of children.

Once in the system, these same enthusiastic teachers were frequently found to be disheartened, disillusioned and stuck with unfulfilled expectations. They were encountering a "tough" hierarchical structure where administrators above them controlled their professional lives.

Most teachers are aware of the inconsistencies between the imposed policies and procedures, imposed by standardized tests and a standard core curriculum and what they intuitively sense are important matters of individual human development and behavior. Those who maintain their employment, hope for change and improvement; they often encounter the "intimidation rituals. Many who survive have either left the profession or succumbed to the forces of intimidation. No wonder we have seen resistance to innovation and change in the way we educate our youth.

Keep in mind that those who practice intimidation rituals are part of a system that creates a need for the employment of survival techniques even if their results are hurtful. These participants are seldom "bad" people; they are members of a system that encourages this behavior.

"The reaction of authority in social systems to the reform initiatives of a subordinate is viewed as a series of intimidation rituals. These rituals divide into two major phases, each involving two distinct steps. The first phase, Indirect Intimidation, includes the rituals of nullification and isolation; the second, Direct Intimidation, rituals of defamation and expulsion. Why these rituals for protest-suppression in organizations are powerful tools in the hands of the middle manager is discussed. Attention is also given to various images projected by the organizational reformer and reasons for resistance to reform from within an organization.

This paper characterizes the reactions of superiors in social systems to a reform-minded subordinate as a series of intimidation rituals. Each successive "ritual of control" represents an escalation in the effects of authority to discourage an individual (and those who may support him *or her* (emphasis added) from continuing to seek reform.

Middle Management's Mechanism of Control

The rituals of intimidation satisfy the two primary concerns of authorities confronted by a subordinate who appears not only able to articulate the grievances of a significant number of other system members but also capable of proposing solutions to them. Their first concern is, of course, to control the reformer so that he (or she) does not succeed in recruiting support. Their other concern is to exercise this control in ways that absolve them of any wrongdoing in the matter.

The individual in question must be controlled in such a way that he or she neither continues to be an effective spokesman nor becomes a martyr. When superiors are confronted with a reform minded subordinate, they want his silence or his absence, whichever is easier to achieve, The "authorities" must also preserve their carefully managed image of reasonableness, and would prefer that the reformer leave voluntarily rather than be removed officially.

For purposes of illustration, this presentation will describe intimidation rituals used by various organizations in the service of protest-suppression, for organizational authorities prefer to intimidate a reform-minded individual rather than commit organizational energy to the structural and personal changes required to transform a "nonconforming enclave" into a legitimate subunit (1). It is further suggested that an organization undergoes major changes that incorporate and accommodate a group of dissidents only when the intimidation rituals do not succeed in silencing the individuals who constitute the "leading edges" of the reform movement.

In the discussion that follows, I will be concerned primarily with the reformer who emerges from the lower hierarchy in an organization and challenges the middle hierarchy. A reformer threatens middle management in three distinctly different ways. The first threat is a function of the validity of his accusations about the inadequacy of specific actions of middle level members and his suggestions for correcting them. If the reformer is correct, those in the middle will fear that those at the top will punish them when they discover the truth. The second threat comes from the moral challenge presented by such a reformer, for his demand for action will reveal the strength or weakness of middle management's commitment to the organization. And thirdly, the reformer's challenge may indicate to people at the top that middle management is unable to maintain order in its own jurisdiction. To protect their Interests, middle-level bureaucrats therefore feel their only defense against reform-minded subordinates is intimidation (2). The rituals of intimidation involve two phases: Indirect Intimidation, which has two steps, nullification and isolation; and Direct Intimidation, which also comprises two steps, defamation and expulsion.

PHASE I: INDIRECT INTIMIDATION
Step 1: Nullification

When a reformer first approaches his immediate superiors, they will assure him that his' accusations or suggestions are invalid-the result of misunderstandings and misperceptions on his part. His superiors, in this phase, hope that the reformer will be so awed by authority that he will simply take their word that his initiative is based on error. **If** however, the reformer insists, his superiors will often agree to conduct an "investigation." The results of such an investigation will convince the reformer that his accusations are groundless and that his suggestions for organizational effectiveness or revising organizational goals have been duly noted by the appropriate authorities.

Bureaucratic justification for this response usually rests on the argument that this method copes with the system's "crackpots" and "hotheads," discouraging them from disturbing the smooth, routine functioning of the organization with their crazy ideas and their personal feuds. But middle management also uses these rituals of nullification to handle a potentially explosive (for them and others in the organization) situation quickly and quietly, in order to prevent unfavorable publicity, maintain the organization's state of pluralistic ignorance, and prevent the development of a sympathetic and concerned audience for the reformer's ideas. The explicit message is: "You don't know what you're talking about, but thank you anyway for telling us. We'll certainly look into the matter for you." Members of the middle hierarchy then proceed to cover up whatever embarrassing (for them) truth exists in the reformer's arguments.

The protest-absorption power of the ritual of nullification derives from an element inherent in bureaucracies: the always-attractive opportunity to avoid personal responsibility for one's actions. Thus, if people attempt reform at all, they generally do not proceed beyond the first ritual, which is a process designed to quash the reformer and allow his superiors to reaffirm the collective wisdom of the organization, while clearing their consciences of wrongdoing. Nullification even gets the would-be reformer off the hook—and he may remain grateful to the organization for this added convenience. This shedding of personal responsibility allows the reformer and the authorities alike to compromise in the belief that although it might not be a perfect organizational world, it is nevertheless a self-correcting one.

Repeated exposure to the nullification ritual (the "beating your head against the wall" phenomenon") is expected to convince any sane organizational member that a reformist voice or presence is unwelcome. He is expected to take the hint and stop pestering his superiors with his misguided opinions. Gestures of generosity on the part of the middle hierarchy are not unusual if he decides to leave the organization—and such concern is usually expressed by offering to help the individual find employment opportunities elsewhere.

Step 2: Isolation

If the reformer persists in his efforts, middle management will separate him from his peers, subordinates, and superiors, thereby softening his impact on the organization and making it extremely difficult for him to mobilize any support for his position.

Middle managers argue that these procedures represent the exercise of their rights of office in the service of protecting the organization. But these attempts to isolate the reformer can also be seen as a show of force, as a way of reassuring their own superiors (if they are paying attention), their subordinates, and perhaps themselves that they can maintain order in their own jurisdiction.

Attempts at isolating the reformer include closing his communication links, restricting his freedom of movement, and reducing his allocation of organization resources. If these do not neutralize the reformer, he will be transferred to a less visible position in the organization. In these rituals, the bureaucratic message is: "If you insist on talking about things which you do not understand, then we will have to prevent you from bothering other people with your nonsense."

Systematic unresponsiveness to a reformer's criticism and suggestions is a particularly interesting form of isolation. This lack of response is meant to convince the reformer of the invalidity of his position; but if he presses his right to be heard, it may be used to create a feeling of such impotence that the reformer overreacts in order to elicit a response from his superiors. This over reaction may then be used to demonstrate the reformer's psychological imperfections.

When subjected to organizational isolation, most people come to see the error of their ways or the handwriting on the wall. When an individual learns that there is still time to mend his ways, he usually steps back in line and becomes a silent participant in the organization. When he realizes his career in the organization is at a standstill, he may decide to leave as gracefully as possible while he can still leave under his own steam. Middle managers closest to him then often offer him assistance in finding a new job, with the assurance that "we only want what is best for you."

Most forms of isolation are designed to persuade the reformer of the futility of trying to initiate change until such time as he is instructed by his superiors to concern himself with change. The reformer practically guarantees his defeat if he reacts to systematic organizational unresponsiveness by confronting his superiors in ways that violate policy or law. The temptation to confront administrative unresponsiveness in dramatic and often self-defeating ways stems in large part from the intense frustration induced by the reformer's belief that systematic unresponsiveness violates his basic rights of freedom of expression and carries with it the implication that he is personally ineffectual (Turner, 1973). Administrative unresponsiveness to what the reformer believes are crucial issues both for himself and for the organization may be sufficiently frustrating to compel him to act, however rashly, in order to clarify the situation. From the administration's point of view, this can be seen as "flushing the rebels out into the open," "giving them enough rope to hang themselves," or, more formally, deviance-heresy conversion (Harshbarger, 1973).

PHASE II: DIRECT INTIMIDATION
Step 3: Defamation

Should the reformer refuse to remain silent, and instead mobilizes support for his position, middle management will begin to impugn his character and his motives. When legitimate techniques fail—the middle hierarchy might resort to illegitimate or non-legitimate ones" (Leeds, 1964, p. 126). Middle managers will often distort events or even fabricate instances of misconduct in order to intimidate not only the reformer but also those who would listen to or believe him.

Defamation attempts to cut the reformer off from a potentially sympathetic following by attributing his attempts at reform to questionable motives, underlying psychopathology, or gross incompetence. This three-pronged attack is meant to blackmail the reformer into submission and to transform a sympathetic following into a mistrustful crowd of onlookers or an angry mob that feels resentful at having been deceived by the reformer.

From the vantage point of the reformer, the Kafkaesque or Alice-in-Wonderland quality of the rituals of intimidation becomes particularly evident at this time. The reformer finds himself faced with charges which only he and his accusers know are either false or irrelevant in relation to the value of his reform initiatives. The reformer is in a double bind. His superiors will use their offices and positions of trust and responsibility to create the impression in the minds of others in the organization that their accusations of incompetence, self-interest, or psychopathology are true. If the reformer continues in the face of these accusations, he risks being viewed as power hungry or irrational. If he allows himself to be intimidated by the threat of lies, he allows his superiors to win by default.

One tactic of the superior is to accuse the reformer of acting out his Oedipal conflicts. Such a personalization of a subordinate's reform efforts (especially a younger subordinate) permits his superior to present himself as a harassed "father" faced with a troubled "son," and blocks any examination of his conduct that might reveal provocation on his part. In this way the bureaucrat hopes to persuade others in the organization to respond to the reformer as a sick person in need of therapy or as a child in need to nurturing-sa stance that allows him to take on the role of" good father" (or good mother–emphasis added) in relation to other subordinates and to the reformer, if and when the latter capitulates and admits his need for help and guidance.

Rituals of defamation are undertaken by superiors in order to focus attention away from themselves and onto the reformer. The superiors hope that by casting enough doubt on the motives, intentions, and personality of the reformer, enough people in the organization will think that "where there is smoke, there must be fire." The message of this ritual is: "Don't listen to him (his message) because you can't trust a person like him."

Like the rituals of nullification and isolation, the ritual of defamation is both an end in itself and a preliminary to the final ritual of expulsion. The superiors hope by threatening to destroy the reformer's reputation and his character, he will retreat into silence and passivity or leave the organization for greener pastures; if, however, the reformer continues his efforts, his superiors have laid the groundwork for his expulsion.

If the ritual of defamation is undertaken, its target is usually indeed a reformer and not simply a nonconformist or a deviant. His superiors would not need to engage in public tactics of intimidation if there were no substance to his challenge. It is precisely the validity of his reform initiatives that leads his superiors to attempt to destroy his credibility. If this destruction of the reformer's credibility with his peers, subordinates, and top management is effectively conducted, others in the organization will desert his cause and he can be dismissed easily as an undesirable member of the intact organizational team.

Step 4: Expulsion

When neither nullification, isolation, nor defamation can silence the reformer or force his "voluntary withdrawal" from the organization, the middle hierarchy seeks an official decision for his dismissal.

If successful, at least three aims may be achieved thereby. Obviously, by expelling the reformer, his superiors will cut him off from any actual or potential following and weaken any opposition to their authority. An official dismissal also serves as a warning to other budding reformers that middle management has the necessary power and authority to expel troublemakers. Finally, the act of expulsion—a verdict of unfitness—supports the contention that the reformer is an immoral or irrational person.

Of course, the middle hierarchy would prefer the reformer to withdraw voluntarily. Managers want to avoid the public and formal proceedings that often accompany an official request for dismissal of an employee, for the accuser (superior) can often then be scrutinized as carefully as the accused, if the accused person wishes to avail himself of the opportunity. The expulsion ritual involves the formal submission of evidence, the keeping of records, the establishment of independent investigative bodies, and the right of cross-examination, which all function to threaten the image of managers as reasonable, honest, and hardworking servants of the organization. Formal dismissal proceedings are also avoided by middle management because in some fundamental sense they imply that the organization has failed and that they, in particular, have shown themselves unable to maintain order.

The Ritual Cycle Absorbs and Destroys

Indirect Intimidation attempts to absorb the accusations and suggestions of the reformer, first by depriving him of effectiveness or validity, then by treating him as if he were an "invisible person." The object here is to define the reformer as "harmless." It also attempts to absorb protest by psychologically and physically exhausting the reformer so that he comes to doubt his own experience of reality, his abilities to accomplish the task he sets for himself, and its significance. The authorities hope that the reformer will come to believe the task he has set for himself is humanly impossible and that his fatigue and confusion are the result of his inability to accept human nature for what it is. Short of this, they hope that the reformer will come to feel so inadequate that he will be grateful for continued employment by the organization, in any capacity. ("You're welcome to stay aboard as long as you don't rock the boat.")

Direct Intimidation attempts to destroy protest through destruction of the character of the reformer (defamation) or, if necessary, of his position in the organization (expulsion). Direct Intimidation represents middle management's active attempt to destroy the reformer as a source of legitimate grievances and suggestions and to terrorize, if necessary, other organizational members. Successful rituals of defamation create a "bad" person, enabling the "good" organization to close ranks once again and benefit from the curative properties of solidarity when he is cast out of the system. In this sense, the ritual destruction of the person (Garfinkel, 1956) necessarily precedes the destruction of his place in the organization."

" ... It is not possible here to do more than raise the issue of whether one should attempt to change organizations from within or whether one should create alternative organizations. Large formal organizations are going to be with us for a long time to come (Heilbroner, 1972), and their members are going to have to devise ways to make them more democratic, because there really is no place to run to anymore.

The serious reformer should be prepared to take advantage of organizational crises. He (or she) must learn how to recognize, expose, and make concrete those administratively designed arrangements that do not satisfactorily resolve critical problems. For it is in a time of crisis that an organization's members will be (more) eager to adopt new structures that promise to reduce the uncertainty and anxiety generated by a crisis (Shepard, 1969). If an organization has become weak internally, if it contains corruption, and indolence at various levels, if the organization is beset by energy-consuming external pressures, and if the organizational elite lack the resources or the will to initiate changes essential for organizational survival, there an organization might well be ready for successful reform from within (Leeds,1964). Such an organization might not be capable of successfully administering the intimidation rituals.

Internal organizational reform is a difficult process. The

cause for reform as well as constructive revolution cannot be served by deluding ourselves as to the ease of restructuring human society (Heilbroner, 1072), (Schon, 1073). The reformer's life is not an easy one. But neither need he feel doomed from the start by the inevitability of the successes of intimidation rituals mobilized against him."

Achievement of the primary goal of *Remaking Our Schools* requires a realization of the crises in education that may be illuminated by the contents of this book.

About the Author:

Robert (Bob) Arnold, Professor of Education, Emeritus, resides in Willsboro, New York with his wife Mary Sue of fifty-nine years. Willsboro is a rural upstate community, twenty-six miles south of Plattsburgh, New York, across Lake Champlain from Burlington, Vermont. He was invited in the spring of 1966 to implement a new teacher education curriculum at Plattsburgh State University of New York, developed from his many years of teaching experience in the public schools of this State. His ideas reflect experimentation conducted at the State University at Potsdam and Jersey City State College. He designed and implemented experimental studies at several research and demonstration centers, created innovative demonstration projects, work-shopped with parents and faculties in several states and authored many proposals. These many experiences led to a comprehensive analysis of public education and a systemic design for the rational overhaul of our public schools.

For the past several years while in retirement he has been culling through stacks of papers and publications that represent a lifetime of experiences in education and business. He consolidated the highlights of this experience in a single volume aimed at *Remaking Our Schools*. As a professor of education, Bob has observed over the decades the problems in education that have resulted in social, economic, and political difficulties in this country. He has described how schools contribute to troubled youth and what can be done about it.

Professor Arnold holds a fervent hope he'll find opportunities to demonstrate what our public schools could become when his ideas are fully implemented.